step by step to

BETTER KNITTING & CROCHET

CAVENDISH HOUSE

Edited by Dorothea Hall
Art editor: Anita Ruddell

Published by Marshall Cavendish Books Limited
58 Old Compton Street
London W1V 5PA

© Marshall Cavendish Limited 1978, 1979, 1980, 1982, 1983

This material has previously appeared in the
partwork *Stitch by Stitch*

First printing 1980
Second printing 1982
Third printing 1983

Printed in Hong Kong

ISBN 0 85685 790 4

Knitting Contents

Sweater with Swiss darning, see page 35

Mohair scarf in garter stitch, see page 9

Below, crochet hats, see page 216

Crochet Contents

Cosy hooded cape, see page 221

Giant floor cushions, see page 202

Knitting Introduction

Hand knitting combines economy with pleasure and satisfaction in what is one of the most popular pastimes of today. It requires no more than needles and yarn for you to create fashion garments for you and your family or colourful accessories for your home.
If you have always wanted to learn to knit, then these practical, step-by-step courses will show you how. For the more practised knitter there are many new stitch effects, helpful advice and hundreds of ideas for you to use.

Here, in thirty-one graded courses, you are introduced in easy stages to the whole range of knitting techniques and skills, from stitch making to shaping, from pattern adaptation to making-up and pressing.
And in addition, you are given information on Swiss darning and smocking, on using special yarns like mohair, bouclé and cotton, how to use colour in stripes, chevrons and checks, and much more.
Each course is clearly explained with step-by-step photographs and has its own pattern especially designed to use only those stitches and techniques already covered.

The patterns include simple gloves and scarf, sweaters for the family — including baby, a child's dressing gown, chunky jackets, sporty waistcoats and pretty, party dresses. In fact, something for every occasion.

Step-by-step course –1

Classification
Many hand-knitting yarns belong to groups according to their construction.

Baby yarns. Available in 3- and 4-ply weights, also a softly twisted Quick-erknit, which knits to 4-ply tension. These yarns are soft to wear and with-stand repeated washings.

2-, 3-, 4-ply weights. Classic threads for general use. 'Crêpes' are a tightly twisted version that produce a smooth fabric with a characteristic pebbled surface.

Double knitting. A very popular hand knitting as it knits up quickly into a strong fabric with many uses. It has a 4-ply construction, but each thread is about double the thickness of that used in a 4-ply knitting.

Chunky or double double knitting. Twice the thickness of double knitting, this type of yarn makes thick sports or outdoor garments.

Speciality yarns. These have a decorative appearance such as lurex and wool com-bined, flecks and tweed effects or an unusual hairy, crinkly or bouclé texture.

Yarn

This is a term used for any type of thread used as knitting material no matter how it is made. 'Spinners' manufacture yarn for hand knitting: it is usually sold in balls although some very chunky yarns may be in hanks, which need winding into a ball before use.

Check the weight of the ball you are buy-ing, as this varies with different types and brands – 20, 25, 40, 50 and 100 grammes are all standard weights for a ball of yarn. See that the total weight you buy is sufficient rather than relying on the num-bers of balls stated in a pattern. Remember that the colour in different dye-lots can vary quite drastically and it is advisable to see that you have plenty of yarn at the outset to complete any particular article.

Fibres
These fall into two main categories— natural and man-mades. Wool, angora, mohair, cotton and linen are all natural fibres; they are hard-wearing and pleasant to wear and handle. Some are in short supply and therefore very expensive; all of them require careful hand washing. Modern technology has given knitters new, man-made fibres such as acrylic, nylon and polyester. These are often cheaper than the natural fibres and com-bine high bulk with light weight. They wash extremely well, especially in machines. The paper band on a ball of yarn should give washing instructions. Wool and man-made fibres are a popular combination, giving a yarn with the soft texture of wool and the strength plus washability of synthetics.

Ply
All yarns have a ply classification: this is the name of a single spun thread, but is not an indication of the thickness of that thread. The threads are never used singly, but twisted together with other threads to give yarns of recognized thickness— 2 ply, 3 ply, 4 ply. Note that all yarns of the same ply are not necessarily the same thickness; some soft Shetland 2 plys are thicker than a fine 3, or even 4, ply.

Needles

Knitting requires very few basic tools and they are all inexpensive. Needles are the main equipment necessary; these are available in a number of modern materials, such as coated aluminium, plastic and wood, which make them light and easy to work with. The old steel needles are heavy in comparison and slow you down. To get good results take care of your needles; a bent needle distorts your fabric, an old blunt pair of needles will fray the yarn.

Sizing

Each type of yarn demands its own needle size, from very fine needles for speciality work such as lace knitting to very thick needles for heavy garments in chunky yarn. The size of the needle is a metric measurement taken around the body of the shaft: there are 17 stages down from 10 to 2 millimetres.

Pairs of needles

For flat knitting in rows you need a pair of needles with a point at one end and a knob at the other to prevent the stitches sliding off. Needles are available in three lengths — 25, 30 and 35 centimetres. If there is a large number of stitches at some stage in the garment you are knitting you need the longest pair of needles possible; otherwise it is more relaxing to work with shorter ones.

Needle sizes

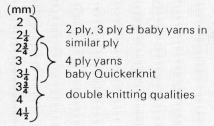
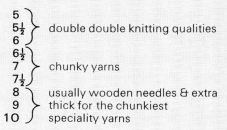

(mm)		
2		
$2\frac{1}{4}$	2 ply, 3 ply & baby yarns in	
$2\frac{3}{4}$	similar ply	
3	4 ply yarns	
$3\frac{1}{4}$	baby Quickerknit	
$3\frac{3}{4}$		
4	double knitting qualities	
$4\frac{1}{2}$		

5	
$5\frac{1}{2}$	double double knitting qualities
6	
$6\frac{1}{2}$	
7	chunky yarns
$7\frac{1}{2}$	
8	usually wooden needles & extra
9	thick for the chunkiest
10	speciality yarns

Sets of needles

Knitting in the round is a method of making a circular fabric without seams: it is widely used for making gloves, hats and socks or any other items that only require a small number of stitches. Circular knitting needs a set of four needles with points at both ends. Three of the needles hold the stitches in a triangular shape and the fourth needle is for working with.

Circular needles

These are also for knitting in rounds, used where there are too many stitches for the set of needles, or for knitting in rows where a large number of stitches is involved. The two needles are linked by a long piece of flexible plastic.

Cable needles

Cable patterns and Aran knitting require a special miniature-length knitting needle with points at both ends. Stitches are transferred to this extra needle at the point in a row when you twist a cable, holding them at the back or front of the knitting while you continue to work the adjacent stitches.

Stitch holders

You need these when you divide your work and leave some stitches until a later stage. Often they are a form of enlarged safety pin with an open end for moving the stitches on and off and a fastening to keep the stitches safe.

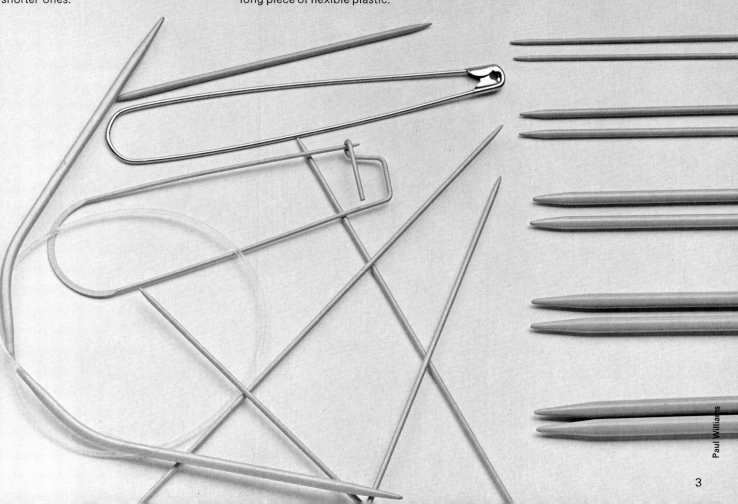

Paul Williams

Step-by-step course – 2

Casting on with two needles

All knitting starts with a foundation row of loops cast on to one needle. To make a fabric you use the second needle to build a series of interlocking loops in rows one above the other.

Generally you hold the needle with the stitches in your left hand and the needle to make the stitches in your right hand. (Left-handed people should work in reverse.) Your way of holding the yarn develops as you practise knitting: as long as you are relaxed it is a case of personal preference. If you are in doubt it helps to control the yarn by winding it round the fingers of your right hand so that it flows evenly, to produce a fabric with firm, even tension.

Cast-on loops form the selvedge of the fabric. If the edge is tighter than the rest of your work and pulls it in, use one size larger needles for casting on only.

There are a number of different casting-on methods. The two-needle method produces a firm edge and can be used for most knitted fabrics. Other ways will be covered in later chapters.

Note : by FRONT we mean the side of the work nearest you ;
by BACK we mean the side of the work away from you.

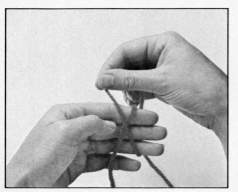

1   Start by making a slip loop about 10cm from the end of the ball of yarn.

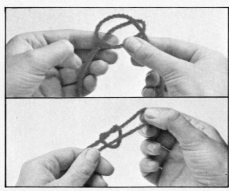

2   Wind the yarn as indicated and pull strand through to form the slip loop.

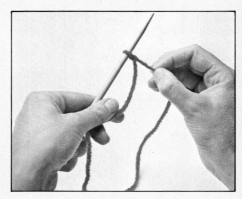

3   Place the loop on the left-hand (LH) needle ; hold needle in left hand.

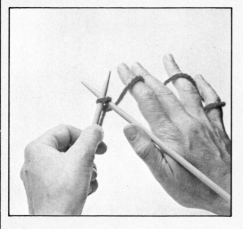

4   Hold the needle to make the stitches in your right hand.
Wind the yarn round the fingers of your right hand so that the index finger remains flexible and controls it.
Insert the right-hand (RH) needle from front to back into the slip loop.

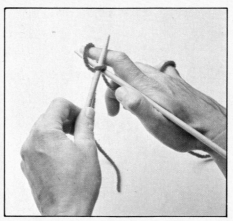

5   Wind the yarn under and over the RH needle point in a clockwise direction. Try to keep the yarn fairly loose or the cast-on edge will be too tight.

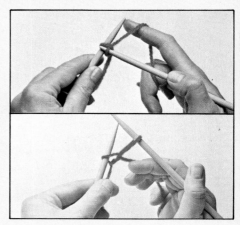

6   Pull the RH needle towards you, drawing a loop of yarn through the slip loop. This forms a new stitch on the RH needle.

David Levin   Paul Williams

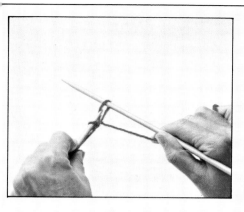

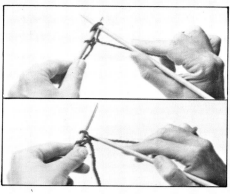

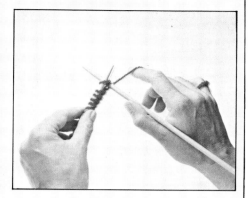

7 Twist the LH needle forwards and insert the point from right to left into the front of the new stitch on the RH needle.

8 Withdraw the RH needle point: the new stitch is now transferred to the LH needle.

9 Always inserting the RH needle from front to back into the last new stitch on the LH needle, repeat steps 4–8, to cast on the number of stitches you require.

Making a garter-stitch fabric

This is the easiest stitch pattern: you knit each stitch in every row to produce a fabric with textured horizontal ridges. The fabric looks the same on both sides and is therefore reversible.

A garter-stitch fabric is neat and firm so that you can use it with the ridges running vertically without the stitches stretching: this creates more variety in garter-stitch designs, as you can knit them from the hem upwards or from side edge to side edge.

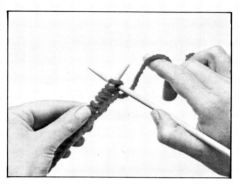

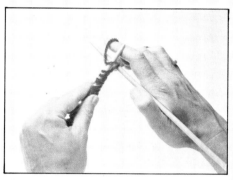

1 Hold the needle with the cast-on stitches in your left hand and the free needle in your right hand. Insert the free needle from front to back into the first stitch.

2 With the yarn at the back of the work throughout, wind it under and over the right-hand (RH) needle point.

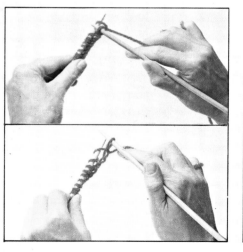

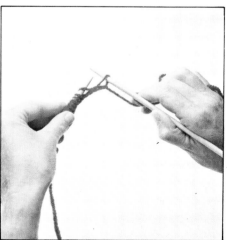

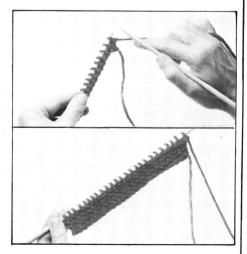

3 Pull the yarn through the stitch on the left-hand (LH) needle to make a new stitch on the RH needle.

4 Drop the stitch from the LH needle and leave the new stitch on the RH needle. Work into each of the cast-on stitches in the same way.

5 At the end of a row transfer the needles so that the one holding the stitches is in your left hand. Knit each stitch in every row to produce a garter-stitch fabric.

David Levin   Paul Williams

Checking simple stitch tension

Before beginning any pattern you must knit a tension sample; individuals knit with different 'tightness', so checking your own tension is the only way to make sure you obtain the exact measurements and get a perfect result.

Each pattern has a tension guide, where it states the number of stitches and rows to a 10cm square using the recommended yarn and needles. Concentrate on getting the correct number of stitches to 10cm. The row tension is not so important at this stage, as you work to reach a given measurement, no matter how many rows it takes.

1 Look at the stitch tension guide at the beginning of the pattern. As an example: 12 stitches to 10cm. Cast on your stitches, plus a few extra, say 17. Knit up a piece at least 10cm long.

2 Count 12 stitches on your sample, and mark with pins. Lay a tape measure along the sample to check what measurement you have achieved with 12 stitches.

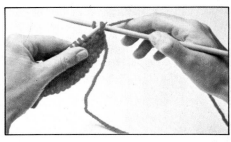

3 This stitch tension is too tight as the 12 stitches make less than 10cm. Make another sample with one size larger needles; if it is still too tight, try even larger needles.

4 Here the stitch tension is too loose as the 12 stitches make more than 10cm. Keep trying progressively smaller needles until you have the right stitch tension.

Casting off

At the end of any piece of work you must secure the stitches so that they do not unravel: do this quite loosely so that the edge does not tighten and distort the fabric.

Sometimes it is easier to make a loose edge if you use a one size larger needle to work the stitches on the cast-off row.

1 Knit the first two stitches in the usual way to transfer them to the RH needle.

2 Use the LH needle point to lift the first stitch knitted over the second.

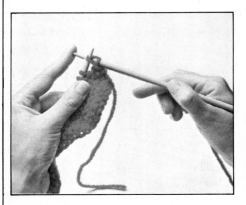

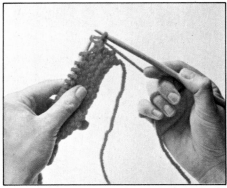

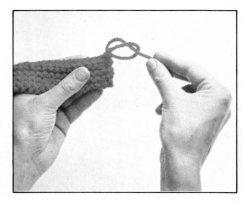

3 Push the RH needle backwards with the LH index finger, at the same time drawing the stitch remaining on the RH needle through the one being lifted.

4 Withdraw the LH needle point from the stitch. One stitch remains on the RH needle and one stitch has been cast off. Knit the next stitch on the RH needle. Insert the LH needle into the first stitch knitted and repeat the process of lifting one stitch over another.

5 Continue until one stitch remains on the RH needle. Break yarn about 10cm from the work. Lengthen the loop on the needle, then drop the stitch from the needle. Draw the cut end through the loop and pull the yarn to tighten the stitch.

David Levin   Paul Williams

6

Joining in a new ball of yarn

Measure the yarn you have left: you need about four times the width of your knitting to complete the row to avoid joining in the middle of a row.

If your yarn does run out in the middle of a row the best thing to do with a simple stitch is to take the stitches back to the beginning of the row.

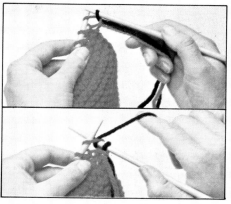

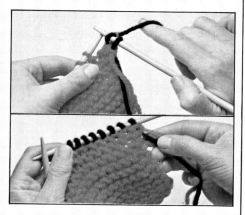

1 Insert RH needle into first stitch as normal. Leaving a 10cm length free, wrap the new yarn around the RH needle.

2 Pull RH needle through stitch to make first stitch in new yarn on RH needle. Insert RH needle into next stitch and wrap new yarn under and over.

3 Pull RH needle through to make second stitch; continue to knit with the new yarn. Pull ends of yarn gently to tighten edge stitches and darn in later.

Joining with a back-stitch seam

This is a common method of joining the main seams such as shoulders, side and sleeve seams on many knitted garments. Welts, cuffs or borders in a different stitch may require another type of seam. When working a back-stitch seam a blunt-ended wool needle is a vital piece of equipment to avoid splitting the stitches. Pull the stitches firmly through the knitting without stretching it; at the same time do not draw the stitches up so tightly that they pucker the fabric.

The join forms a ridge on the wrong side of the fabric which is virtually undetectable when the garment is worn. For a professional finish press the completed seam lightly on the right side. Garter stitch garments should be pressed only *very* lightly, if at all, as pressing can destroy the texture of the fabric.

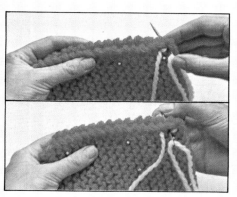

1 Place right sides together, match edge to be joined, and pin at intervals. Secure the yarn at the RH edge — about one knitted stitch in from the edge — using two small stitches, one on top of the other. Move one stitch to the left, and bring the needle through from the back to the front.

2 Re-insert needle from front to back, at the end of the previous stitch. Bring the needle out one knitted stitch to the left. Continue like this until the seam is complete. Fasten off by working two small stitches, draw the yarn a short way back along seam and cut off the excess.

Joining with a flat seam

Use this seam when you want to avoid an extra-bulky ridge. It is equally useful whether you are working with very chunky yarn or fine yarn for baby clothes. This is also the seam to choose for joining sections of ribbing, such as welts or cuffs, as well as sewing on borders or edgings. The seam has a laced effect on the wrong side when the two pieces of knitting are laid flat.

1 Place the two edges of knitting with right sides together, matching ridges at row ends if possible. Secure yarn at the the right-hand edge through both thicknesses of fabric.

2 Oversew through corresponding ridges on each edge being careful not to pull the yarn too tightly.

David Levin   Paul Williams

Great garter stitch!

The very basic techniques covered in this section are all you need to try your hand at a simple pattern.

Scarves are the easiest for a first attempt, but the tops, too, are simply made from straight pieces of garter stitch. Full instructions are on the next page.

In all garter stitch patterns a much neater edge can be achieved by 'slipping a stitch knit-wise'. To do this insert the RH needle into the stitch on the LH needle in the usual way : transfer the stitch to the RH needle without winding the yarn round to make a new stitch.

Scarves

Sizes

Random-dyed bouclé scarf is about 25cm wide × 170cm long.
Mohair scarf is about 18cm wide × 200cm long.
Plain scarf is about 10cm wide × 170cm long.

Materials

Bouclé scarf: 330g of bouclé yarn such as Wendy Fashion Lorraine
One pair 6½mm knitting needles
Mohair scarf: 90g of mohair yarn such as Lister Tahiti
One pair of 10mm knitting needles
Plain scarf: 125g of Aran-type yarn such as Patons Capstan
One pair of 4mm knitting needles

Bouclé scarf

Cast on 35 stitches.
Work 170cm in garter stitch always slipping first stitch of every row.
Cast off.
Darn in all ends of yarn on one side of the knitting.

Mohair scarf

Cast on 18 stitches.
Work 200cm in garter stitch always slipping first stitch of every row. The very large needles produce an open, lacy fabric.
Cast off.
Darn in all ends of yarn on one side of the knitting.

Plain scarf

Cast on 16 stitches.
Work 170cm in garter stitch always slipping first stitch of every row.
Cast off.
Darn in all ends of yarn on one side of the knitting.

Long waistcoat

Sizes

These instructions will give a finished garment about 73cm long, 48cm wide across the back, 22cm wide across each front. These measurements allow for the weight of the yarn in garter stitch pulling the fabric slightly downwards and inwards. The waistcoat fits any bust size between 80 and 92cm. To make it wider or narrower cast on one stitch more or less for each centimetre difference. Remember you may need more or less yarn accordingly.

Materials
900g of extra-chunky yarn such as Patons Pablo
One pair 7½mm knitting needles
2 buttons

Tension
10 stitches and 20 rows to 10cm over garter stitch worked on 7½mm needles.

Back
Cast on 52 stitches.
Work 70cm in garter stitch always slipping first stitch of every row.
Cast off.

Front (make 2)
Cast on 26 stitches. Work as given for back.

To make up
1   Darn in all ends of yarn on one side of the knitting: this will be the wrong side.
2   There is no need to press garter stitch as this destroys the quality of the texture.
3   With right sides of front and back facing inwards and matching cast off edges, join top edge with a flat stitch seam for 16cm from each side edge to form shoulder seams.
4   Leave a 20cm gap for armholes, then join side seams with a flat seam to within 20cm of lower edge.
5   On right side of work, turn back top corners of fronts to form a triangular shape: sew on a button to hold in place.

Caroline Arber

Mother and toddler tops

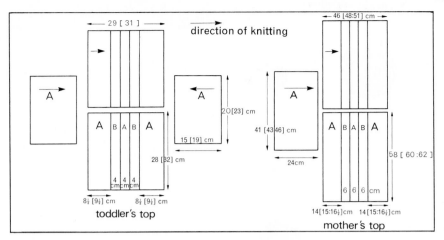

direction of knitting

toddler's top

mother's top

Sizes
These instructions are for the measurements shown on the diagrams.

Toddler's fits a 51 and 56cm chest.

Mother's is in small (81/86cm bust), medium (86/91cm bust) and large (91/97cm bust) sizes.
Note that instructions for larger sizes are in square brackets [ ]; where there is only one set of figures it applies to all sizes.

Materials
Toddler's top:
100 [150]g of mohair-type yarn such as 3 Suisses Aubretia in colour A
50g of colour B
One pair 7mm knitting needles
Mother's top:
250 [300:350]g of colour A
100g of colour B
One pair 7mm knitting needles

Tension
14 stitches to 10cm over garter stitch worked on 7mm needles.

Toddler's top
Back and front (alike)
☐   Using colour A, cast on 39[44] stitches for side edge.
Work 8½[9½]cm in garter stitch always slipping first stitch of every row. Note the number of rows you knit in this section: a row-counter gadget that fits on to your needle is useful.
☐   Break off colour A. Join in colour B and work 4cm in garter stitch: work an even number of rows in each stripe, joining in new yarn at same edge, so that the lines of broken stripes on changing colour are on the wrong side.
☐   Break off colour B. Work another 4cm stripe in colour A, then one in colour B. Break off A.
☐   Join in colour A and work another 8½[9½]cm, knitting the same number of rows as in the previous section.
Cast off loosely.

Sleeves (make 2)
☐   Using colour A, cast on 28[32] stitches for cuff edge.
Work 24cm in garter stitch, always slipping first stitch of every row.
Cast off loosely.

To make up
☐   Darn in all ends on the wrong side of the work. There is no need to press garter stitch.
☐   With wrong sides of back and front together, join top edge with a flat seam for 9[9½]cm from each side edge to form shoulder seams.
☐   Mark centre of cast-off edge of sleeves with a pin. Open front and back sections out flat and with right sides facing, match pin to shoulder seam and pin cast-off edge along side edges of main piece. Sew with a back-stitch seam.
☐   With right sides together, join side seams with a back-stitch seam and sleeve seams with a flat seam, reversing seam for 4cm at lower edge of sleeves (i.e. turn fabric so that wrong sides are together and sew seam on the right side of the work).
☐   Turn sweater with right sides out. Press seams lightly if necessary. Fold back 7cm at sleeve edges to form cuff.

Mother's top
Back and front (alike)
☐   Using colour A, cast on 82[84:86] stitches for side edge.
Work as given for back and front of toddler's sweater, but following measurements on larger diagram.
Sleeves (make 2)
☐   Using colour A, cast on 56[60:64] stitches for cuff edge.
Work as given for toddler's sleeves, but following measurements on larger diagram.
To make up
☐   Follow instructions for toddler's sweater, joining shoulder seams for 15[16:17]cm from side edges and reversing sleeve seam for 7cm at lower edge to form cuff.

Step-by-step course – 3

* Working purl stitches
* Making a stocking stitch fabric
* Blocking and pressing a knitted fabric
* Stocking stitch sweater pattern

Working purl stitches

After learning how to knit stitches, you only need to know how to purl them to be able to construct an infinite number of fabrics and textures. A fabric made completely of purled stitches resembles garter stitch, and is not generally used: usually knit and purl stitches are considered to form a variety of knitted fabrics.

Casting off purlwise

At some stage in a pattern you may need to cast off on a purl row. Do this in exactly the same way as casting off on a knit row, only purl the stitches before lifting one over another.

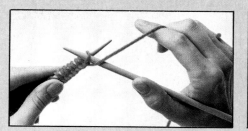

1 Hold the needle with the cast-on stitches in your left hand and the free needle in your right hand. Insert the free needle from right to left into the **front** of the stitch to be purled.

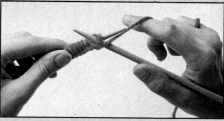

2 With the yarn at the front of the work throughout, wind it over and round the RH needle point.

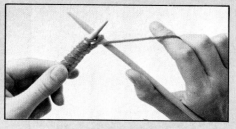

3 Pull the yarn through the stitch on the LH needle to make a new loop on the RH needle.

4 Drop the stitch from the LH needle and leave the new stitch on the RH needle. Work into each stitch to be purled in the same way.

Making a stocking stitch fabric

With the second basic stitch, purl, you now know enough to knit in stocking stitch, the most widely used knitted fabric. Originally it was used for knitted stockings; now it is found in many classic designs including sweaters and cardigans. Knit and purl rows alternate to produce a smooth-textured fabric. The right side of the work faces you when you are doing the knit rows. The formation of stocking stitch is easily reproduced by machines, so increasing its popularity especially for ready-made knitwear.

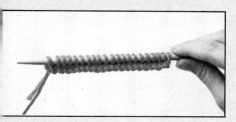

1 Take the needle with the cast-on stitches and knit each stitch in the first row.

2 Purl each stitch in the second row: the wrong side of the fabric faces you.

3 Knit one row, then purl one row alternately to produce a stocking stitch fabric. The 'right' side of the fabric has interlocking V shapes.

Paul Williams

11

Blocking and pressing a knitted fabric

Blocking is the method of pinning down pieces of knitting before pressing to ensure correct shape and size. It is especially helpful with a stocking stitch fabric, where edges tend to roll under. The amount of pressing required depends upon the type of yarn used and directions are often given on the yarn ball band.

1 Place knitting with wrong side up on a flat padded surface. If your ironing board is too small improvise with old folded blankets on a flat surface such as the floor or a table top.

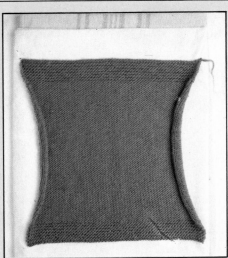

2 Ease piece into shape, then check measurements. Hold in position with plenty of pins – this is called 'blocking'.

As you pin the knitting down see that the stitches and rows run in straight lines and the fabric is not pulled out of shape.

3 Use a clean pressing cloth – slightly damp or dry according to the type of yarn. Many modern yarns need no pressing, but in general press synthetics with a cool iron over a dry cloth, and natural fibres with a warm iron over a slightly damp cloth. Heavy pressing destroys the quality of many textured yarns, or stitch patterns such as garter stitch. Leave garter stitch borders free

when pressing. Press evenly and lightly, lifting and lowering the iron over the surface. Take out pins and make sure that knitting is dry before lifting it up.

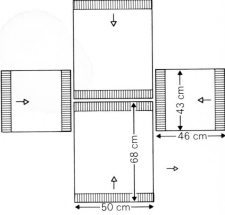

A sweater for all seasons

Our stocking stitch sweater is made from simple pieces with garter stitch borders. It's a really versatile top that looks good over shirts, polos or just on its own !

Sizes
These instructions are for the measurements shown on the diagram : the sweater fits a range of bust sizes between 83 and 92cm.
Lengthen or shorten the sweater by working more or less stocking stitch between the garter stitch borders on each piece. Remember that you may need more or less yarn if you alter the length.

Materials
1000g chunky yarn such as Jaeger Naturgarn.
One pair 5½mm knitting needles

Tension
14 stitches and 20 rows to 10cm over stocking stitch worked on 5½mm needles.

To make sweater
Back
Cast on 72 stitches. Work 6cm in garter stitch for border.
☐ Beginning with a knit row, continue in stocking stitch until work measures 62cm from cast-on edge, ending with a purl row.
☐ Work another 6cm in garter stitch. Cast off loosely.

Front
Follow the instructions for the back.

Sleeves (make 2)
Cast on 62 stitches. Work 6cm in garter

stitch for cuff.

☐ Beginning with a purl row, continue in stocking stitch until work measures 40cm from cast-on edge, ending with a purl row.

☐ Work another 6cm in garter stitch. Cast off loosely.

To make up

Press each section, omitting garter stitch borders, according to type of yarn.

☐ With right sides of back and front facing inwards and matching cast-off edges, join top edge with a back stitch seam for about 17cm from each side edge to form shoulder seams.

☐ Mark centre of cast-off edge of sleeve with a pin.

☐ With right sides of knitting facing inwards, match centre of sleeve top to shoulder seam and sew sleeve top in position with back stitch seam.

☐ Again with right side of knitting facing inwards and using a back stitch seam, join side and sleeve seams : if you want to turn back the garter stitch cuff, you must reverse the seam on this section by joining on the right side of the work.

☐ Press seams. Fold back cuffs.

Neil Kirk/shirts by Marx

Step-by-step course – 4

* Using reverse stocking stitch
* Picking up dropped stitches
* Pattern for a waistcoat

Using reverse stocking stitch

The wrong side of stocking stitch – that is the side facing you as you purl a row – is a fabric in its own right. It has a densely looped texture in horizontal ridges which resembles garter stitch, but is less sculptured.

Work a classic-style garment in this fabric as a change from the more usual stocking stitch: it is also a useful background for cable and Aran patterns.

Picking up dropped stitches

Even experienced knitters drop stitches, so don't panic when it happens to you. One dropped stitch may be easy to cope with, but a number of stitches running down through the rows to leave a 'ladder' are more of a problem. To prevent the stitches going farther, insert a safety pin from left to right to hold the stitches behind the ladder at the back of the work. You can now take the stitches one at a time and deal with them individually.

Method for garter stitch
Note If you have an even number of rows of knitting when you drop a stitch, follow the directions *in brackets* below.

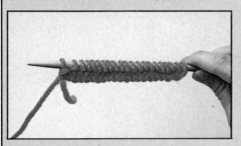

1 Always purl the first row of reverse stocking stitch.

1 As the stitch unravels down through the rows it leaves horizontal strands of yarn.

2 With the horizontal strand of yarn lying across the front (back) of the stitch, insert the RH needle through the back (front) of the dropped stitch.

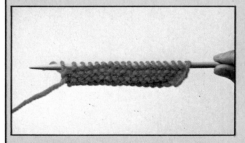

2 Alternate knit and purl rows exactly as in stocking stitch. This is the right side of the fabric.

3 Push the RH needle from back (front) to front (back) under the horizontal strand of yarn.

4 Insert the LH needle through the back (front) of the dropped stitch.

3 Note the finished piece of reverse stocking stitch resembles garter stitch.

5 Use the LH needle to lift the dropped stitch over the horizontal strand of yarn and off the needle.

6 The strand of yarn forms a stitch on the RH needle: transfer it to the correct knitting position on the LH needle by inserting the LH needle through the stitch back and withdrawing the RH needle.

Paul Williams

Method for stocking stitch
Picking up a ladder on the right side

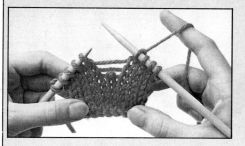  

1 The unravelled stitches will leave horizontal strands of yarn.

2 On the right side of the knitting insert a crochet hook through the front of the loop at the bottom of the ladder, pulling the lowest strand through to the front.

3 Work up the ladder in this way until you have the original stitch. Remove the crochet hook and replace the dropped stitch on the LH needle ready to be knitted. Make sure that the stitch is not twisted and that you work it as a knit stitch.

Picking up a ladder on the wrong side

1 Use a crochet hook, as before, to hook the bottom-most strand through the front of the lowest loop in the ladder.

2 Work up the ladder, but remove the crochet hook each time you move up to the next loop.

3 Replace the dropped stitch on the LH needle, making sure that it is not twisted, and work the stitch in purl.

Pretty casual waistcoat

This little waistcoat is an invaluable addition to any wardrobe. The textured stripe effect is achieved by knitting bands of stocking stitch and reverse stocking stitch.

Sizes

These instructions are for the measurements shown on the diagrams: the waistcoat fits a woman with an 83 to 87cm bust.
Lengthen or shorten the waistcoat in multiples of 8cm by adding or subtracting a pattern repeat – 4cm stocking stitch, 4cm reverse stocking stitch – between the garter stitch borders at top and bottom.
Make the sections wider or narrower by casting on two stitches more or less for each cm difference.
Remember that you need more or less yarn according to the size you make and whether you alter the length: in general allow approximately 25g for each 5cm added to the bust size.

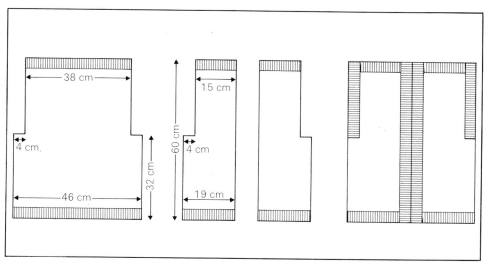

Materials
250g of double knitting yarn such as Pingouin Confortable
One pair 4mm knitting needles

Tension
21 stitches and 30 rows to 10cm over pattern on 4mm needles.

Back
Cast on 96 stitches for lower edge of back. * Work 4cm in garter stitch.
☐ Beginning with a knit row, work 4cm in stocking stitch ending with a purl row.
☐ Beginning with a purl row, work 4cm in reverse stocking stitch, ending with a knit row.
☐ Repeat 8cm of pattern until back measures 32cm from cast-on edge, ending with last row of a stocking stitch stripe. Take care to stretch fabric open when measuring as stripes of different textures make a fabric 'concertina up. *
☐ Cast off 8 stitches at the beginning of the next 2 rows for armholes. 80 stitches remain.
** Continue in the 8cm pattern repeat until back measures 56cm from cast-on edge, ending with last row of a stocking stitch stripe.
☐ Work 4cm garter stitch for top border Cast off loosely to form top edge. **

Left front
Cast on 40 stitches for lower edge. Make in same way as back by repeating instructions in section marked at beginning and end by an asterisk (*).
☐ Cast off 8 stitches at the beginning of the next row for armhole. 32 stitches remain.
☐ Now complete as given for the back by repeating instructions in section marked by 2 asterisks (**)

Right front
Work as given for left front, but work 1 more row before the cast-off group for armhole.

Borders
Cast on 9 stitches for one front border.
☐ Work in garter stitch always slipping the first stitch of each row to give a neat edge, until border fits along front from lower edge to top.
☐ Cast off loosely.
Make another border in the same way.
☐ Using the same number of stitches, make two 56cm strips of garter stitch for armhole borders.

To make up
Block front and back sections as stripes of stocking stitch and reverse stocking stitch make a fabric concertina up.
☐ Press, omitting garter stitch borders. With right side of both fabrics facing inwards and using a flat seam, sew front borders in position : match cast-on edges of both sections being sewn.
☐ With right side of both fabrics facing inwards and using a back stitch seam, join cast-off edges of fronts and back for about 10cm from each side edge to form shoulders.
☐ Fold armhole borders in half : with right side of both fabrics facing inwards, match centre of one edge of border to each shoulder and using a flat seam, sew borders in position.
☐ With right side of fabric facing inwards, use a back-stitch seam to join side seams.
☐ Turn waistcoat with right side out and lightly press seams.

Step-by-step course – 5

Working a single rib

The use of both knit and purl stitches in the same row forms an elastic fabric called ribbing. A single rib is the most common of a number of rib patterns: it consists of knitting, then purling one stitch alternately across the first row. On subsequent rows each stitch that you knitted in the previous row is purled and each one that you purled is knitted.

The vertical 'knit' ribs predominate, creating a stretchy fabric, which springs back into shape. It is ideal for the sections of a garment that need to grip, such as cuffs, welts and neckbands.

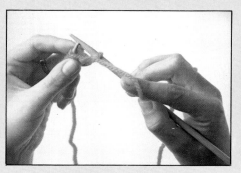

1 Cast on an even number of stitches. Knit the first stitch in the usual way: take the yarn forwards between the two needles so that it is at the front.

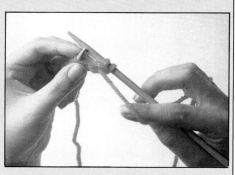

2 Purl the next stitch on the LH needle in the usual way.

3 Take the yarn from the front to the back between the two needles.

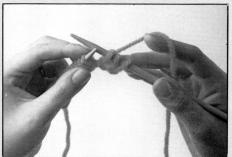

4 Knit the next stitch.

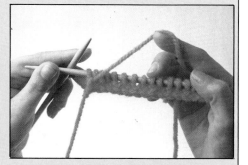

5 Continue in this way, alternately purling, then knitting a stitch, until the first row is complete, ending with a purled stitch.

6 Knit the first stitch on subsequent rows.

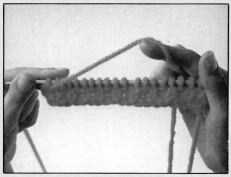

7 Work in the same alternate knit and purl sequence on every row.

8 Stretch the fabric slightly open to see that the knit stitches form raised vertical lines whilst the purl stitches recede.

Paul Williams

17

Casting off in rib

To retain the elasticity of any piece of ribbing you must cast off in rib: knit or purl the stitches in their correct sequence before lifting one stitch over another.

Don't press any ribbed fabric unless you are specifically told to do so: this again destroys its elastic qualities. Use a flat seam for joining ribbing especially welt or cuff sections on a garment.

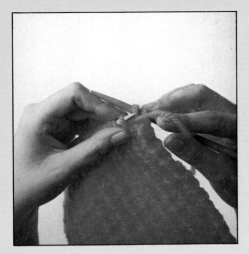

1 Keep the ribbed pattern correct by knitting the first stitch on the LH needle and purling the second.

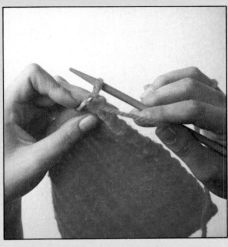

2 Use the LH needle point to lift the first stitch knitted over the second: keep the stitches fairly loose.

3 Knit the next stitch.

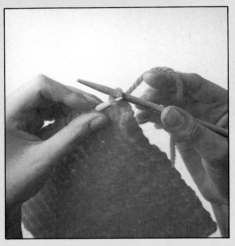

4 Cast off in the usual way.

5 Purl the next stitch to keep rib sequence correct.

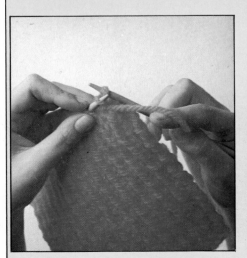

6 Cast off this stitch.

7 Continue in this way, alternating knit and purl.

8 The cast-off edge is as elastic as the main piece of knitting.

Paul Williams

Step-by-step course – 6

*Double rib
*Moss stitch
*Basket stitch
*Pattern for cot blanket

Double rib

Altering the number of stitches in the knit and purl 'ribs' adds variety to ribbed patterns. Double rib is a popular fabric, not quite as elastic as single rib, but with similar uses ; it can also be used as an all-over pattern for close-fitting sweaters.

Double rib requires a multiple of four stitches plus two extra to make the pattern balance across the row. In the first row you knit two stitches and then purl two stitches alternately. Subsequent rows are worked in the same way as single rib by knitting all purled stitches and purling all knitted stitches in the previous row.

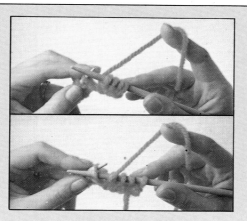

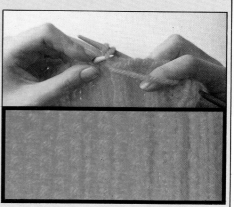

1 To make sample cast on any number of stitches that is a multiple of 4 (e.g. 12, 16, 20, 24) plus 2 extra stitches. For the **1st row** knit 2 stitches, then purl 2 stitches, continue in this way until you reach the last 2 stitches, knit 2.
2 To work the **2nd row** purl 2 stitches then knit 2 stitches, continue in this way until you reach the last 2 stitches, purl 2.

3 Repeat the 1st and 2nd rows for the length that you require, ending with a 2nd pattern row. Cast off in pattern, knitting or purling each stitch accordingly.
4 The finished fabric requires no pressing : it stretches slightly open when it is worn so that the vertical 'ribs' are clearly visible.

Moss stitch

This is another simple variation of ribbing which produces a neat, all-over pattern with a light 'seeded' texture. You work the first row in the same way as single rib : on subsequent rows each stitch that you knitted in the previous row must be knitted again and each one that you purled must be purled again. Both sides of the fabric have the same appearance, so it is reversible.

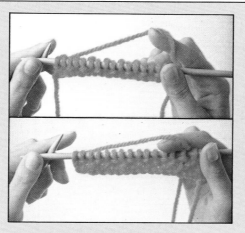

1 To make sample cast on any even number of stitches (e.g. 16, 18, 20). For the **1st row** knit 1 stitch then purl 1 stitch, continue in this way until you reach the end of the row.
2 To work the **2nd row**, purl 1 stitch then knit 1 stitch, continue in this way until you reach the end of the row.

3 Repeat the 1st and 2nd rows for the length that you require, ending with either row. Cast off in pattern so that you knit or purl each stitch accordingly.
4 The finished fabric is flat, unlike ribbing. Lightly press if necessary taking care not to flatten the texture.

Paul Williams

Basket stitch

Larger multiples of stitches and rows form blocks of stocking stitch and reverse stocking stitch in a familiar basketweave pattern. You can make other fabrics by altering the number of stitches and rows in the blocks: remember that this may affect the multiple of stitches that you cast on.

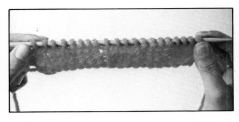

1 To make sample cast on any number of stitches that is a multiple of 8 (e.g. 16, 24, 32) plus 4 extra stitches. For the **1st row** knit 4 stitches then purl 4 stitches, continue in this way until you reach the last 4 stitches, knit 4.

2 To work the **2nd row** purl 4 stitches then knit 4 stitches, continue in this way until you reach the last 4 stitches, purl 4.

3 For the **3rd and 4th rows** repeat the instructions for the 1st and 2nd rows.

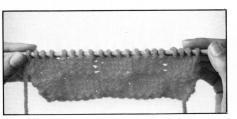

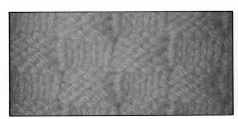

4 Alternate the blocks of pattern in the **5th to 8th rows** by repeating the 2nd, 1st, 2nd, 1st rows in that order.

5 Repeat these 8 rows for the length that you require, ending with either pattern row 4 or 8. Cast off in pattern, knitting or purling each stitch accordingly.

6 The pattern is reversible: it may require a light press depending on the yarn that you use.

Baby's favourite blanket

This bright, modern cot blanket is really fun to make. Made from different-textured patches, it's an excellent way to practise simple-stitch patterns.

Size
These instructions are for the measurements shown on the diagram: the blanket is approximately 84cm long x 56cm wide.

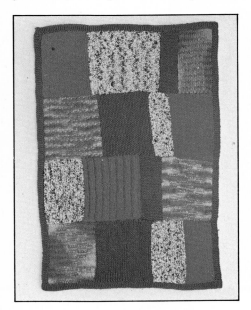

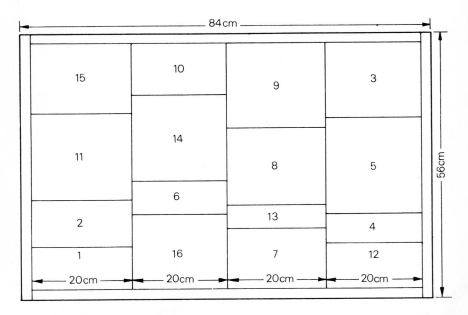

20

Materials
125g of double knitting yarn such as
  Lister/Lee Target Motoravia —
  code A
100g of bouclé tweed yarn such as
  Lister/Lee Target Knoppy Knit —
  code B
80g of bouclé yarn such as
  Lee Target Poodle — code C
75g of random-dyed mohair yarn such
  as Lister/Tahiti —
  code D
One pair each 4mm, 5mm and 6mm
  knitting needles

To make blanket
The blanket consists of 16 pieces, which all measure 20cm in length. Number each patch as you finish it to make it easy when you sew them together.

Patches 1-3 are in stocking stitch.
6mm needles and C, cast on 13 stitches.
5mm needles and B, cast on 18 stitches.
6mm needles and C, cast on 22 stitches.

Patches 4-6 are in garter stitch.
4mm needles and A, cast on 13 stitches.
5mm needles and B, cast on 36 stitches.
4mm needles and A, cast on 15 stitches.

Patches 7-9 are in moss stitch.
6mm needles and C, cast on 18 stitches.
4mm needles and A, cast on 35 stitches.
6mm needles and D, cast on 25 stitches.

Patches 10-12 are in single rib (K1, P1 rib)
5mm needles and B, cast on 22 stitches.
4mm needles and A, cast on 50 stitches.
6mm needles and D, cast on 18 stitches.

Patches 13 and 14 are in double rib (K2, P2 rib)
5mm needles and B, cast on 10 stitches.
6mm needles and C, cast on 32 stitches.

Patches 15 and 16 are in basket stitch.
6mm needles and D, cast on 20 stitches.
6mm needles and D, cast on 24 stitches.

Borders
Using 4mm needles and A, cast on 5 stitches.
Work 2 pieces in garter stitch each 80cm long and another 2 pieces each 56cm long.

To make up
Darn in all ends on the wrong side of the work. Only the sections in stocking stitch require pressing. Oversew the patches together on the wrong side in the order shown in the chart : make sure that the knitting is in the same direction by having all cast-on edges at the same edge of each strip. Sew on the 2 long borders, then the 2 short ones.

George Wright/cot, John Lewis

Step-by-step course -7

*What is 'tension'?
*Getting the correct tension for a pattern
*Learn your first abbreviations
*Using tension to shape a pullover

What is 'tension'?

Tension is one of the most important aspects of knitting, yet it is so often overlooked. An understanding of tension is the key to successful knitting: it involves the relationship of yarn to needle sizes and the way you control the yarn. Knitting is an enjoyable pastime, not a chore; relax and allow the yarn to run easily over your fingers — they have a function similar to the tension control of a sewing machine. As you practise with different types of yarn you will notice that thicker yarns require a slacker control of tension whilst thinner yarns need a tighter one: any variation in control within a piece of knitting gives it an irregular appearance.

Above all, remember that the tension of your work is personal to you, as two people rarely work to the same tension; this is why it is unwise to let another person complete a piece of knitting you have started. To see — and feel — what tension is about, try this experiment with a ball of yarn and a range of needle sizes.

You need a ball of double knitting yarn and a selection of knitting needles, preferably a complete set ranging down from 7½mm to 2mm. Using 7½mm needles cast on 24 stitches and work six rows in stocking stitch. (To prevent the fabric curling, purl the second and next to last stitches on every knit row).

Change to one-size-smaller needles. Mark the change by working one purl row to make a ridge across the right side. Work five rows in stocking stitch. Continue in this way until you have worked through the whole range of needles.

The tapering look of the finished sample indicates that you can shape a piece of knitting without complicated increasing and decreasing — simply by changing the needle size. The pattern for the baggy top puts this method into practice.

mm, 2¾mm, 2¼mm and 2mm needles
he smallest needle sizes give a hard,
tiff fabric with minute crowded stitches.

½mm, 4mm, 3¾mm and 3¼mm needles
his range of needles sizes work per-
ctly in conjunction with this yarn, to
roduce neat, firm stitches in a soft
astic fabric. 4mm or 3¾mm needles are
e most popular sizes to use with
ouble knitting yarn.

mm, 5½mm and 5mm needles
ese sizes are too large for this double
nitting yarn. It is hard to control the neat
ppearance of the stitches and the quality
f the pattern is lost.

½mm, 7mm and 6½mm needles
ese needles are extra large for the
arn: they produce a soft fabric unsuitable
r most garments as it has difficulty in
taining the shape. Using a softer yarn,
ch as mohair, results in a warm fabric
ith an almost cellular quality.

Getting the correct tension for a pattern

Most patterns give a tension guide that states the number of stitches and rows to a measurement (usually 10cm) using the recommended yarn and needles. This is the designer's tension, all measurements for the knitting pattern are based on it.

If you want to end up with a correctly fitting garment, then you must achieve the same tension as the designer. Even one stitch more or less every 10cm makes a significant difference in the size of a piece of knitting. This is especially important with a thick yarn where ten stitches might measure 10cm; if you have only nine stitches to 10cm then the front of a sweater that should measure 50cm across is going to be 5cm too big. The back of the sweater will be the same and the finished garment 10cm bigger than intended.

Making a tension sample to check the measurements is vital before you start work. Knitting course 3 gives details of checking a simple tension; more so-phisticated patterns require both stitch and row tension to be correct.

Stitch tension is necessary in most patterns to obtain the correct width; in some instances the row tension is the most important, too. There are two main examples of this: where you are in-creasing or decreasing over a specific measurement to shape a garment; where you are working a garment from side edge to side edge where the number of rows, not stitches, form the width of the garment.

If you obtain the correct stitch tension, but the number of rows are slightly more or less than stated, then ignore the difference and continue to work — unless the circumstances are special, as described above. Only make more sam-ples if the row tension is drastically wrong; in this case it is fairly certain that the stitch tension also needs amending.

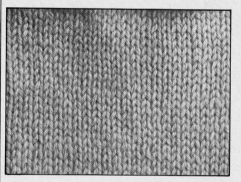

1 Patterns often quote the tension over a stocking stitch fabric, e.g. 21 sts and 27 rows to 10cm over st st. Make a 12cm stocking stitch sample using a few more stitches than stated in the tension guide.

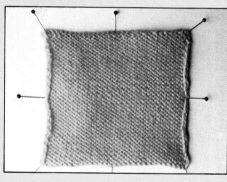

2 Pin the sample down, without stretching it, on a flat surface such as an ironing board. The stitches and rows are more distinctive on the reverse side of stocking stitch.

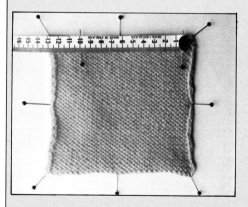

3 Count 21 stitches on your sample and mark with pins. Check their measurement with a tape measure. If there are less than 21 to 10cm, use a smaller needle, if there are more than 21, use a larger one.

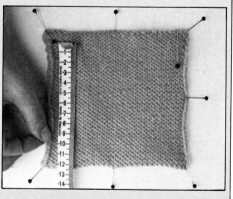

4 Each horizontal ridge represents a row of stocking stitch. Insert 1 pin between ridges and count out 27 rows, inserting the second pin in the hollow after the last ridge counted. Use a tape measure to check the measurement of these rows.

continued

Paul Williams

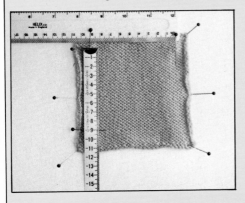

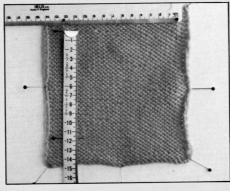

5 This sample is too tight as the 27 rows make less than 10cm : also the stitch tension is incorrect. Make another sample with one-size-larger needles : try progressively larger needles until the tension is absolutely correct.

6 Here the knitting is too loose as the 27 rows measure more than 10cm : again the stitch tension is wrong. Use smaller needles to make another sample. It doesn't matter how many times you change the needle size as long as you end up with the correct tension.

Learn your first abbreviations

Knitting has its own technical terms and a special language – a kind of shorthand – for describing instructions in a clear, concise way. Without this shorthand, the instructions for any but the simplest knitting are far too long and tedious to follow.

The abbreviations given here are for simple techniques that you already know : gradually these and other general knitting notation will be introduced into patterns in the courses. As you become more practised at your knitting, you will find following the abbreviations becomes quite easy and automatic.

K = knit
P = purl
st(s) = stitch(es)
g st = garter stitch
st st = stocking stitch
rev st st = reverse stocking stitch
K1, P1 rib = knit 1, purl 1 (single) rib

Big, baggy pullover

This loose, cuddly pullover is shaped simply by changing the size of your needles. Exactly the same both back and front, it can be made up in no time.

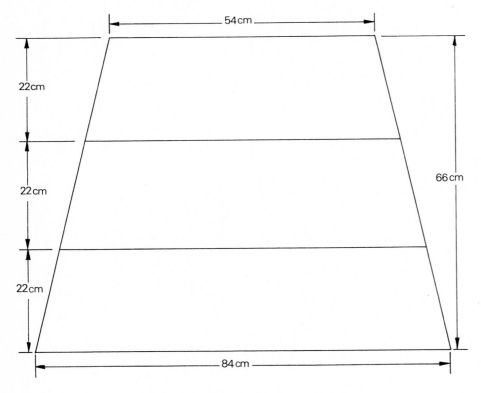

Measurements
These instructions are for the measurements shown on the diagram. The top is very loose and fits a range of bust sizes from 83 to 92cm. If you want to make the top larger or smaller, cast on about two stitches more or less for each centimetre difference. Knit the top to any length you like. Remember you need more or less yarn according to the size you make and whether you alter the length : in general allow approximately 25g for each 5cm you add to the bust size.

Materials
Total of 200g of fine mohair-type yarn such as 3 Suisses Barbara
1 pair each 3¾, 5½ and 7½mm knitting needles
1½m of narrow ribbon

Tension
18 sts and 40 rows to 10cm over g st worked on 3¾mm needles.

Front
Using 3¾mm needles cast on 98 sts for neck/shoulder edge. Always slipping first st of every row, work 22cm in g st.
☐ Change to 5½mm needles. Work another 22cm in g st.
☐ Change to 7½mm needles. Continue in g st until work measures 66cm from cast-on edge. Cast off very loosely : if possible, use one size larger needle.

Back
Make the back the same as the front.

To make up
Do not press at any stage.
☐ Using a back stitch seam, join shoulder seams for approximately 18cm from each armhole edge. Using a flat seam, join side seams leaving 22cm open for armholes.
Gather lower edge by threading a 1½m length of ribbon through spaces between stitches above first g st ridge.

Step-by-step course – 8

*Simple increasing on knit and purl rows
*Simple decreasing on knit and purl rows
*Pattern for a jacket

Simple increasing on knit and purl rows

At some stage in your knitting you will need to shape the fabric to make it wider; by increasing the number of stitches in the row.

There are various ways of making extra stitches, depending on how you want the finished increase to look. Making two stitches out of one is the simplest, most popular way and can be worked anywhere in the row. It is a convenient way to shape side edges, either increasing into the first or last stitches in a row, or increasing one stitch from the end, to maintain a slightly neater edge.

The abbreviation for this technique is 'inc one st'. If a pattern stipulates 'increase a stitch' then use this method; if another means of increasing is required, you must follow the precise instructions given in the pattern.

To make two stitches out of one on a knit row

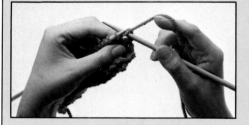

1 Insert RH needle from front to back into first stitch in a knit row.

2 Wind yarn under and over RH needle in a clockwise direction.

3 Draw a new stitch through the loop on the LH needle in the same way as knitting.

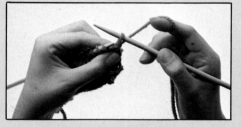

4 Twist RH needle point in a clockwise direction until it lies behind LH needle point: there is a new loop on the RH needle and the stitch you are working into remains on the LH needle.

5 Insert RH needle from right to left into back of stitch on LH needle.

6 Wind yarn under and over RH needle in a clockwise direction.

7 Draw a new stitch through the loop on the LH needle in the same way as knitting.

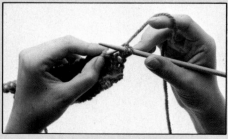

8 Slip the first stitch off the LH needle in the usual way.

9 There are now two stitches on the RH needle made by increasing in the first stitch of the row.

Paul Williams

To make two stitches out of one on a purl row

1 Insert RH needle from back to front into front of the first stitch in a purl row.

2 Wind yarn over top and round RH needle in an anti-clockwise direction.

3 Use LH thumb to gently push RH needle point back through loop on LH needle.

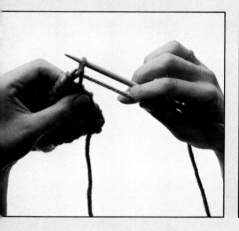

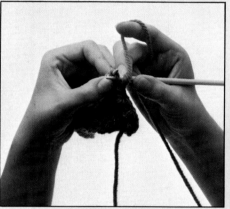

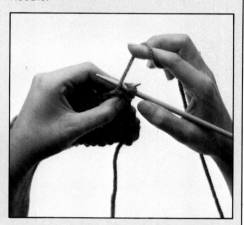

4 There is a new loop on the RH needle, and the stitch you are working into remains on the LH needle.

5 Insert RH needle from left to right into back of stitch on LH needle : hold top of loop clear with left thumbnail until needle is well inserted between front and back strands.

6 Wind yarn over top and round RH needle in an anti-clockwise direction.

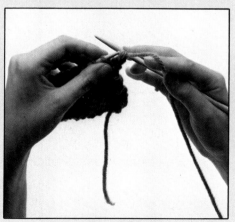

7 Use LH thumb to gently push RH needle point back through loop on LH needle.
8 Twist RH needle upwards and forwards.

9 Slip the first stitch off the LH needle in the usual way.

10 There are now two stitches on the RH needle made by increasing in the first stitch in the row.

Paul Williams

Simple decreasing on knit and purl rows

The usual way to decrease a stitch is to knit or purl two stitches together; combining them to form a single stitch. This technique is abbreviated as 'K2 tog' on a knit row or 'P2 tog' on a purl row. You can use this method at any point in a row, as well as for shaping side edges. The steepness of shaped edges, such as a raglan armhole or the triangular form-ation of the squares in the jacket pattern given at the end of this course, depends on the frequency of decreasing. Working stitches together at the beginning and end of every fourth or more rows gives a gradually tapering edge, whilst de-creasing on every row or alternate rows gives a sharper incline. Sometimes at the end of a piece of shaping there may be three stitches remaining. The pattern will specify that you knit or purl them together. Do this in the same way as you would when working two stitches to-gether, but insert the right-hand needle through three stitches instead of two. Cut off the yarn and thread through the stitch remaining on the needle to fasten off the work.

Decreasing by knitting two stitches together

1 Insert RH needle tip from left to right through front of second stitch on LH needle.

2 Push RH needle farther, taking it from front to back of first stitch on LH needle : the RH needle is now inserted from front to back through first two stitches.

3 Wind yarn under and over RH needle in a clockwise direction.

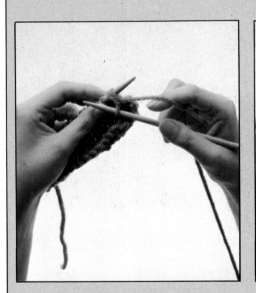

4 Draw a new stitch through the two loops on the LH needle in the same way as knitting.

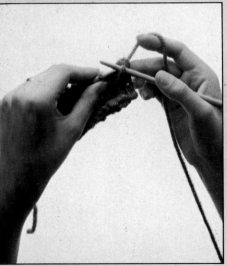

5 Slip the two knitted-together stitches off the LH needle as if knitting a single stitch.

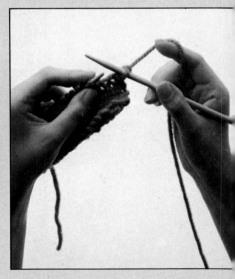

6 The single stitch formed by knitting the first two stitches together is now on the RH needle.
Work to the end of the row as directed in the pattern.

7 To knit three stitches together, insert RH needle from left to right through front of first three stitches on LH needle.

8 Wind the yarn round the RH needle and knit in the usual way, drawing one new stitch through the three loops on the LH needle.

9 Cut off the yarn about 10cm from the needle. Loosen the remaining stitch on the needle ; thread the yarn through and draw the stitch up tightly in the same way as finishing off the last stitch of a cast-off edge.

Decreasing by purling two stitches together

1 Insert RH needle from right to left through front of first two stitches in a purl row.

2 Wind yarn over top and round RH needle in an anti-clockwise direction.

3 Use left thumb to gently push RH needle point back through two loops on LH needle in the same way as purling.

4 Twist RH needle upwards and forwards : there is a new loop on the RH needle and the stitches you are working into remain on the LH needle.

5 Slip the two purled-together stitches off the LH needle as in purling a single stitch.

6 The single stitch formed by purling the first two stitches together is now on the RH needle. Work to the end of the row as directed in the pattern.

Loose and chunky jacket

Wear this loose, open jacket when you need a cover-up on cooler days. It's made from only twelve squares, just pieced together. The intriguing triangular effect is achieved by reversing the right and wrong sides of the work half-way through each square.

Sizes
These instructions are for the measurements shown on the diagram. The jacket is very loose and fits a range of bust sizes from 83 to 92cm.

Materials
Total of 700g of chunky yarn such as Pingouin Iceberg
1 pair each of 6mm and 6½mm knitting needles

Tension
13 sts and 16 rows to 10cm over st st worked on 6½mm needles.

To make square
Using 6½mm needles cast on 3 sts.
☐ Inc one st, K to end of row. Inc one st, P to end of row. Inc one st, K to last st of 3rd row, inc one st. Inc one st, P to last st of 4th row, inc one st. There are now 9 sts.
☐ Repeat these 4 rows 6 times more, then the first and 2nd rows again. There are now 47 sts.
☐ P2 tog, P to end of row. This P row reverses the st st pattern. K2 tog, K to end of row. P2 tog, P to last 2 sts, P2 tog. K2 tog, K to last 2 sts, K2 tog.
☐ Repeat the last 4 rows 6 times more, then the first 2 again. There are now 3 sts. P these 3 sts tog. Fasten off yarn. Make 12 squares in all.

To make up
Block each piece so that it measures 25cm square. Press lightly, taking care not to destroy the texture of the knitting.
☐ Overcast the squares together, positioning them as shown in diagram, apart from neck and front opening indicated by dotted line. Press seams carefully.
☐ Join x . . . . x to x . . . . x to form under-arm seams and y . . . . y to y . . . . y to form side seams.

Borders
Using 6mm needles cast on 4 sts.
☐ Always slipping first st of every row, work in g st until strip fits all round neck edge, beginning and ending at centre front opening. Cast off.
☐ Make a similar border to fit all round lower edge. Cast off. Using overcasting, sew on borders : reverse seam on front neck edges, sewing together on right side of work. Make borders to fit up front edges.
☐ Sew front borders in position, reversing seam for 16cm at top edge. Make borders for lower edges of sleeves : join ends of border to form a circle and sew in position.

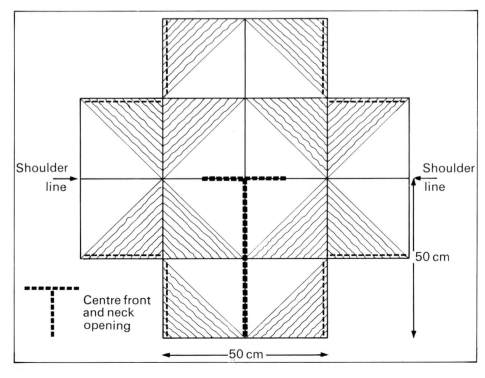

Shoulder line

Shoulder line

50 cm

Centre front and neck opening

◀— 50 cm —▶

Step-by-step course – 9

Swiss darning and how to work it

An effective way of working different coloured patterns into ordinary knitting is to Swiss darn it – it is easy to do and avoids the complications of working with lots of different-coloured yarns while you are knitting. Work it before the garment pieces are sewn together.

All kinds of designs are suitable – you could try anything from numbers and names to a rose in full bloom. Use it to bring a forgotten old sweater back to life or make use of the extra thickness to strengthen places that get a lot of wear and tear, such as elbows.

A solid fabric such as stocking stitch is the best background – as you embroider, each knitted stitch is individually covered with a new colour, so that the finished result looks just like the original knitting, but the embroidered area is double the thickness. Choose a yarn of the same thickness as the background – don't try to cover a thick yarn with a thinner one or vice versa, as this will distort the fabric.

1 Thread a large blunt-ended needle with yarn of the same ply as the background. Secure yarn by working two or three stitches on top of each other on the back of the first stitch at lower RH corner of motif (the LH side of fabric when you are working on the back).

2 Insert the needle from the back to the front of the work through the base of the first stitch.

3 On the front of the fabric, thread the needle from right to left under the two vertical loops of the same stitch, but one row above.

4 Pull the yarn through. A stitch is formed, covering the RH vertical loop of the knitted stitch. (Don't pull the yarn too tightly ; the darning must be kept at the tension of the background.)

5 Re-insert the needle into the base of the stitch you are covering and out to the front again through the base of the next stitch to the left.

6 Pull the yarn through. A stitch is formed covering the LH vertical loop of the knitted stitch ; one Swiss-darned stitch is now complete.

7 To complete the first line of a block of colour, continue working from right to left along a row, repeating steps 3 to 7 for the number of stitches required. Finish with the needle at the base of the work.

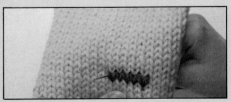

8 To work the row above when the LH edge of the block is a straight line, insert the needle from the back to the front through the centre of the last stitch worked.

9 It is easier to work the second and alternate rows if you turn the knitting upside down. On the front of the fabric, thread the needle under the two vertical loops of the same stitch, but one row below.

continued

continued

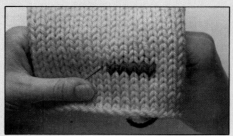

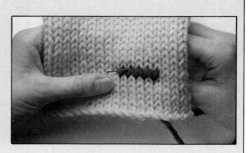

10 Swiss darn the stitch in the usual way. To work the next stitch bring the needle to the front of the fabric, through the base of the next stitch to the left. Continue in this way until you come to the end of the row. Turn your work the other way up before beginning the next row.

11 If the first Swiss-darned stitch of the second row is located one stitch to the left, begin the row by re-inserting the needle through the centre of the next unworked stitch at the end of the first row.

12 To move the first stitch of the second row one stitch to the right, re-insert the needle through the centre of the second to last Swiss-darned stitch on the first row.

Following a chart for Swiss darning

Sometimes a knitting pattern will include a selection of motifs that can be Swiss-darned on the garment. These motifs are usually shown in chart form, on a graph. Each square of the graph represents an individual stitch. Each horizontal line of squares represents a row of knitting; each vertical line, the number of rows. On some charts the different colours are indicated by various symbols — circles, crosses and so on.

Another method of showing the different colours is for the chart to be printed with the actual colours to be used, leaving the background grid visible, so that you can check the number of stitches and rows. Do not be misled by charts on graph paper. The proportions of knitted stitches are not square and most stitches are wider than they are tall, so that a design on graph paper appears to be wider and shorter when you transfer it on to

the garment. To see the design as it will look on your knitting you will have to draw your own grid representing the stitches in their actual proportion, then block in the design on your new grid. Before you begin darning find the correct position for the design on the garment. Some patterns specify an exact spot; otherwise, mark where you want the centre of the design and locate your first stitch from that point.

KEY:
✗ apple green
Ꝺ red
· pink
✛ leaf green
╱ brown

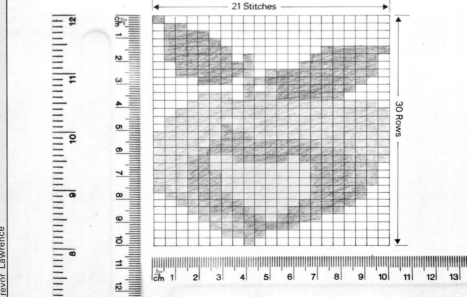

21 Stitches

30 Rows

Trevor Lawrence

Paul Williams

1 The design to be Swiss darned is usually printed in chart form in either of these two ways: one uses symbols to represent the colours and the other has the appropriate colours on the background grid.

2 To see what the design will look like on your knitting, draw a grid showing the stitches in proportion. This grid is based on a fabric that has 21 stitches and 30 rows to 10cm.

3 Colour in the design exactly from the squared chart. The true proportions of your finished design are now visible. If the design flattens too much you can add extra rows to make it taller.

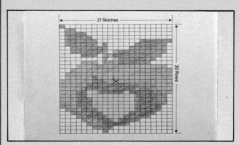

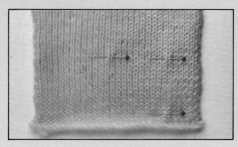

4 Mark the centre of the design so that you can position it correctly on the knitting. Note that the lower RH corner of the area occupied by the motif is located 10 stitches across to the right and 14 rows down.

5 Mark the approximate centre stitch on the area of knitting that you are darning. Count the necessary number of stitches across and rows down to the right to mark the lower RH corner of the area on the fabric.

6 when you finish a block in the first colour, work an adjacent block in another colour. Don't be tempted to work all the blocks in the same colour first : it is easy to lose your place if you make isolated islands of colour.

Designing your own motif or pattern

For a really personal look, design your own motif or pattern. Use your own drawing or a picture from a book as reference, but remember to keep it simple. It is usually difficult to represent fine details with Swiss darning and the degree of detail possible depends on the type of yarn used for the background fabric. Fine 3 or 4 plys have more stitches and rows to a certain measurement than double knitting or chunky yarns. This will give you more scope for details. Check the number of stitches and rows available in the area that you want to darn. Beware of drawing a chart that has many more stitches and rows than you have room for.

1 Find a simple stylized drawing or transfer for an embroidery design. Remember that the type of fabric you are darning dictates the amount of detail you can depict. In general don't attempt too detailed a design.

2 Transfer the main outlines on to tracing paper. Think in terms of areas of colour rather than linear detail.

3 Place carbon paper shiny side down on a piece of graph paper. Position the tracing paper on top of the carbon and pencil over the outlines of the design, transferring them to the graph paper.

4 Go over the outline, deciding as it passes through each square whether to include that stitch in the darning. Where the outline divides a square, if the greater part of the square is within the design, then include the whole square in the darning. Use a pencil for the outline at this stage so that you can amend it if necessary.

5 Lightly colour in the design so that you can see the background grid : this enables you to count the stitches and rows in each block of colour.

6 This simple stylized design has been enlarged to two and three times the size. To do this replace each square in the original chart with four squares for twice the size — nine for three times the size — arranged to form a square block. The symmetry of the design is maintained.

Picture a sweater

Here's proof that a simple sweater needn't be plain. Knit these sweaters in vivid colours, then decorate them with your chosen motifs in easy-to-work Swiss darning.

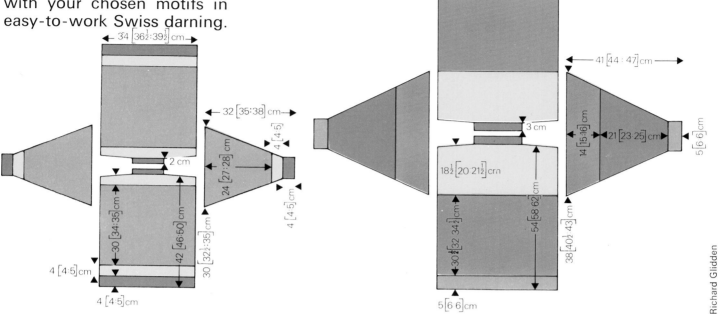

Sizes
The instructions are for the measurements shown on the diagrams.
To fit a 66 [71 :76 :83 :87 :92]cm chest/bust.

Note that instructions for larger sizes are in square brackets [ ] ; where there is only one set of figures it applies to all sizes.

Materials
Total of 250 [300 :350 :400 :450 : 500]g of double knitting yarn such as Madame Pingouin
Child's sweater requires 3 [4 :5] x 50g balls of blue
1 [2 :2] balls each of yellow and green
Adult's sweater requires 4 [4 :5] balls of pink
2 [2 :3] balls each of yellow and green
1 [1 :2] balls of blue
1 pair each 3¼mm and 4mm knitting needles

Tension
22sts and 30 rows to 10cm over st st.

Back and front (alike)
Using 3¼mm needles and green [green : green :blue :blue :blue] cast on 75 [81 : 87 :93 :99 :105]sts.

☐ **1st rib row** K first st, then P one st and K one st alternately to the end of the row.

☐ **2nd rib row** P first st, then K one st and P one st alternately to the end of the row.

☐ Repeat these 2 rows for 4 [4 :5 :5 :6 :6] cm ending with a 2nd rib row.

Above, a set of numbers for you to copy, enlarge if necessary.
Below, motif for the child's sweater (not taken from above set).

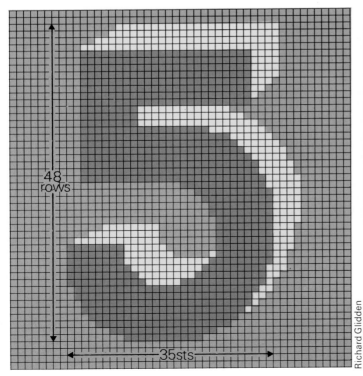

48 rows

35sts

☐ Change to 4mm needles. Beginning with a K row, proceed in st st working in colours as shown on diagram for the size you are making, until work measures 42 [46:50:54:58:62]cm from cast-on edge, ending with a P row.

☐ Shape shoulders by casting off 6 [7: 7:8:8:9]sts at the beginning of next 4 rows and 6 [6:8:8:10:10]sts at the beginning of following 2 rows. 39 [41: 43.:45:47:49]sts.

☐ Change to 3¼mm needles and work the 2 rib rows for 2 [2:2:3:3:3]cm for neck band.

☐ Cast off loosely in rib.

Sleeves (make 2)

Using 3¼mm needles and green [green: green:blue:blue:blue] cast on 35 [39: 43:47:51:55]sts. Work the 2 rib rows of back and front for 4 [4:5:5:6:6]cm, ending with a 2nd rib row.

☐ Change to 4mm needles. Beginning with a K row, proceed in st st working in colours as shown on diagram for the size you are making, increasing one st at each end of next and every following 6th row until there are 65 [71:77:83:89:95]sts.

☐ Now work straight until sleeve measures 32 [35:38:41:47]cm from cast-on edge, ending with a P row. Cast off loosely.

To make up

Do not press.

☐ Darn in all ends on the wrong side of the work.

☐ With right sides of back and front together, join shoulder and neckband seams using a back stitch seam.

☐ Swiss darn on motifs as shown in charts.

☐ Mark centre of cast-off edge of sleeves with a pin. Open front and back sections out flat and with right sides together, match pin to shoulder seam and pin cast-off edge along side edges of main piece. Sew sleeve to body sections with a back stitch seam.

☐ With right sides together, join side and sleeve seams, joining welts and cuffs with a flat seam and the remainder with a back stitch seam.

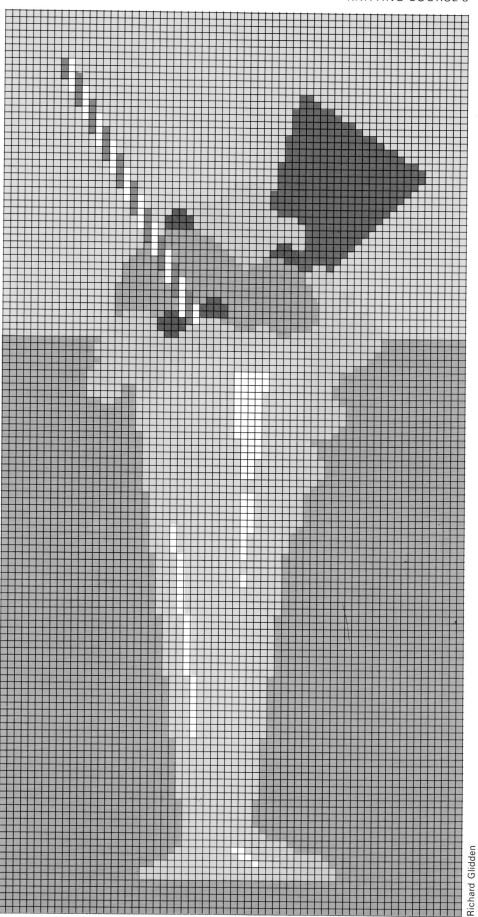

Richard Glidden

Step-by-step course – 10

*Working narrow horizontal stripes
*Horizontal stripes in garter and stocking stitch
*Working narrow vertical stripes

Working narrow horizontal stripes

Narrow horizontal stripes are easy to work in a variety of knitted fabrics and are particularly popular in stocking stitch and garter stitch. To avoid having to darn in lots of loose ends, don't break off the yarn, but carry it up the right-hand edge of the work and resume knitting with it where necessary. Be careful not to pull the yarn so tightly between stripes that the fabric is distorted and the rows draw together at the right-hand edge. This method is practicable only if the stripes are close together, say 2cm to 3cm apart.

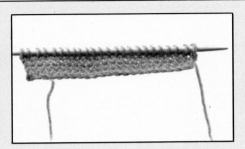

1 To make a regular striped stocking stitch fabric in three colours, cast on the required number of stitches with one of the colours. Work an even number of rows in stocking stitch – here there are four. Limit yourself to three or four colours: the distance won't be too great for you to carry the yarn up the side of the work.

2 Without breaking off the first colour, take a ball of the second colour and begin knitting with it. The ends of yarn are at the RH edge.

3 Work four rows in stocking stitch using the second colour. Note the row of broken stripes immediately below the one you are working; this effect occurs on the wrong side of the fabric when you change colour.

4 Take a ball of yarn in the third colour and begin knitting with it. The ends of both the first and second colours are at the RH edge.

5 Complete four rows in the third colour. Hold the needle with the stitches in your left hand ready to begin the next row with the first colour. Untangle the first colour and hold in your right hand: keep the other ends clear at the back of the work.

6 Insert the RH needle into the first stitch to knit it. Wind the first colour round the RH needle. Keep the loop of yarn at the RH edge fairly loose – pulling it tight distorts the row tension. Work four rows as usual.

7 Continue in this way, changing colour every four rows until the knitting is the depth you require. Don't let the ends of yarn become too tangled and keep the loops of yarn carried up the side at an even tension.

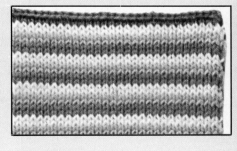

8 Cut off the two colours you have finished with, leaving 10cm ends (darn these in later). Cast off with the colour used for the last stripe.

Horizontal stripes in garter and stocking stitch

Simple stitches and colourful yarns combine to produce a variety of interesting effects in narrow horizontal stripes. Create your own design by using a pattern for a plain garter stitch or stocking stitch garment, such as a sweater, and adding stripes to it. Unlike substituting one stitch for another, adding stripes to a pattern does not affect the tension, so you needn't worry about variations in size. Striping is also an ideal way to use up oddments of left-over yarn. Choose yarn of similar thicknesses for a neat, even fabric.

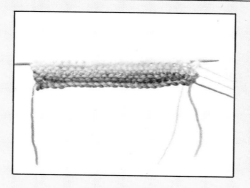

1 Choose three colours and knit an even number of rows with each (here there are two), carrying the yarns up the side of the work.

2 Note that the two rows in a single colour form one horizontal ridge.

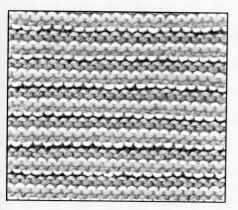

3 The reverse side of the garter stitch fabric looks attractive and can be used as the right side of the work if you prefer. Each horizontal ridge here is a broken stripe made with two colours: these automatically form on the back as you change colours on the other side of the work.

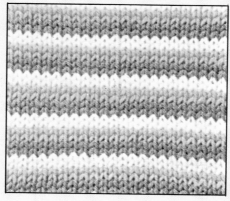

4 Here is the same two-row stripe pattern worked in stocking stitch. Change colours on a knit row to avoid lines of broken colour on the right side of the work; in this way the yarns are always at the RH edge of the knitting so they can be carried up to the next stripe.

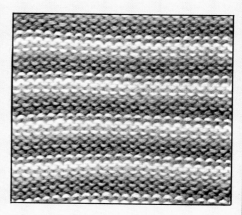

5 Broken stripes occur where you change colours on the reverse side of the stocking stitch fabric. It is similar to the garter stitch version except that there is one row of plain-coloured stitches separating the broken stripes.

Working narrow vertical stripes

To make a stocking stitch fabric with vertical stripes in two colours you must use both balls of yarn within the same row of knitting. Each hand holds one colour, and the colour not in use strands across the back of the work. Keep the strands loose so that the stitch tension doesn't become distorted. This method of stranding is only suitable if the stripe is no more than five stitches wide; with more stitches the strands of yarn become too long and are likely to be caught and pulled. The stranding on the wrong side produces a fabric that is double the normal thickness, making it ideal for heavier or outdoor garments.

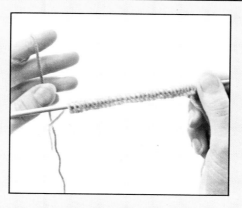

1 To make a stocking stitch fabric with regular vertical stripes in two colours (A and B), cast on the required number of stitches with A. Wind B round the fingers of your left hand as shown.

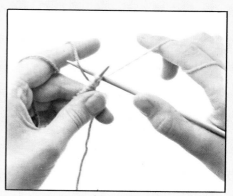

2 Hold needle with cast-on stitches in your left hand and wind A round the fingers of your right hand ready to begin knitting. The first stripe is in B: insert RH needle into first stitch, then from left to right under front of loop of yarn in B on left index finger.

continued

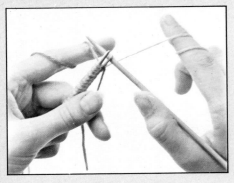

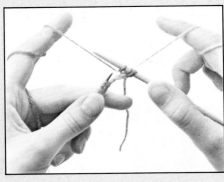

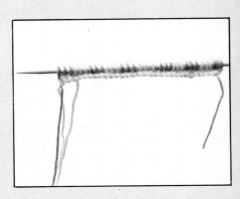

3 Twist RH needle forwards so that yarn in B forms a loop round the needle. Use the RH needle to pull the loop in B through the stitch on the LH needle.

4 Allow the stitch in A to fall from the LH needle. Continue in this way, looping B through the required number of stitches (here it is three) on the LH needle.

5 Knit the next three stitches with A in the usual way. Don't pull the yarn at the back of the work too tightly across the stitches in B. Work alternate stripes in B, then A, to the end of the row.

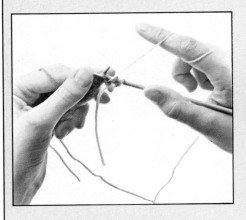

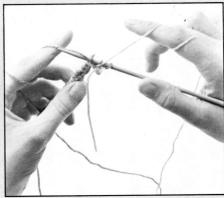

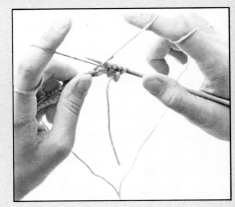

6 At the start of the second (purl) row, loop B round A to bring both yarns to RH edge. Holding yarns as before, wind B with your left hand from the front of the work over the top and round the RH needle point in an anti-clockwise direction.

7 Pull a new loop in B through the stitch on the LH needle. Place the tip of your left thumb on the RH needle point as you pull it backwards to help guide the new loop through the stitch and prevent it falling off the needle.

8 Allow the stitch to fall from the LH needle in the usual way. Work three stitches in B, then three in A, keeping B out of the way at the LH side of your work.

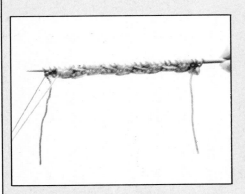

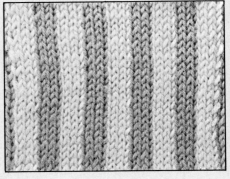

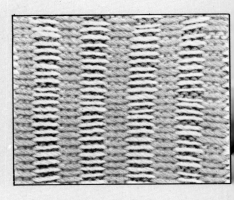

9 Purl to the end of the row, working the appropriate stitches in A and B. Keep checking that the yarn lies loosely across the wrong side of the knitting.

10 Always keeping A in your right hand and B in your left hand, work in stocking stitch for the depth that you require. Cast off in the normal way using one colour only.

11 The stranded threads look very neat on the wrong side of the work : they have a regular under and over appearance without any twisting.

Step-by-step course – 11

Keep baby snug in this gaily coloured robe, worked in horizontal and vertical stripes. Ribbon binding at the neck and front opening simplifies the making up, as does the ribbon-tie fastening.

Kim Sayer

Joining shoulder seams

Most knitted garments have shaping to give a sloping line from the armhole edge up to the neck, along the shoulders. Patterns give specific instructions for shaping. Keep the continuity of the sloping line by joining the shoulder seams carefully.

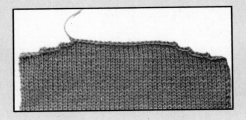

1 Begin shaping the shoulders six to eight rows below the final group of cast-off stitches for the back neck. The cast-off stitches form an edge at each side, sloping from the armhole edge up to the stitches cast off in the centre for the neck.

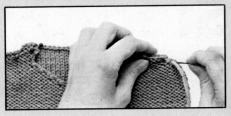

2 When the front is complete join the shoulder seams. Match cast-off edges, right sides together, and pin in a straight line as shown. Sew with a back stitch seam following the line of pins.

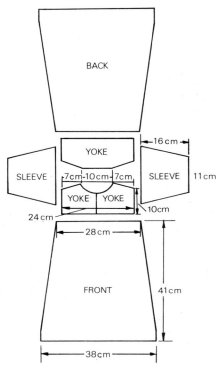

Roy Flooks

Sizes
To fit 46 to 51cm chest: other measurements are shown on the diagram.

Materials
Total of 200g of double knitting crêpe yarn such as Robin Columbine Crêpe Double Knitting
This garment took 3 x 20g balls in each of colours A (pink) and B (ivory) 2 balls in each of 4 other colours C (blue), D (green), E (red) and F (yellow)
1 pair each 3mm and 3¾mm needles
50cm of 15mm-wide ribbon for binding
1m of 6mm-wide ribbon for ties

Tension
24 sts and 32 rows to 10cm over st st worked on 3¾mm needles.

Horizontal stripe sequence
This consists of four rows each in colours F, C, B, E, D and A; repeat this sequence as directed in the pattern. Cut off yarn after finishing each colour; the distance between stripes of the same colour is too great to permit carrying the yarn up the side of the work.

Skirt back
□ Using 3mm needles and A, cast on 92 sts. Work 4 rows g st.
□ Change to 3¾mm needles. Beginning with a K row, continue in st st and horizontal stripe sequence.
□ Dec one st at each end of 25th and every following 8th row until 68 sts remain.
□ Work a total of 116 rows in stripes, finishing after last row of D in the 5th repeat.
□ Change to 3mm needles. Using A, work 4 rows g st. Cast off.

Skirt front
□ Work as given for skirt back.

Sleeves
□ Using 3mm needles and A, cast on 28 sts. Work 4 rows g st.
□ Change to 3¾mm needles. Beginning with a K row, continue in st st and stripe sequence.
□ Inc one st at each end of 5th and every following 4th row until there are 48 sts.
□ Work a total of 44 rows in stripes, finishing after last row of D in the 2nd repeat.
□ Change to 3mm needles. Using A, work 4 rows g st. Cast off.

Yoke back
□ Using 3¾mm needles and B, cast on 57 sts.
□ Begin vertical stripe pattern. Using B, K3 sts, using A, K3 sts; alternately K3 sts using B and A to end of row.
□ Continue in st st and vertical stripes as above until work measures 10cm, ending with a P row.
□ Cast off 4 sts at beginning of each of next 8 rows to shape shoulders.
□ Cast off remaining 35 sts.

Yoke left front
□ Using 3¾mm needles and B, cast on 29 sts.
□ Begin vertical stripe pattern. Using B, K3 sts, using A, K3 sts; alternately K3 sts using B and A to last 5 sts, using B, K3 sts, using A, K2 sts.
□ Continue in vertical stripes until there are 11 rows less than back before the shoulder shaping, ending at front edge.
□ Shape neck by casting off at beginning of next and every alternate row (i.e. same edge at start of P rows) 6 sts once, 2 sts twice, one st 3 times. The last row is a P row and 16 sts remain.
□ Cast off at the beginning of next and every alternate row (i.e. same edge at start of K rows) 4 sts 4 times to shape shoulders.

Yoke right front
□ Using 3¾mm needles and B, cast on 29 sts.
□ Begin vertical stripe pattern. Using A, K2 sts, using B, K3 sts, using A, K3 sts; alternately K3 sts using B and A to end of row, finishing with 3 sts in B.
□ Continue in vertical stripes until there are 10 rows less than back before the shoulder shaping, ending at front edge.
□ Continue as given for left front yoke, reversing position of neck shaping by casting off at beginning of K rows. Reverse shoulder shaping by casting off at beginning of P rows.

To make up
□ Press lightly with a cool iron over a dry cloth.
□ Using a back stitch seam throughout join shoulder seams.
□ Mark centre of sleeve top with a pin and match to shoulder seam. Sew sleeve tops in position along sides of yoke.
□ Sew yoke to top of skirt, easing skirt slightly to fit yoke.
□ Join side and sleeve seams. Press finished seams.
□ Bind neck and front opening with ribbon. Sew on ribbon to tie at top of front opening.

Step-by-step course – 12

*Knitting a background for smocking
*Smocking a knitted fabric
*Knitting in smocking
*Pattern for toddler's smocked party dress
*More abbreviations to learn

Knitting a background for smocking

Smocking is a technique normally used in dressmaking to control fullness in a fabric: similar techniques applied to knitting are particularly successful since knitted fabrics are naturally elastic. Garments knitted in fine yarns lend themselves to smocking; those made of thick yarns are too bulky. A ribbed fabric is a perfect background for smocking, as the vertical knit ribs serve as a guide for the stitching. The most popular background is single knit ribs with three stitches between them. To make a fabric of the required width after smocking you must first knit one measuring one and a half times the finished width. Specific details, including the number of stitches, normally appear in a pattern. The following steps can be used in working your own design for a smocked panel for a bodice, yoke or cuffs on a dress or blouse.

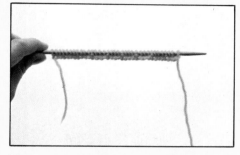

1 Make a tension sample to calculate the number of stitches required. Cast on a multiple of 8 stitches (e.g. 16, 24, 32) plus 3 extra stitches. Try 35 stitches for double knitting yarn. To work the row (this is the right side of the fabric), P3 sts, K1 st alternately until 3 sts remain, P3,

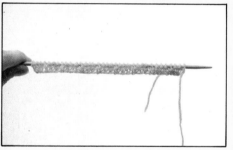

2 To work the 2nd row K3 sts, then P1 st alternately until 3 sts remain, K3. The wrong side of the work is facing you.

3 Repeat the 2 pattern rows until the fabric is about 6cm deep, ending with a 2nd row.

4 Cast off, keeping the rib sequence correct.

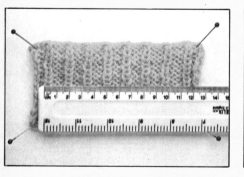

5 Pin the sample down and measure 10cm across the centre. Count the number of stitches to 10cm: on our sample it is 25.

Finished width = 40cm
Width before smocking = 40cm x $1\frac{1}{2}$ = 60cm
Stitch tension is 25sts to 10cm
No. of stitches to 60cm = 25 x 6 = 150
Total no. must be divisable by 8 + 3
150 ÷ 8 = 18 with 6 left over
Take 3 away from total (150) to
give 147 which is a multiple of 8 + 3

6 Calculate the number of stitches to cast on. For example, if you want the completed work to measure 40cm across, you would use the figures given here to determine the number of cast-on stitches.

7 Cast on the necessary number of stitches and make the background fabric the depth you require. The vertical ribs are an ideal guide for the smocking.

Smocking a knitted fabric

After the background fabric is complete, work horizontal lines of stitching across it using a contrasting coloured yarn of the same quality. The stitching draws pairs of ribs together across the fabric: their position alternates on every other row to form the characteristic honeycomb effect.

1 To work the 1st row, first locate the stitch on the 2nd rib from RH edge in the 4th row. Thread a blunt-ended wool needle with the smocking thread; secure with 2 or 3 small stitches, one on top of another, on the wrong side.

2 Bring needle from back to front just before the 2nd knit rib: reinsert from front to back after 3rd knit rib. The strand of yarn covers 5 stitches – 2 knit ribs and 3 purl stitches between them.

3 Wind yarn once or twice round the stitches again, finishing with the needle at the back. Pull yarn gently, drawing the ribs together.

4 Carrying yarn across back of work, bring needle from back to front immediately before the next knit rib to the left. Miss this rib, 3 purl stitches and following rib; reinsert needle from front to back.

5 Continue in this way, winding yarn round pairs of ribs and drawing them together until 1st row is complete. Fasten off.

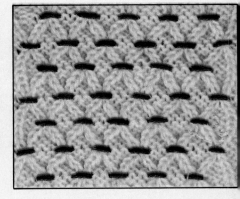

6 To work 2nd row, first miss 4 rows; rejoin yarn behind 1st rib at RH edge. Bring needle from back to front just before the 1st rib; reinsert from front to back after 2nd rib (i.e. 1st rib of 1st pair drawn together on previous row).

7 Wind yarn round the stitches again, finishing with the needle at the back. Pull yarn gently drawing the ribs together. Continue in the same way as on the previous row, always taking LH rib of pair below together with RH rib of the next pair.

8 Always missing 4 rows between lines of smocking, work 1st and 2nd rows alternately for the depth you require. The lines of stitching draw the ribs together into a textured honeycomb pattern.

Knitting in smocking

Rather than applying smocking after the background is complete, you can add it simultaneously when working the background. Use a cable needle to hold the stitches to be drawn together separate from the remainder of the work whilst you wind the smocking thread round them. Keep the strands of yarn threaded loosely across the wrong side of the background; draw them up when you have finished all the rows of smocking.

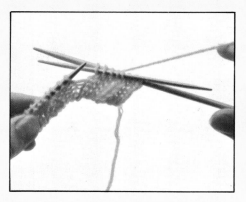

1 Cast on a multiple of 8 stitches (e.g. 16, 24, 32) plus 3 extra stitches. Work 4 rows in rib (see steps 1 and 2 of 'knitting a background for smocking').
To work the 1st row of smocking, knit the first 8 stitches in pattern. Take a cable needle and insert it from left to right through the front of the last 5 sts.

2 Withdraw the RH needle from the stitches on the cable needle. Position the cable needle at the front of the work with RH and LH needles behind it.

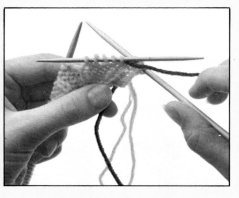

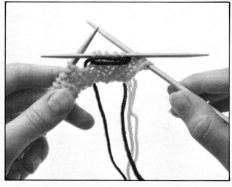

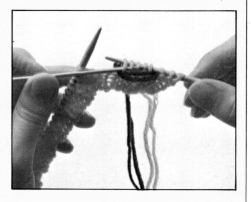

3 Take the yarn for smocking, leaving a 10cm end, from the back of the work to the front between the RH needle and cable needle.

4 Use your right hand to wind the yarn for smocking twice round the front of the 5 stitches on the cable needle in a clockwise direction. Leave the yarn at the back of the work.

5 Insert the RH needle from right to left through the stitches on the cable needle. Withdraw the cable needle returning the 5 stitches to the RH needle.

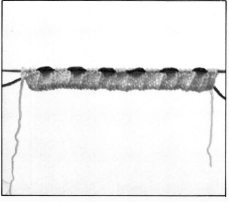

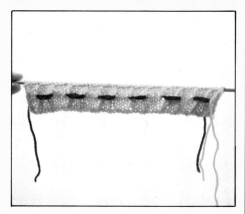

6 Leaving the smocking yarn at the back of the work, pattern another 8 stitches of background. Draw the ribs together at a later stage.

7 Repeat these steps threading the smocking yarn across the back of the work until you reach the end of the row. Cut off the smocking yarn leaving a 10cm end.

8 Pattern 3 rows : you can vary the number of rows between smocking as long as it is uneven (3, 5, 7). The right side of the work faces you as you start the 2nd smocking row.

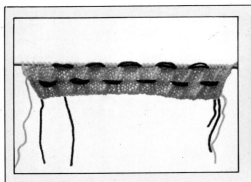

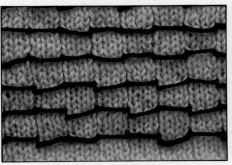

9 To work the 2nd smocking row pattern 12 stitches before slipping the last 5 stitches worked on to a cable needle and winding round the smocking yarn as before. Note that 1 knit rib at each end is left unworked and the smocked stitches alternate with those in the 1st row.

10 Continue in pattern with smocking rows (alternate 1st and 2nd smocking rows) at regular intervals until the fabric is the depth you require. Work 3 rows clear after last smocking row. Cast off in ribbed pattern.

11 Draw up each row of smocking: secure the smocking yarn on the back of the work at one edge. Gently pull the ribs together individually before securing at the opposite edge.

More abbreviations to learn

K = knit
P = purl
st (s) = stitch (es)
g st = garter stitch
st st = stocking stitch
rev st st = reverse stocking stitch
K1, P1 rib = knit 1, purl 1 (single rib)

At left are the abbreviations that you already know; most refer to special knitting techniques. To keep instructions short and concise, a number of frequently recurring ordinary words are abbreviated to form part of the special knitting shorthand. Here is a list of some of these words in alphabetical order: they will now appear in the patterns in the knitting courses so that you can become familiar with them.

beg = begin(ning)
dec = decreas(e)(ing)
inc = increas(e)(ing)
patt = pattern
rem = remain(ing)
rep = repeat
tog = together

Pretty-up for a party

A charming silky, smocked dress like this will be a big hit for party time. The smocking gives it a delicate, traditional look, but the dress will stand up to plenty of wear and tear.

Sizes
To fit 51 [56 :61] cm chest : other measurements are shown on the diagram. The figures in brackets, [], refer to the 2nd and 3rd sizes respectively.

Materials
Total of 180 [200 :220] g of silky rayon yarn such as Twilley's Lystwist
Extra yarn in each of 2 colours for embroidery, or oddments of embroidery silks
1 pair each 2¾mm and 3mm knitting needles
1.5m of ribbon for ties

Tension
30 sts and 40 rows to 10cm over st st worked on 3mm needles.

Front
☐ Using 2¾mm needles cast on 193 [201 :209] sts. Work 4 rows g st.
☐ Change to 3mm needles. Beg with a

K row, continue in st st until work measures 5cm from beg, ending with a P row.
☐ Continue in ribbed pattern for background. An asterisk, *, in a pattern row is another form of knitting shorthand: it means repeat the sequence of stitches following it as directed.
☐ To work the next row P2 sts, *K1 st, P3 sts, rep from * (i.e. K1 st and P3 sts alternately) to last 3 sts, K1 st, P2 sts.
☐ To work the following row K2 sts, *P1 st, K3 sts, rep from * to last 3 sts, P1 st, K2 sts.
☐ Rep the last 2 rows 8 times more, then the first row again (19 rows in all).
☐ Change to 2¾mm needles. To work the next row K3 sts, *K3 sts tog, K5 sts, rep from * to last 6 sts, K3 sts tog, K3 sts. 145 [151 :157] sts rem.
☐ Work 4 rows g st. Change to 3mm needles. To work the next row K1 [2 :3] sts, *K2 sts tog, K3 [3 :4] sts, K2 sts tog, K2 [3 :3] sts, rep from * to end, but on

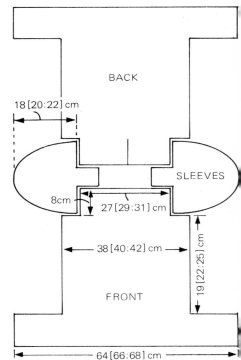

BACK

18 [20 :22] cm

SLEEVES

8cm

27 [29 :31] cm

38 [40 :42] cm

19 [22 :25] cm

FRONT

64 [66 :68] cm

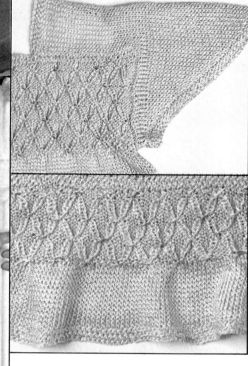

Kim Sayer

Sleeves
☐ Using 2¾mm needles cast on 18[24 :30] sts for neck edge of shoulder section. Work 4 rows g st.
☐ Change to 3mm needles. Beg with a K row, continue in st st until work measures 8[9 :10]cm from beg, ending with a P row.
☐ Shape sleeve by casting on 24 sts at beg of next 2 rows. Shape frill as follows :

K next row to last 2 sts, leave these sts unworked ; turn and P following row to last 2 sts, leave these sts unworked ; turn and K next row to last 4 sts, leave these sts unworked. Continue to work 2 sts less on every row until 6[8 :10] sts rem in centre, then K to end.
☐ Change to 2¾mm needles. Work 4 rows g st. Cast off.

2nd size only finish with K2 sts instead of K3. 113[121 :129] sts rem.
☐ Beg with a P row, continue in st st until work measures 29[32 :35]cm from beg, ending with a P row. **.
☐ Work 31 rows in ribbed pattern as before, ending with right side of work facing.
☐ Change to 2¾mm needles. To work the next row K3 sts, *K3 sts tog, K5, rep from * to last 6 sts, K3 sts tog, K3 sts. 85[91 :97] sts rem.
☐ Work 3 rows g st. Cast off.

Back
☐ Work as given for front until you reach the point in the instructions marked with a double asterisk, **. Now follow the instructions given here.

☐ To divide for the back opening, work 54[58 :62] sts in rib, then K2 sts, slip rem sts on LH needle on to a stitch holder, turn and continue on first set of 56[60 :64] sts.
☐ To work the following row K2 sts, rib to end of row. Work 29 more rows, ending with right side of work facing.
Change to 2¾mm needles.
☐ To work the next row K2[6 :2] sts, *K3 sts tog, K5 sts, rep from * to last 6 sts, K3 sts tog, K3 sts. 40[44 :46] sts.
☐ Work 3 rows g st. Cast off.
☐ Return to sts on spare needle and slip them back onto LH needle. With right side of work facing, rejoin yarn to first st, K2 sts tog, K1 st, rib to end.
☐ Complete to match other side of opening, reversing rib and shaping.

To make up
☐ Block pieces of knitting to correct size. Lightly dampen with fine spray and leave to dry.
☐ Starting from top of ribbed background on yoke, work smocking on every 6th row alternating lines of stitching in 2 different colours.
☐ Beg at armhole edges and using a back stitch seam throughout, sew straight edges of sleeves to cast-off edges of back and front.
☐ Sew cast-on sts at each side of sleeves to sides of smocking on back and front. Join side seams.
☐ Work smocking on frill.
☐ Press all seams with a cool iron over a damp cloth.
☐ Sew on ribbons to form ties at top of centre back opening.

Step-by-step course – 13

*Casting on with one needle
*A new decreasing technique

Casting on with one needle

Try this quick and simple method of casting on; you may prefer it to the two-needle method. It produces a firm but elastic selvedge suitable for most general knitting purposes.

Use a single needle from the pair required for the knitting: hold it in your right hand to make and hold the cast-on stitches.

Your left thumb acts as a flexible 'needle' for winding the yarn round and forming stitches.

1 Make a slip loop in the yarn some distance from the end (the short end of yarn is for making the cast-on stitches – 1 m of double knitting yarn makes approximately 60 stitches). Place the slip loop on the needle.

2 Hold the needle in the normal way in your right hand. Insert your left thumb under the shorter end of yarn from the back so that the yarn travels in an anti-clockwise direction from the slip loop around the thumb.

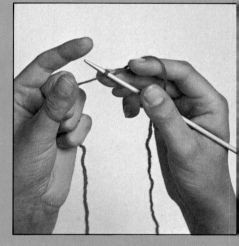

3 Hold the yarn round your thumb down across your left palm with the fingers of that hand, keeping the index finger free for working. Wind the yarn from the main ball round the fingers of your right hand in the usual way.

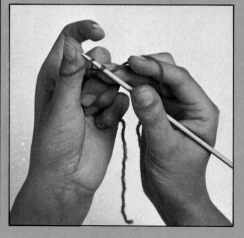

4 Use your left thumb as a form of needle: insert the needle into the loop on the part of the thumb facing you.

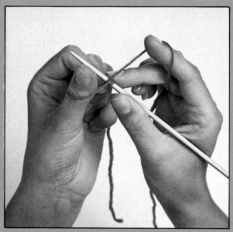

5 Wind the yarn from the main ball under and over the needle point in a clockwise direction.

6 Draw a loop of yarn through the loop on your thumb to form a new stitch on the needle.

Frederick Mancini

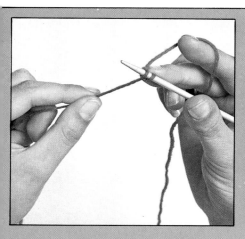

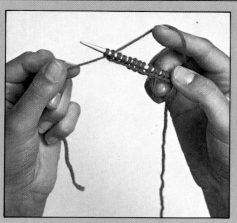

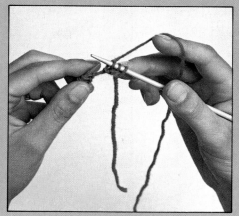

7 Withdraw your thumb from the loop of yarn around it. Pull the short end of yarn gently to tighten the stitch on the needle.

8 Continue to wind the yarn from the short end round your left thumb. Work as described in steps 4 to 7 until you have cast on the required number of stitches.

9 Transfer the needle with the cast-on stitches to your left hand. Take the second needle in your right hand and begin knitting in the usual way. There are 2 ends of yarn at the beginning of your first row : remember to knit with the yarn from the main ball.

Decreasing by working two stitches together through the back of the loops.

Often when shaping a simple raglan arm-hole you must knit two stitches together through the back of the loops – abbreviated as 'K2 tog tbl'. This type of decrease is often found at the end of right-side rows – sometimes within a one- or two-stitch border : it produces a neat edge with a distinctive slope to the right. The same technique can also be applied to purl stitches.

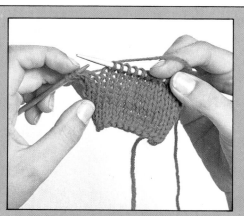

1 On the right side of a stocking stitch fabric, knit to the position of the decrease – in this case when 3 stitches remain on the LH needle.

2 Insert the RH needle from right to left through the back of the next 2 stitches.

3 Knit the 2 stitches together in the usual way – called K2 tog tbl ; knit the last stitch.

4 A line of this type of decrease on every knit row has a neat appearance with a distinctive slant to the stitches.

5 To purl 2 stitches together through the back of the loops – P2 tog tbl – insert the RH needle from left to right through the back of the 2 stitches. Purl the stitches together in the usual way.

Frederick Mancini

Step-by-step course – 14

*Cross stitch
*Chain stitch
*Pattern for an evening cardigan
*Pattern for a check jacket

Cross stitch

Cross stitch is a very effective way to embroider a stocking stitch fabric. Apply the stitching after the fabric is complete, but plan the design beforehand. Each cross covers a square section of background; each square has slightly more stitches than rows. By covering two stitches and three rows of knitting, or three stitches and four rows, you make small and large crosses respectively.

The position of the needle as you work is important; always insert it to the side of the stitches over which you are working. If you insert the needle through the centre of a stitch, the natural elasticity of the knitting pulls the embroidery out of shape.

1 Mark perimeter of area to be embroidered with pins inserted after every four rows and between every three stitches. The design on the evening cardigan in this course has an additional two free rows between lines of crosses.

2 Using a blunt-ended wool needle threaded with sewing cotton, tack lines of stitching on to the background to form a grid of squares. Each square will eventually have a cross covering it.

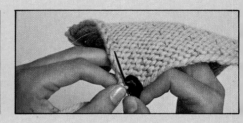

3 Thread a blunt-ended needle with your chosen yarn. Yarn used for embroidery on knitting is usually similar in thickness to the background yarn. Secure yarn to back of work at lower RH corner of design (this is on the left when the wrong side of the work is facing you).

4 Bring needle from back to front at side of first marked stitch (i.e. *between* this stitch and next stitch to the right) at lower RH corner of first box.

5 Working from right to left, re-insert needle from front to back after third stitch four rows above – at corner of box diagonally opposite where yarn is joined.

6 Bring needle to front again at lower RH corner of next box to the left, making sure that you always insert the needle between stitches.

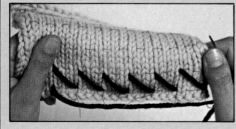

7 Continue in this way, working one diagonal line of each cross, until you reach the end of the first line of pattern. Finish with the yarn at the lower LH corner of the last box.

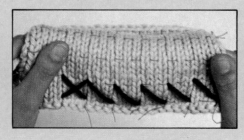

8 Working from left to right, re-insert the needle from front to back at corner of box diagonally opposite. One cross stitch is complete.

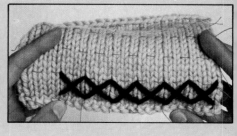

9 Bring the needle to the front again at lower LH corner of next box to the right. Repeat steps 8 and 9 to complete first line of crosses.

Frederick Mancini

50

Chain stitch

Chain stitch looks best worked in a contrasting colour against a stocking stitch background. It is particularly effective as horizontal and vertical lines dividing the background into large check patterns. To keep the checks square you must work individual chains over slightly more rows than stitches. The chains on the check jacket included in this chapter are worked over two stitches and three rows. This can be varied according to the thickness of the knitted yarn; some finer yarns may require chains to be worked over every stitch horizontally and every two rows vertically.

1 Using a blunt-ended wool needle threaded with sewing cotton, tack lines of stitching on to the background to form a guide for the embroidery. Work vertical lines through centre of stitches and horizontal lines across the stitches of one row of knitting.

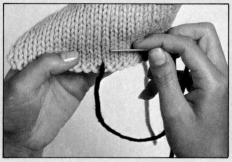

2 Thread a blunt-ended needle with yarn for the embroidery; this is usually similar in thickness to the background. Secure yarn to the back of work at lower edge of marked vertical line. Bring needle from back to front through centre of first stitch and pull yarn through.

3 Form the yarn into a wide circle above the line of stitching. Hold the yarn with your left thumb; re-insert the needle through the centre of the first stitch and out again through the centre of the corresponding stitch three rows above.

4 Pull the yarn through drawing the large circle in to make one chain stitch. Keep the embroidery yarn at a relaxed tension so that it does not pucker the knitted background.

5 Repeat the process of making chains over every three rows until the line of embroidery is as long as you require. Insert the needle from front to back immediately above last stitch worked and fasten off on the back of the work.

6 To embroider horizontal lines, turn work so that side edge of background becomes the lower edge. Secure yarn to back of work at lower edge of marked line. Bring needle from back to front between first and second stitches.

7 Form the yarn into a wide circle above the line of stitching and hold yarn down with your left thumb. Re-insert the needle between the first and second stitches and out again after the third stitch.

8 Pull the yarn through, drawing the large circle in to make one chain stitch. Make chains over every two stitches until the line of embroidery is as long as you require. Fasten off on the wrong side.

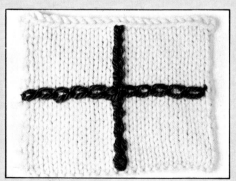

9 On a large piece of fabric, work all the lines in the same direction first; in this way the lines of chain always cross in the same order.

Frederick Mancini

Evening sparkle

Add a little sparkle to your evenings with this attractive cover-up. Cross stitches worked over the knitted fabric form intriguing pyramids round the sleeves and the lower front edge. The borders are in garter stitch.

Sizes

To fit 83 [87:92:97]cm bust; other measurements are shown on the diagram. The figures in brackets [] refer to the 2nd, 3rd and 4th sizes respectively.

Materials

Total of 275 [300 :300 :325]g of glitter yarn such as Twilleys Goldfingering
Extra yarn in another colour for embroidery
1 pair each 2¾mm and 3¼mm knitting needles

Tension

28 sts and 36 rows to 10cm over st st worked on 3¼mm needles.

Back

Using 2¾mm needles cast on 114[122 : 130 :138] sts. Work 10 rows g st.
☐ Change to 3¼mm needles. Beg with a K row, continue in st st until work measures 41cm from beg, ending with a P row.
☐ Beg armhole shaping by casting off 7 sts at beg of next 2 rows.
☐ To work the next row, K1 st, K2 sts tog, K to last 3 sts, K2 sts tog tbl, K1 st. To work the following row, P to end.
☐ Rep the last 2 rows until 34[36 :38 : 40] sts rem, ending with a P row. Cast off.

Left front

Using 2¾mm needles cast on 57[61 :65 : 69] sts. Work 10 rows g st.
☐ Change to 3¼mm needles. Beg with a K row, cont in st st until work measures same as back to armholes, ending with a P row.
☐ Begin shaping armhole by casting off 7 sts at beg of next row. P the following row.
☐ Shape front edge at same time as armhole edge : to work the next row K1 st, K2 sts tog, K to last 3 sts (front edge), K2 sts tog tbl, K1 st.
☐ Continue to dec at front edge on every 4th row 14[15 :16 :17] times more, **at the same time** dec at armhole edge on every alternate row until 2 sts rem, ending with a P row. Cast off.

Right front

Work to match left front, reversing shaping at armhole and front edges by ending with K row before beg armhole shaping; omit the P row following the row where you cast off 7 sts for underarm and start front edge shaping on next row.

Sleeves

Using 2¾mm needles cast on 78[84 :88 : 94] sts. Work 10 rows g st.
☐ Change to 3¼mm needles. Beg with a K row, continue in st st, inc one st at each end of 5th and every foll 6th row until there are 90[96 :100 :106] sts.
☐ Continue without shaping until sleeve measures 12cm (in a straight line down centre of sleeve) from beg, ending with a P row.
☐ Beg shaping raglan sleeve top by casting off 7 sts at beg of next 2 rows.

☐ Rep the 2 rows of back armhole shaping until 10[10 :8 :8] sts rem, ending with a P row. Cast off.

Front border

Using 2¾mm needles cast on 8 sts.
☐ Work in g st until border reaches up front edge, round back neck and down other front. Cast off.

Ties (make 2)

Using 2¾mm needles cast on 6 sts. Work in g st for 25cm. Cast off.

To make up

☐ Join all raglan seams using a back stitch seam.
☐ Join side and sleeve seams.
☐ Using a flat seam, sew on front border. Sew ties in position.
☐ Work cross stitch embroidery. First row, over 3 sts and 4 rows, goes all round lower edge, 5 rows above g st border.
☐ On each front work a pyramid of 10, 8, 6, 4 and 2 crosses with 2 rows of knitting between each line.
☐ Work a similar pattern on the sleeves.

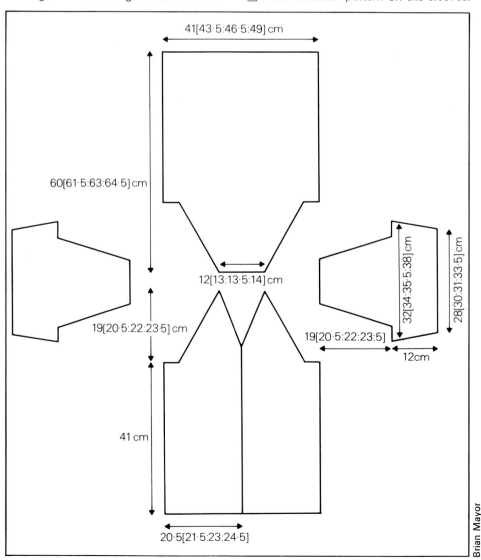

41[43·5:46·5:49] cm

60[61·5:63:64·5]cm

12[13:13·5:14] cm

19[20·5:22:23·5] cm

41 cm

20·5[21·5:23:24·5]

32[34:35·5:38]cm

28[30:31:33·5]cm

19[20·5:22:23·5]

12cm

Brian Mayor

Checks, chains and crosses

A simple jacket in stocking stitch takes on an ethnic look with the addition of cross stitch and chain stitch embroidery. The style is basically the same as the glittery evening jacket on page 52, but slightly longer and with full-length sleeves.

Sizes

To fit 83[87:92:97]cm bust: other measurements are shown on the diagram below.
The figures in brackets [] refer to the 2nd, 3rd and 4th sizes respectively.

Materials

*Total of 500[550:600:650]g of chunky yarn such as Phildar Shoot
Extra yarn in two contrasting colours for embroidery
1 pair each 4mm and 5mm knitting needles*

Tension

16 sts and 22 rows to 10cm over st st worked on 5mm needles.
If your tension is wrong, use a different needle size.

Back

Using 4mm needles cast on 70[74:78:82] sts. Work 8 rows g st.
☐ Change to 5mm needles. Beg with a K row, continue in st st until work measures 45cm from beg, ending with a P row.
☐ Beg armhole shaping by casting off 3 sts at beg of next 2 rows.
☐ To work the next row, K1 st, K2 sts tog, K to last 3 sts, K2 sts tog tbl, K1 st. To work the following row, P to end.
☐ Rep the last 2 rows until 20[20:22:22] sts rem, ending with a P row. Cast off.

Left front

Using 4mm needles cast on 35[37:39:41] sts. Work 8 rows g st.
☐ Change to 5mm needles. Beg with a K row, continue in st st until work measures same as back to armholes, ending with a P row.
☐ Beg armhole shaping by casting off 3 sts at beg of next row. P the following row
☐ Shape front edge at same time as armhole edge: to work the next row K1 st, K2 sts tog, K to last 3 sts (front edge), K2 sts tog tbl, K1 st.
☐ Continue to dec at front edge on every 4th row 7[7:8:8] times more, *at the same time* dec at armhole edge on every alternate row until 2 sts rem, ending with a P row. Cast off.

Right front

Work to match left front, reversing shaping at armhole and front edges by ending with a K row before beg armhole shaping; omit the P row following the row where you cast off 3 sts for underarm and start front edge shaping on next row.

Sleeves

Using 4mm needles cast on 36[38:40:42] sts. Work 8 rows g st.
☐ Change to 5mm needles. Beg with a K row, continue in st st, inc one st at each end of 7th and every foll 6th row until there are 58[62:64:68] sts.
☐ Continue without shaping until sleeve measures 43[44:45:46]cm (in a straight line down centre of sleeve) from beg, ending with a P row.
☐ Beg shaping raglan sleeve top by casting off 3 sts at beg of next 2 rows.
☐ Rep the 2 rows of back armhole shaping until 8 sts rem, ending with a P row. Cast off.

Front border

Using 4mm needles cast on 6 sts.
☐ Work in g st until band reaches up front edge, round back neck and down other front. Cast off.

Ties (make 2)

Using 4mm needles cast on 4 sts. Work in g st for 25cm. Cast off.

To make up

Press pieces (except g st borders and ties) under a dry cloth with a cool iron.
☐ Work chain stitch embroidery, dividing pieces of knitting into large checks: see diagram for approximate position of lines. As far as possible, divide the area equally so that there are about the same number of sts and rows in each check.
☐ Use first contrast colour to work a cross stitch over centre 3 sts and 4 rows of each check. With 2nd contrast colour work 4 more crosses 2 sts and 4 rows distant from the first cross.
☐ Join all raglan seams using a back stitch.
☐ Join side and sleeve seams.
☐ Using a flat seam, sew on front border. Sew ties in position. Press seams.

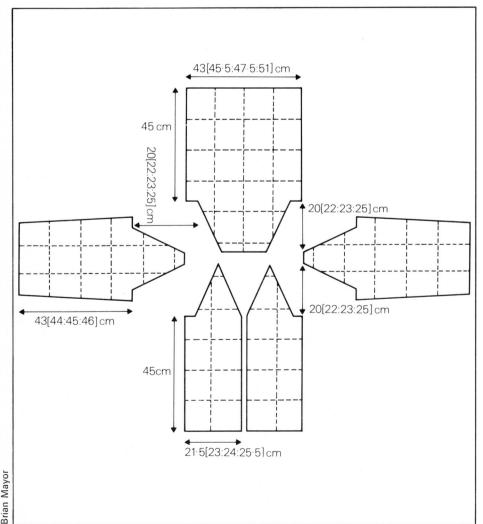

43[45·5:47·5:51]cm

45 cm

20[22:23:25]cm

20[22:23:25] cm

43[44:45:46]cm

20[22:23:25]cm

45cm

21·5[23:24:25·5]cm

Brian Mayor

Step-by-step course – 15

Paired decreasing on a right-side row

Most methods of decreasing leave a stitch that lies at an angle, which may be used as a decorative feature of the garment. Raglan armhole shaping uses pairs of decreases – one at each end of the row or side of the armhole. The first decrease follows the eventual slope of the edge to the left, while the second decrease slopes to the right. A one- two- or three-stitch border between the edge and decrease accentuates the shaping.

In this course we introduce a new method of decreasing. The decrease is made by means of a slipped stitch, and the knitting terminology for it is 'slip one, knit one, pass slipped stitch over (sl1, K1, psso)'. It makes a slope to the left on the right side of the work.

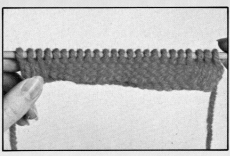

1 Here the raglan edges are emphasized by means of borders consisting of three stocking stitches; these contrast with the main fabric in reverse stocking stitch. The decreases are made where the border meets the main fabric.

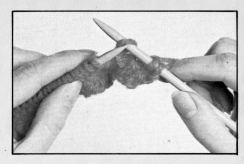

2 On a right-side row the first decrease needs to slope to the left. Knit the first two border stitches, then slip the next stitch knit-wise.

3 Knit the next stitch – even though it is part of the main fabric. As the decreasing progresses the number of stitches in the main fabric is reduced, while the 3-stitch border remains constant.

4 Insert the LH needle point from left to right through the front of the slipped stitch to begin the first decrease.

5 Slide the stitches towards the end of the RH needle. Lift the slipped stitch over the last knitted stitch and off RH needle : withdraw LH needle point. Steps 2-5 form the decrease called 'slip one, knit one, pass slipped stitch over (sl1, K1, psso)'.

6 Work – in this case purl – to within one stitch of the border at the other end. The decreasing must start one stitch before the border to maintain the correct number of edge stitches.

7 On a right-side row, the last decrease must slope to the right : an ordinary decrease is sufficient here. Knit the next two stitches (ie. one stitch from the main fabric and the first of the border stitches) together. Work to the end of the row.

8 This picture shows the effect of this type of decreasing worked on alternate right-side rows (ie. three rows between decreasing). The border at the beginning of the row slopes to the left and the one at the end slopes to the right.

Paired decreasing on a wrong-side row

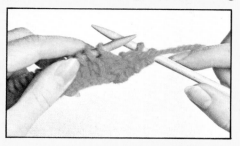

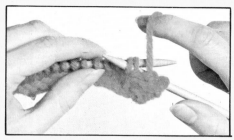

1 At the beginning of a wrong-side row you need a decrease that slopes to the right on the right side of the work : this is the opposite of how the border slopes on the wrong side. Purl the first two border stitches.

2 Purl the next two stitches (the last border stitch and the first stitch from the main fabric) together. This ordinary decrease gives the required effect on the right side.

3 Work to within one stitch of the border at the end of the row. For a border that slopes to the left on the right side of the work, purl the next two stitches together *through the back of the loops.*

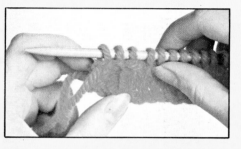

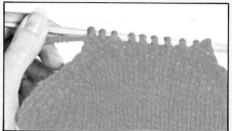

4 Work to the end of the row. Notice that the fabric is definitely not reversible. It is quite acceptable, however to have a stocking stitch main fabric with a stocking stitch border if you prefer.

5 This is how the wrong side of the work looks when you decrease on every row, alternating instructions for paired decreasings on wrong-side rows with those for decreasing on right-side rows.

6 This shows the finished effect of this type of decreasing worked on every row. The edges incline much more sharply than when you decrease on every fourth row (see step 8, page 379) ; for a moderately sloped edge decrease on every right-side row.

Sewing in a zip fastener

There are a number of occasions when you may need to fit zip fasteners to knitted fabrics. Back neck openings (especially useful on children's sweaters for extra room when pulling them on) and skirt side or back seams need the ordinary type of zip, which is closed at the bottom. Open-ended zips are ideal for the fronts of cardigans and jackets. Use the same zips for knitting as you would for dressmaking : you may need heavier zips in some cases, as knitted fabrics tend to be heavier than dress fabrics.

Match the length of the opening and that of the zip exactly : sewing a zip that is too short into an opening makes the seam bulge while one that is too long will drag the sides of the opening.

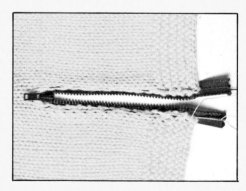

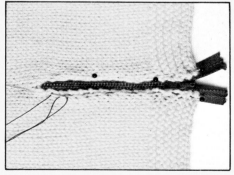

1 Working on the right side of the fabric, pin zip into opening with teeth facing upwards. Take care to match both sections of the garment exactly, and avoid stretching the knitting. Pin the zip so that the sides of the opening meet and the teeth are concealed. With thicker fabrics, such as those for outdoor wear, leave the zip teeth exposed.
Tack along both sides of the zip, using ordinary sewing thread.

2 Remove pins. Thread sewing needle to match the colour of the fabric. Open the zip carefully. Secure thread at back of top RH side of zip. Bring needle through to front and back into the fabric a minute distance to the right. This is called a 'stab' stitch.

Fred Mancini

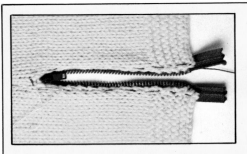

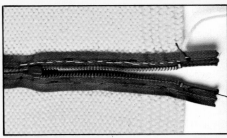

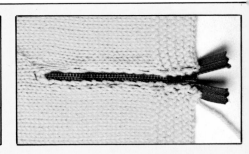

3 Bring the needle through to the front again about 5mm to the left of the previous stitch. Repeat these stab stitches down as close as possible to the edge of the work.

4 The stitches are invisible on the right side of the knitting, as the fine thread sinks down into the thicker yarn. On the back of the zip are the longer strands of thread between the stitches.

5 For a back neck or skirt side seam opening, work a few extra stitches across the bottom of the zip before continuing up the other side ; work the second side separately. It is easier to work the second side with the zip closed.

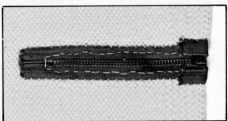

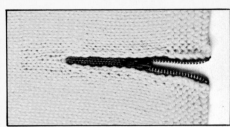

6 To finish off the wrong side of the work, fold the extended tapes back so that the fold is level with the top of the zip : angle them slightly to the side to avoid obstructing the zip slider. Pin in position. If the zip is being inserted into neckband that folds to the inside, the top of the zip itself will reach only to the fold line and the tapes will be enclosed between the layers.

7 Neaten the tapes and keep them in position by oversewing all round the outer edges ; this is normally done with matching yarn. Catch down the folded-back tapes at the top in the same way.

8 The finished zip must open easily on the right side of the work without the opening slider catching any knitted edge ; if this does happen then you have stitched too close to the teeth of the zip.

Warm for winter

Here's a dressing gown any child will warm to — a snug, soft-coloured robe with a jolly, pixie-style hood. It's easy to knit, in reverse stocking stitch, and fastens with a zip.

Sizes
To fit 51 [56 :61] cm chest.
Length, 73 [80 :87] cm.
Sleeve seam, 20 [23 :26] cm.

Note Instructions for larger sizes are in square brackets [ ] : where there is only one set of figures it applies to all sizes.

Materials
13 [15 :16] x 50g balls of Phildar Kadischa
1 pair each 5mm and 6mm knitting needles
46 [51 :56] cm open-ended zip fastener

Tension
13 sts and 19 rows to 10cm over st st on 6mm needles.

Back
Using 6mm needles cast on 67 [73 :79] sts.
1st row K1, (P1, K1) to end.
2nd row P1, (K1,P1) to end.
Rep these 2 rows twice more. Beg with a P row, cont in reverse st st, work 16 rows. Dec one st at each end of next and every foll 6th row until 37 [41 :45] sts rem. Cont without shaping until work measures 61 [66 :71] cm from beg, ending with a K row.
Shape raglan armholes
**Cast off 2sts at beg of next 2 rows.
Next row K3, P to last 3 sts, K3.
Next row P3, K to last 3 sts, P3.
Next row K2, sl1, K1, psso, P to last 4 sts, K2tog, K2.
Keeping 3 sts at each end in st st throughout cont to dec in the same way on every foll 4th row 1 [2 :3] times more,

then on every alt row until 13[15 :17]sts rem, ending with a WS row.** Cast off.

Left front
Using 6mm needles cast on 35[37 :41]sts.
1st row (K1, P1) to last 3 sts, K3.
2nd row K2, P1, (K1,P1) to end.
Rep the last 2 rows twice more but inc one st at end of last row on 2nd size only. 35[38 :41]sts.
Next row P to last 2 sts, K2.
Next row K to end.
Rep the last 2 rows 7 times more. Keeping the 2 sts at front edge in g st, dec one st at beg of next and every foll 6th row until 20[22 :24] sts rem. Cont without shaping until work measures the same as back to armholes, ending with a WS row.
Shape raglan armhole
Cast off 2 sts at beg of next row. Work 1 row.
Next row K3, P to last 2 sts, K2.
Next row K to last 3 sts, P3.
Next row K2, sl1, K1, psso, P to last 2 sts, K2.
Dec at beg of every 4th row 1 [2 :3] times more, then at beg of every alt row until 14[15 :16]sts rem, ending with a RS row.
Shape neck
Next row Cast off 2[3 :4]sts, K to last 3 sts, P3.

Next row K2, sl1, K1, psso, P to last 2 sts, P2tog.
Next row K to last 3 sts, P3.
Rep the last 2 rows 3 times more. 4 sts.
Next row K2, sl1, K1, psso.
Next row P3.
Next row K1, sl1, K1, psso.
Next row P2tog. Fasten off.

Right front
Using 6mm needles cast on 35[37 :41]sts.
1st row K3, (P1,K1) to end.
2nd row (P1,K1) to last 3 sts, P1, K2.
Rep the last 2 rows twice more but inc one st at beg of last row on 2nd size only. 35[38 :41]sts.
Next row K2, P to end.
Next row K to end.
Work to match left front, reversing shaping.

Sleeves
Using 5mm needles cast on 21[23 :25]sts. and work 6 rows rib as given for back. Change to 6mm needles and beg with a P row, cont in reverse st st inc one st at each end of first and every foll 8th row until there are 29[33 :37]sts. Cont without shaping until sleeve measures 20[23 :26] cm from beg, ending with a K row.
Shape raglan armhole
Rep from ** to ** of back, but dec until 7 sts rem, ending with a WS row.

Next row K2,sl 1, K2 tog, psso, K2.
Next row P5. Cast off.

Hood
Using 5mm needles cast on 53[57 :61]sts and work 6 rows in rib as back. Change to 6mm needles and beg with a P row cont in reverse st st until work measures 14[16 :18]cm from beg, ending with a K row and dec one st at centre of last row. 52[56 :60]sts.
Shape back
Next row P1, *P2tog, P10[11 :12], rep from * 3 times more, P2tog, P1. 47[51 :55]sts. Work 3 rows.
Next row P1, *P2tog, P9[10 :11], rep from * twice more, P2tog, P8[9 :10], P2tog, P1. 42[46 :50]sts.
Cont to dec in this way, working one st less between each decrease on every 4th row until 12[11 :10]sts rem. Cut off yarn, thread through sts, draw up and fasten off.

To make up
Press work lightly with a cool iron over a dry cloth. Join raglan seams. Join side and sleeve seams. Sew hood to neck edge then join rem part of hood seam. Sew in zip placing the top of zip at neck edge and leaving bottom part of front edge free. Make a tassel and sew to end of hood. Press seams.

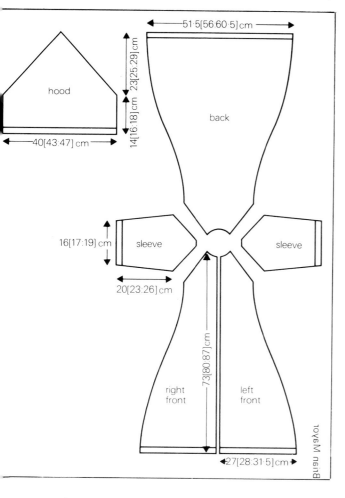

S. Wells

Step-by-step course – 16

*Checking measurements
  for T-shaped designs
*Adapting basic T-shaped
  pieces
*Planning your own design
*Double crochet edging
*Pattern for 3 children's
  sweaters

Checking measurements for T-shaped designs

In this chapter we introduce the popular T-shaped design – easy to make and almost as easy to vary to suit your own taste and requirements. The name, of course, derives from the way the garment, with arms outstretched, resembles a large letter T.

Patterns for three children's T-shaped sweaters are given on page 67; these step-by-step instructions show you how to check the child's measurements, and if necessary, how to alter the pattern accordingly.

The diagram shows the pieces required for the children's sweaters – basically there are two shapes – the back and front are alike and so are the sleeves. The measurement chart gives a number of points on the sweaters that grade larger or smaller according to the chest size. First find the chest size that you want to make (i.e. measured without garments on). Check that the other measurements for this size (in centimetres) are suitable; if not, they can be altered to suit particular requirements by lengthening or shortening body and sleeves.

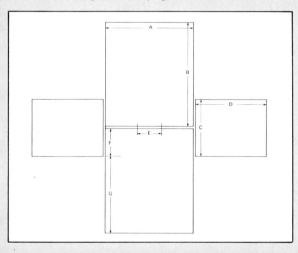

Chest size		50	56	61	66	71	76
	Code on diagram						
Width across front/back	A	28	30	33	35	38	40
Total length of sweater	B	29	33	37	41	45	49
Width all round sleeve	C	21	23	26	28	31	33
Sleeve length	D	18	22	25	29	32	36
Approximate width of neck opening	E	15	16	17	18	19	20
Armhole depth	F	10.5	11.5	13	14	15.5	16.5
Underarm length front/back	G	18.5	21.5	24	27	29.5	32.5

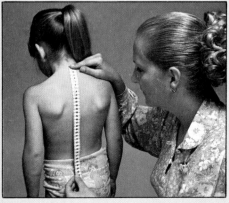
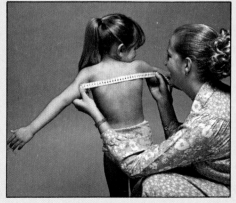
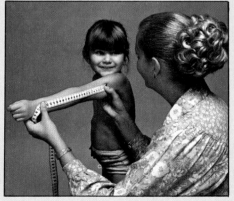

Fred Mancini

1 Referring to the pattern, note the finished lengths of the sweater for the chest size you are making. Check this against the child, placing the beginning of the tape against the centre-back neck and measuring downwards.

2 To check the sleeve measurement the child should stand with arms outstretched. Hold the tape with back measurement across his shoulders and note where side edge of sweater will fall on his arms; this is called a dropped shoulder line.

3 Measure the sleeve length from the dropped shoulder line downwards along the arm. For a short sleeve, subtract the necessary amount: make the sleeve longer for a turn-back cuff by adding extra length. (You can work to the length given and then turn back a cuff, as on the garter stitch sweater, but this shortens the length of the sleeve).

Adapting the basic T-shaped pieces

You can easily alter a T-shape pattern in several ways. For example, you can vary the direction of the knitting: instead of knitting the body and sleeve pieces from lower edge to top, as you normally would, you can knit them from one side edge to the other. You can knit the body vertically and the sleeves horizontally, or vice versa. Choose garter stitch, with its definite ridges, if you want to create strong directional emphasis.

It is also fairly easy to alter the lengths of basic pieces, making them longer or shorter where necessary to suit individual requirements.

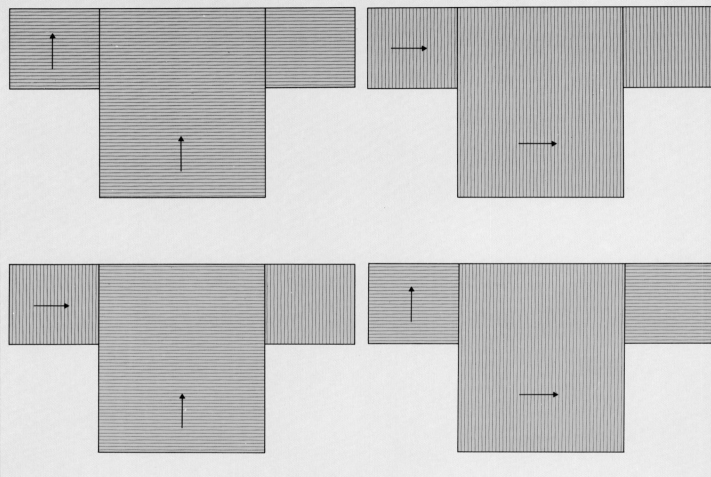

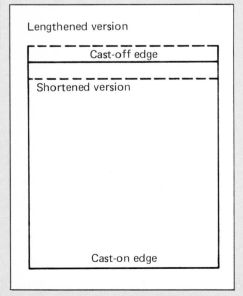

Lengthened version

Cast-off edge

Shortened version

Cast-on edge

1 If you are working the back and front of a sweater from lower edge to top and want to lengthen or shorten it, simply work to the measurement you require.

2 To lengthen or shorten a sleeve knitted from wrist to top edge, work to the length you require then cast off. Extra length for a turn-back cuff is added in the same way.

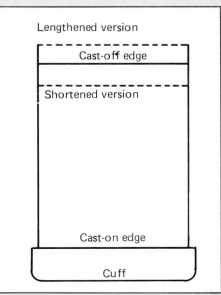

Lengthened version

Cast-off edge

Shortened version

Cast-on edge

Cuff

Total length of sweater = 45cm

Number of cast-on stitches for side edge = 54

You want to add 5cm in length

Look at the stitch tension; in this pattern it is 12 stitches to 10cm.

Here an extra 6 stitches give the extra 5cm required.
Cast on (54 + 6) 60 stitches in all.

.3 Altering the length of a sweater is more difficult if you are working from side edge to side edge : here the number of cast-on stitches dictate the length. The calculations here show the procedure for lengthening or shortening the back and front of such a sweater. The figures will of course vary in each particular case.

Total length of sleeve = 32cm

Number of cast-on stitches for seam = 38sts

You want to add 3cm in length.

Look at the stitch tension; in this pattern it is 12 stitches to 10cm (ie. 1⅕ stitches = 1cm)

For an extra 3cm length, you need 1⅕ stitches x 3 = 3¾ (4 stitches is nearest whole number)

Cast on (38 + 4) = 42 stitches in all.

4 The length of a sleeve worked from seam to seam also depends on the number of cast-on stitches. Add more or fewer stitches according to whether you want to lengthen or shorten the sleeve : follow the process shown in our example to see how to calculate this.

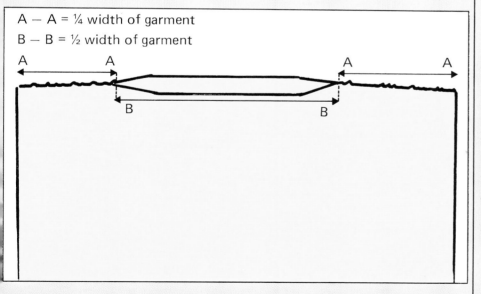

A — A = ¼ width of garment
B — B = ½ width of garment

5 The length of the neck opening can be varied again to suit individual requirements. Generally the neckline should be about half the width of the back or front. Join the shoulder seams for the same distance from each side edge, leaving an opening in the centre large enough for the head to go through.

Planning your own design

The basic pattern pieces and measurements for the T-shaped sweater can easily be used as a basis for your own designs. You can choose different stitch patterns or change direction of knitting, but you must calculate the number of stitches to cast on. Don't assume, for example, that the number of stitches cast on for the back of the garter stitch sweater will be the same number if you knit it in moss stitch ; the finished piece of knitting will not be the correct size, since different stitch patterns and different yarns create their own, widely varying, tensions. You must always first make a tension sample to work out the number of stitches to cast on according to your tension.

1 Choose the yarn and appropriate needles for that yarn. Make a tension sample in the stitch pattern for the design. The sample shows a moss stitch fabric knitted in a chunky yarn.

2 Measure the stitch tension : here it is 15 stitches to 10cm. The row tension is unimportant if you are using the basic pattern pieces : you work to a given measurement rather than to a number of rows.

continued

Fred Mancini

3 Calculate the number of stitches to cast on. Suppose you are making the 65cm size sweater and want to knit the back from lower edge to top – follow the calculations shown in the diagram. Apply the same method to each piece of knitting.

Stitch tension – 15 stitches to 10cm	
Number of stitches to 1cm – $\dfrac{15}{10}$ = 1½	
Width of piece of knitting must be 35cm	
Number of stitches to cast on – 1½ stitches x 35 = 52½ stitches	
Cast on 53 stitches (the nearest whole number) to achieve the correct width	

4 Don't assume that the same number of cast-on stitches necessarily works with a different stitch pattern, even if you use the same yarn and needles. Compare the width of 15 stitches in moss stitch with the same number in garter stitch. The difference is more pronounced with a greater number of stitches.

5 The calculation in step 3 applies to moss stitch in *chunky* yarn. If you decide on the same stitch but want to use a different weight of yarn – say double knitting – you must make a tension sample to find out the number of cast-on stitches. Note the difference between an equal number of stitches and rows in chunky yarns and double knitting yarns.

Double crochet edging

Give your T-shaped designs a touch of originality with various edgings or embroidery. Outline all the knitted pieces with crochet before joining them together, as in the garter stitch sweater; or use crochet to neaten outer edges after the garment is sewn up. You need no previous knowledge of crochet to attempt this edging: it is suitable for many other knitted fabrics besides the garter stitch shown here. Choose a plain yarn to contrast with a tweedy or multi-coloured fabric. Double knitting yarn is a suitable weight for trimming chunky fabrics: use a medium-sized hook with this type of yarn. On our sweater there is some distance between the double crochet stitches; bridge the spaces with single chain. Some less chunky fabrics may not require extra stitches.

1 Hold the piece of knitting so that cast-off edge is at top. Insert crochet hook from front to back through knitting at RH edge about 3cm from top.

2 Fold over end of yarn for crochet for about 10cm: hold this folded end with your left hand. Insert crochet hook in the loop of yarn; draw the hook with the loop on it through to the front of the knitting.

3 Secure yarn by inserting hook from left to right under double strand of yarn at back of work. Draw strands of yarn through loop on hook.

4 Continue working with one strand of yarn from the ball, leaving the tail end free. It is easier to work if you wind the yarn round the fingers of your left hand as shown. Keep your left index finger flexible to tension the yarn.

5 Insert hook from front to back under strand of yarn and draw through loop on hook; this is called one chain.

6 Insert hook from front to back through next stitch in knitting, about 3cm from top. Put hook under and over yarn at back of work and draw a loop through to the front: keep work relaxed and draw loop level with top edge of work.

7 Insert hook from front to back under strand of yarn and draw through both loops on the hook. One double crochet edge stitch is now complete.

8 Continue working one double crochet edge stitch into each knitted stitch – with one chain between stitches – to within about one stitch of LH edge.

9 To turn the corner, work (one chain and one double crochet edge stitch) twice: insert hook each time into base of last stitch at LH edge.

10 The side edge of the knitting now forms the top edge. Continue working edging as before, working about one double crochet edge stitch between garter stitch ridges.

11 Work edging round sides as required. To finish off in this case, insert hook into first stitch worked and draw yarn through both loops on hook. Cut off yarn about 10cm from hook and draw cut end through loop on hook; pull end gently to secure loop.

Fred Mancini

Knitting for child's play

There are lots of exciting ways of adapting this basic T-shaped top. We start the ball rolling with three very simple ideas which make distinctive sweaters.

Sizes
To fit 50[56 :61 :66 :71 :76]cm chest : other measurements are shown on the diagram.
The figures in brackets, [], refer to the 2nd, 3rd and 4th sizes respectively.

Materials
Garter stitch sweater : total of 550[600 :600 :650 :700 :700]g of chunky tweed-effect yarn such as 3 Suisses Nanouk ; oddments of double knitting yarn for edging
1 pair 6mm knitting needles
5.00mm crochet hook
Stocking stitch sweater : total of 300[300 :350 :350 :400 :400]g of chunky yarn such as 3 Suisses Suizasport ; oddments of contrast chunky yarn for embroidery
1 pair 4½mm knitting needles
Multi-stitch sweater : total of 250[300 :300 :350 :350 :400]g of chunky yarn such as 3 Suisses Suizasport
1 pair 4½mm knitting needles

Tension
Garter stitch sweater 12 sts and 24 rows to 10cm over g st worked on 6mm needles.
Stocking stitch sweater 15 sts and 22 rows to 10cm over st st worked on 4½mm needles.
Multi-stitch sweater As stocking stitch sweater.

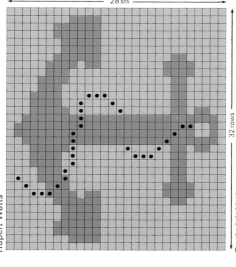

Garter stitch sweater

Back and front (alike)
Using 6mm needles cast on 35[40:45:
50:55:60] sts for side edge.
☐ Work in g st for 28[30:33:35:38:40]
cm. Cast off.

Sleeves
Using 6mm needles cast on
22[26:30:34:38:42] sts for seam.
☐ Work in g st for 21[23:26:28:31:33]
cm from seam to seam. Cast off.

To make up
Using 5.00mm hook and contrast yarn,
work a double crochet edging all round
back and front (see Knitting Course 14,
p.280).
☐ Work a similar edging along top and
lower edge of sleeves (i.e. along row
ends at side edges of sleeves). Work
lower edging on opposite side of fabric
to the other edging.
☐ Join back and front at shoulders by
oversewing, leaving approximately

15[16:17:18:19:20]cm open in centre
for neck.
☐ Mark centre of sleeve top edge with a
pin : match pin to shoulder seam and
oversew sleeves in position. Note that
wrong side of double crochet at lower
edge must be on the outside so that cuff
can be turned up on the right side.
☐ Join side and sleeve seams (side
seams by oversewing and sleeves with a
back-stitch seam), reversing seam at cuff
edge. Leave slits in side seams if required.

Stocking stitch sweater

Back and front (alike)
Using 4½mm needles cast on 44[50 :56 :62 :68 :74] sts for side edge. Work 4 rows g st.

☐ Beg with a K row and keeping 3 sts at each end of row in g st, continue in st st until work measures 26[28 :31 :33 :36 : 38]cm from beg, ending with a K row.

☐ Work 4 rows g st. Cast off.

Sleeves
Using 4½mm needles cast on 32[35 :38 :42 :46 :50] sts for wrist edge. Work 4 rows in g st.

☐ Beg with a K row, continue in st st until work measures 16[20 :23 :27 :30 : 34]cm, ending with a K row.

☐ Work 4 rows g st. Cast off.

To make up
Press work if required, according to instructions on ball band, omitting g st borders.

☐ Swiss darn anchor and embroider rope in chain stitch on front as shown in diagram on page 67 : remember that stitches lie sideways.

☐ Join shoulder seams with a flat seam, leaving approximately 15[16 :17 :18 :19 : 20]cm open in centre for neck.

☐ Mark centre of cast-off sleeve edge with a pin : match pin to shoulder seam and sew in sleeves with a flat seam.

☐ Join side and sleeve seams.

Rupert Watts

Multi-stitch sweater

Back and front (alike)
Using 4½mm needles cast on 44[48 : 56 :60 :68 :72] sts. Work 3[5 :5 :7 :7 :9] cm moss st.

☐ Work 16 rows in K4, P4 basket st, alternating blocks of st st and rev st st every 4 rows.

☐ Beg first row (right side of work) with K4, continue in K4, P4 rib until work measures 20[22 :26 :28 :32 :36]cm from beg, ending with a wrong-side row.

☐ Beg next row with P4, work 16 rows in K4, P4 basket st.

☐ Work 3[5 :5 :7 :7 :9]cm in moss st. Cast off loosely.

Sleeves
Using 4½mm needles cast on 28[32 :36 :40 :44 :48] sts for wrist edge. Work 3[5 :5 :7 :7 :9]cm in moss st.

☐ Work 32[32 :40 :40 :48 :48] rows in K4, P4 basket st.

☐ Work 3[5 :5 :7 :7 :9]cm in moss st. Cast off loosely.

To make up
Moss st and basket st sections do not require pressing : it may be necessary to lightly press the ribbed section open.

☐ Complete in same way as stocking stitch sweater, omitting Swiss darning and embroidery.

Step-by-step course – 17

* Adapting T-shaped designs for adult sizes
* Multiple increasing and decreasing at beginnings of rows
* Using a circular needle for working in rows
* Sewing on a patch pocket
* Making a twisted cord
* Patterns for sweater and jacket

Adapting T-shape designs for adult sizes

Kim Sayer/accessories from Fenwicks

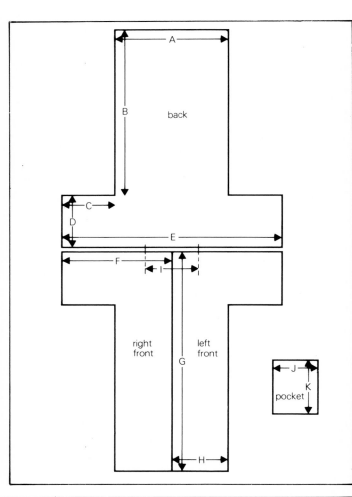

Continuing to explore the possibilities of the T-shape, introduced in Knitting Course 16, we offer, on pages 75-76, designs for two adult sweaters.

These designs develop the T-shape idea one stage further than in the basic children's designs given earlier. They include pockets and – in the case of the man's sweater – a collar.

If you prefer, however, you can adapt these designs – by using a different stitch, by altering the proportions, or by

Bust/chest size for jacket (in cm)	Code on diagram	83	87	92	97	102	107
Width across back	A	43	45	48	51	53	56
Underarm length	B	49	50	51	52	53	54
Sleeve length	C	37	39	41	43	45	47
Armhole depth	D	18	20	22	24	26	28
Width sleeve edge to sleeve edge	E	117	123	130	137	143	150
Width from sleeve edge to centre front	F	59	62	65	69	72	75
Total length of jacket	G	67	70	73	76	79	82
Width across front	H	22	23	24	25	26	27
Width of neck opening	I	19	19	20	21	21	22
Pocket width	J	12	13	14	15	16	17
Pocket depth	K	15	16	17	18	19	20

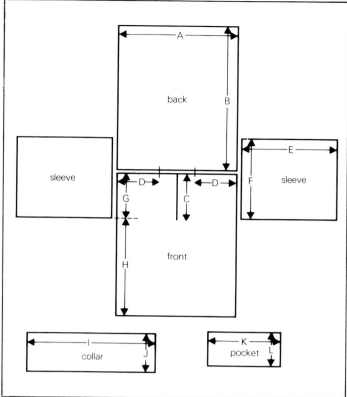

Brian Mayor

Bust/chest size for sweater (in cm)	Code on diagram	83	87	92	97	102	107
Width across front/back	A	43	45	48	51	53	56
Total length of sweater	B	57	60	63	66	69	72
Depth of front opening	C	17	19	21	23	25	27
Shoulder seam (from each side edge)	D	12	13	14	15	16	17
Sleeve length	E	37	39	41	43	45	47
Width all round sleeve	F	34	38	42	46	50	54
Armhole depth	G	17	19	21	23	25	27
Underarm length front/back	H	40	41	42	43	44	45
Collar width	I	36	38	40	42	44	46
Collar depth	J	20	20	20	20	20	20
Pocket width	K	18	18	18	23	23	23
Pocket depth	L	13	15	15	17	17	19

adding or subtracting a collar or pockets. The diagrams and measurements given here are slightly more detailed than those included with the pattern and may be used as a guide in adapting the designs, if you so choose. Making minor adjustments on a simple pattern is a good way to begin learning the basics of pattern design.

If you want to use a different stitch remember to make a tension square using your chosen yarn and needles. Use the measurement chart to determine the number of stitches to cast on and cast off in shaping the garment, as explained in Knitting Course 16 page 61.

If you are altering the proportion of the garment, remember to take into consideration the possible effect this will have on another part of the garment. For example, if you want to widen the neck opening on the man's sweater you must also increase the width of the collar so that it will fit round the entire neck edge. You may also want to increase the depth of the collar.

Similarly, a pocket should also vary in size according to the garment. If you prefer to substitute two patch pockets for the single horizontal pocket on the man's pullover, you should first complete the front piece, then make two paper templates and lay them on the finished piece of knitting to check their size. Trim the templates if necessary, and knit the

pockets to that measurement.

On some T-shaped designs the sleeve and bodice are knitted in one piece, as on the woman's jacket. You can apply this technique to other T-shaped designs. There are two ways of doing this. If you are knitting the garment from bottom to top, you proceed as usual up to the armhole point, then cast on the required extra stitches for the length of each sleeve. You then continue knitting across the entire width from one wrist to the

other (measurement 'E' on the diagram) until you reach the upper edge. Alternatively, if you are knitting the garment sideways, you cast on the required number of stitches for the sleeve width, knit the sleeve, then cast on the required extra stitches for the bodice front and back. You then continue knitting across the bodice (casting off, if necessary, for a front opening), cast off the bodice stitch at the side seam and complete the other sleeve.

Multiple increasing and decreasing at beginning of rows

Sometimes a pattern will include a design feature that requires you to cast on or cast off a number of stitches at a time. For example, garments in which the sleeves are worked in one piece with the body involve this multiple increasing and decreasing in order to form sleeve or side edges, depending on the direction of the knitting.

Essentially the same technique is used in making a centre front slit for a neckline, as illustrated in the following steps.

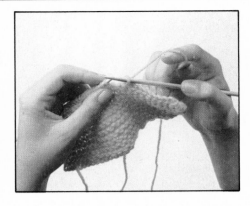

1 To make an opening for the neck in a fabric being knitted sideways, cast off the required number of stitches at the beginning of a row in the usual way. One stitch remains on the RH needle.

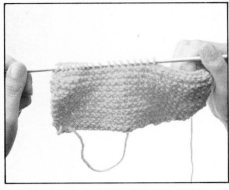

2 Work to the end of the row. The first stitch (the one remaining on the RH needle after casting off) counts as one of the stitches in that row.

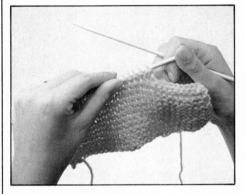

3 Now, work the following row. The cast-off stitches are now to your left. Transfer the needle with the stitches to your left hand to start the next row.

4 Using the two-needle method (see Knitting Course 2, p.4), cast on the number of stitches required. For an opening, the cast-on stitches must correspond in number to those cast off previously.

5 Work into each of the cast-on stitches, then continue knitting across the main piece of fabric.

Using a circular needle for working in rows

A circular needle consists of two small rigid needles joined by a length of flexible nylon wire. This type of needle is generally used for working in rounds to form a seamless piece of knitting; it does, however, have advantages in flat knitting (that is, working backwards and forwards in rows).

Whenever you've got a large number of stitches in a piece of knitting, the work eventually becomes heavy and unwieldy; when most of a row has been worked, the needle holding the new stitches is difficult to handle. A circular needle, however, can hold a great number of stitches, and because there is only one needle, the weight of the work is evenly distributed between both your hands.

1 When making a garment from cuff edge to cuff edge, use an ordinary pair of needles to make the sleeves and the cast-on stitches for side seams. On the next row, transfer the stitches to a circular needle; use one point of the circular needle in your right hand and knit in the usual way.

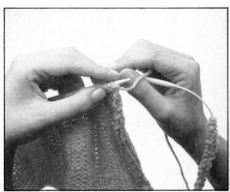

2 At the end of the row, when all the stitches are on the circular needle, transfer the point with the stitches to your left hand. The opposite side of the work must be facing you for the next row – in this case it is a purl row.

3 Work stitches from left needle point to right in the usual way. Once the RH needle is full of stitches move them on to the wire.

4 During the course of a row you will need to keep a constant supply of stitches to be worked on the LH needle. Move the stitches along the wire accordingly.

5 After each row, turn the work round so that the opposite side is facing for the next row, in the same way as in using a pair of needles. Continue in this way for the depth you require : cast off stitches in the usual way.

Sewing on patch pockets

Patch pockets are easy to make in a variety of stitches : they are simply squares or rectangles knitted separately from the main garment and sewn on later. The pocket must, however, be sewn on correctly so that it looks neat and attractive. Don't rely on your eye to set the pocket on the fabric accurately ; follow the pointers given here for a professional finish.

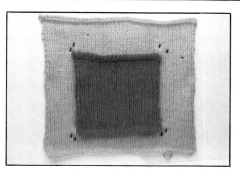

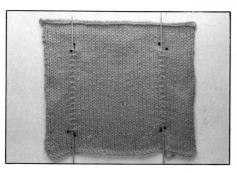

1 Make a pocket of the required size and cast off as usual. Position the pocket on the main fabric and mark the corners with pins. Remove the pocket for the time being.

2 Check that the pins run in straight lines along the rows and stitches. Use fine knitting needles, pointed at both ends, to pick up alternate stitches of the main fabric just outside the vertical lines of pins. This is a useful guide for a straight edge.

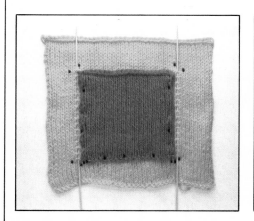

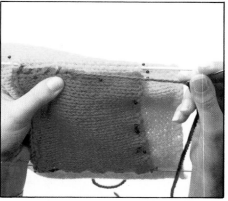

3 Pin pocket in position just inside the knitting needles. Check that the lower edge runs across a straight line of stitches on the main fabric.

4 Thread a blunt-ended wool needle with matching yarn (we have used a contrasting colour for clarity) and secure to back of work. Oversew the pocket to the main fabric round three sides, taking one stitch from the edge of the pocket and one stitch from the needle alternately down sides of pocket.

5 The finished pocket is sewn neatly in position. Strengthen either side of opening with a few stitches worked over the first line of oversewing.

Paul Williams

Making a twisted cord

For this simple trimming, strands of yarn are twisted together to form a cord; the cord varies in thickness according to the quality of yarn and number of strands used.

Fine cords make pretty and inexpensive ties on babies' garments, and because they are round, they are more comfortable than ribbon. Threaded through eyelet holes, a cord makes an effective drawstring on many kinds of garment. Fine yarns are suitable for cords on evening wear; thicker yarns and more strands make sturdy ties for outdoor clothes. Make an extra-thick cord to form the handle of a tote bag.

Usually, cords are made in the same yarn as the garment itself. You can experiment with different-coloured strands of yarn — perhaps including a different texture — to obtain some unusual effects.

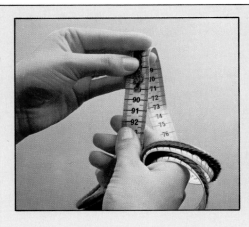

1 Cut the required number of strands of yarn; we have used three. Each strand must be three times the length of the finished cord (i.e. 90cm long to make a 30cm cord). Knot the strands together about 2cm from each end.

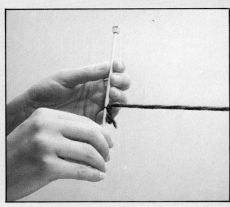

2 Insert a small knitting needle through each knot. Enlist the help of a friend for the next operation. Each of you should take one end of the strands and stand facing each other. Use the knitting needles to twist the strands in a clockwise direction.

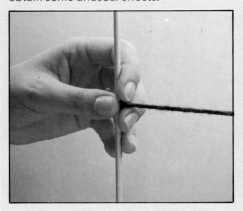

3 Keep turning — for what seems like ages — until the strands are tightly twisted and it is impossible to turn any more without the cord twisting back on itself.

4 Still holding the strands and keeping them taut, fold them in half at the centre. Without letting go of the ends, remove the knitting needles and knot the two ends together just above the previous knots.

5 Hold the knot and give the cord a sharp shake; smooth it down from the knot to the folded end to even out the twists.

6 Undo the original knots at the ends of the strands and even out the yarn in the tassel. Neaten the tassel by trimming ends. If you are using the cord as one of a pair of ties, sew the folded end to the garment.

7 To use the cord as a drawstring, make another tassel at the folded end. Knot the cord, leaving enough length at the end to make a matching tassel. Cut through the loops and smooth out the ends.

8 The finished cord is about one third the length of the original strands of yarn, including the tassels.

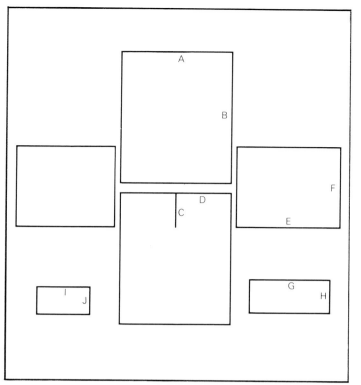

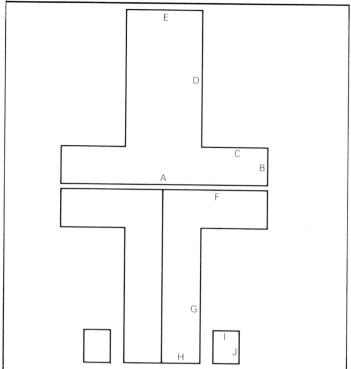

Brian Mayor

T-shape for two

Here are two more ingenious ways with the versatile T-shape. The man's pullover and woman's jacket are both worked in garter stitch in chunky yarn. Vertical patch pockets are smart as well as practical.

Woman's T-shaped jacket

Size

To fit 83 [87 :92 :97 :102 :107]cm bust : other measurements are shown on the diagram.

Note instructions for larger sizes are in square brackets [] ; where there is only one set of figures it applies to all sizes.

Materials

Total of 1000[1050 :1100 :1150 : 1200 :1250]g of chunky yarn such as Sirdar Pullman
2 x 5g of double knitting yarn in a contrasting colour for trimming
1 pair 6½mm knitting needles
6½mm Twin Pin
4.00mm crochet hook

Tension

14sts and 28 rows to 10cm over gst on 6½mm needles.

Back

Using the pair of 6½mm needles and chunky yarn, cast on 60[63 :67 :70 :74 : 77] sts and work in g st for 49[50 : 51 :52 :53 :54]cm.
☐ For the sleeves, cast on 51[54 :57 : 60 :63 :66] sts at beg of next 2 rows. 162[171 :181 :190 :200 :209] sts.
☐ Change to 6½mm Twin Pin and continue in g st until work measures 67 [70 :73 :76 :79 :82]cm from beg. Cast off.

Left front

Using the pair of 6½mm needles and chunky yarn cast on 30 [32 :34 :35 :37 : 39]sts and work in g st for 49[50 :51 :52 : 53 :54]cm.
☐ For the sleeve, cast on 51[54 :57 : 60 :63 :66]sts at beg of next row. 81[86 :91 :95 :100 :105] sts.
Continue in g st until work is same length as back. Cast off.

Right front

Work as given for left front ; the work is reversible.

Pockets (make 2)

Using the pair of 6½mm needles and chunky yarn, cast on 21[22 :24 :25 : 27 :29] sts and work in g st for 12[13 : 14 :15 :16 :17]cm. Cast off.

To make up

☐ Do not press.
☐ Join upper sleeve and shoulder seams by oversewing, leaving 19[19 :20 : 21 :21 :22]cm free for neck.
☐ Join side and underarm seams by oversewing.

Measurements for woman's T-shaped jacket	
(see diagram above)	
A	117(123 :130 :137 :143 :150)cm
B	18(20 :22 :24 :26 :28)cm
C	37(39 :41 :43 :45 :47)cm
D	49(50 :51 :52 :53 :54)cm
E	43(45 :48 :51 :53 :56)cm
F	59(62 :65 :69 :72 :75)cm
G	67(70 :73 :76 :79 :82)cm
H	22(23 :24 :25 :26 :27)cm
I	12(13 :14 :15 :16 :17)cm
J	15(16 :17 :18 :19 :20)cm

☐ With right side facing, join on double knitting yarn and, using the crochet hook, work a row of double crochet evenly all round outer edge.
☐ With wrong side facing, work a row of double crochet round lower edge of sleeves.
☐ Turn back 10cm at lower edge of each sleeve to form cuff.
☐ Work double crochet round the four edges of pockets, then sew pockets to fronts, placing one edge at side seam and leaving top 2/3 of this side open.
☐ Using 4 strands of double knitting make two twisted cords each 50cm long and sew one to each front to tie as shown in picture overleaf.

Next row Cast off 28[31:34:37:40:43] sts for neck opening, K to end of row.
Next row K to end, then turn and cast on 28[31:34:37:40:43] sts for neck opening. 91[96:101:106:111:116] sts.
☐ Continue in g st until front measures same as back. Cast off.

Sleeves (worked from wrist)
Using 6mm needles cast on 54[61:67:74:80:87] sts and work in g st for 37[39:41:43:45:47]cm. Cast off loosely.

Collar
Using 6mm needles cast on 32[32:32:32:32:32] sts and K 2 rows.
Next row (Right side) K6, then (P4, K4) to the last 2 sts, K2.
Next row K2, P4, (K4, P4) to the last 2 sts, K2.
☐ Rep these 2 rows until work measures 35[37:39:41:43:45] cm from beg, ending with a right-side row.
☐ K 2 rows, then cast off.

Pocket
Using 6mm needles cast on 32[32:32:40:40:40] sts.
☐ Work the 2 rows of K4, P4 rib with 2 sts at each end in g st as given for collar for 13[15:15:17:17:19] cm. Cast off loosely.

To make up
☐ Do not press.
☐ Join shoulder seams for 12[13:14:15:16:17]cm.
☐ Mark centre of sleeve top edge with a pin : match pin to shoulder seam and join sleeves to body by oversewing.
☐ Join side and sleeve seams by oversewing.
☐ Sew cast-on edge of collar to neck.
☐ Sew on pocket, sewing along cast-on and cast-off edges.
☐ Press seams.

Kim Sayer/accessories from Fenwicks

Man's T-shaped sweater

Sizes
To fit 83[87:92:97:102:107]cm chest : other measurements are shown on the diagram.
Note instructions for larger sizes are in square brackets [] ; where there is only one set of figures it applies to all sizes.

Materials
Total of 1400[1500:1500:1600:1600:1700]g of chunky yarn such as Sirdar Norsgarn 1 pair 6mm knitting needles

Tension
16sts and 32 rows to 10cm over g st on 6mm needles.

Back (worked sideways)
Using 6mm needles cast on 91[96:101:106:111:116] sts for side edge and work in g st for 43[45:48:51:53:56] cm. Cast off.

Front (worked sideways)
Using 6mm needles cast on 91[96:101:106:111:116] sts for side edge and work in g st for 21.5[22.5:24:25.5:26.5:28] cm.

Measurements for man's T-shaped sweater
(see diagram on page 75, top left)

A	43(45:48:51:53:56)cm
B	57(60:63:66:69:72)cm
C	17(19:21:23:25:27)cm
D	12(13:14:15:16:17)cm
E	37(39:41:43:45:47)cm
F	34(38:42:46:50:54)cm
G	36(38:40:42:44:46)cm
H	20(20:20:20:20:20)cm
I	18(18:18:23:23:23)cm
J	13(15:15:17:17:19)cm

Step-by-step course – 18

*The advanced T-shape
*Working a neckshaping
*Using a pair of needles to
 pick up stitches round neck
*Finishing off a crew
 neckband
*Honeycomb slip stitch
*A T-shaped pullover

The advanced T-shape

The sweater included in this course is more advanced in style than the basic T-shapes included in previous courses. This design features a shaped neck finished with a crew neckband or polo collar to make it sit comfortably round the neck. It also has a ribbed welt to draw in the lower edge and ribbed cuffs so that it fits the body more closely.

The diagram and measurement plan give a whole range of children's and adults' sizes. If you want to add neck shaping to the T-shaped designs shown in previous chapters, refer to the chart on this page and find measurements G, H, I and J for the size you are making. Calculate the number of stitches and rows on the shaping using the instructions given in Knitting Course 16, page 64.

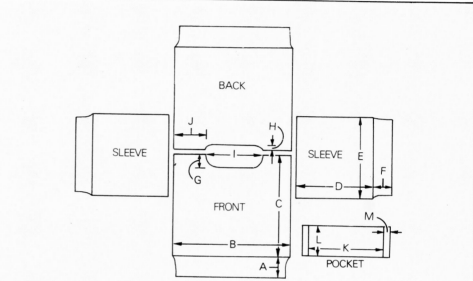

Basic measurements for designing T-shaped pullover (in centimetres)

Chest/bust sizes	Code	51	56	61	66	71	76	83	87	92	97	102	107
Depth of welt	A	4	4	4	5	5	5	5	6	6	7	7	7
Width across front/back	B	28	30.5	33	35.5	38	40.5	43	45.5	48.5	51	53.5	56
Length from welt to shoulder	C	26	30	34	38	42	46	50	54	58	60	62	64
Sleeve length from cuff to top	D	18	22	26	29	32	35	37	39	41	42	44	46
Width all round sleeve	E	26	28	30	32	34	36	38	40	42	44	46	48
Depth of cuff	F	2	2	2	3	3	3	4	4	4	5	5	5
Depth of front neck shaping	G	5	5	5	6	6	6	7	7	7	8	8	8
Depth of back neck shaping	H	1	1	1	1.5	1.5	1.5	2	2	2	2.5	2.5	2.5
Width of front/back neck	I	15.5	16	16.5	17	17.5	18	18.5	19	19.5	20.5	21	21.5
Shoulder seam	J	5	6	7	8	9	10	11	12	13	14	15	16
Width of pocket	K	16	16	16	18	18	18	20	20	20	22	22	22
Depth of pocket	L	10	10	12	12	14	14	16	16	18	18	20	20
Width of pocket border	M	1	1	1	1.5	1.5	1.5	2	2	2	2.5	2.5	2.5
Depth of crew neck (after folding in half)	N	1.5	1.5	1.5	2	2	2	2.5	2.5	2.5	3	3	3
Depth of polo neck	O	10	10	12	12	14	14	16	16	18	18	20	20

continued : The advanced T-shape

A shaped neck usually requires some kind of a finish to make it grip. This is usually a ribbed neckband – a polo collar is simply an extended neckband – which is worked directly on to the fabric by picking up the stitches round the neck.

A welt can be added to T-shaped designs by one of two methods, depending on the direction of the knitting. If you are working from the lower edge to the top it is simple : just cast on the required number of stitches with needles two sizes smaller than those used for the main fabric. Work the depth of rib you want – see the chart on page 77 – then change to the larger needles and continue in pattern. If you are knitting the sweater sideways, first make the main front and back pieces. Later, pick up stitches along the lower edge for the welt and work downwards in rib to the depth you require.

The number of stitches to cast on for a ribbed cuff is slightly more difficult to calculate. Refer to the chart on page 77 and find the number to cast on for the sleeve edge of an existing T-shaped design. You should cast on approximately two-thirds of this number for the cuff. Again, use needles two sizes smaller than for pattern, and end with a right-side row. Now knit one more row of ribbing (wrong side), increasing to obtain the number of stitches required for the sleeve ; do this evenly across the row. To increase by one-third, increase on every other stitch. (See the detailed pattern row given in the instructions on pages 81-82 for precise details for making up the pullover.)

Working neck shaping

Most patterns give detailed instructions on how to work any neck shaping. Here we explain the general principle of the technique. Our sample is the front of a garment and shows how to divide the work and retain stitches for working at a later stage with the aid of a spare needle and stitch holder. In some patterns the centre front stitches may be cast off and neckband stitches picked up from this edge rather than picking them up from the spare needle as described here.

1 Work to point where shaping is to begin. (Usually, as here, you end with a wrong-side row.) On the next row, pattern the required number of stitches for one side of the neck. Leave the remaining stitches on a spare needle with points at both ends ; there are too many stitches to fit on to a holder. Buy special rubber stops to prevent the stitches falling off the ends, or improvize with corks or rubber bands.

2 Turn the work for the next row. Complete one side of the neck first. Here, the left side has been completed, as the piece is the front of the work. If you're making the back you normally complete the right side first. A series of decreased stitches at the neck edge produce a shaping line from the front neck to the shoulder.

3 Return to the stitches on the spare needle ; a number of these across the centre front neck are left unworked until you add the neckband. With the right side of the work facing you, begin at the RH edge of the stitches on the spare needle and slip the required number for the centre front on to a holder.

4 Transfer the stitches still remaining on the spare needle to one of a pair of needles, slipping them on to this needle from the LH edge. You are now ready to begin knitting the RH side of the front neck shaping, beginning with a right side row. Rejoin the yarn to inner end of sts on needle and work to the end of the row (armhole edge).

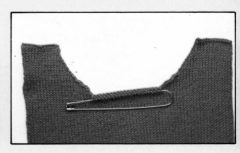

5 Complete the second side of the neck to match the first. Precise instructions may be given in the pattern ; if not reverse the neck shaping by decreasing at the RH edge instead of the LH edge.

Using a pair of needles to pick up stitches round neck

It is possible to make a neckband by knitting it separately and then sewing it on to the garment, but this may produce a hard, bulky seam across the throat. To prevent this, use the technique of picking up the stitches at the neck edge and knitting the neckband or collar directly on to the garment.

Join one shoulder seam only before beginning the neckband; in this way the back and front open out flat and you can use a pair of needles for picking up the stitches instead of using a circular needle or a set of four needles, which are slightly more difficult to use. The needles used for a neckband are usually two sizes smaller than those used for the main fabric.

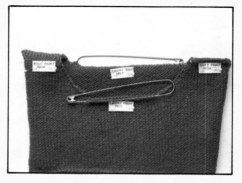

1 Take the front and back sections of the garment and join the right shoulder seam. Turn the work right side out and hold it so that the front is on top; the unjoined shoulder seam is to your right.

2 With the right side of the work facing you, begin picking up stitches for neckband at the left front (un-seamed) shoulder. Insert the LH needle from front to back through the first vertical loop of a stitch at the end of the row.

3 Hold your yarn ready for knitting, leaving an end of about 10cm. Insert the RH needle into the loop on LH needle; wind the yarn round the RH needle tip in the usual knit position and draw a stitch through the loop on the LH needle. This action is called 'knitting up' (K up).

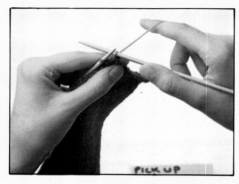

4 There is now one stitch on the RH needle. Insert the LH needle into the next long vertical loop to the left and knit up another stitch.

5 Continue picking up stitches in this way until you reach the shaped section. (On some patterns, the shaping goes right up to the shoulder.) The decreased stitches form a sloping loop: insert the LH needle into this loop. In general pick up one stitch for every two row ends on a shaped edge.

6 Pick up stitches down left front neck until you reach the centre front neck stitches on the holder. Transfer the stitches to the LH needle, open the stitch holder at the LH edge and, working from left to right, slip the stitches on to the needle one by one.

7 When all the centre front neck stitches are on the LH needle, knit across them in the usual way.

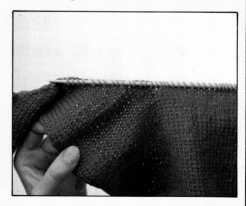

8 Continue round neck, picking up stitches up right front neck and down right back neck, knitting across centre back neck stitches on holder and picking up stitches up left back neck so that all stitches are on one needle.

Finishing off a crew neckband

For a professional finish and a comfortable fit round the neck, a crew neckband should be worked to twice the required depth and then folded over to the inside. Knit up stitches round neck (with right shoulder seamed) and work in rib to twice the depth that you require. Cast off very loosely. Join the shoulder seam that was left open; also join the ends of the neckband in a continuous line with the shoulder seam. The neckband now forms a complete circle.

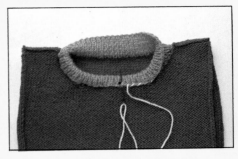

1 Fold the neckband in half to the wrong side of the work. The cast-off edge is very pliable so that you can easily stretch it to fit all round the inner neck edge. Pin the edge in position exactly on top of the ridges where stitches were picked up round neck.

2 Thread a blunt-ended wool needle with matching yarn – a different colour has been used here for clarity. Slipstitch the edge of the neckband in position, taking care that the ridges are just hidden.

Honeycomb slip stitch

This is another useful basic stitch pattern: it produces a neat, textured fabric with an all-over honeycomb effect. You can use this stitch pattern as a substitute for garter stitch, stocking stitch, moss stitch and others when you are designing your own T-shaped sweaters. Remember to work a tension square first; although the stitch may substitute for other stitches this doesn't mean that it is equal in tension to them.

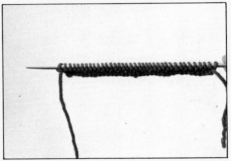

1 Cast on an uneven number of stitches (e.g. 17, 19, 21). To work the first row, P the first st, insert the needle into the next st as if to purl it and transfer the stitch to the RH needle without working it – called sl 1 P-wise; P1 st, alternately sl 1 P-wise, then P1 st to the end of the row.

2 Purl each stitch in the 2nd row. Here the wrong side of the work is facing you.

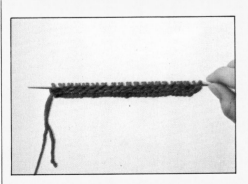

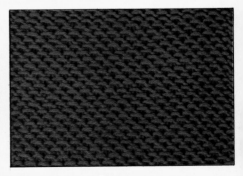

3 To work the 3rd row, P2 sts, then sl 1 P-wise, P1 st alternately until you reach the last stitch; P1 st. This is the right side of the work.

4 Purl the 4th row. Repeat these 4 rows until the fabric is the depth you require. Cast off, preferably, on a wrong-side (i.e. purl) row.

5 The finished fabric has horizontal strands of yarn on the right side formed by passing over slipped stitches. The alternating positions of strands of yarn and purled stitches throughout the fabric creates a three-dimensional texture similar to a honeycomb.

Final list of abbreviations

beg = begin(ning)
dec = decreas(e)(ing)
g st = garter stitch
inc = increas(e)(ing)
K = knit
P = purl
patt = pattern
rem = remain(ing)
rep = repeat
rev st st = reverse stocking stitch
st(s) = stitch(es)
st st = stocking stitch
tog = together

On the left is an alphabetical list of abbreviations that you know so far. To complete your knowledge of knitting shorthand, the final abbreviated terms are given on the right (there are a few more special knitting abbreviations : these will be introduced in a course with the techniques to which they apply). From now on patterns will include the full range of abbreviations.

alt = alternate
cont = continu(e)(ing)
foll = follow(ing)
K up = pick up and knit
K-wise = knitwise
P-wise = purlwise
RS = right side
sl = slip
tbl = through back of loop(s)
WS = wrong side

Suit your family to a 'T'

Here's a pattern to please every member of your family — an easy-to-wear pullover in the easy-to-make T-shape. A whole range of sizes is given, and you can choose either a crew neck or a polo neck to finish off the sweater.

Sizes
To fit 53[56 :61 :66 :71 :76 :83 :87 :92 : 97 :102 :107]cm chest/bust. Instructions for larger sizes are in square brackets [] ; where there is only one set of figures it applies to all sizes.

Materials
*Total of 225 [275: 300: 350: 375: 425: 450: 500: 525: 575: 600: 650] g of double knitting yarn
For polo collar, allow an extra 25 [25: 25: 25: 50: 50: 50: 50: 75: 75: 75: 75] g
1 pair each 3¼ mm and 4 mm knitting needles*

Tension
24 sts and 40 rows to 10cm over patt worked on 4mm needles.

Note
In a pattern containing instructions for a large number of sizes it is easy to mistake the figures for the size you are making : before knitting go through the pattern and circle all the figures that apply to your size.

Back
Using 3¼mm needles cast on 67[73 :79 : 85 :91 :97 :103 :109 :115 :121 :127 :133] sts.
☐ Beg and ending 1st row with K1 and 2nd row with P1, work 2 rows K1, P1 rib. Rep these 2 rows for 4[4 :4 :5 :5 :5 :6 :6 :6 : 7 :7 :7]cm, ending with a 2nd row.
☐ Change to 4mm needles. Cont in honeycomb slip stitch (see page 80) until work measures 29[33 :37 :41.5 : 45.5 :49.5 :54 :58 :62 :64.5 :66.5 : 68.5]cm from beg, ending with a P row.
☐ Beg neck shaping on next row : patt 16[18 :21 :24 :27 :29 :33 :35 :38 :41 :44 : 46] sts, turn and leave rem sts on a spare needle.
☐ Cont in patt, dec one st at beg (neck

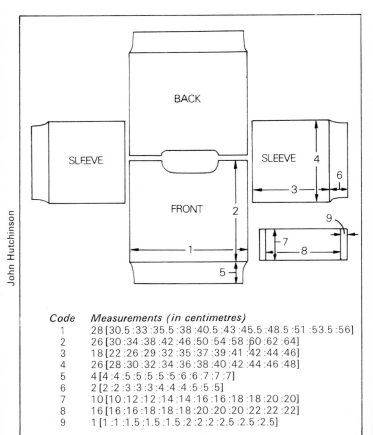

Code	Measurements (in centimetres)
1	28 [30.5 :33 :35.5 :38 :40.5 :43 :45.5 :48.5 :51 :53.5 :56]
2	26 [30 :34 :38 :42 :46 :50 :54 :58 :60 :62 :64]
3	18 [22 :26 :29 :32 :35 :37 :39 :41 :42 :44 :46]
4	26 [28 :30 :32 :34 :36 :38 :40 :42 :44 :46 :48]
5	4 [4 :4 :5 :5 :5 :6 :6 :7 :7 :7]
6	2 [2 :2 :3 :3 :3 :4 :4 :4 :5 :5]
7	10 [10 :12 :12 :14 :14 :16 :16 :18 :18 :20 :20]
8	16 [16 :16 :18 :18 :18 :20 :20 :20 :22 :22 :22]
9	1 [1 :1 :1.5 :1.5 :1.5 :2 :2 :2 :2.5 :2.5 :2.5]

John Hutchinson

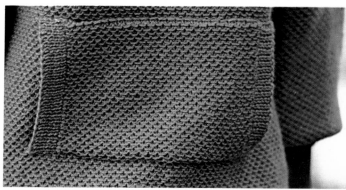

edge) of next and foll 1 [1 :1 :2 :2 :2 :3 : 3 :3 :4 :4 :4] alt rows, ending with a P row.

☐ Cast off rem 14 [16 :19 :21 :24 :26 :29 : 31 :34 :36 :39 :41] sts.

☐ Return to sts on spare needle ; sl first 35 [37 :37 :37 :37 :39 :37 :39 :39 :39 :39 : 41] sts onto a holder for back neck, rejoin yarn to next st and patt to end.

☐ Cont in patt, dec one st at end (neck edge) of next and foll 1 [1 :1 :2 :2 :2 :3 :3 : 3 :4 :4 :4] alt rows, ending with a P row. Cast off.

Front

Work as given for back until front measures 25 [29 :33 :37 :41 :45 :49 :53 : 57 :59 :61 :63] cm from beg, ending with a P row.

☐ Beg neck shaping on next row : patt 23 [25 :28 :31 :34 :36 :41 :43 :46 :49 :52 : 54] sts, turn and leave rem sts on a spare needle.

☐ Cast off 2 sts at beg (neck edge) of next and foll 1 [1 :1 :1 :1 :1 :2 :2 :2 :2 :2 :2] alt rows, then dec one st at same edge on foll 5 [5 :5 :6 :6 :6 :6 :6 :6 :7 :7 :7] alt rows.

☐ Cont without shaping until front measures same as back to shoulders, ending with a P row.

☐ Cast off rem 14 [16 :19 :21 :24 :26 :29 : 31 :34 :36 :39 :41] sts.

☐ Return to sts on spare needle ; sl first 21 [23 :23 :23 :23 :25 :21 :23 :23 :23 :23 : 25] sts onto holder for front neck, rejoin yarn to next st and patt to end.

☐ P one row, then cont to match first side.

Sleeves

Using 3¼mm needles cast on 41 [45 :47 :51 :53 :57 :61 :65 :67 :71 :73 : 77] sts.

☐ Work 2 [2 :2 :3 :3 :3 :4 :4 :4 :5 :5 :5] cm rib as given for back, ending with a 1st row and inc one st at end of last row on 3rd-6th and 9th-12th sizes.

☐ Inc to width of sleeve on next row : P1 [1 :2 :0 :0 :1 :1 :2 :2 :0 :0] sts, then P twice into next st and P1 st alternately to end of row. This makes 61 [67 :71 :77 : 81 :87 :91 :97 :101 :107 :111 :117] sts.

☐ Change to 4mm needles. Cont in honeycomb slip stitch until work measures 20 [24 :28 :32 :35 :38 :41 :43 : 45 :47 :49 :51] cm from beg. Cast off very loosely.

Pocket

Using 4mm needles cast on 39 [39 :39 : 43 :43 :43 :47 :47 :51 :51 :51] sts. Work 10 [10 :12 :12 :14 :14 :16 :16 :18 : 18 :20 :20] cm in honeycomb slip stitch. Cast off.

☐ Work pocket borders : using 3¼mm needles and with RS of work facing, K up 29 [29 :35 :35 :41 :41 :47 :47 :53 :53 :59 : 59] sts along side edge of pocket.

☐ Work 1 [1 :1 :1.5 :1.5 :1.5 :2 :2 :2 : 2.5 :2.5 :2.5] cm rib as given for back. Cast off in rib.

☐ Rep along other side edge.

Neckband

Join right shoulder seam. Using 3¼mm needles and with RS of work facing, K up 16 [16 :17 :19 :19 :19 :22 :22 :23 :25 :25 : 25] sts down left front neck, K front neck sts from holder, K up 15 [15 :16 :18 : 18 :18 :21 :21 :22 :24 :24 :24] sts up right front neck, 3 [3 :4 :5 :5 :5 :7 : 7 :8 :9 :9 :9] sts down right back neck, K back neck sts on holder, then K up 3 [3 :4 :5 :5 :5 :7 :7 :8 :9 :9 :9] sts up left back neck. This makes 93 [97 :101 :107 :107 :111 :115 :119 : 123 :129 :129 :133] sts.

☐ Cont in K1, P1 rib ; work 3 [3 :3 :4 : 4 :4 :5 :5 :5 :6 :6 :6] cm for crew neck or 10 [10 :12 :12 :14 :14 :16 :16 :18 : 18 :20 :20] cm for polo neck. Cast off loosely in rib.

To make up

Press work if necessary with a warm iron over a damp cloth.

☐ Join left shoulder and neckband seams
☐ Join left shoulder seam and neckband, reversing seam on top half of polo collar.
☐ Fold crew neckband in half to inside and slip stitch in position.
☐ Mark centre of cast-off sleeve edge with a pin : match pin to shoulder seam and sew sleeves in position.
☐ Sew on pocket along top and lower edges, stitching along side opening for a short distance. This leaves an opening for hands in top of side edge.
☐ Join side and sleeve seams. Press.

Step-by-step course – 19

Understanding a knitting pattern

Although the style in which knitting patterns are presented varies slightly according to the publisher, most patterns have certain basic similarities. A pattern is normally divided into three different sections: information about sizes, materials and tension, working instructions for each section and instructions for assembling the sections. Full use is made of the abbreviations you already know, and the language is very concise, in order to give a maximum of information in a small space. From this point onward the patterns in the Knitting Course will be written in normal knitting style.

To help the knitter, everything is written in logical order. Read the pattern through before you begin knitting, so that you have a general understanding of the work. Don't worry if a particular detail or instruction isn't crystal clear at first reading: many techniques only become obvious when you have the work in front of you.

Sizes

These usually include the chest or bust sizes and other major measurements: scale drawings given in some patterns help you to see at a glance the number of pieces and their measurements. Check the finished lengths of individual pieces and read the working instructions to see if they allow you to make any alterations. A pattern is usually given in a variety of sizes: instructions for the larger sizes are in square brackets. Read through the complete pattern and circle the figures relevant to your size.

Materials

This section states the amount, brand and quality of yarn used for the garment shown in the photograph. Where possible, in our patterns, the type of yarn is quoted, in case you are unable to obtain the original and have to make a substitution. Remember that the quantity stated applies only to the original yarn; you may need more or less yarn if you use a different brand or type.

Also listed under 'materials' is everything else you will need for the pattern, from knitting needles to zip fasteners.

Tension

Every pattern gives the recommended tension that you need to achieve in order to make an item of the correct size. Always make a tension sample before you begin, whether you use the original yarn or a substitute.

Working instructions

Instructions for each section of the garment are given under the appropriate headings: 'back', 'front', and so on. Work the pieces in the order in which they appear in the instructions; different pieces may have to be joined before you can continue knitting, or specific instructions may be given in full in the first section and referred to more briefly later on in the pattern.

An asterisk, *, is often used to avoid repetition; in a pattern row it means that you should repeat the sequence of stitches from that point as instructed. A whole section of instructions may be marked with single or double asterisks at the beginning and end: these must be repeated at a later stage in the pattern; for example: 'Back: work as given for front from * to *.'

Making up

Pay particular attention to this section; it it easy to spoil a beautifully-knitted garment by careless making up. Here you will find details of pressing the yarn; if, however, you have used a substitute yarn, you should follow the instructions on the ball band instead.

The pattern instructions also tell you the order in which pieces should be sewn together to form the base for any final edgings or trimmings – details of which are also included here.

Abbreviated version

1st row (RS) K2, *yfwd, K1, yfwd, sl 1, K1, psso, K9, K2 tog, yfwd, K1, yfwd, K3, rep from * to end, but finish last rep K2 instead of K3. 241 sts.
2nd row P5, *P2 tog, P7, P2 tog tbl, P9, rep from * to end, but finish last rep P5 instead of P9. 217 sts.

Here is proof of the practicality and economy of knitting pattern language. This excerpt from a Stitch by Stitch knitting pattern for a Shetland shawl (above left) is only seven lines long. Written out in normal English (on the right), the same instructions occupy 18 lines. The final effect (right) is the same.

Full length version

First row (Right side) knit 2, bring yarn forward, knit 1, bring yarn forward, slip 1, knit 1, pass slip stitch over, knit 9, knit 2 together, bring yarn forward, knit 1, bring yarn forward, knit 3. Repeat this sequence of stitches – beginning with the first 'bring yarn forward' – to the end of the row, but on the last repeat knit 2 instead of 3. You now have 241 stitches on the needle.
Second row Purl 5, purl 2 together, purl 7, purl 2 together through the backs of the loops, purl 9. Repeat this sequence of stitches – beginning with the first 'purl 2 together' – to the end of the row, but on the last repeat, purl 5 instead of 9. You now have a total of 217 stitches on the needle.

Making buttonholes in a ribbed border

A buttonhole is made by casting off a number of stitches in the centre of one row (the number varying with the size of the button) and replacing them with the same number of stitches in the following row. Work as neatly as possible, otherwise you will spoil the appearance of the garment. Patterns tell you precisely how to make the buttonholes and the distance to work between each one. On a garment such as the V-neck cardigan on page 87 the first buttonhole is just above the lower edge, the last level with the beginning of the front edge shaping and the others evenly spaced between them.

1 Cast on the number of stitches specified; in the cardigan pattern it is 10. Work in rib until you reach the position for the first buttonhole, ending with a wrong-side row.

2 The first buttonhole row reads 'rib 4 sts, cast off 2 sts, rib to end'. Work the first 4 stitches to reach the cast-off position: rib two stitches, then lift the first over the second in the usual way.

3 Rib 1 more stitch, casting it off in rib as usual. On the RH needle there are 4 stitches before the cast-off group and one stitch remaining from casting off.

4 Work to the end of the row; there should be the same number of stitches on each side of the buttonhole. On the 2nd buttonhole row, rib up to the last stitch before the cast-off group.

5 Cast on the same number of stitches as those cast off in the previous row. Do this by increasing into the front and back of the next stitch. Make the first stitch by knitting into the front of the next stitch.

6 Do not allow the stitch you are working into to fall from the LH needle. Twist the RH needle to the right so that it lies behind the LH needle: make the next stitch by knitting into the back of the stitch on the LH needle.

7 Increase again by knitting into the front of the same stitch. You now have 2 extra stitches on the RH needle – the number cast off in the previous row. (If more stitches have been cast off, continue increasing alternately into the front and back of the same stitch until you have the required number.)

8 Work in rib to the end of the row. On the next row, which is on the right side of the work, continue in rib pattern to end. Work in correct rib sequence over cast-on stitches in the centre.

Sewing on a ribbed border

Ribbed borders, worked separately, are often used to finish a knitted edge. Usually the edge you are finishing off consists of the row ends at the sides of a piece of knitting such as those along the front opening of a cardigan or jacket. Often, say on a V-neck cardigan, the border fits up one front edge, then extends round the entire neck and down the other front; this type of border may include buttonholes and forms a base for sewing on buttons.

Following pattern, work the border on smaller needles than the main fabric, just as you would for a welt or cuffs at the lower edge (which are normally knitted in one piece with the main fabric). Make the border very slightly shorter than the edge. Check the tension by holding it against the edge. Now stretch the border on to the edge before pinning and sewing it in position: this helps to keep the knitting firm and prevent it sagging.

1 Before sewing on the border, press the main piece of knitting. With right side of border (if there is one) against right side of fabric, stretch border slightly to fit edge. Pin in position along outer edge.

2 Use a blunt-ended wool needle threaded with matching yarn (we have used a contrasting yarn for clarity) to work a flat seam. Work through edge stitches on both pieces of knitting.

3 If you open the work flat with wrong side uppermost and gently ease the stitches apart you will see that this type of seam makes a laced effect through the stitches.

4 This is the finished seam on the right side of the work. The yarn used for stitching makes regular, neat bars across the seam: these are indistinguishable when you work the seam in a matching yarn.

Paul Williams

Setting in a sleeve

Setting a sleeve into a garment is an important part of the making up. Two different shapes must be fitted together; this requires some skill and practice in order to obtain a neat finish.

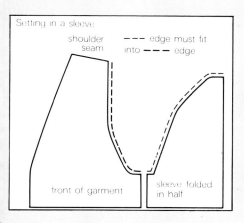

Setting in a sleeve

shoulder seam — — — edge must fit
into — — — edge

front of garment / sleeve folded in half

1 Join shoulder and side seams on back and front of garment in the usual way. Leave garment wrong side out.

2 Join the sleeve seam and turn the completed sleeve right side out. Fold the sleeve in half with the seam forming one side edge. Mark the centre of the sleeve top on the opposite edge to the seam with a pin.

continued

3 Position sleeve in armhole. With right side of sleeve to right side of garment, match underarm seams and pin. Also match pin at centre of sleeve top to shoulder seam and secure with a pin.

4 Always working on edge just inside *sleeve top* (on wrong side of fabric), pin sleeve in position all round ; match any decreased edges at underarm and ease in fullness on sleeve top if necessary.

5 Sew sleeve in position with a back stitch seam, following the line of pins inside the sleeve top edge. The finished sleeve fits neatly into the armhole without puckering. Press gently on the right side of the work if so instructed in pattern.

Perennial favourite

Here's a cardigan you'll wear again and again and never tire of. Gently shaded bouclé yarn gives textural interest to its classic lines and makes it extra soft. You can dress it up or down to suit almost any occasion.

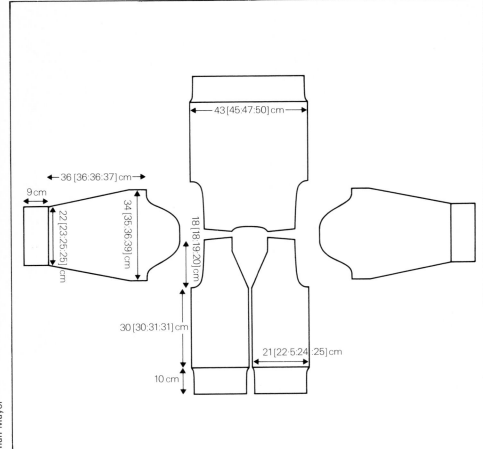

Sizes
To fit 83[87 :92 :97]cm bust.
Length, 60[60 :61.5 :62]cm.
Sleeve seam, 45[45 :45 :46]cm.
Note Instructions for larger sizes are in square brackets [] ; where there is only one set of figures it applies to all sizes.

Materials
8[9 :9 :10] x 50g balls of Patons Mona Lisa (a double bouclé yarn)
1 pair each 3¾mm and 5mm knitting needles
5 buttons

Tension
16sts and 30 rows to 10cm over g st worked on 5mm needles.

Left front
**Using 3¾mm needles cast on 33[35 :37 :39]sts.
1st row (RS) K2, *P1, K1, rep from * to last st, K1.
2nd row *K1, P1, rep from * to last st, K1.
Rep these 2 rows for 10cm, ending with a 2nd row and inc one st at end of last row. 34[36 :38 :40]sts. Change to 5mm needles. Cont in g st until work measures 38[38 :39 :39]cm from beg, ending with a WS row. **
Shape front edge
Next row K to last 2sts, K2 tog, K 5 rows.
Shape armhole
Next row Cast off 2[3 :3 :4]sts, K to last

2sts, K2 tog.

K 1 row. Dec one st at front edge on every 6th row from previous dec, *at the same time* dec one st at armhole edge on the next 3 rows, then foll 2[2:3:3] alt rows. Keeping armhole edge straight, cont to dec at front edge only until 17[18:19:20]sts rem. Cont without shaping until armhole measures 18[18:19:20]cm from beg, ending at armhole edge.

Shape shoulder
Cast off at beg of next and foll alt rows 4[5:4:5]sts once, 4[4:5:5]sts twice and 5sts once.

Right front
Work as given for left front from ** to ** but inc at beg instead of end of last row of ribbing.

Shape front edge
Next row K2 tog, K to end. K 5 rows.
Next row K2 tog, K to end.

Shape armhole
Next row Cast off 2[3:3:4]sts, K to end. Complete to match left front, working 1 more row before shaping shoulder.

Back
Using 3¾mm needles cast on 69[73:77:81]sts. Work 10cm rib as given for left front, ending with a 2nd row and inc one st at each end of last row. 71[75:79:83]sts. Change to 5mm needles. Cont in g st until back measures same as fronts to armholes, ending with a WS row.

Shape armholes
Cast off 2[3:3:4]sts at beg of next 2 rows. Dec one st at each end of next 3 rows, then foll 2[2:3:3] alt rows. Cont without shaping until armholes measure same as fronts, ending with a WS row.

Shape shoulders and back neck
Cast off 4[5:4:5]sts at beg of next 2 rows.
Next row Cast off 4[4:5:5]sts, K until there are 12[12:13:13]sts on right-hand needle, cast off next 17sts, K to end. Cont on last set of sts as foll:
1st row Cast off 4[4:5:5]sts, K to last 2sts, K2 tog.
2nd row K2 tog, K to end.
3rd row As 1st.
K 1 row. Cast off rem 5sts.
Rejoin yarn to rem sts at neck edge.
1st row K2 tog, K to end.
2nd row Cast off 4[4:5:5]sts, K to last 2sts, K2 tog.
3rd row As 1st.
Cast off rem 5sts.

Sleeves
Using 3¾mm needles cast on 35[37:39:39]sts. Work 9cm rib as given for left front, ending with a 2nd row. Change to 5mm needles. Cont in g st, inc one st at each end of 9th and every foll 10th[10th:10th:8th] row until there are 53[55:57:61]sts. Cont without

Caroline Arber/accessories from Harvey Nichols

shaping until sleeve measures 45[45:45:46]cm from beg, ending with a WS row.

Shape top
Cast off 2[3:3:4]sts at beg of next 2 rows. Dec one st at each end of next and every foll alt row until 21sts rem, then at each end of every row until 13sts rem. Cast off.

Border
Join shoulder seams. Using 3¾mm needles cast on 10sts.
1st row K2, *P1, K1, rep from * to end. This row forms the rib. Work 3 more rows.
1st buttonhole row Rib 4sts, cast off next 2sts, rib to end.
2nd buttonhole row Rib to end, casting on 2sts over those cast off in the previous row.
Make 4 more buttonholes in this way with 8cm between each. Cont in rib until border, when slightly stretched, fits up right front, across back of neck and down left front. Cast off in rib.

To make up
Press lightly, following instructions on ball band. Sew border in position. Join side and sleeve seams. Set sleeves into armholes. Press seams lightly. Sew on buttons.

Step-by-step course – 20

*Shaping a V-neckline
*Making a traditional neckband using a pair of needles
*Making a cross-over neckband
*Pattern for a V-neck slipover and sweater

Shaping a V-neckline

When you make a garment with a V-neckline you must divide the front of the work in the centre and shape each side of the neck separately. The depth of the V may vary according to taste, but generally it is level with, or slightly lower than, the armhole shaping. Some patterns include precise instructions for both sides of the neck; others give you instructions for one side, then tell you to complete the second side to match the first; if this is the case, make sure you work the shaping at the correct edge.

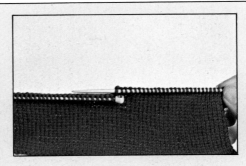

1 The neck shaping begins in the centre of the front. On the right side row, work half the total number of stitches; leave the remainder of the row on a spare needle.

2 Turn and continue on first set of stitches for left side of neck. In our sample there are 27 stitches, 15 of which are required for the shoulder shaping; so 12 stitches must be decreased. The frequency of decreasing depends on the row tension of the fabric.

3 When you have decreased to the necessary number of stitches for the shoulder you may have to work a small amount without shaping to reach the required armhole depth.

4 End at the armhole (outer) edge before beginning the shoulder shaping. Work the shoulder shaping as instructed in the pattern. The left side of the neck is complete here.

5 Return to the stitches left on a spare needle for the right side of the neck. Transfer the stitches on to a working needle; the needle-point should be at the centre front.

6 With the right side of the work facing you, rejoin the yarn at the centre front and knit to the end of the row.

7 Complete the second side of the neck to match the first. Take care to work the neck shaping at the correct edge; don't confuse the neck and armhole shapings and work them the wrong way round.

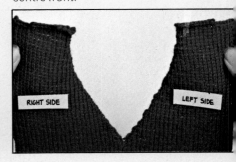

8 This is the completed front with the V-neckline: it still requires some form of neckband to finish it. The labels denote the right and left sides of the neck when the garment is worn.

Making a traditional neckband using a pair of needles

A ribbed neckband, worked directly on to the V-neck using picked-up stitches, neatens the edges of the neckline so that it fits correctly without gaping. The easiest method of working the neckband is with a pair of needles. By leaving open one shoulder seam – usually the left – you can knit the entire neckband backwards and forwards in rows. Afterwards you must join the row ends of the neckband in line with the open shoulder.

Stitches decreased at either side of the V-point at the centre front neck help to maintain the neck shape. Often the decreases are at either side of a central stitch to give the effect of diagonal lines of rib converging on a central point. The centre front stitch is repeated up through the neckband to form a vertical knit rib.

1 Join the right shoulder seam in the usual way. Take a pair of needles (generally two sizes smaller than those used for the main fabric) and the yarn for the neckband; with the right side of the work facing you, start picking up stitches at the left front shoulder.

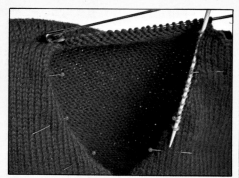

2 Some patterns tell you how many stitches to pick up in each section of the neck; others merely state the total number. When there is only a total number, divide each side of the neck into smaller, equal sections and concentrate on picking up approximately the same number of stitches within each section. Generally you must pick up about two stitches to every three row ends.

3 Pick up an odd number of stitches down the left side of the neck until you reach the point of the V. Tie a marker loop of contrast-coloured yarn on the RH needle. Pick up a stitch from the point of the V; insert LH needle from front to back under the horizontal loop of yarn lying between stitches at centre front and knit it up in the usual way.

4 Tie another marker loop on to the RH needle after the centre front stitch: these markers enclose the centre front stitch and are slipped on every row. Continue up to the right shoulder, picking up the same number of stitches as on the other side of the neck.

5 Slip the back neck stitches from the holder on to the LH needle. In some cases, back neck stitches are previously cast off. In this case you would knit up the necessary number of stitches across the cast-off edge.

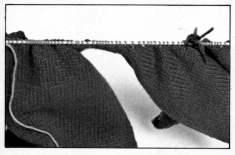

6 Knit across the back neck stitches from the needle, finishing at the open left shoulder. All the neck stitches are now on one needle. Notice that the neckline appears very distorted at this stage, having been put on one straight needle.

7 The wrong side of the work is now facing for the first (WS) row. Work in K1, P1 rib as directed to within two stitches of first marker; knit next two stitches together. Slip first marker; purl centre stitch. Slip second marker. Knit next two stitches together. Rib to end.

8 Work the second row on the right side of the fabric. There is no decrease on this row. Instead, work in rib as set, remembering to slip the markers as before. Here the centre front stitch is always knitted on a right-side row and purled on a wrong-side row.

9 Repeat the last 2 rows for the depth you require; generally a neckband is about 3 to 4cm deep on an adult's garment. Finish with a wrong-side row.

10 Cast off in rib to give a flexible edge. Concentrate on keeping an even tension throughout, so that the ribs lie smoothly without slanting to the right or to the left. This takes a little practice. In some patterns you may have to decrease at either side of the centre front stitch before casting off the resulting single stitch. Discard the markers.

11 This is the finished neckband with a knit rib running up the centre front neck and neat decreases at either side of it. Complete the neckline by joining the left shoulder and neckband seams.

Making a cross-over neckband

A cross-over neckband is a classic variation of the traditional type; it is worked in a similar rib, but overlaps at the centre front. This is an easy style to work, as it requires no shaping. Again, you can leave an open shoulder and use a pair of needles for working the band in rows.
Pick up stitches down one side of the front neck and complete this side first; then use stitches from the other side of the front neck, plus the back neck stitches, to make another similar band. Afterwards, overlap the neckband row ends at the centre front and neatly sew them down.

1 Join the right shoulder seam in the usual way. Follow steps 1 and 2 of making a traditional neckband until you have picked up the required number of stitches down the left side of the neck only.

2 Work in rows of K1, P1 rib on the left side of the neck until the band is the required depth. Cast off in rib.

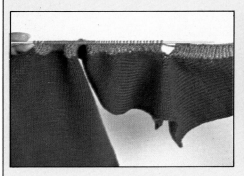

3 With the right side of the work facing you, begin at the centre front neck and work along the right side of the neck to the shoulder. Pick up the same number of stitches as before, then slip back neck stitches on to the LH needle and knit across them.

4 Continue in K1, P1 rib on these stitches: work the same number of rows as for the other side of the neck. Cast off in rib.

5 Finish the cross-over at the centre front neck as follows: lap the right neckband over the left. Secure the left edge first by slipstitching the row ends of the neckband along the ridge of picked up stitches on the wrong side of the work. On the right side of the work, sew down the row ends of the right neckband in the same way as neatly as possible.

Winter Woollies

A must for your winter wardrobe, these classic styles have been updated by using a fashionable bouclé yarn with interesting combinations of colour and texture.

Sizes
To fit 83 [87 :92 :97]cm bust.
Length, 58 [59 :60 :61]cm.
Sleeve seam, 43 [44 :46 :47]cm.

Note Instructions for larger sizes are in square brackets [], where there is only one set of figures it applies to all sizes.

Materials
Slipover : 4[5 :5 :5] x 50g balls of Lee Target Poodle in main colour ;
[3 x 25g balls of Lister/Lee Target Motoravia double knitting in a contrasting colour
Sweater : 7[7 :8 :8] x 50g balls of Lee Target Poodle in main colour ;

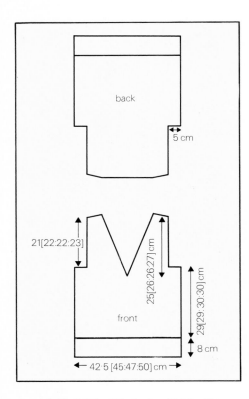

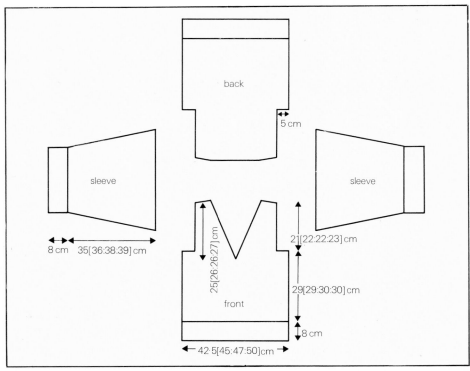

2 [2 :3 :3] x 25g balls of Lister/Lee
Target Motoravia double knitting in
a contrasting colour
1 pair each 4mm and 5mm knitting
needles

Tension
16 sts and 24 rows to 10cm over rev st st.

Slipover
Back
Using 4mm needles and DK yarn, cast on
68 [72 :76 :80] sts. Work in K1, P1 rib for
8cm. Change to 5mm needles and
Poodle yarn. Beg with a P row, cont in
rev st st until back measures 37
[37 :38 :38] cm from beg, ending with a
K row.
Shape armholes
Cast off 8 sts at beg of next 2 rows. 52
[56 :60 :64] sts. Cont without shaping
until armholes measure 21 [22 :22 :23]
cm from beg, ending with a K row.
Shape shoulders
Cast off 8 [9 :10 :10] sts at beg of next 4
rows. Leave rem sts on a holder.

Front
Work as given for back until 33
[33 :34 :34] cm have been completed
from beg, ending with a K row.
Divide for neck
Next row P34 [36 :38 :40] sts, turn and
leave rem sts on a spare needle.
Complete left side of neck first. Dec one st
at neck edge on next and every foll 4th
row until 31 [33 :35 :37] sts rem, ending
with a K row.
Shape armholes
Cast off 8 sts at beg of next row. 23
[25 :27 :29] sts. Keeping armhole edge

straight, cont to shape front edge on every
4th row until 16 [18 :20 :22] sts rem.
Cont without shaping until armhole
measures 21 [22 :22 :23] cm from beg,
ending at armhole edge.
Shape shoulder
Cast off 8 [9 :10 :10] sts at beg of next
row. Work 1 row. Cast off.
With RS of work facing, join yarn to inner
end of sts on spare needle and complete
to match first side, reversing shapings.

Neckband
Join right shoulder seam. Using 4mm
needles, DK yarn and with RS of work
facing, K up 41 [43 :45 :47] sts along left
front neck. Tie a loop of contrast coloured
yarn to act as a marker on RH needle, K
up one loop from centre front neck, add
another marker loop, K up 41
[43 :45 :47] sts along right front neck,
then K the back neck sts from holder.
103 [107 :111 :119] sts.
1st row (WS) K1, (P1, K1) to within 2 sts
of 1st marker, K2 tog, sl 1st marker, P
centre front st, sl 2nd marker, K2 tog, K1,
(P1, K1) to end.
2nd row Keeping ribs correct as set, work
to end.
Rep these 2 rows 3 times more, then work
the 1st row again.
Cast off loosely in rib.

Armhole borders (alike)
Join left shoulder and neckband seam.
Using 4mm needles, DK yarn and with
RS of work facing, K up 82 [82 :84 :84]
sts along straight edge of armhole,
omitting cast-off sts. Work in K1, P1 rib
for 5cm, ending with a WS row. Cast off
loosely in rib.

To make up
Join side seams. Join short edges of
armhole borders to cast-off sts at
underarm.

Sweater
Work front and back as given for back and
front of slipover.

Sleeves
Using 4mm needles and DK yarn, cast on
36 [38 :40 :42] sts. Work in K1, P1 rib for
8cm. Change to 5mm needles and
Poodle yarn. Beg with a P row, cont in
rev st st, inc one st at each end of next and
every foll 5th row until there are 64
[66 :68 :68] sts. Cont without shaping
until sleeve measures 43 [44 :46 :46]cm
from beg.
Cast off.

Neckband
Join right shoulder seam. Using 4mm
needles, DK yarn and with RS of work
facing K up 42 [44 :46 :48] sts along left
front neck. Work in K1, P1 rib for 4cm.
Cast off loosely in rib.
Using 4mm needles, DK yarn and with
RS of work facing, K up 42 [44 :46 :48] sts
along right front neck, then K the back
neck sts from holder. 62 [64 :66 :72] sts.
Work in K1, P1 rib for 4cm. Cast off
loosely in rib.

To make up
Join left shoulder and neckband seam.
Join side seams. Join sleeve seams
leaving 5cm open at top. Set in sleeves,
sewing open ends to cast-off sts at
underarm. Sew short ends of neckband
into position, lapping right over left.

Step-by-step course – 21

*Sewn-in hem
*Knitted-in hem
*Eyelet holes
*Picot hem
*Pattern for a child's smock and skirt

Sewn-in hem

The lower edges of skirts, dresses, coats and jackets often benefit from having extra weight – such as that provided by a hem – to help them hang properly.

There are two main ways of turning up a horizontal hem worked in one with the main fabric. In one method you turn up the hem after the garment is complete and then stitch it in place. In the other method you knit the cast-on edge into the fabric, so forming the hem as you knit the garment.

For a particularly neat appearance a pattern will sometimes instruct you to use one size smaller needles to work the underside of the hem and then change to the larger needle size after the row that marks the hemline.

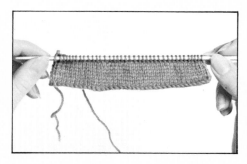

1 Cast on the required number of stitches using the two-needle method. Beginning with a knit row, work an odd number of rows – here it is nine – in stocking stitch to give the necessary depth for the underside of the hem.

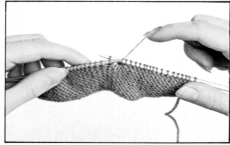

2 Instead of purling the next row, knit each stitch through the back of the loop.

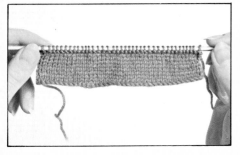

3 This makes a garter stitch-type ridge on the right side of the knitting to mark the foldline (or lower edge) of the hem.

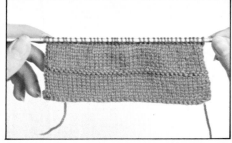

4 Beginning with a knit row, continue working in stocking stitch for the depth stated in the pattern. You need at least one more row than the number worked on the underside of the hem.

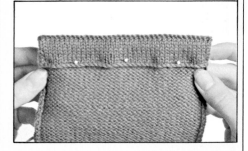

5 After the garment is complete, turn the hem to the wrong side at the fold-line : pin in position keeping the cast-on edge straight in line with a row of knitting.

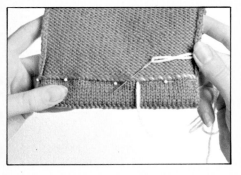

6 Using matching yarn (here it is contrast-coloured for clarity), slip stitch the hem in position.

7 The picture shows the finished hem on the wrong side of the work. Note that the stitching is practically indistinguishable.

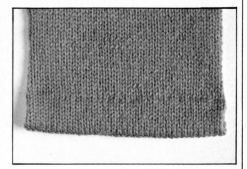

8 Here is the finished hem on the right side of the work ; it has a slightly scalloped appearance where the hem is folded back.

Knitted-in hem

This is the other popular way of working a hem. It appears similar to the sewn-in hem on the right side of the work, but the hem is knitted into the fabric instead of being stitched. Use an extra needle to pick up loops from the cast-on edge. Pick up the same number of stitches as you are working and then knit the two sets together so that you automatically knit the edge of the hem into the fabric. At a later stage, when you join the side seams of the fabric, seam through both thicknesses of the hem.

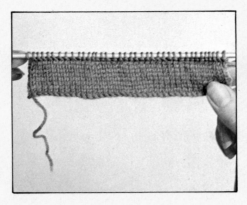

1 Cast on the required number of stitches using the two-needle method. Work as given for sewn-in hem until you have completed step 2.

2 Beginning with a knit row, continue in stocking stitch. Work one row less than for the underside of the hem — here it is eight — so ending with a purl row.

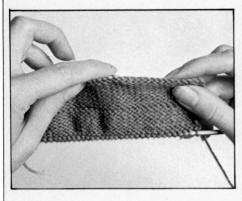

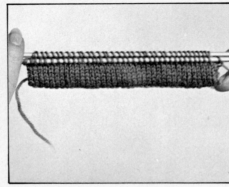

3 Take a spare needle the same size as the pair you are using. With the wrong side of the work facing and cast-on edge at the top, work from left to right and use the spare needle to pick up loops from the cast-on edge. Slip the needle from front to back through each loop. Check that you have the same number of stitches as you cast on originally.

4 Fold the work in half so that the two stitches are level, with both needle points facing in the same direction. The needle holding the loops from the cast-on edge is at the back and the foldline is at the lower edge.

5 Insert RH needle knit-wise through the first stitch on needle at the front of the work. Push needle-point further and insert it knit-wise through the first stitch on the needle at the back of the work. Knit both stitches simultaneously so that there is one stitch on the RH needle.

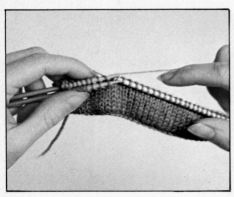

6 Continue knitting across the row, taking one stitch from the front needle and one from the back (cast-on loops) each time.

7 Beginning with a purl row continue in stocking stitch or pattern as directed.

8 The photograph shows the finished hem on the wrong and right sides of the work. The wrong side is particularly neat where the edge of the hem is knitted into the fabric. The right side appears similar to a sewn-in hem.

Eyelet holes

An eyelet is a hole made in the fabric by a technique known as 'decorative increasing'; this type of increasing is the basis of many lace patterns which require a decorative eyelet – you can see how they could be used on the smock and skirt page 97.

Apart from being attractive, eyelets have other, more functional purposes. Thread a drawstring in and out of the holes, then draw it up to gather the fabric for a simple, yet stylish method of shaping the fabric and fastening the garment at the same time.

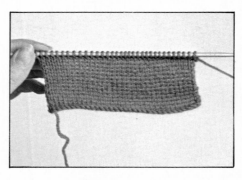

1 Work a stocking stitch fabric on an odd number of stitches as the basis for the eyelet holes. Start to work the eyelet holes with the right side of the fabric facing you.

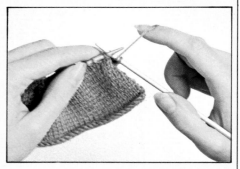

2 For eyelet-hole row, knit first two stitches together. Bring yarn forward – abbreviated as 'yfwd' – to the front of the work between the two needles, then knit the next two stitches together. The yarn brought forward is taken back over the needle to do this, making an extra loop on the RH needle, so cancelling out the stitch you lose by decreasing.

3 Continue in this way, bringing the yarn forward and knitting two stitches together, until you reach the last stitch; bring the yarn forward and knit this in the usual way, so increasing one stitch to balance the decrease at the start of the row.

4 Beginning with a purl row, continue in stocking stitch. The stitches made by bringing the yarn forward in the previous row are merely long loose strands; when you purl them the hole appears in the fabric.

5 This shows the finished effect of the eyelet holes on the right side of the work. In some patterns – such as the smock and skirt in this course – the holes are spaced farther apart and a drawstring is threaded through the holes to gather up the fabric.

Picot hem

This variation of a stocking stitch hem can either be knitted in or sewn up at a later stage. A row of eyelet holes mark the foldline; when the hem is folded in half, the eyelets form a dainty, pointed – or picot – edging.

Picots are small loops of yarn with a twisted appearance that often decorate lacy edgings: babies' garments often feature picot hems as the loops are particularly effective worked in the more delicate yarns and patterns.

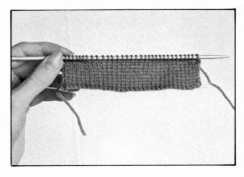

1 Cast on an odd number of stitches using the two-needle method. Beginning with a knit row, work an even number of rows – here it is 10 – in stocking stitch, ending with a purl row.

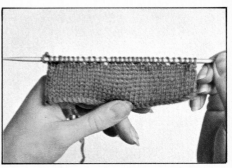

2 Work eyelet holes in the next row as described in steps 2 and 3 of 'Eyelet holes'.

Fred Mancini

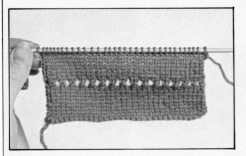 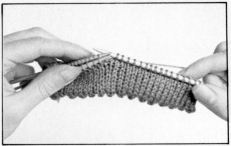 

3 Beginning with a purl row, work one row less – here there are nine rows – than in underside of hem, so ending with a purl row.

4 Knit in the hem as given for steps 4, 5 and 6 of 'Knitted-in hem'. Fold hem in half at eyelet-hole row.

5 The photograph shows the finished effect of the hem on the wrong and right sides of the work. The eyelet-hole row folds in half to give the serrated effect of picot points.

Pretty as a picture

This pretty smock and skirt can be worn together or separately. They are based on a simple rectangular shape and have a dainty picot edging. Both are drawn up with a twisted cord.

Sizes
Smock to fit, 66[71 :76]cm chest.
Length of smock to underarm, 26[29 : 32]cm.
Skirt length, 46[50 :54]cm.
Note Instructions for larger sizes are in square brackets []; where there is only one set of figures it applies to all sizes.

Materials
Smock 5[6 :7] x 20g balls of Wendy Darling 4 ply
Skirt 12[12 :13] x 20g balls of Wendy Darling 4 ply
1 pair of 3¼mm knitting needles

Tension
28 sts and 36 rows to 10cm over st st on 3¼mm needles.

Smock (back and front alike)
Using 3¼mm needles and two-needle method, cast on 129[137 :145]sts.
** Beg with a K row, work 10 rows st st.
Picot row *K2tog, yfwd, rep from * to last st, K1.
Beg with a P row, work 9 rows st st.
Hem row Fold work in half with the cast on edge behind work and K tog one st from needle with one st from cast-on edge, rep this to end of row. You have now completed the hem.
Beg with P row, work 15 rows in st st.

SMOCK (back and front alike) — 46 [49 :52] cm — 26 [29 :32] cm (hemmed)

SKIRT (back and front alike) — 46 [50 :53] cm (hemmed) — 52 [57.5 :63] cm

John Hutchinson

Commence patt
1st row K4, *yfwd, K2tog, K6, rep from * to last 5sts, yfwd, K2tog, K3.
2nd-6th rows Beg with a P row, work in st st.
7th row K8, *yfwd, K2tog, K6, rep from * to last st, K1.
8th-12th rows Beg with a P row, work in st st.
13th row As 1st row. ******
Cont in st st until work measures 25[28 :31]cm from hem, ending with a P row.
Eyelet-hole row K4, *yfwd, K2tog, K6, rep from * to last 5sts, yfwd, K2tog, K3.
Work 3 rows st st.
Picot row *K2tog, yfwd, rep from * to last st, K1.
Work 3 rows in st st.
Eyelet-hole row K4, *yfwd, K2tog, K6, rep from * to last 5sts, yfwd, K2tog, K3.

Work 3 rows st st. Cast off.

To make up
Press work with a cool iron over a damp cloth. Join side seams. Fold top hem in half at picot row and slipstitch in position. Press seams.
Using 4 strands of yarn together make a twisted cord 120cm long and thread through eyelet holes in top hem.
Using 4 strands of yarn make 8 cords 70cm long, thread one cord through 2 eyelet holes on front and another cord through corresponding 2 eyelet holes on back to form shoulder strap. Make other shoulder strap in the same way.

Skirt (back and front alike)
Using 3¼mm needles and two-needle method, cast on 145[161 :177] sts and work as given for smock from ** to **.
Cont in st st until work measures 45[49 :53]cm from hem, ending with a P row.
Next row K4, *cast off 2, K until there are 6 sts on right-hand needle after cast-off group, rep from * to last 5 sts, cast off 2, K to end.
Next row P to end, casting on 2 sts over each 2 cast off.
Work 10 rows st st.
Picot row *K2tog, yfwd, rep from * to last st, K1.
Beg with a P row, work 9 rows st st.
Cast off.

To make up
Press as for smock. Join side seams. Fold top hem in half at picot row and slipstitch in position. Press seams.
Using 4 strands of yarn together, make a twisted cord 140cm long and thread through holes at waist.

Step-by-step course – 22

Bobble stitches

The raised stitches of a bobble make an unusual and highly textured fabric. Bobble stitches are often used in Aran knitting to symbolize a rock or boulder in a sea-scape. They can form an all-over pattern, such as Trinity Stitch, or, spaced out, combine with cables in beautiful designs.

There are various ways of making a bobble; all are based on the principle of creating a number of stitches out of one. Here we describe two methods. One of the methods involves working the bobble stitches over several rows—while working the main fabric—and then decreasing to a single stitch.

Alternatively, you can work the bobble stitches separately from the main fabric; in this case you work several rows on the bobble stitches only and reduce them to the original one before carrying on with the background.

Basic method of making a bobble

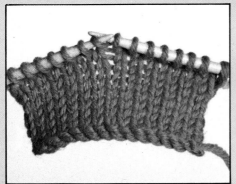

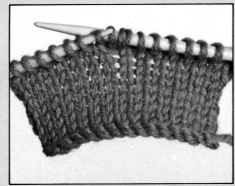

1 This technique makes a reverse stocking stitch bobble, worked over a number of rows, against a background of the same fabric. First, work to the position of the bobble on a wrong-side (knit) row. Knit the next stitch in the usual way, but without dropping the loop from the LH needle.

2 Bring the yarn forward and purl the loop on the LH needle : take the yarn to the back again and knit the loop. There are now three loops on the RH needle.

3 Purl and knit again—still keeping the loop on the LH needle—to make five loops on the RH needle. Allow the original loop to drop from the LH needle.

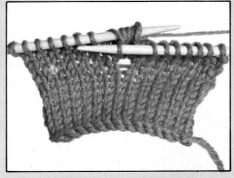

4 Continue to the end of the row, then work three rows in reverse stocking stitch, ending with a P row. At this stage the increased stitches form a slight bump on the right side of the work.

5 On the following (knit) row, work to the position of the five bobble stitches and reduce them to their original stitch by knitting them all together. Knit to the end of the row, then continue in reverse stocking stitch.

6 The bobble formed resembles a large 'blister' on the right side of the fabric. Using this method you can position bobbles at random or make an all-over fabric. On the wrong side the bobble makes a dent in the fabric.

Alternative method of making a bobble

1 This technique makes a reverse stocking stitch bobble, based on a single stitch, against a stocking stitch background. On a knit row, make five stitches out of one (see steps 1 and 2 of basic method). Turn and knit these stitches : turn the work and purl them.

2 The five bobble stitches are now on the RH needle. Use the LH needle point to lift the second bobble stitch over the first and off the RH needle ; repeat this process with the third, fourth and fifth stitches until a single bobble stitch remains.

3 A small, neat bobble resembling those in Popcorn stitch (see Stitch Wise) is formed on the right side of the fabric. The only sign of the bobble on the back of the fabric is a slight irregularity in the knitting at the position of the bobble.

Cluster stitches

Cluster stitches are very similar to—and often confused with—bobble stitches. The basic method of working clusters is the same as for bobbles : increasing a number of stitches out of one, then either working the cluster in one with the background or finishing it separately.

Generally cluster patterns are larger than for bobbles : the shaping is much more gradual than for a bobble and so requires more rows of knitting. Because of their size, some cluster patterns are often used quite separately on a fabric. They are also ideal for border patterns, like the one used on the chunky jacket, page 101.

Basic method of making a cluster

  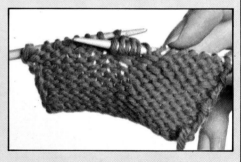

1 Make a detached cluster in reverse stocking stitch against a stocking stitch background. Work to cluster position on a purl row ; keep the yarn at front and knit next stitch to increase one stitch.

2 Don't drop the original stitch from the LH needle. Bring the yarn forward again and knit the original stitch.

3 Repeat the last sequence to make six loops on the RH needle out of one stitch. Allow the original stitch to drop from the LH needle.

4 Turn the work so that right side is facing. Always slipping first stitch and beginning with a purl row, work four rows in reverse stocking stitch on the six cluster stitches.

5 Turn and purl two stitches together three times across next right-side row. On the following row, slip one, knit two stitches together, then pass the slipped stitch over ; one cluster stitch remains.

6 The finished cluster is attached to the main fabric by a single stitch at the start and finish ; the back of the fabric is slightly marked by an irregular stitch at the position of the cluster.

Fred Mancini

99

Alternative method of making a cluster

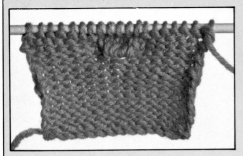

1 This technique makes a stocking stitch cluster worked over a number of rows against a reverse stocking stitch background. On a purl row make five stitches out of one as described in steps 1 and 2 of basic method of making a bobble; work to the end of the row. Now work three more rows, reversing the background pattern over the five cluster stitches.

2 Decrease over the next three rows to shape the cluster and reduce the five stitches to one. On the next row (right side) slip the first cluster stitch, knit one, then pass the slipped stitch over; knit the next stitch, then knit the last two stitches together. Purl the three cluster stitches on the following row. Finally, on the third row (RS), slip the first stitch, knit the two stitches together and pass the slipped stitch over.

3 Although this cluster is worked flat over a number of rows, it is quite distinct against the background. The cluster covers the same area on the wrong side of the work, but it looks smaller, as the reverse side of the stitches recedes into the background.

Stitch Wise

Trinity stitch

Cast on a multiple of 4 sts.
1st row (WS) *(K1, P1, K1) all into next st, P3 tog, rep from * to end.
2nd row P to end.
3rd row *P3 tog, (K1, P1, K1) all into next st, rep from * to end.
4th row As 2nd.
These 4 rows form the pattern.

Detached cluster

Cast on a multiple of 6 stitches plus 5 extra.
1st row (WS) P to end.
2nd row K to end.
3rd row *P5, (yfwd to make one st, K next st) 3 times into same st, so making 6 sts out of one, turn and P these 6 sts, turn and sl 1, K5, turn and sl 1, P5, turn and sl 1, K5, turn and (P2 tog) 3 times, turn and sl 1, K2 tog, psso—called make cluster (MC), rep from * to last 5 sts, P5.
4th row K to end.
5th row P to end.
6th row K to end.
7th row P2, *MC, P5, rep from * to last 3 sts, MC, P2.
8th row K to end.
These 8 rows form the pattern.

Popcorn stitch

Cast on a multiple of 6 sts plus 5 extra.
1st row (WS) P to end.
2nd row K2, (K1, P1, K1, P1, K1) all into next st, turn and K these 5 sts, turn and P5. Using point of LH needle, lift 2nd, 3rd, 4th and 5th sts over first st and off RH needle—called make bobble (MB), *K5, MB, rep from * to last 2 sts, K2.
3rd row P to end.
4th row *K5, MB, rep from * to last 5 sts, K5.
These 4 rows form the pattern.

A peal of bells

This jacket, with its decorative border of bell clusters, is long enough to replace a coat on a cool spring day. The attractive ribbed circular yoke echoes the border motif, and the outfit is completed with a matching scarf.

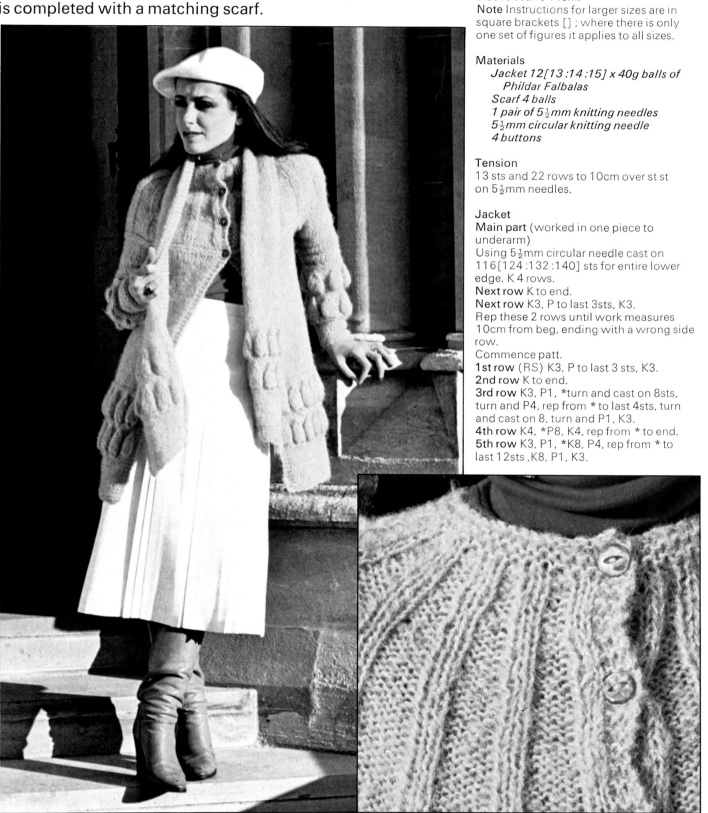

Sizes

Jacket To fit 82[87 :92 :97]cm bust.
Length, 83[85 :87 :89] cm.
Sleeve seam, 44cm.
Note Instructions for larger sizes are in square brackets [] ; where there is only one set of figures it applies to all sizes.

Materials

Jacket 12[13 :14 :15] x 40g balls of Phildar Falbalas
Scarf 4 balls
1 pair of 5½mm knitting needles
5½mm circular knitting needle
4 buttons

Tension

13 sts and 22 rows to 10cm over st st on 5½mm needles.

Jacket

Main part (worked in one piece to underarm)
Using 5½mm circular needle cast on 116[124 :132 :140] sts for entire lower edge. K 4 rows.
Next row K to end.
Next row K3, P to last 3sts, K3.
Rep these 2 rows until work measures 10cm from beg, ending with a wrong side row.
Commence patt.
1st row (RS) K3, P to last 3 sts, K3.
2nd row K to end.
3rd row K3, P1, *turn and cast on 8sts, turn and P4, rep from * to last 4sts, turn and cast on 8, turn and P1, K3.
4th row K4, *P8, K4, rep from * to end.
5th row K3, P1, *K8, P4, rep from * to last 12sts ,K8, P1, K3.

101

6th row As 4th row.
7th row K3, P1, *sl1, K1, psso, K4, K2 tog, P4, rep from * to end, but finish last rep P1, K3.
8th row K4, *P6, K4, rep from * to end.
9th row K3, P1, *sl 1, K1, psso, K2, K2 tog, P4, rep from * to end, but finish last rep P1, K3.
10th row K4, *P4, K4, rep from * to end.
11th row K3, P1, *sl1, K1, psso, K2 tog, P4, rep from * to end, but finish last rep P1, K3.
12th row K4, *P2, K4, rep from * to end.
13th row K3, P1, *K2 tog, P4, rep from * to end, but finish last rep P1, K3.
14th row K4, *P1, K4, rep from * to end.
15th row K3, P1, *P2 tog, P3, rep from * to end, but finish last rep P2 tog, K3.
16th row As 2nd row.
17th row K3, P3, *turn and cast on 8, turn and P4, rep from * to last 6sts, turn and cast on 8, turn and P3, K3.
18th row K6, *P8, K4, rep from * to end, but finish last rep K6.
Patt a further 12 rows keeping 'bell' shaping above cast-on sts as before.
Keeping 3 sts at each end in g st, beg with a K row, proceed in st st until work measures 58cm from beg, ending with a K row.

Divide for armholes
Next row K3, P25[27 :29 :31], cast off 4, P until there are 52[56 :60 :64] sts on right-hand needle after cast-off group, cast off 4, P to last 3 sts, K3. Cont on last set of 28[30 :32 :34] sts for right front.
Next row K to last 3 sts, K2 tog, K1.
Next row P to last 3 sts, K3.
Rep the last 2 rows 0[2 :4 :6] times more. 27 sts. Leave sts on a holder.
With RS facing rejoin yarn to inner end of sts on needle and work on next 52[56 :60 :64] sts for back.
Next row K1, sl1, K1, psso, K to last 3 sts, K2 tog, K1.
Next row P to end.
Rep the last 2 rows 0[2 :4 :6] times more. 50 sts. Cut off yarn and leave sts on a holder.
With RS facing rejoin yarn to inner end of sts on needle and work on rem 28[30 :32 :34] sts for left front.
Next row K1, sl1, K1, psso, K to end.
Next row K3, P to end.
Rep the last 2 rows 0[2 :4 :6] times more. 27 sts and leave sts on a holder.

Sleeves
Using 5½mm needles cast on 24[28 :28 :32] sts. K 4 rows.
Beg with a K row, cont in st st until work measures 7cm from beg, ending with a P row, and inc one st at each end of last row. 26[30 :30 :34] sts.
Commence patt.
1st row P to end.
2nd row K to end.
3rd row P1, *turn and cast on 8, turn and

P4, rep from * to last st, turn and cast on 8, P1.
Cont in patt as set so omitting the g st border at each end until the 30 rows have been completed. Beg with a K row, cont in st st but inc one st at each end of next and every foll 8th[8th :6th :6th] row until there are 38[42 :46 :50] sts. Cont without shaping until work measures 44cm from beg, ending with a P row.

Shape top
Cast off 3 sts at beg of next 2 rows.
Next row K1, sl1, K1, psso, K to last 3 sts, K2 tog, K1.
Next row P to end.
Rep the last 2 rows 0[2 :4 :6] times more. 30 sts. Cut off yarn and leave sts on a holder.

Yoke
Using 5½mm circular needle and with RS facing K the sts of right front, sleeve, back sleeve and left front, knitting 2 sts tog at each seam. 160 sts. K 1 row.
Buttonhole row K1, K2 tog, yfwd, K to end.
K 2 rows.
Next row K3, P to last 3 sts, K3. Now cont in rib as foll :
1st row K5, *P6, K2, rep from * to last 3 sts, K3.
2nd row K3, P2, *K6, P2, rep from * to last 3 sts, K3.
3rd to 12th rows Work 1st and 2nd rows 5 times.
13th row K1, K2tog, yfwd, K2, *P2, P2 tog, P2, K2, rep from * to last 3 sts, K3. 141sts.
14th row K3, P2, *K5, P2, rep from * to last 3 sts, K3.
15th to 22nd rows Work in rib as set.
23rd row K5, *P1, P2 tog, P2, K2, rep from * to last 3 sts, K3. 122 sts.
24th row K3, P2, *K4, P2, rep from * to last 3 sts, K3.
25th to 28th rows Work in rib as set.
29th row K1, K2tog, yfwd, rib to end.
30th row Work in rib as set.

31st row K5, *P1, P2 tog, P1, K2, rep from * to last 3 sts, K3. 103 sts.
32nd row K3, *P2, K3, rep from * to end.
33rd to 36th rows Work in rib as set.
37th row K5, *P1, P2 tog, K2, rep from * to last 3 sts, K3. 84 sts.
38th row K3, P2, *K2, P2, rep from * to last 3 sts, K3.
39th to 42nd rows Work in rib as set.
43rd row K5, *P2 tog, K2, rep from * to last 3 sts, K3. 65 sts.
K 1 row.
Next row K1, K2 tog, yfwd, K to end.
K 2 rows. Cast off knitwise.

To make up
Press with a cool iron over a dry cloth. Join underarm and sleeve seams. Press seams. Sew on buttons.

Scarf
Using 5½mm needles cast on 5 sts.
Cont in g st, cast on 3 sts at beg of 3rd and every alt row until there are 26 sts.
K 1 row.
Next row K to end.
Next row K3, P to last 3 sts, K3.
Rep the last 2 rows for 7cm, ending with a WS row.
Commence patt.
1st row K3, P to last 3 sts, K3.
2nd row K to end.
3rd row K3, P2, *turn and cast on 8, turn and P4, rep from * 3 times more, turn and cast on 8, turn, P2, K3.
Keeping edge sts and 'bell' shaping as set, cont in patt as first 16 rows of jacket.
Next row K3, P4, *turn and cast on 8, turn and P4, rep from * to last 3 sts, K3.
Cont in patt as set, complete border.
Keeping the 3 sts at each end in g st, cont in st st, dec inside the edge sts by working K3, sl1, K1, psso, K to last 5 sts, K2 tog, K3 on every 20th row until 16 sts rem.
Cont without shaping until work measures 76cm from top of the g st shaped edge, ending with a WS row. Cast off.
Work a second piece, reversing shaping.
Join cast-off edges together. Press seam.

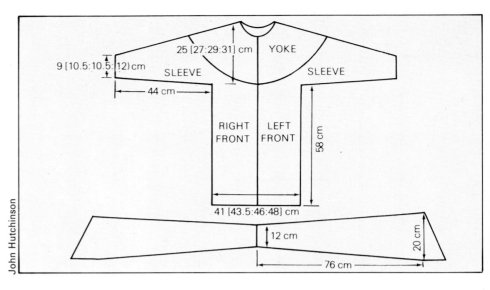

25 [27:29:31] cm   YOKE
9 [10.5:10.5:12] cm   SLEEVE   SLEEVE
44 cm
RIGHT FRONT   LEFT FRONT   58 cm
41 [43.5:46:48] cm
12 cm   20 cm
76 cm
John Hutchinson

Step-by-step course – 23

Decorative increasing

This method of increasing involves winding the yarn over or round the needle to create an extra stitch. The combination of stitches immediately before and after the increased stitch determines whether you must bring the yarn forward (yfwd), or bring it over the needle (yon) or wind it round the needle (yrn). You can use these techniques for shaping a garment; but more commonly they form the basis of lace patterns, as they make a small eyelet hole in the fabric — hence the name 'decorative increasing'.

In the section entitled 'Stitch Wise' we give you two lace stitch patterns that incorporate decorative increasing techniques. The bed jacket on page 107 also uses these techniques.

Increasing between two knit stitches

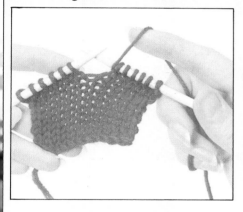

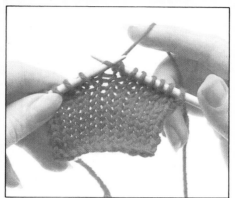

1 To make a stitch between two knit stitches, bring the yarn forward to the front of the work between the two needles – called yarn forward (yfwd).

2 Knit the next stitch in the usual way. Notice that the yarn makes an extra loop on the RH needle as you wind it from the front and over the needle point.

3 On the following – in this case, purl – row, work as usual into each stitch including the extra loop. This makes a hole in the fabric.

Increasing between a purl and a knit stitch

1 To make a stitch between a purl and a knit stitch – for example, in a ribbed fabric – proceed as follows : note that as you begin the increase the yarn is already at the front of the work from purling the previous stitch.

2 Instead of taking the yarn to the back, as you would normally do before knitting the next stitch, simply proceed to knit the stitch. As you do so, you automatically bring the yarn over the needle – called 'yarn over needle' (yon), so creating an extra loop.

3 On the next row, work into the extra loop as directed in the pattern ; if you are making eyelet holes in a rib you may have to purl the extra loop together with the stitch before it to keep the number of stitches and pattern correct.

continued

Mike Berend

103

Increasing between two purl stitches

1 To make a stitch between two purl stitches take the yarn completely round the RH needle point and to the front again between the two needles. This is called 'yarn round needle (yrn)'.

2 Purl the next stitch in the usual way. The yarn previously wound round the RH needle forms an extra loop.

3 On the following – in this case, knitted row – work into the extra loop in the usual way, so making a hole in the fabric.

Increasing between a knit and a purl stitch

1 To make a stitch between a knit and purl stitch bring the yarn forward to the front between the two needles.

2 Now take the yarn over the top of the RH needle point and round to the front again between the two needles ; again, this is called 'yarn round needle (yrn)'.

3 Purl the next stitch in the usual way. The 'yarn round needle' leaves a characteristic hole in the fabric when the following row has been worked.

Introduction to simple lace patterns

A lacy knitted fabric usually consists of a small pattern that repeats across a row : any decorative increase within a pattern repeat must be counter-balanced by a decrease to keep the number of stitches within a row constant. The combination of holes, stitches and decreases forms a lacy pattern.

The correct balance of yarn and needles is important in lace knitting. It is pointless using thick yarn, as the holes produced will be indistinct ; using too-small needles will also create this effect. When you make practice samples, try using 4 ply – or finer – yarn with needles one or two sizes larger than those you would nor-

mally use for that particular quality of yarn.

The following step-by-step pictures show various stages of making the 'falling leaf' pattern used in the bedjacket on page 107. Detailed instructions for working the 'falling leaf' pattern appear in the instructions for the bed jacket.

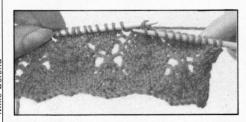 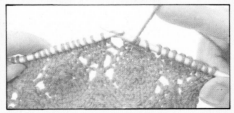 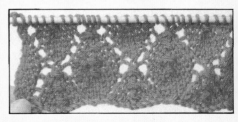

1 Many lace patterns include the direction 'sl 1, K2 tog, psso' ; it occurs in all the right-side rows in the 'falling leaf' pattern. Here, the slipped stitch is being lifted over the knitted-together stitches. As well as shaping the 'falling leaf', this action makes an interesting design when it is repeated in a vertical line up the centre of the leaf.

2 Here the pattern instructions say 'yfwd, K7' (see the 15th row). In this case the yarn has been put forward before knitting the *first* of the seven stitches, so increasing one stitch. Don't put the yarn forward before each of the seven stitches individually.

3 The leaves in this pattern are staggered, so that during the course of one row of knitting you are decreasing to shape the top of some leaves and increasing to form the base of others. Here, alternate leaves are being completed – as in the 1st and 8th pattern rows : the other leaves are half formed at this stage.

Stitch Wise

Cat's paw pattern

Cast on a multiple of 12 sts plus 1 extra.
1st row (RS) K5, *yfwd, sl 1, K2 tog, psso, yfwd, K9, rep from * to last 8 sts, yfwd, sl 1, K2 tog, psso, yfwd, K5.
2nd and every alt row P to end.
3rd row K3, *K2 tog, yfwd, K3, yfwd, sl 1, K1, psso, K5, rep from * to last 10 sts. K2 tog, yfwd, K3, yfwd, sl 1, K1, psso, K3.
5th row As 1st.
7th row K to end.
9th row K2 tog, *yfwd, K9, yfwd, sl 1, K2 tog, psso, rep from * to last 11 sts, yfwd, K9, yfwd, sl 1, K1, psso.
11th row K2, *yfwd, sl 1, K1, psso, K5, K2 tog, yfwd, K3, rep from * to last 11 sts, yfwd, sl 1, K1, psso, K5, K2 tog, yfwd, K2.
13th row As 9th.
15th row As 7th.
16th row As 2nd.
These 16 rows form the pattern.

Checked mesh pattern

Cast on a multiple of 10 sts plus 4 extra.
1st and every alt row (WS) P to end.
2nd row K4, *yfwd, sl 1, K1, psso, (K2 tog, yfwd) twice, K3, rep from * to end.
4th row *K3, (yfwd, sl 1, K1, psso) twice, K1, K2 tog, yfwd, rep from * ending with K4.

6th row K2, *(yfwd, sl 1, K1, psso) 3 times, K4, rep from * ending with yfwd, sl 1, K1, psso.
8th row K1, *(yfwd, sl 1, K1, psso) 4 times, K2, rep from * ending with yfwd sl 1, K1, psso, K1.
10th row As 6th.
12th row As 4th.
14th row As 2nd.
16th row K2 tog, yfwd, *K4, (K2 tog, yfwd) 3 times, rep from * ending with K2.
18th row K1, K2 tog, yfwd, *K2, (K2 tog, yfwd) 4 times, rep from * ending with K1.
20th row As 16th row.
These 20 rows form the pattern.

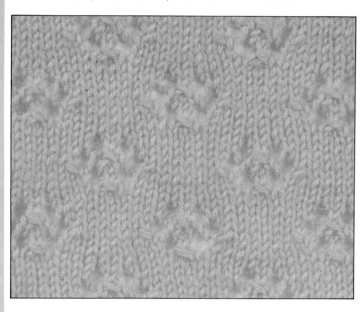

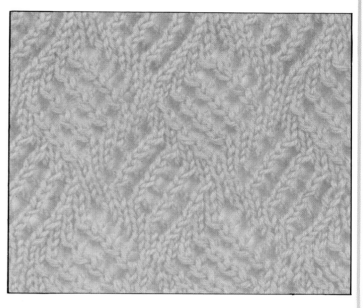

Lace for lounging

Now you have learned some of the basic techniques of knitting lacy patterns, why not try knitting a comfortable bed jacket. It is just the thing to wear for extra warmth when you are reading — or being served breakfast — in bed.

Sizes

To fit, 83-87[92-97]cm bust.
Length, 47[49]cm.
Sleeve seam, 43cm.
Note Instructions for larger sizes are in square brackets []; where there is only one set of figures it applies to both sizes.

Materials

6[7] x 40g balls of 3 Suisses Barbara
1 pair each 3¾mm and 4mm needles
3¾mm circular needle
4 buttons
1.50m of ribbon

Tension

20 sts and 28 rows to 10cm over patt using 4mm needles.
22 sts and 44 rows to 10cm over g st using 3¾mm needles.

Back

Using 4mm needles cast on 121[141] sts.
**Beg with a K row, work 3 rows st st.
Picot row K1, *yfwd, K2 tog, rep from * to end.
Beg with a K row, work 4 rows st st.
Commence patt.
1st row K1, *yfwd, K3, sl 1, K2 tog, psso,

K3, yfwd, K1, rep from * to end.
2nd and alt rows P to end.
3rd row K2, *yfwd, K2, sl 1, K2 tog, psso, K2, yfwd, K3, rep from * to end, ending last rep K2 instead of K3.
5th row K3, *yfwd, K1, sl 1, K2 tog, psso, K1, yfwd, K5, rep from * to end, ending last rep K3 instead of K5.
7th row K4, *yfwd, sl 1, K2 tog, psso, yfwd, K7, rep from * to end, ending last rep K4.
9th row K2 tog, *K3, yfwd, K1, yfwd, K3, sl 1, K2 tog, psso, rep from * to end, ending last rep sl 1, K1, psso.

11th row K2 tog, *K2, yfwd, K3, yfwd, K2, sl 1, K2 tog, psso, rep from * to end, ending last rep sl 1, K1, psso.
13th row K2 tog, *K1, yfwd, K5, yfwd, K1, sl 1, K2 tog, psso, rep from * to end, ending last rep sl 1, K1, psso.
15th row K2 tog, *yfwd, K7, yfwd, sl 1, K2 tog, psso, rep from * to end, ending last rep sl 1, K1, psso.
16th row As 2nd row.
These 16 rows form the patt. Rep them 3 times more. **

Shape armholes
Dec one st at each end of next and foll 3 alt rows by omitting the yfwd at beg and end of rows. 113[133] sts.
P1 row.
Cut off yarn and leave sts on a holder.

Left front
Using 4mm needles cast on 61[71] sts.
Work as for back from ** to **.

Shape armhole
Dec one st at beg of next and foll 3 alt rows by omitting the yfwd at beg of rows. 57[67] sts.
P 1 row.
Cut off yarn and leave sts on a holder.

Right front
Work as left front, but reverse shaping at armhole by decreasing at the end of each alt row.

Sleeves
Using 4mm needles cast on 61[71] sts

and work as for back from ** to **. Cont in patt, work 48 more rows.

Shape top
Dec one st at each end of next and foll 3 alt rows by omitting the yfwd at beg and end of rows. 53[63] sts.
P 1 row.
Cut off yarn and leave sts on a holder.

Yoke
Using 3¾mm circular needle and with RS facing, knitting 2 sts tog at each seam, K the sts of right front 57[67] sts, right sleeve 53[63] sts, back 113[133] sts, left sleeve 53[63] sts and left front 57[67] sts. 329[389] sts.
Next row K4[1], * K2 tog, K3[2], rep from * to end. 264[292] sts.
1st buttonhole row K2, cast off 2 sts, K to end.
2nd buttonhole row K to end, casting on 2 sts over the sts that were cast off on the previous row.
K 14 rows.
Next row K5, *K2 tog, K5, rep from * to end. 227[251] sts.
K 15[17] rows, working a buttonhole over the 6th and 7th[8th and 9th] rows.
Next row K5, *K2 tog, K4, rep from * to end. 190[210] sts.
K 15[17] rows, working a buttonhole over the 12th and 13th[14th and 15th] rows.
Next row K2, *K2 tog, K3, rep from * to last 3 sts, K2 tog, K1. 152[168] sts.
K 15[17] rows.

Next row K1, *K2 tog, K2, rep from * to last 3 sts, K2 tog, K1. 114[126] sts.
K 15[17] rows, working a buttonhole over the 2nd and 3rd rows.
Next row K1, *K2 tog, K3, rep from * to last 3[5] sts, K2 tog, K1[3]. 91[101] sts.
K 4 rows.
Eyelet-hole row (WS) K1, *yfwd, K2 tog, rep from * to end.
K 7 rows.
Picot row K1, *yfwd, K2 tog, rep from * to end.
K 4 rows. Cast off.

Front borders
Using 3¾mm needles and with RS facing,

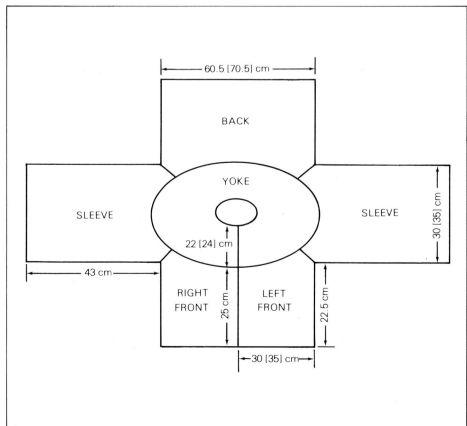

60.5 [70.5] cm

BACK

YOKE

SLEEVE

SLEEVE

30 [35] cm

43 cm

22 [24] cm

RIGHT FRONT

LEFT FRONT

25 cm

22.5 cm

30 [35] cm

beginning at picot row on right front, K up 105[109] sts along front edge. Beg with a P row, work 2 rows st st.
Next row (hemline) K1, *yfwd, K2 tog, rep from * to end. Beg with a K row, work 4 rows in st st.
Cast off knitwise.
Work along left front in the same way.

To make up
Do not press. Sew in sleeves. Join side and sleeve seams. Turn in all edges along picot row and sl st in place. Sew on buttons.
Thread ribbon through eyelet holes at neck.

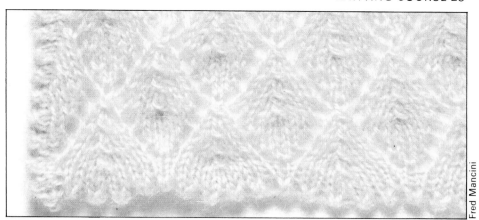

Fred Mancini

Step-by-step course – 24

*Working a chevron-striped fabric
*Working a herringbone casing over elastic
*Stitch Wise: more chevron patterns
*Pattern for chevron skirt and scarf

Working a chevron-striped fabric

The zig-zag pattern of chevrons is formed by alternately increasing and decreasing stitches at intervals across the right-side rows throughout the fabric. Some patterns emphasize the upward and downward points of the chevrons with decorative vertical lines of shaping.

Another way of heightening the effect of a chevron fabric is to use different colours for the stripes. The various colours are added in the same way as for simple horizontal stripes, but the finished appearance is completely different.

In our sample, stocking stitch is used for the basic fabric. Garter stitch and some lacy patterns – which naturally entail a mixture of increasing and decreasing – can also be adapted effectively to make chevron stripes. (See shale pattern and shale and rib pattern in Stitch Wise, page 110.)

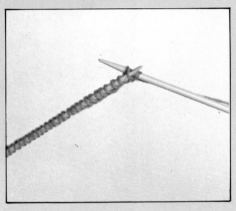

1 Cast on a multiple of 13 stitches plus 2 extra (e.g. 28, 41, 54). Work the 1st row as follows : * knit 2, them make 1 by picking up the horizontal loop lying between the needles and knitting through the back of it.

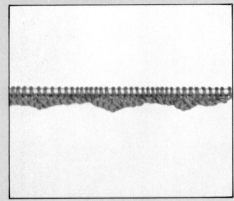

2 Complete the first row : knit 4, slip 1 purlwise, knit 2 together, pass slipped stitch over, then make 1 as in step 1. Repeat this sequence from * to last 2 stitches ; knit 2.

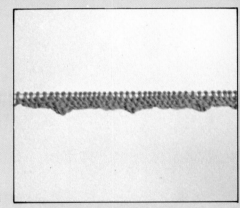

3 On the 2nd row and all following wrong-side rows – simply purl every stitch to the end of the row.

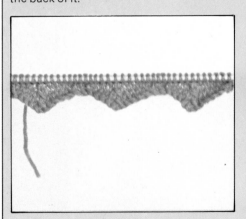

4 The 1st and 2nd rows are repeated throughout to create the chevron fabric. Work two more rows before joining in the next colour.

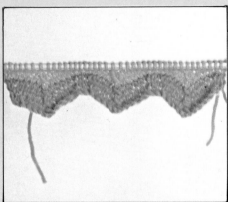

5 At the beginning of the next row join in the new colour in the same way as for working horizontal stripes (see Knitting Course 10, page 38). Work four rows in pattern with the new colour.

6 Continue working in four-row stripes carrying the colours not in use up the side of the work. You can vary the number of rows in each stripe as long as it is an even number. You must always change colours on a right-side row so that the colour change does not show.

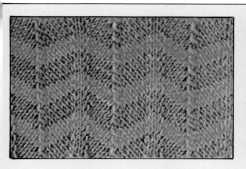

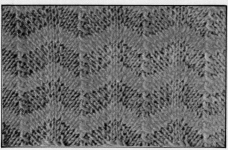

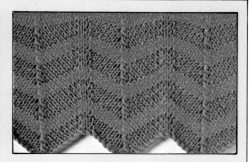

7 Cast off when you reach the length you require. Note the distinctive lower edge of the fabric as the chevrons dip at the points where stitches have been decreased and rise where stitches have have been increased.

8 To make deeper chevron points, work fewer stitches between the shaping position. To do this you must cast on a different number of stitches. For example, cast on multiples of 11 stitches instead of 13, and knit 3 stitches instead of 4 between shaping.

9 Chevron points can be made shallower by increasing the number of stitches between shaping points. Here multiples of 17 stitches have been cast on and 6 stitches (instead of 4) separate the shaping positions.

Working a herringbone casing over elastic

The most popular finish for a skirt waistband is a length of elastic placed just inside the upper edge and held in position with herringbone stitches. The elastic should be specially made for waistbands – flat and at least 2.5cm wide. Cut it to fit your waist measurement – not the finished waistband.

After the herringbone stitching is complete, the elastic should move freely within the casing and not be caught down.

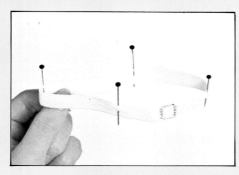

1 Cut the elastic to your waist measurement plus an extra 3cm. Overlap the ends for 1.5cm to make a circle. Secure ends by oversewing. Mark circle into four equal quarters with pins.

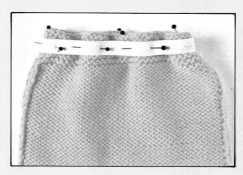

2 Join the skirt sections. Divide the upper edge into quarters marking the four points with pins. On the wrong side of the waistband pin the elastic in position matching the quarter-section pins on elastic and skirt. You may need to stretch the elastic slightly to fit. Remove quarter pins before sewing.

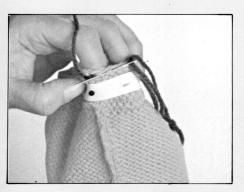

3 Thread a blunt-ended wool needle with matching yarn (here it is contrast-coloured for clarity) ; secure yarn to LH side seam. Hold the waistband and slightly stretched elastic over the fingers of your left hand. Insert the needle from right to left through two stitches at the top of the elastic.

4 Work the herringbone stitches from left to right. Take the yarn diagonally down across the elastic to the lower edge and insert the needle from the right to left through the next two stitches to the right. Make another stitch above the elastic, diagonally to the right, catching the next two stitches at the top of the elastic.

5 Continue in this way, alternating stitching on each side of elastic until it is secured all round waistband. Take care to distribute the knitting evenly and not to catch the elastic in the stitching.

Fred Mancini

Stitch Wise

Shale pattern

Two colours are required for this pattern. Using the first colour, cast on a multiple of 11 sts.

1st row (RS) *(K2 tog) twice, (yfwd, K1) 3 times, yfwd, K2 tog, K2 tog, rep from * to end.

2nd row P to end.

3rd row K to end.

4th row K to end.

Join in the second colour and repeat the 4 patt rows in stripes throughout.

Shale and rib pattern

Five toning colours are required for this pattern. Using the first dark colour, cast on a multiple of 17 sts plus 2 extra.

1st row (RS) *K2, P2, K2 tog tbl, (K1, yfwd) 6 times, K1, K2 tog, P2, rep from * to last 2 sts, K2.

2nd row P2, *K2, P15, K2, P2, rep from * to end.

3rd row *K2, P2, K3 tog tbl, K9, K3 tog, P2, rep from * to last 2 sts, K2.

4th row P2, *K2, P11, K2, P2, rep from * to end.

Work from dark to light colours. Join in the second colour and repeat the 4 patt rows in stripes throughout, then repeat the sequence with the remaining five colours.

Note When changing colours you must knit the stitches in the 1st row that you previously purled in order to keep unbroken lines of colour on the right side of the work.

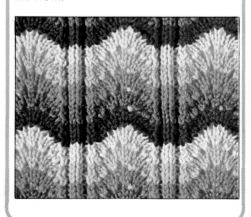

Shapley chevrons

Chevrons are flattering to any figure. Make this gently flared skirt in harmonizing shades, as we have, or in one of your favourite colours, and pair it with a dashing chevron-striped scarf.

Sizes
Skirt to fit 86[91:97]cm hips.
Length, 75cm.
Scarf 18cm wide x 147.5cm long, excluding fringe.

Note Instructions for larger sizes are in square brackets []; where there is only one set of figures it applies to all sizes.

Materials
Skirt : *Hayfield Beaulon 4 ply :*
  6[7:8] x 25g balls in main colour (A)
  2 balls of contrast colour (B)
  4[4:5] balls of contrast colour (C)
  5[6:6] balls of contrast colour (D)
  1 pair each 2¾mm and 3¼mm knitting needles
  Waist length of 1.5cm-wide elastic
Scarf : *3 balls of yarn as above in A, 1 ball in B, 1 ball in C and 2 balls in D*
  3¼mm circular knitting needle

Note The scarf is knitted in rows on a circular needle because the number of stitches to be cast on would make it impracticable to use ordinary needles. The circular needle is used as ordinary needles would be.

Tension
30 sts and 40 rows to 10cm over patt on 3¼mm needles.

Skirt
Back
Using 2¾mm needles and A, cast on 101 [101:115] sts for waist edge and work 10 rows in g st.
Change to 3¼mm needles. Join on B. Commence patt.
1st row (RS) Using B, K1, sl 1, K1, psso, *K5, yfwd, K1 yfwd, K5, sl 2 tog K-wise, K1, p2sso, rep from *ending with K2 tog, K1 instead of sl 2 tog, K1, p2sso.
2nd row K7, *K1 tbl, K1, K1 tbl, K11, rep from *ending with K7.
Rep these 2 rows throughout in stripe patt of 2 rows A, 4 rows C, 2 rows A, 6 rows D, 2 rows A, 2 rows B. Work 10 rows in patt.

SCARF

18 cm

147.5 cm

67 [72:76] cm
width all around waist

76 cm

SKIRT

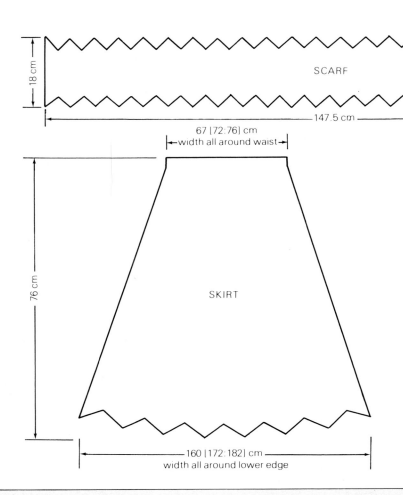

160 [172:182] cm
width all around lower edge

John Hutchinson

Shape skirt

Next row K8, *yfwd, K1, yfwd, K13, rep from * ending with K8.

Next row K to end, knitting into back of all 'yfwd' in previous row.

Next row K1, sl 1, K1, psso, *K6, yfwd, K1, yfwd, K6, sl 2 tog, K1, p2sso, rep from * ending as 1st patt row.

Work 7 rows as set.

Next row K9, *yfwd, K1, yfwd, K15, rep from * ending with K9.

Cont to inc in this way on every 10th row until there are 241 [241 :275] sts. Cont without shaping until work measures approximately 75cm from beg, ending with 6 rows in D. Using A, work 9 rows in patt. Cast off *very loosely.*

Front

Using 2¾mm needles and A, cast on 101 [115 :115] sts and work as given for back, inc to 241 [275 :275] sts.

To make up

Do not press. Join side seams. Work herringbone casing over elastic on WS of waistband as shown on page 109.

Scarf

Using 3¼mm circular needle and A, cast on 443 sts and work backwards and forwards in rows thus :

1st row K1, sl 1, K1, psso, *K8, yfwd, K1, yfwd, K8, sl 2 tog, K1, p2sso, rep from * ending with K2 tog, K1.

2nd row K to end, knitting into back of all 'yfwd' in previous row.

Rep these 2 rows throughout in stripe patt of (2 rows B, 2 rows A, 4 rows C, 2 rows A, 6 rows D, 2 rows A) 4 times, then 1 row in A. Cast off *very loosely.*

Fringe Cut 30cm lengths in each of the 4 colours. For each tassel take 1 strand in each colour and knot tassels into every 6th row end along short ends of scarf.

Step-by-step course – 25

Twisting stitches

The technique of twisting stitches – though a simple one – forms the basis of a number of interesting and varied patterns. You can use twisted stitches as a substitute for cables – or in conjunction with them – in Aran designs, either as an all-over pattern or in panels. Twisted stitches can also be used to form 'travelling lines' across the surface of a fabric, making diagonal and check patterns. One of these – double diagonal pattern – is used in the man's sweater at the end of this course.

Twisted stitches are usually worked over a small number of stitches – either two or three. They work well with most weights of yarn as long as the needles are the correct size for the yarn. Over-large needles open up the pattern and make it too sloppy.

The following sequences of step-by-step photographs show you how to work stitches twisting either to the left or to the right.

Twisting stitches to the left

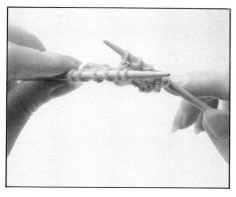

1 Work the twist over two knitted stitches. To work a twist that lies to the left, knit the *second* stitch on the LH needle through the back of the loop. At this stage the original stitch remains on the needle.

2 Now, with the new stitch on the RH needle, knit the first stitch (the one that you missed) on the LH needle in the usual way.

3 Slip both stitches off the LH needle and continue in pattern. This is called 'twist two left (T2L)'. Here a series of left twists have been worked on every 4th row to create a miniature cable effect.

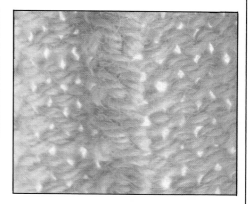

4 You can vary the number of rows between twists to give a tighter or looser 'cable'. On one side of this sample, left twists have been worked on alternate rows : the other side is twisted on every 6th row.

5 In some cases you may need to work a left twist on wrong-side rows to produce a tight twist. Purl the *second* stitch on the LH needle through the back of the loop, then purl the first stitch (the one that you missed) on the LH needle in the usual way.

6 Slip both stitches off the LH needle and continue in pattern. This is called 'twist two left back (T2LB)'. Here a series of left twists have been worked on every row to give a tightly twisted cable effect.

Paul Williams

Twisting stitches to the right

1 To work a twist that lies to the right, knit the *second* stitch on the LH needle through the front of the loop in the usual way. At this stage the original stitch remains on the LH needle.

2 Now, with the new stitch on the RH needle, knit the first stitch (the one that you missed) on the LH needle in the usual way.

3 Slip both stitches off the LH needle and continue in pattern. This is called 'twist two right (T2R)'. Here a couple of right twists have been worked on every 4th row to create a miniature cable effect.

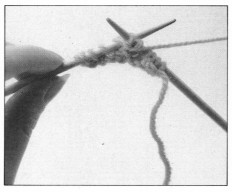

4 To produce a right twist on the right side of the fabric when you are working a wrong-side row, purl the *second* stitch on the LH needle through the front of the loop in the usual way.

5 Now, with the new stitch on the RH needle, purl the first stitch on the LH needle in the usual way. Take care to keep the remaining loop of the second stitch on the left of the first stitch while you are working into it.

6 Slip both stitches off the LH needle together and continue in pattern. This is called 'twist two right back (T2RB)'. Here a series of right twists have been worked on every row.

Working a mock cable

Twisted stitches are an ideal way of producing a very realistic cable pattern without the use of a cable needle: the mock cable pattern in Stitch Wise is an example of this. The cable here is worked over four stitches and the method of twisting them is slightly complicated: it involves twisting two pairs of stitches left, but working the second pair before the first; the step-by-step sequence here describes this clearly. When worked in a vertical line, as in mock cable patterns, twisted stitches tend to pull the work together in the same way as ribbing does. Most patterns will compensate for this by instructing you to cast on more stitches than would be normally required.

1 The 5th pattern row of mock cable pattern in Stitch Wise describes how to twist the four cable stitches to make a mock cable. Start to work the first T2L by knitting the fourth stitch on the LH needle through the back of the loop.

2 To complete the first T2L, bring the RH needle completely round to the front of the fabric and knit the third stitch on the LH needle in the usual way.

114

3 With the original stitches still on the LH needle and two new loops on the RH needle, start to work the second T2L by knitting the second stitch on the LH needle through the back of the loop.

4 Complete the second T2L by knitting the first stitch on the LH needle in the usual way. Note that the original four stitches still remain on the LH needle.

5 Here the 'double twist' is complete with the four cable stitches on the RH needle : the four loops that were left on the LH needle are dropped simultaneously.

Stitch Wise

Twisted rib
Cast on a multiple of 5 sts plus 3 extra.
1st row (RS) P3, *K2, P3 rep from * to end.
2nd row K3, *P2, K3, rep from * to end.
3rd row As 1st.
4th row As 2nd.
5th row P3, *T2L, P3, rep from * to end.
6th row As 2nd. 6 rows form pattern.

Mock cable pattern
Cast on a multiple of 14 sts plus 2 extra.
1st row (RS) P2, *T2L, P2, K4, P2, T2L, P2, rep from * to end.
2nd row K2, *P2, K2, P4, K2, P2, K2, rep from * to end.
3rd row As 1st row.
4th row As 2nd row.
5th row P2, *T2L, P2, work T2L into

4th and 3rd sts on LH needle leaving sts on needle, then work T2L into 2nd and 1st sts and sl all 4 sts off needle tog, P2, T2L, P2, rep from * to end.
6th row As 2nd. 6 rows form pattern.

Latticed warmth

So casual and comfortable, this sweater will please any man. It has a patterned back and front and a snug polo collar.

Sizes
To fit 97[102:107]cm chest.
Length, 67cm.
Sleeve seam, 47cm, with cuff turned back.
Note Instructions for larger sizes are in square brackets []; where there is only one set of figures it applies to all sizes.

Materials
27[28:29] x 25g balls of Lister/Lee Target Motoravia Double Knitting
1 pair each 3¾mm, 4mm and 5mm knitting needles

Tension
22 sts and 28 rows to 10cm over st st on 4mm needles.
26 sts and 27 rows to 10cm over patt on 5mm needles.

Front
Using 3¾mm needles, cast on 136[142:148 sts] and work in K1, P1 rib for 10cm.
Change to 5mm needles. Commence patt.
1st row *K 2nd st on left-hand needle tbl, then K the first st, let both sts drop from left-hand needle – called twist 2 left or T2L, (K 2nd st on left-hand needle, then K the first st, let sts drop from left-hand needle – called twist 2 right or T2R) twice, rep from * to last 4 sts, T2L, T2R.
2nd and alt rows P to end.
3rd row K1, T2L, *T2R, (T2L) twice, rep from * to last st, K1.
5th row (T2L) twice, *K2, (T2L) twice, rep from * to end.

Gary Warren

7th row K1, *(T2L) twice, T2R, rep from * to last 3 sts, T2L, K1.
9th row T2R, T2L, *(T2R) twice, T2L, rep from * to end.
11th row K3, *(T2R) twice, K2, rep from * to last st, K1.
12th row P to end.
These 12 rows form the patt. Cont in patt until work measures 57cm from beg, ending with a WS row.
Shape neck
Next row Patt 54[56:58], turn and leave rem sts on a spare needle. Complete this side of neck first.
Dec one st at neck edge on next and foll alt rows until 47[49:51] sts rem, ending at side edge.
Shape shoulder
Cast off 5[7:9] sts at beg of next row and 7 sts at beg of foll 5 alt rows.
Work 1 row.
Cast off.
Return to sts on spare needle. Place next 28[30:32] sts on a holder, join yarn to next st and patt to end of row. Complete to match first side.

Back
Work as given for front, omitting neck shaping, until back is same length as front to beg of shoulder shaping, ending with a WS row.
Shape shoulders
Cast off 5[7:9] sts at beg of next 2 rows

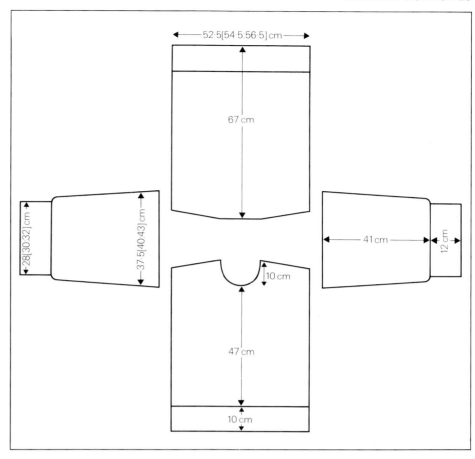

and 7 sts at beg of foll 12 rows. Cut off yarn and leave rem 42[44:46] sts on a holder.

Sleeves
Using 3¾mm needles cast on 48[52:56] sts and work in K1, P1 rib for 12cm.
Inc row (Rib 3, inc in next st) to end. 60[65:70] sts.
Change to 4mm needles. Cont in st st inc one st at each end of 7th and every foll 8th row until there are 84[89:94] sts. Cont without shaping until work measures 53cm from beg. Cast off loosely.

Polo collar
Join right shoulder seam. With RS facing and using 3¾mm needles K up 27 sts from left front neck, K the sts from holder, K up 27 sts from right front neck, then K the back neck sts from holder. 124[128:132] sts.
Working in K1, P1 rib, work 22 rows, change to 5mm needles and work 28 more rows. Cast off.

To make up
Press st st sections only. Join left shoulder and collar seam. Mark centre of cast-off edge of sleeves with a pin, match pin to shoulder seams, then sew sleeves to back and front. Join side and sleeve seams reversing seam on cuffs. Turn back cuffs. Press seams lightly.

Step-by-step course – 26

Introducing cable patterns

Cables are among the most popular and adaptable of knitting motifs. They derive from 'fisherman's knitting', such as that done in the Aran Islands, off the coast of Ireland, and in other coastal areas of Britain, and they suggest the ropes used in fishing. Many variations of cable patterns have been devised over the years. You can use a cable singly as a panel, or combine several cables in an all-over pattern. A single cable – usually worked against a purl background – is a versatile form of decoration for a plain cardigan or sweater. You can add a cable detail up the centre of a sleeve or at each side of the front bands of a cardigan. Plan the style and position of the cable before you begin knitting.

Producing a cable twist involves moving a group of stitches from one position within the cable to another during the course of one row. The move is made with the help of a special, short double-pointed cable needle that holds the stitches during the transfer. There are very few sizes of cable needle; if you are unable to find the same size as the needles you are using, choose a thinner cable needle, so as not to stretch and spoil the appearance of the stitches.

The following step-by-step pictures show the basic cable techniques used in all cable patterns.

Twisting cables from right to left

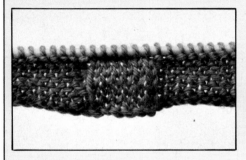

1 Cables, worked over a number of knitted stitches, show up in sharp relief against a purl background. For this sample, work six rows straight before working the cable twist. Here there are six stitches in the cable panel, but there could be any even number (four, six or eight are the most usual) depending on how wide you want the cable to be.

2 On the right side of the work, purl to the start of the cable panel. To make a twist, take the cable needle and insert it from right to left through the next stitch. Slip this stitch off the LH needle. Repeat for the next two stitches. Three stitches are now on the cable needle.

3 Leave the cable needle (with the stitches in the middle of it) at the front of the work, so that both LH and RH needles are behind it. Take the yarn to the back of the work and knit the next three stitches of the cable panel.

4 Now work the stitches on the cable needle. First, slide them to the RH end of the needle. Now you need your left hand free to guide the cable needle, and this means letting go of the LH needle.

5 Push the stitches down the needle to prevent their falling off. Knit the three stitches on the cable needle from right to left.

6 The cable twist – called 'cable six front (C6F)' – is finished. It looks odd at this stage, as all the cable stitches are crowded together. Continue with the background stitches and purl to the end of the row.

7 Work seven straight rows between cable twists. Always twist the cable on the right side of the work by repeating steps 2 to 6. Here you can see the finished effect of cable twists worked from right to left on every 8th row.

8 You can vary the number of rows between twists to produce a 'rope' with tighter or looser twists. This picture shows the difference between C6F worked on every 6th row – on the right – and every 10th row – on the left.

9 This photograph shows the varied effects produced if you work the cable over four stitches (on the right) and eight stitches (on the left).

Twisting cables from left to right

1 Work the first 2 steps as given for twisting cables from right to left. Leave the cable needle (with the stitches in the middle of it) at the *back* of the work so that both LH and RH needles are in front of it. Take the yarn to the back of the work and knit the next three stitches on the LH needle.

2 Now work the stitches on the cable needle; slide them to the RH end of the needle. Knit the three stitches on the cable needle from right to left in their correct order. See steps 4 and 5 of 'Twisting cables from right to left' for hints on doing this. The cable twist is called 'cable six back (C6B)'.

3 In this picture there are seven straight rows between cable twists. The rope effect is similar to that made by twisting cables from right to left, only in this case the 'strands' twist in the opposite direction.

Alternating twists

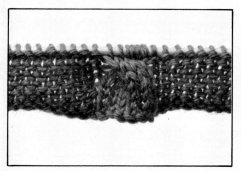

1 Work the first 6 steps as given for 'Twisting cables from right to left' to produce a cable six front (C6F).

2 Work seven rows straight. On the next row twist the cable in the opposite direction – called C6B.

3 Continue to alternate the direction of the cable twists to produce a 'rope' with a completely different look. Here one of the 'strands' winds continuously on top of the section below.

Paul Williams

119

Stitch Wise

Plaited cable
This cable is worked over 9 sts.
1st row (RS) K9.
2nd row P9.
3rd row S1 next 3 sts on to cable needle and leave at back of work, K3, then K the 3 sts from cable needle – called C6B, K3.
4th row P9.
5th and 6th rows As 1st and 2nd.
7th row K3, sl next 3 sts on to cable needle and leave at front of work, K3, then K the 3 sts from cable needle – called C6F.
8th row P9.
These 8 rows form the pattern.

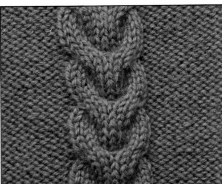

Horseshoe cable
This cable is worked over 12 sts.
1st row (RS) K12.
2nd row P12.
3rd and 4th rows As 1st and 2nd.
5th row S1 next 3 sts on to cable needle and leave at back of work, K3, then K the 3 sts from cable needle – called C6B, sl next 3 sts on to cable needle and leave at front of work, K3, then K the 3 sts from cable needle.
6th row P12.
7th and 8th rows As 1st and 2nd.
These 8 rows form the pattern.

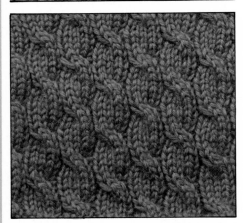

Cable panel pattern
Cast on a multiple of 10 sts plus 1 extra.
1st row (RS) P1, *K4, P1, rep from * to end.
2nd row K1, *P4, K1, rep from * to end.
3rd row P1, *K4, P1, sl next 2 sts on to cable needle and leave at front of work, K next 2 sts, then K the 2 sts from the cable needle – called C4F, P1, rep from * to end.
4th row As 2nd.
5th and 6th rows As 1st and 2nd.
7th row P1, *C4F, P1, K4, P1, rep from * to end.
8th row As 2nd.
These 8 rows form the pattern.

Honeycomb pattern
Cast on a multiple of 8 sts.
1st row (RS) * S1 2 sts on to cable needle and leave at back of work, K2 sts, then K the 2 sts from cable needle – called C4B, sl next 2 sts on to cable needle and leave at front of work, K2 sts, then K the 2 sts from cable needle – called C4F, rep from * to end.
2nd row P to end.
3rd row K to end.
4th row P to end.
5th row *C4F, C4B, rep from * to end.
6th row P to end.
7th and 8th rows As 3rd and 4th.
These 8 rows form the pattern.

Cable fashion

This smart jacket trimmed with cables has its own matching hat and scarf – perfect for a trip to the zoo or a walk in the country.

Sizes
Jacket to fit 66[71 :76]cm chest.
Length, 42[46 :50]cm.
Sleeve seam, 38[40 :42]cm.
Hat to fit average size head.
Scarf 20cm wide by 90cm long, excluding fringe.

Note Instructions for larger sizes are in square brackets [] ; where there is only one set of figures it applies to all sizes.

Materials

Jacket *6[7 :8] x 50g balls of Patons Beehive Shetland style Chunky*
Hat *2 balls*
Scarf *3 balls*
1 pair each 5mm and 6mm knitting needles
1 cable needle
5mm circular needle 100cm long
5 buttons for jacket

Tension

15sts and 20 rows to 10cm over st st on 6mm needles.

Jacket

Back

Using 5mm needles cast on 54[58 :62] sts.

1st rib row P2, *K2, P2, rep from * to end.
2nd rib row K2, *P2, K2, rep from * to end.
Rep these 2 rows for 7cm, ending with a 2nd rib row and inc 1 [2 :3] sts evenly on last row 55[60 :65] sts. Change to 6mm needles. Commence patt.
1st row K10[11 :12], P2, K6, P2, K15[18 :21], P2, K6, P2, K10[11 :12].
2nd row P10[11 :12], K2, P6, K2, P15[18 :21], K2, P6, K2, P10[11 :12].
3rd and 4th rows Rep 1st and 2nd rows.
5th row K10[11 :12], P2, sl next 3 sts on to cable needle and leave at back of work, K3, then K the sts from cable needle – called 'cable 6 back' or C6B ; P2, K15[18 :21], P2, sl next 3 sts on to cable needle and leave at front of work, K3, then K the sts from cable needle – called 'cable 6 front' or C6F ; P2, K10[11 :12].
6th row As 2nd row.
7th and 8th rows Rep 1st and 2nd rows. These 8 rows form the patt. Cont in patt until work measures 28[30 :32]cm from beg, ending with a WS row.
Shape raglan armholes
Keeping patt correct, cast off 2 sts at beg of next 2 rows.
**Next row K1, sl 1, K1, psso, patt to last 3 sts, K2 tog, K1.
Work 3 rows.
Rep the last 4 rows 4[5 :6] times more, then work the first of these 4 rows again. Work 1 row. ******. 39[42 :45] sts.
Next row Cast off 13[14 :15]sts, K to last 13[14 :15] sts, cast off last 13[14 :15] sts. Leave centre 13[14 :15] sts on a holder.

Left front

Using 5mm needles cast on 25[29 :33] sts.
1st rib row *P2, K2, rep from * to last st, P1.
2nd rib row K1, *P2, K2, rep from * to end.
Rep these 2 rows for 7cm, ending with a 2nd rib row and inc 2[1 :0] sts on last row. 27[30 :33] sts. Change to 6mm needles.
Commence patt.

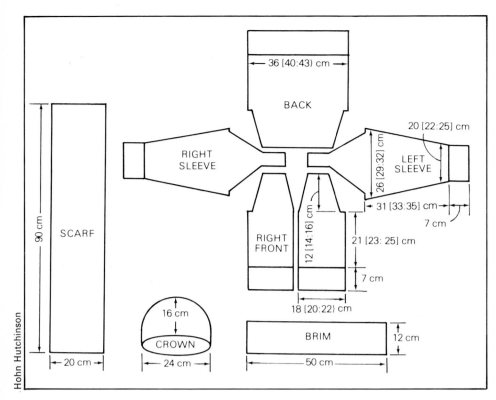

1st row K10[11:12], P2, K6, P2, K7[9:11].
2nd row P7[9:11], K2, P6, K2, P10[11:12].
3rd and 4th rows As 1st and 2nd rows.
5th row K10[11:12], P2, C6B, P2, K7[9:11].
6th row As 2nd row.
7th and 8th rows Rep 1st and 2nd rows.
These 8 rows form the patt. Cont in patt until work measures 28[30:32] cm from beg, ending with a WS row.
Shape raglan armhole and front edge
Cast off 2 sts at beg of next row.
Next row Patt to end.
Rep from ** to ** of back. 13[14:15] sts. Cast off.

Right front
Using 5mm needles cast on 25[29:33] sts.
1st row P1, *K2, P2, rep from * to end.
2nd row *K2, P2, rep from * to last st, K1.
Rep these 2 rows for 7cm, ending with a 2nd rib row and inc 2[1:0] sts on last row. 27[30:33] sts. Change to 6mm needles.
Commence patt.
1st row K7[9:11], P2, K6, P2, K10[11:12].
2nd row P10[11:12], K2, P6, K2, P7[9:11]. Cont in patt as set, work to match left front but work C6F instead of C6B and reverse all shaping.

Left sleeve
Using 5mm needles cast on 30[34:38] sts and work the 2 rib rows of back for 7cm, ending with a 2nd rib row. Change to 6mm needles.

Commence patt.
1st row K10[12:14], P2, K6, P2, K10[12:14].
Cont in patt as set, working C6B and inc one st at each end of 9th and every foll 10th row until there are 40[44:48] sts. Cont without shaping until sleeve measures 38[40:42] cm from beg, ending with a WS row.
Shape raglan armhole
Cast off 2 sts at beg of next 2 rows.
Next row K1, sl 1, K1, psso, patt to last 3 sts, K2 tog, K1.
Next row Patt to end.
Rep these 2 rows until 14 sts rem. Cont straight on these 14 sts until saddle shoulder extension fits along the 13[14:15] sts that were cast off on back and fronts, ending with a WS row. Cut off yarn and leave sts on a holder.

Right sleeve
Work as given for left sleeve but work C6F instead of C6B.

Front border
Sew saddle shoulder extensions to cast off groups on back and fronts. With RS facing and using the 5mm circular needle join on yarn and K up 52[54:56] sts along right front to beg of shaping, 19[21:23] sts to shoulder, then knit 2 sts tog at each back seam and inc one st at centre of back neck on 1st size and dec one st at centre on 3rd size, K the right sleeve, back neck and left sleeve sts from holders, then K up 19[21:23] sts along left front to beg of shaping and 52[54:56] sts to lower edge. 182[190:198] sts.

Next row K4, (P2, K2) to last 2 sts, K2.
Next row K2, (P2, K2) to end.
Rib 1 more row.
1st buttonhole row K2, (cast off 2, rib until there are 10 sts on right-hand needle after cast-off group) 4 times, cast off 2, rib to end.
2nd buttonhole row Rib to end, casting on 2 sts over those cast off on previous row.
Rib 3 rows. Cast off in rib.

To make up
Press as instructed on ball band. Join raglan seams, then join side and sleeve seams. Press seams. Sew on the buttons.

Hat
Main part
Using 6mm needles cast on 73 sts. Work in st st for 9cm, ending with a P row.
Shape top
1st row *K7, K2 tog, rep from * to last st, K1.
2nd row P to end.
3rd row *K6, K2 tog, rep from * to last st, K1.
Cont to dec in this way, working one st less between each dec, on every alternate row until 17 sts rem, ending with a P row.
Next row (K2tog) to last st, K1.
Cut off yarn, thread through rem sts, draw up tightly and secure.

Brim
Using 6mm needles cast on 18 sts.
1st row K2, P5, K6, P5.
2nd row K5, P6, K7.
3rd and 4th rows Rep 1st and 2nd rows.
5th row K2, P5, C6B, P5.
6th row As 2nd row.
7th and 8th rows Rep 1st and 2nd rows.
These 8 rows form the patt. Cont in patt until work measures approx. 50cm from beg. Cast off.

To make up
Press as instructed on ball band. Join back seam of main part. Join cast-on and cast-off edges of brim. Sew the P edge to main part so that brim turns up to right side and the g st edge turns in at top. Press seams.

Scarf
Using 6mm needles cast on 31 sts.
1st row K2, P4, K6, P7, K6, P4, K2.
2nd row K6, P6, K7, P6, K6.
3rd and 4th rows Rep 1st and 2nd rows.
5th row K2, P4, C6B, P7, C6F, P4, K2.
6th row As 2nd row.
7th and 8th rows Rep 1st and 2nd rows.
These 8 rows form the patt. Cont in patt until work measures 90cm from beg, ending with an 8th row. Cast off.

Fringe
Using two 32cm lengths of yarn tog, knot fringe into every alternate stitch along each short end. Trim the ends.

Step-by-step course – 27

Knitting in rounds with four needles

Knitting in rounds is the method used in making socks, gloves and anything else in which a seamless fabric is required. A circular needle is normally used for this purpose if the fabric is wide, but on a narrow fabric – for socks or a polo neck, for example – the knitting is normally done with a special set of four needles which are pointed at both ends. Three of the needles hold the stitches in a triangular shape; the fourth needle is held in the right hand and used to knit the stitches. When all the stitches from one needle have been knitted, that needle becomes the working needle. As you work, the right side of the fabric is always facing you. At first, you will find it quite difficult to work in this way, as the needles are awkward to manage, but it becomes easier with practice.

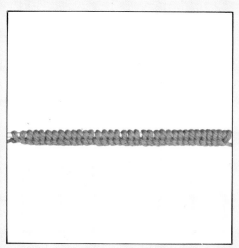

1 Using the two-needle method, cast the total number of stitches required on to one of the four needles. Here there are 36 stitches.

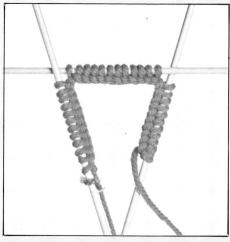

2 Divide the stitches equally between three needles – 12 on each – taking great care not to twist the stitches. These three needles represent the LH needle in flat knitting. Tie a marker loop of contrast-coloured yarn to the LH end of the stitches to denote the beginning of new rounds.

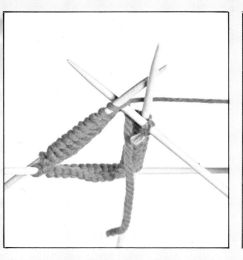

3 Arrange the stitches in a triangle – they must not be twisted – ready to begin knitting; the marker loop is at the RH end of the third needle. Take the fourth – or RH – needle and slip the marker loop on to it.

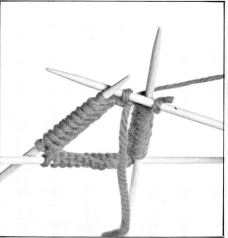

4 Insert the fourth needle into the first stitch on the third needle and knit it in the usual way. The triangle is now joined. Pull the yarn across tightly from the previous stitch whenever changing needles to avoid having a loose stitch at the corner.

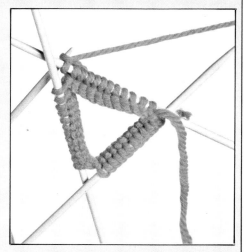

5 Continue knitting each stitch from the third needle on to the fourth. When all these stitches have been knitted, the third needle is free and in turn becomes the working needle.

continued

Fred Mancini

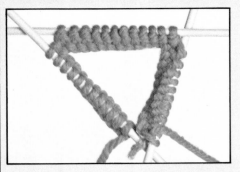

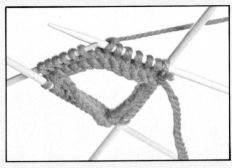

6 Continue to work in a clockwise direction, knit the stitches on the second needle until it becomes free : use this free needle to knit the stitches on the first needle. One round is now complete.

7 Remember that the right side of the fabric is always on the outside (facing) as you work a tubular fabric. To continue in stocking stitch, slip the marker loop and knit each stitch in the second round. If the 'purl' ridge of the wrong side of the knitting is facing outwards on any of the needles, then the stitches are twisted.

8 Always slipping the marker loop at the beginning of each round so that you don't lose your place, continue to knit each stitch in every round until the fabric is the depth you require. The smooth side of the stocking stitch fabric must always be on the outside. Finish after a complete round (at the marker).

9 Before casting off, discard the marker loop. Knit the first two stitches of the next round on to the fourth needle : cast off by the usual method of using the LH (or third) needle point to lift the first stitch knitted over the second and off the fourth needle.

10 Continue casting off across the third needle until one stitch remains on the RH needle ; use this needle holding the single stitch to cast off the stitches on the second needle and so on across the first needle until one stitch remains. Fasten off in the usual way.

11 This picture shows a continuous piece of tubular fabric without any side seams. The smooth side of the stocking stitch fabric is on the outside. For a reverse stocking stitch fabric, turn the work inside out.

Making a pompon

Pompons are ornamental tufts of yarn, which make excellent trimmings for hats, berets, scarves and babies' and children's clothes. Making them is easier than you might think – in fact, children find them great fun to make. The only materials you need, apart from the yarn, are a blunt-ended wool needle and two cardboard discs. Both discs must be the same size ; their diameter governs the size of the finished pompon.

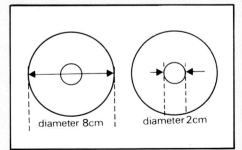

diameter 8cm   diameter 2cm

1 Cut out twin cardboard rings with a diameter about 2.5cm greater than the finished size of the pompon. The hole in the centre should be one quarter the diameter of the circle.

2 Place the circles together. Thread a long length of yarn into a blunt-ended wool needle ; wind the yarn evenly round and round the rings, using more yarn as required, until the hole is full. Plenty of yarn is needed in order to make a good thick pompon. For a mottled effect, use two different yarns.

Knitting in rounds to make stitch patterns

Knitting in rounds differs from flat knitting in that the right side of the work is always facing you. This produces some interesting results if you try to produce the basic stitch patterns in the normal way. By following the instructions given below, you will discover the special characteristics of circular knitting and learn how to form the basic fabrics, including striped patterns, by working in this way.

One advantage of working stitch patterns in rounds is that you can always keep track of the pattern as it forms on the right side. Also, there is no need for the extra edge stitches allowed for seams in flat knitting. Simply use an exact multiple of the stitches in the pattern repeat.

Garter stitch Just as the garter stitch method for flat knitting produces stocking stitch when knitted in rounds, so the stocking stitch method, knitted in rounds, produces garter stitch. You must knit one round and purl one round alternately to produce the characteristic horizontal ridges.

Stripes Join in a new colour to the first stitch of a round. Work as many rounds as you like for each stripe. If your stripes are relatively narrow, as they are here, you can carry the strands loosely up the fabric, rather than breaking off the yarn after each stripe. Notice that the stripes have a slightly staggered effect at the colour change; as the knitting forms a spiral, the last stitch in the old colour is side by side with the first stitch in the new colour.

Stocking stitch This is formed by knitting every round, as shown in detail on pages 123-124. The exterior of the tube has the familiar chain stitch effect, while the interior is ridged in the same way as reverse stocking stitch.

Ribbing In every round you must knit each knitted stitch and purl each purled stitch. Remember that there is no selvedge, so the total number of stitches must be a multiple of the number of stitches in each rib, or – if you are working a pattern with different numbers of knit and purl stitches – a multiple of each pattern repeat. Ribbing worked in rounds is a good way of finishing the neckband on a garment.

This photo shows the wrong side of the striped fabric, with the yarn carried up from one stripe to another. Note that you can work an uneven number of rows in a stripe and still have the yarn in the right place for picking up when you next need to knit with it.

3 Insert the scissor point between the two pieces of cardboard at the outer edge and cut the threads all round. Take care not to let the threads slip through the hole.

4 Gently separate the cardboard rings and wind a long piece of yarn (we have used a contrasting yarn for clarity) around the centre, then tie it to secure the pompon. You can leave a long end to use for attaching the pompon at a later stage. Ease the cardboard discs over the strands at each side of pompon.

5 Shake the pompon gently so that the strands form a sphere, concealing the yarn used for tying. Trim any protruding ends to give the pompon a smooth shape.

Fred Mancini

Plié perfect

You don't have to be a Pavlova to appreciate the comfort of these easy-to-knit leg warmers. Pair them with a matching hat — also knitted in rounds — for outdoor wear.

Sizes
To fit approximately 5-8 years [9-12 years : average woman's size].
Leg warmers length, 40[50 :60]cm, adjustable.

Note Instructions for larger sizes are in square brackets [] ; where there is only one set of figures it applies to all sizes.

Materials
Hayfield Beaulon Double Knitting :
Garter stitch hat *1 [1 :2] x 25g balls each in white, pale green, dark green, pale pink and dark pink*
Hat with ribbed brim *3[4 :4] balls in dark pink*
Moss stitch hat *2[3 :3] balls in dark green ; 1 ball each in white, pale green, pale pink and dark pink*
Striped stocking stitch hat *1 [1 :2] balls in pale green ; 1 ball each in white, dark green, pale pink and dark pink*
Set of four, double-pointed 4mm needles
Leg warmers *5[6 :7] balls*
Set of four, double-pointed 3mm, 3¼mm, 3¾mm and 4mm needles

Tension
22 sts and 30 rows to 10cm over st st on 4mm needles.

Garter stitch hat
Using set of 4mm needles and white, cast on 96[104 :112] sts. Cont in rounds of g st, working 4 rounds each in white, pale pink, dark green, pale green and dark pink throughout, until work measures 12[14 :16]cm from beg, finishing at the end of a stripe. Turn work inside out to reverse for turn-up brim and cont in stripes as before until work measures 28[31 :34]cm from beg, finishing at the end of a stripe. Cut off yarn, thread through sts, draw up and fasten off.

Hat with ribbed brim
Using set of 4mm needles and dark pink, cast on 96[104 :112] sts and work 12[14 :16]cm in rounds of K2, P2 rib. Cont in rounds of st st until work measures 28[31 :34]cm from beg. Cut off yarn, thread through sts, draw up and

Serge Krouglikoff/accessories from The Dance Centre and John Lewis

fasten off.
Make a pompon and attach it to top of the hat.

Moss stitch hat
Using set of 4mm needles and white, cast on 96[104:112] sts. Cont in rounds of g st, working 2 rounds each in white, pale pink, dark green, pale green and dark pink, until work measures 12[14:16]cm from beg. Cont in moss stitch with dark green only until work measures 28[31:34]cm from beg. Cut off yarn, thread through sts, draw up and fasten off.

Striped stocking stitch hat
Using set of 4mm needles and pale green, cast on 96[104:112] sts. Cont in rounds of st st, working 36[41:46] rounds in pale green, 18[19:20] rounds in pale pink, 14[15:16] rounds in dark green, 10[11:12] rounds in dark pink and 6[7:8] rounds in white.
Cut off yarn, thread through sts, draw up and fasten off.

Leg warmers
Using set of 3mm needles cast on 56[64:72] sts. Work 8[9:10]cm in rounds of K2, P2 rib. Change to 3¼mm needles and cont in rib until work measures 18[22:25]cm. Change to 3¾mm needles and rib until work measures 28[25:40]cm. Change to 4mm needles and rib until work measures 40[50:60]cm or length required. Cast off *loosely* in rib.

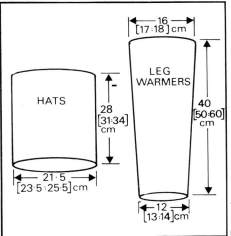

HATS — 28 [31:34] cm — 21·5 [23·5:25·5]cm

LEG WARMERS — 16 [17:18]cm — 40 [50:60] cm — 12 [13:14]cm

Trevor Lawrence

Step-by-step course – 28

Every knitter knows the frustration of being unable to obtain the yarn stated in a pattern. Substitution *may* be possible providing you are aware of the pitfalls. Once you understand the basic principles of tension and how they apply in patterns, then you can guard against an unsuitable choice of yarn.

Always choose another yarn in the same category as the original, e.g. 4 ply, chunky, mohair; assistants in wool shops are often a good source of advice on possible substitute yarns.

It is then essential to check the tension with the recommended needles. The ply and thickness of yarns is not standardized; even if a pattern requires widely available double knitting yarn, individual brands often vary in thickness. If you are substituting a different yarn, buy one ball first to see if it will work before you purchase the complete amount.

Note Whenever possible avoid trying to substitute a different stitch from the one used in the pattern. Even if you use the same yarn and needles as the original design, different stitch patterns create their own, widely varying tensions, and you usually need to alter the number of stitches throughout the pattern.

Substituting alternative yarns

1 This sample shows the correct tension for a sweater that you want to knit using the yarn (double knitting), needles (4mm) and stitch pattern (moss stitch) recommended in the pattern. Here there are 19 stitches and 34 rows to 10cm, as quoted in the pattern: all the designer's calculations are based on this tension.

2 You want to make the sweater in a bouclé yarn that appears roughly similar in thickness to double knitting.

3 Make a tension sample in moss stitch with the bouclé yarn and needles recommended in the pattern.

4 As the yarn is so textured it is difficult to distinguish the stitches and rows in this 10cm square. The yarn texture also counteracts that of the moss stitch. This type of yarn is therefore unsuitable for this particular pattern.

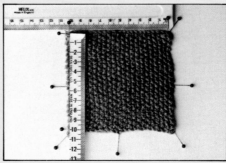

5 Next, you decide to try substituting some Shetland-type yarn. Make another sample using the recommended needles. The tension here is 22 stitches and 38 rows to 10cm: this is too tight and your sweater will be too small. You must knit another sample using larger needles.

6 Try one size larger to begin with. This time there are 19 stitches and 34 rows to 10cm – the same as in the original double knitting. The moss stitch looks as attractive in this Shetland-type yarn as it does in the original design.

128

Step-by-step course – 29

*Choosing a circular needle
*Knitting in rounds with a circular needle to make a tubular fabric
*Increasing between stitches
*Pattern for a woman's dress

Choosing a circular needle

When you work a seamless tubular fabric, the scale of the garment – as well as the number of stitches – will determine whether you require a set of four double-pointed needles or a circular needle. Generally, circular needles are ideal for large-scale tubular knitting; you are able to work in a continuous round, without the risk of possibly stretching the stitches, as when working with four needles. You must, however, use a set of four needles for items such as seamless socks or gloves which involve fewer than about 80 stitches. Here are some points to bear in mind when you are planning to use a circular needle.

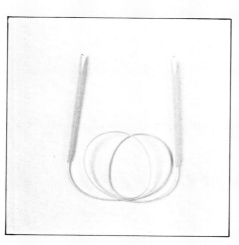

1 A circular needle usually consists of two small rigid needle-shaped sections joined by a length of flexible nylon 'wire'. The needle sections are available in various sizes corresponding to those of ordinary knitting needles.

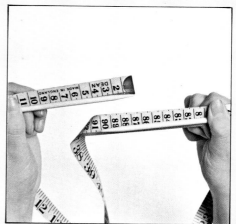

Fred Mancini

2 Besides varying in diameter, circular needles also vary in length. The length is given as an overall measurement including the needles themselves and the wire; the one shown measures 90cm. The needle sections are always the same length; only the length of the wire varies.

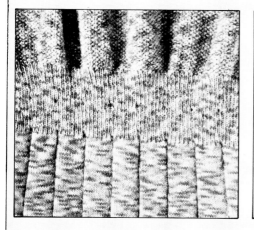

Tension	Length of needle (cm)				
(sts to 10cm)	40	60	80	90	100
20	80	120	160	180	200
22	88	132	176	198	220
24	96	144	192	216	240
26	104	156	208	234	260
28	112	168	224	252	280
30	120	180	240	270	300
32	128	192	256	288	320
34	136	204	272	306	340
36	144	216	288	324	360

3 The length of needle you require depends on the minimum number of stitches in the garment and your stitch tension. First find the smallest number of stitches in the garment, or garment section to be knitted in rounds. For example, if you are making the dress in this course, look through the instructions and you will find that in the smallest size the minimum number of stitches is 256. This is where the bodices join at the waist.

4 The chart above shows the minimum length of needle you require, according to the number of stitches, so that the stitches reach from one needle point to the other without stretching. Note that any circular needle can comfortably hold up to four times its minimum number of stitches; there is no need to change to a larger needle as the stitches increase.

5 You must also allow for stitch tension. For the dress that follows, the tension is 25 stitches to 10cm; ring the figure '26' in the LH column. Follow the horizontal line of numbers to the right until you come to one that is less than the minimum number of stitches (256). In this case the number is 234, and the longest needle you should buy is one measuring 90cm. A shorter needle would also serve the purpose.

Knitting in rounds with a circular needle to make a tubular fabric

The method of knitting in rounds with a circular needle is similar to using four double-pointed needles : the outside of the fabric is always facing you and all the rules regarding the formation of stitch patterns (as described on page 125) are the same. The advantage of a circular needle is that it is much more manageable and easier to hold than a set of needles. With only two needle points, instead of eight, there's no risk of losing stitches from the ends and there are no awkward joins between needles.

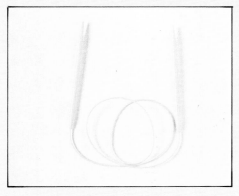

1 You may find that the length of flexible wire joining the two needle sections is twisted when you unpack the circular needle.

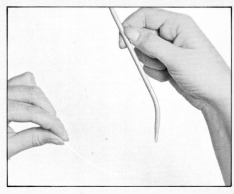

2 Straighten the twist by immersing the wire in warm water for a short time ; then draw the wire between finger and thumb until it lies in a gradual curve.

3 Cast the required number of stitches on to the section of the needle held in your right hand. When the rigid needle section is crowded with stitches, allow them to overflow on to the wire. If you cast on with one needle, a rubber band wound around the other end will prevent the stitches from slipping off.

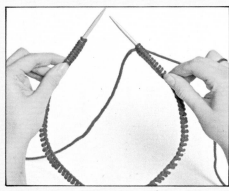

4 The total number of cast-on stitches should reach comfortably from RH needle point to LH needle point. The cast-on edge is likely to twist round the needle ; to eliminate this, begin by working three rows in the normal way, as instructed in steps 5 and 6.

5 To work in rows, transfer the RH needle to the left hand and vice versa so that the first stitch, with the yarn ready to knit it, is in the left hand. Knit each of the cast-on stitches.

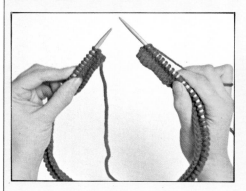

6 To work subsequent rows of a stocking stitch fabric, transfer the needle points to opposite hands so that the first stitch to be worked is always in your left hand (as in normal knitting). Purl the second row, and knit the third.

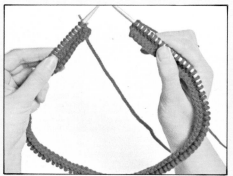

7 The ball of yarn is now at the RH needle section. Before joining the work and knitting in rounds, tie a marker loop of contrasting-coloured yarn to the LH needle section. The marker is always slipped from one needle point to the other at the beginning of a round to prevent your losing your place.

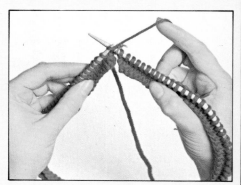

8 As you begin the first round the yarn is already attached to the stitch at the end of the RH needle and the right side of the fabric is facing outwards. Slip the marker loop on to the RH needle, then knit the first stitch on the LH needle ; pull the yarn across quite tightly to avoid making a loose stitch at this join.

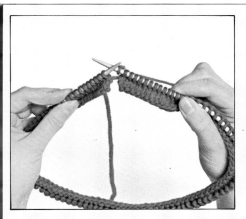

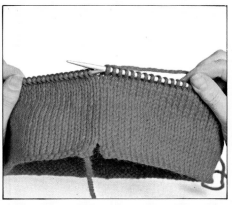

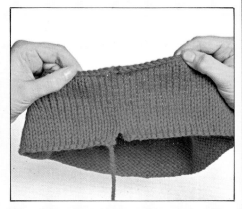

9 You have come to the end of the first round when you reach the marker loop on the LH needle; slip the marker before beginning the second round. At this point there is only a single horizontal strand across the join of the rounds.

10 Continue to work round in a circle; remember to knit each stitch in every round to form a stocking stitch fabric. (For methods of working other stitch patterns in rounds see page 125.)

11 Cast off at the start of a new round. First, discard the marker loop, then knit the first two stitches of the next round, cast off the first, and continue to cast off in the usual way to the end of the round. The finished fabric is tubular except for the slit at the first three row ends; these may be seamed together.

Increasing between stitches

This is known as 'making a stitch' and has the abbreviation 'M1'. The instructions here are for making a stitch on either a knit row or a purl row.

The method described here involves picking up the loop between two stitches and using this to form a new stitch. This method of shaping is often used in tailored garments; the resulting increase is virtually invisible.

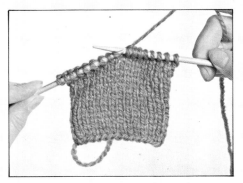

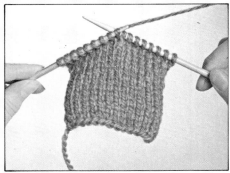

1 Work to the position of the increase. Insert the LH needle from front to back under the horizontal strand of yarn lying between the next stitch on the LH needle and the one just knitted on the RH needle.

2 At this stage the picked-up loop makes a hole in the fabric. Knit the extra loop through the back to close the hole.

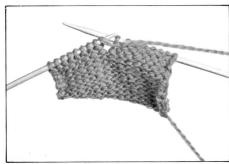

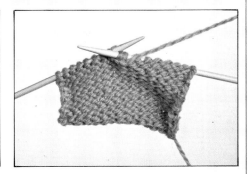

3 Several rows later the increase is practically invisible, except that a new stitch appears to have emerged from between the existing stitches.

4 On a purl row work to the position of the increase. Pick up a loop on the LH needle by inserting it from front to back under the horizontal strand of yarn lying between the two needles.

5 Now you must purl this loop through the back. Take care to insert the RH needle from left to right through the back loop: the RH needle must always be behind the front loop.

Fred Mancini

Knit yourself the well dressed look

This elegant dress will see you through the afternoon and on to an evening in town. It's knitted in a random-dyed wool, which is particularly effective on the bodice, knitted in moss stitch. The ribbed skirt is gently flared.

Sizes
To fit 83[87:92:97]cm bust. Length, 115[116:117:118]cm adjustable.

Note Instructions for larger sizes are in square brackets [] ; where there is only one set of figures it applies to all sizes.

Materials
10[11:11:12] x 50g balls of Phildar Contraste
1 pair each 2¾mm and 3mm knitting needles
2mm, 2¼mm, 2¾mm and 3mm circular needles

Tension
23 sts and 36 rows to 10cm over moss st on 3mm needles.

Back bodice
Using 3mm needles cast on 126[140:154:168] sts for neckline and work downwards. Work 4cm K1, P1 rib. Commence moss st patt.
1st row *K1, P1, rep from * to end.
2nd row *P1, K1, rep from * to end. Cont in patt until work measures 39[40:41:42]cm from beg. Cut off yarn and leave sts on a spare needle.

Front bodice
Work as given for back bodice, but do not cut off yarn.

Skirt
Join front and back bodice : using 2mm circular needle work in rib across sts of front bodice, then across sts of back bodice. 252[280:308:336] sts. Work 5cm in rounds of K1, P1 rib.
Next round (eyelet-hole round) *(K1, P1) 6 times, yon, K2 tog, rep from * to end.
Work 5cm more in rib. Change to 2¼mm circular needle. Commence wide rib patt.
1st round *K12, P2, rep from * to end. Rep the last round for 14cm. Change to 2¾mm circular needle and work 14cm in rib. Change to 3mm circular needle and work a further 14cm in rib.

Next round *K6, pick up loop lying between needles and K tbl – called make one, or M1 –, K6, P2, rep from * to end. 18[20:22:24] sts increased.
Next round *K13, P2, rep from * to end. Rep the last round for 14cm.
Next round *K7, M1, K7, P2, rep from * to end. 18[20:22:24] sts increased.
Next round *K14, P2, rep from * to end. Rep the last round for 13cm or until dress is 2cm less than required length. Work 6 rounds moss st, dec one st on 1st round. Cast off.

Armhole borders
Join shoulder seams for approximately 16cm from each side edge. Using 2¾mm needles and with RS of work facing, beg 25cm down side seam and K up 128 sts round armhole. Work 4cm K1, P1 rib. Cast off in rib.

To make up
Join underarm seams. Press lightly as directed on ball band. Make a twisted cord approx 180cm long and thread through eyelet holes at waist.

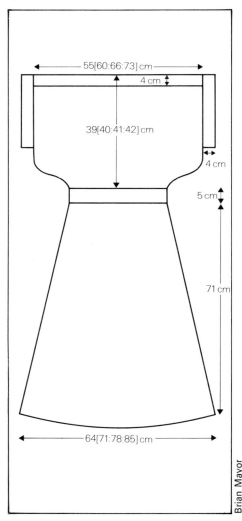

55[60:66:73] cm
4 cm
39[40:41:42] cm
4 cm
5 cm
71 cm
64[71:78:85] cm

Brian Mayor

Victor Yuan/photographed at Fern's Coffee Shop

Step-by-step course – 30

Narrow vertical and diagonal stripes

We have already shown you one method of working narrow vertical stripes (see Knitting Course 10, page 39). That method involves using both hands to control the two colours. Here is another way of working vertical stripes in two colours, which can be adapted to produce diagonal stripes. In this method, like the first one, the colours not in use are carried across the back of the work; but both yarns are controlled by the right hand. Keep narrow stripes five stitches wide, or less. If the stripes are more than five stitches wide, the strands of yarn are likely to be pulled too tightly across the work.

1 To make a two-colour striped stocking stitch fabric with three stitches in the main colour (A) and two in the contrast yarn (B), first cast on the required number of stitches with the main colour. Use B to knit the first two stitches.

2 Leave colour B at the back of the work; pick up A and bring it loosely across from the RH row end (over the top of B) to knit the next three stitches. Leave A at the back of the work, pick up B and take it under A to knit the following two stitches. Continue in this way to the end of the row.

3 At the beginning of every row you must have both strands of yarn at the RH row end. In this case, colour B is already in position, but you must move A to the right over the top of B. Purl the first two stitches with B, catching in A with the first stitch.

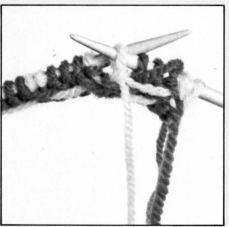

4 After purling the first two stitches, leave B at the front of the work. Pick up A and take it loosely across from the RH row end (over the top of B) to purl the next three stitches. Leave A at the front of the work, but over the top of the RH needle, pick up B and take it under A to purl the following two stitches. Continue in this way to the end of the row.

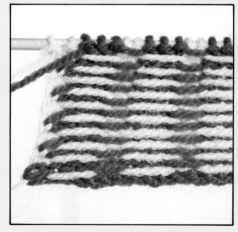

5 Remember to keep the strands of yarn at the back of the work fairly loose; if you pull them tightly you will distort the tension of the knitting. On every row you should strand one colour above the other consistently (here it is A); this prevents the yarns from becoming tangled.

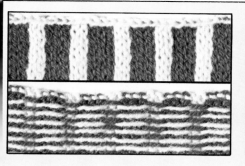

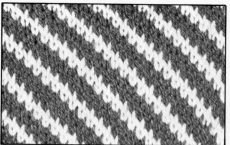

6 The finished fabric looks neat on the right side.
On the wrong side of the work the stranded yarns have a regular under and over appearance. The stranded yarns double the thickness of the fabric.

7 Essentially the same method can be used to make narrow diagonal stripes. The stripes can either slope to the left, as in this picture, or to the right. In this sample the stripes have been moved one stitch to the left on right-side rows and one stitch to the right on wrong-side rows. To do this you change colour one stitch *after* you would do so if working vertical stripes on right-side rows and one stitch *before* on wrong-side rows.

8 In this sample the diagonal stripes are sloping to the right. To achieve this gradual slope, you move the stripes one stitch to the right on right-side rows only. You can make an even more gradual slope by working more rows between moving stripes.

Wide vertical and diagonal stripes

If there are more than five stitches in a vertical stripe or if you are using more than two colours, the yarn cannot be stranded across the back from one stripe to the next without distorting the tension of the fabric. Instead, each stripe requires a separate ball of yarn. Unless the stripes are very wide, the separate balls of yarn need only be quite small. The most important thing to remember in using individual balls of yarn is to twist each yarn as you start to use it with the one just used, in order to avoid making a hole in the fabric.

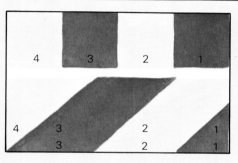

1 Wind small separate balls of yarn, corresponding in number to the maximum number of times you change colour across a row. To work the combination of vertical stripes shown at the top, you need four small balls of yarn. The illustration with diagonal stripes requires three balls for the cast-on edge. As new stripes are formed you will need to add new balls at the edge where they begin

2 To work wide vertical stripes, using the first colour, called 'A', cast on the required number of stitches for the first stripe; here, 10 stitches are required. Using colour B, cast on 10 more stitches. As you work the first stitch of each cast-on group, loop the ball of yarn under and over the colour no longer in use.

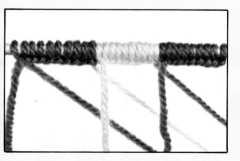

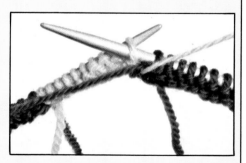

3 Continue in this way until you have cast on the total number of stitches required; for this sample it is 30. The cast-on edge forms a solid line, instead of each group of stitches being separate, for the stripes have been linked together at each colour change.

4 To work the first row of a stocking stitch fabric, using the appropriate ball of yarn, knit to the end of the first stripe. At the back of the work, pick up the second ball of yarn and take it from left to right under and over the first colour before knitting next stripe. Continue to end.

5 On the second purl-row use the appropriate ball of yarn to purl to the end of the first stripe. Leave the first colour slightly to the left at the front (WS). Take second colour to the right and over the top of the first colour before purling the first stitch in the second stripe.

continued

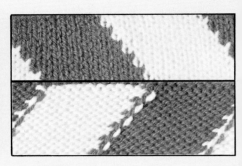

6 Continue in stocking stitch, always twisting the yarns at each colour change ; without the twist each stripe would be a separate length of knitting with nothing to link it to the next stripe. The stripe joins must be very neat, without the twisted colours showing through on the right side. To ensure this, tighten the yarns each time you change colour.

7 The right side of the finished fabric : apart from the colour change there is no other visual sign of a change of yarn. The wrong side of the fabric is also neat, with the twisted yarns forming a two-colour 'rope' effect at the join.

8 Wide diagonal stripes are worked on the same principle. The diagonal effect is created by gradually moving the stripes to the right or left, one stitch at a time. The desired angle of the slope and the stitch and row tension of the fabric will determine whether you move a stripe one stitch on every row or move it only every two or more rows.

Working a button loop

Button loops are a simple kind of fastening to make, for unlike buttonholes they are not an integral part of the fabric. Instead, they are sewn on to the edge of the opening, opposite the button, after the garment is complete. A button loop is ideal for fastening a single button used, for example, at the top of a slash-type neck opening. Only rarely is a number of button loops used to fasten a long row of buttons ; in this case, buttonholes are generally preferred.
Obviously, the size of loop varies according to that of the button; generally, the foundation strands of the loop should barely allow the button to pass through ; for the loop enlarges when covered with close loop stitches.

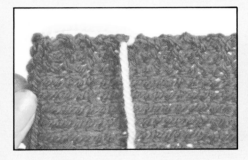

1 Thread a blunt-ended wool needle with yarn matching the garment. Turn the edge of the opening so that it lies horizontally, and join the yarn to the back of the work at the left of the loop position. Insert the needle through edge of the fabric the necessary width to the right. Keep the loop fairly taut ; secure it at the RH edge with a small back stitch.

2 Bring the needle back to the first position and make another small stitch, making sure the second strand formed is the same length as the first. Secure the yarn with a small backstitch. Finally repeat this process at the RH end of the loop, so that the foundation has three strands.

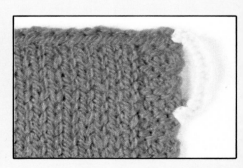

3 Turn the work around so that the edge with the loop is facing downwards. The yarn is now at the LH edge of the strands. Form it into a large circle below them. Insert the needle from front to back through loop ; draw it down and out through the front of the large circle. Tighten the circle over the three strands to form one loop stitch.

4 Continue to work loop stitches over the three strands until they are completely covered. Although the loop may soon appear full of stitches, you must keep gently pushing them to the LH end so that they are tightly packed.

5 The finished loop overlaps the edge of the opening. It must look neat and tidy, with evenly-worked stitches. Pushing the stitches together prevents their separating later on when the loop has become more pliable with use.

Squares and stripes

These chunky slipovers are made up from simple panels, cleverly arranged to emphasize the diagonal stripes. Worn over a sweater, they will keep the children warm when the weather turns chilly.

Gary Warren/accessories from John Lewis

John Hutchinson

Sizes
To fit 66[71 :76]cm chest.
Length, 43[47 :51]cm.

Note Instructions for the larger sizes are in square brackets [] ; where there is only one set of figures it applies to all sizes.

Materials
Narrow-striped top 6[6 :7] x 50g balls of Emu Fiord in main colour (A)
4[4 :5] balls in a contrasting colour (B)
Wide-striped top 5[5 :6] x 50g balls of Emu Fiord in main colour (A)

4[4 :5] balls in a contrasting colour (B)
1 pair 5½mm knitting needles
One button

Tension
18 sts and 20 rows to 10cm over narrow-striped patt on 5½mm needles.
16 sts and 20 rows to 10cm over wide-striped patt on 5½mm needles.

Narrow-striped top

Back
Note Back is worked in four sections.

Lower right-hand section Using 5½mm needles and A, cast on 30[32 :36] sts.
1st row (RS) *K 2 A, 4 B, rep from * to last 0[2 :0] sts, 0[2 :0] A.
2nd row PO [1 :0] A, 3[4 :3] B, *2 A, 4 B, rep from * to last 3 sts, 2 A, 1B.
3rd row K2 B, *2 A, 4 B, rep from * to last 4[0 :4] sts, 2[0 :2] A, 2[0 :2] B.
4th row P1[3 :1]·B, *2A, 4 B, rep from * to last 5 sts, 2 A, 3 B.
5th row *K4 B, 2 A, rep from * to last 0[2 :0] sts, 0[2 :0] B.
6th row PO [1 :0] B, 1[2 :1] A, *4 B, 2 A, rep from * to last 5 sts, 4 B, 1 A.
These 6 rows form patt. Rep them 5[6 :6] times more, then work 5[1 :5] rows more. Cast off P-wise using A.
Upper left-hand section Work as given for lower right-hand section.
Lower left-hand section Using 5½mm needles and A, cast on 30[32 :36] sts.
1st row (RS) KO[2 :0] A, *4 B, 2 A, rep from * to end.
2nd row P1 B, 2 A, *4 B, 2 A, rep from * to last 3[5 :3] sts, 3[4 :3] B, 0[1 :0] A.
3rd row K2[0 :2] B, 2[0 :2] A, *4 B, 2 A, rep from * to last 2 sts, 2 B.
4th row P3 B, 2 A, *4 B, 2 A, rep from * to last 1[3 :1] sts, 1[3 :1] B.
5th row KO[2 :0] B, *2 A, 4 B, rep from * to end of row.
6th row P1 A, 4 B, *2 A, 4 B, rep from *

137

to last 1[3:1] sts, 1[2:1] A, 0[1:0] B.
These 6 rows form patt. Rep them
5[6:6] times more, then work 5[1:5]
rows more.
Cast off P-wise using A.
Upper right-hand section Work as given
for lower left-hand section.

Front

Lower left-hand section Work as given
for lower right-hand section of back.
Lower right-hand section Work as given
for lower left-hand section of back.
Upper left-hand section Work 24 rows as
given for lower left-hand section of
back. Work neck edge as follows:
Next row Patt to last 4 sts, K4 A.
Next row K4 A for neck border, patt to
end of row.
Complete as given for lower left-hand
section of back, working a 4-st border in
g st at neck edge using A.
Upper right-hand section Work 24 rows
as given for lower right-hand section of
back. Work neck edge:
Next row K4 A, patt to end of row.
Next row Patt to last 4 sts, K4 A.
Complete this section as given for lower
right-hand section of back, working a
4-st border in g st at neck edge using A.

Lower bands (make 2)
Using 5½mm needles and A, cast on 5 sts.
Work 33[36:38]cm in g st. Cast off.

Neckband
Using 5½mm needles and A, cast on
5 sts. Work 28[31:33]cm in g st.
Cast off.

Side bands (make 2)
Using 5½mm needles and A, cast on 5
sts. Work 25[28:31]cm in g st.
Next row Cast on 5 sts, K to end. 10 sts.
Cont in g st until band measures
36[38:40]cm from cast-on sts, ending at
same edge as cast-on sts.
Next row Cast off 5 sts, K to end. 5 sts.
Work a further 25[28:31]cm in g st.
Cast off.

To make up
Pin out each section to correct
measurements – approximately
16 x 20[18 x 21:19 x 24]cm. Press with
a cool iron over a damp cloth. Join front
and back section using a back stitch
seam: take in cast-on and cast-off edges
so that they don't show on the RS. Join
shoulders for 9[10:11]cm from each
armhole edge. Sew lower bands in
place using a flat seam. Sew side bands in
position with unshaped edge along side
of garment. Sew neckband in position,
placing each end to front opening. Make
a buttonhole loop at neckband: sew
button to other side to correspond. Beg
14[15:16]cm from lower edge, join
side seams to end of each armhole. Press
seams lightly.

Gary Warren/accessories from John Lewis

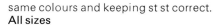

Wide-striped top

Back

Note Back is worked in four sections.

Lower right-hand section Using 5½mm needles cast on 27[30:33] sts as foll: 9[10:11] A, 9[10:11] B, 9[10:11] A.

Next row (WS) P9[10:11] A, 9[10:11] B, 9[10:11] A.

Commence patt.

1st row (RS) K9[10:11] A, 9[10:11] B, 9[10:11] A.

2nd row P8[9:10] A, 9[10:11] B, 9[10:11]A, 1 B.

3rd row K1 B, 9[10:11] A, 9[10:11] B, 8[9:10] A.

4th row P7[8:9] A, 9[10:11] B, 9[10:11] A, 2 B.

5th row K3 B, 9[10:11] A, 9[10:11] B, 6[7:8] A.

6th row P6[7:8] A, 9[10:11] B, 9[10:11] A, 3 B.

Cont in this way, moving the diagonals one st to the left on K rows and to the right on P rows on the 1st, 2nd, 4th and 5th rows of each 6-row patt as before. Work 7[9:10] rows. The corner diagonal is now complete. Cont in this way, moving the rem diagonals one st to the left on K rows and to the right on P rows as before, until 41[45:50] rows have been worked from beg. The diagonal should now be complete.

1st and 3rd sizes only

Rep last row worked once more, using same colours and keeping st st correct.

All sizes

Using B, cast off.

Lower left-hand section Work as given for lower right-hand section, reversing patt by reading row from end to the beg and moving the diagonal one st to the right on K rows and to the left on P rows as before.

Upper right-hand section Using 5½mm needles and B, cast on 27[30:33] sts.

Next row (WS) P1 A, 26[29:32] B.

Commence patt.

1st row (RS) K26[29:32] B, 1 A.

2nd row P2 A, 25[28:31] B.

3rd row K25[28:31] B, 2 A.

4th row P3 A, 24[27:30] B.

5th row K23[26:29] B, 4 A.

6th row P4 A, 23[26:29] B.

Work 34[38:43] more rows in this way, moving the diagonals one st to the right on K rows and to the left on P rows on the 1st, 2nd, 4th and 5th rows of each 6-row patt as before. (A new diagonal must be started at the centre edge on the 29th[31st:35th] row from beg.)

1st and 3rd sizes only

Rep the last row worked once more, using the same colours and keeping the st st correct.

All sizes

Cast off using the colours of previous row.

Upper left-hand section Work as given for upper right-hand section, reversing patt by reading rows from end to beg and moving the diagonal one st to the left on K rows and to the right on P rows as before.

Front

Lower left-hand section Work as given for lower right-hand section of back.

Lower right-hand section Work as given for lower left-hand section of back.

Upper left-hand section Patt 24 rows as given for lower left-hand section of back. Work neck edge as follows:

Next row Patt to last 4 sts, K4 A for border.

Next row K 4A for border, patt to end of row.

Complete as given for upper right-hand section of back, working a 4-st border at neck edge using A.

Upper right-hand section Patt 24 rows as given for lower right-hand section of back. Work neck edge:

Next row K4 A, patt to end of row.

Next row Patt to last 4 sts, K4 A.

Complete this section as given for upper left-hand section of back, working a 4-st border in g st at neck edge using A.

Lower, neck and side bands

Work as given for narrow-striped top.

To make up

Complete as given for narrow-striped top.

Step-by-step course – 31

*Double casting on
*Mosaic pattern effects
*Stitch Wise : more mosaic
 patterns
*Pattern for man's waistcoat

Double casting on

Experiment with this unusual method of casting on – you may find it easier than the one you are already using. The working method appears to be a combination of previous techniques – using your thumb to cast on with two needles. Both needles are held in your right hand throughout and operate as a single needle. A double-cast-on is often used by professional knitters wherever a strong, but elastic, edge is required. It makes an ideal cast-on edge for the ribbed back of the man's waistcoat on page 142.

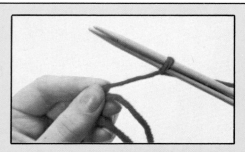

1 Hold the two needles together in your right hand. Make a slip loop some distance from the end of a ball of yarn and place it on the needles. (1 metre of double knitting makes about 60 stitches). The short end is for making the stitches in the same way as casting on with one needle.

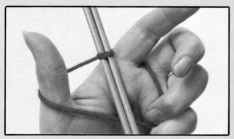

2 Take both ends of yarn – that from the main ball and the short end – and hold them together across the palm of your left hand. The short end is round your thumb and the yarn from the main ball round your forefinger.

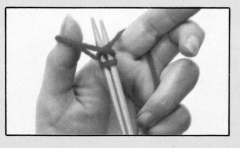

3 Use both needles together to cast on the stitches : put them up through the loop on the front of the thumb and down through the loop on the forefinger, drawing a new stitch through the loop on the thumb.

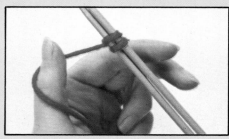

4 Release the loop on your thumb ; without letting go of either end of yarn in your left hand, tighten the new loop on the needles by re-inserting your thumb under the short end and pulling it gently downwards.

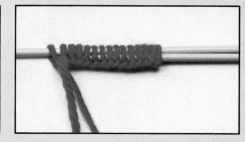

5 Repeat steps 3 and 4 until you have cast on the required number of stitches. Withdraw one of the needles. Transfer the needle with the stitches to your left hand and hold the free needle in your right hand ready to begin knitting.

Mosaic pattern effects

Mosaic patterns are a sophisticated version of slip stitch design. They use two colours of yarn, which alternate every two rows ; the colours are worked with slip stitch techniques to create unusual geometric shapes. The design forms when part of the pattern in one colour is hidden behind slip stitches of a different coloured yarn, coming from a row below. The slip stitches span two rows and are caught up again by their own colour on the third row. Mosaic designs are very versatile : they can be worked over any number of stitches as there are no special instructions for wrong-side rows.

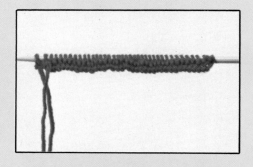

1 You require two colours of yarn, A and B. Colour A forms the pattern, whilst B is the background. Using B, cast on a multiple of 6 stitches plus 2 extra. Knit the first 2 rows.

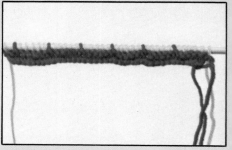

2 Join in A and use it to work the 3rd row (RS) K6, *sl 1, K5, rep from * to last 2 sts, sl 1, K1. Note that on all right-side rows you must keep the yarn at the back when slipping stitches.

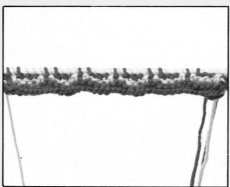

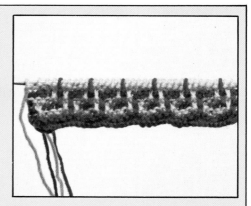

3 On the 4th row and all other wrong-side rows, use the same colour as the previous row to knit the same stitches as before; slip the same stitches, remembering to keep the yarn at the front of the work.

4 Use B to work the 5th row K1, sl 1, *K3, sl 1, K1, sl 1, rep from * ending last rep with K2. For the 7th row using A, K4, *sl 1, K1, sl 1, K3, rep from * ending with K1. The pattern is now beginning to form.

5 Use B to work the 9th row K3, *sl 1, K1, sl 1, K3, rep from * ending with K2. For the 11th row. Using A, K4, *sl 1, K5, rep from * ending with K3. Work the next wrong-side row to complete 12 pattern rows.

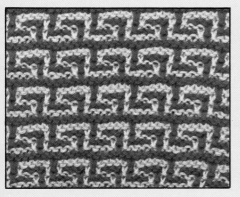

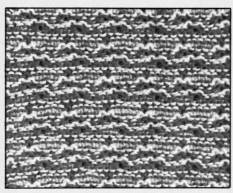

6 Repeat the 12 pattern rows throughout until the fabric is the required depth. Cast off after working the first two rows using B. Colour A makes horizontal bands of a formal, 'key-type' pattern.

7 The back of a mosaic-patterned fabric is very neat. The fabric is only a single thickness unlike the double thickness of Fair Isle knitting where two yarns are carried across a row of knitting.

8 You can achieve an interesting, and often completely different, effect if you reverse the colours in the design. Here the previous colour A has been used for the background, whilst B forms the design. Choose two, contrasting light and dark colours to give the most pronounced results.

9 Give a greater emphasis to the pattern by having the design in garter stitch against a stocking stitch background. Simply purl the wrong-side rows worked in B, the background colour.

10 Most mosaic patterns are entirely in garter stitch, but there is no rule against working them in stocking stitch. The finished fabric is not textured and the tension of the work makes the designs taller and thinner.

11 You can experiment with different types of yarn to achieve varying effects and textures. Here a mohair pattern has been worked against a double knitting background. Below, a shiny crepe yarn is used against a 4-ply background.

Mike Berend

Stitch Wise

Alternating checks

You require two colours, A and B. Using A, cast on a multiple of 14 sts plus 2 extra. Note that on all rows, you must slip stitches with the yarn at the back.

1st and 2nd rows Using A, K to end.

3rd, 7th, 11th and 15th rows (RS) Using B, K1, *K7, (sl 1, K1) 3 times, sl 1, rep from * to last st, K1.

4th and foll alt rows K all sts knitted in previous row with same colour and sl all slipped sts with yarn in front.

5th, 9th and 13th rows Using A, K1, *(sl 1, K1) 3 times, sl 1, K7, rep from * to last st, K1.

17th and 18th rows Using A, K to end.

19th, 23rd, 27th and 31st rows Using B, as 5th.

21st, 25th and 29th rows Using A, as 3rd.

32nd row As 4th.

These 32 rows form the patt. Rep them throughout.

Fancy border pattern

You require two colours, A and B. Using A, cast on a multiple of 16 sts plus 2 extra. Note that on all right-side rows you must slip stitches with the yarn at the back.

1st row (RS) Using B, K1, *K4, sl 1, K11, rep from * to last st, K1.

2nd and every foll alt row P or K (depending on whether you want a st st or g st fabric) all sts knitted in previous row with the same colour and sl all slipped sts with yarn in front.

3rd row Using A, K1, *(K3, sl 1) twice, (K1, sl 1) 3 times, K2, rep from * to last st, K1.

5th row Using B, K1, *K2, sl 1, K3, sl 1, K7, sl 1, K1, rep from * to last st, K1.

7th row Using A, K1, *K1, (sl 1, K3) twice, sl 1, K1, sl 1, K3, sl 1, rep from * to last st, K1.

9th row Using B, K1, *K4, (sl 1, K3) 3 times, rep from * to last st, K1.

11th row Using A, K1, *(K3, sl 1) 3 times, K4, rep from * to last st, K1.

13th row Using B, K1, *sl 1, K3, sl 1, K1, (sl 1, K3) twice, sl 1, K1, rep from * to last st, K1.

15th row Using A, K1, *K1, sl 1, K7, sl 1, K3, sl 1, K2, rep from * to last st, K1.

17th row Using B, K1, *K2, (sl 1, K1) 3 times, (sl 1, K3) twice, rep from * to last st, K1.

19th row Using A, K1, *K11, sl 1, K4, rep from * to last st, K1.

20th row As 2nd.

These 20 rows form the patt. Rep them throughout.

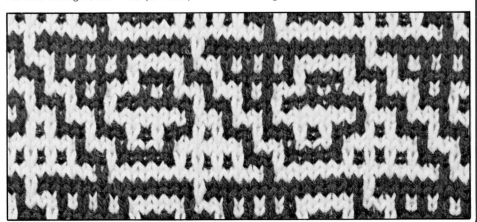

Sporting colours

A simple slip stitch pattern gives you sporting colour combinations. The back is worked in rib to give a trim fit.

Sizes
To fit 92[97:102:107]cm chest.
Length to shoulder, 54[55:56:57]cm.

Note Instructions for larger sizes are in square brackets [] ; where there is only one set of figures it applies to all sizes.

Materials

- 8[9 :9 :10] x 25g. balls of Bernat Ladyship Renown Superwash 4 ply in main colour (A)
- 2[3 :3 :3] balls in a contrasting colour (B)
- 1 pair each 2¾mm and 3¼mm knitting needles
- 5 buttons

Tension

32 sts to 10cm over main rib patt on 3¼mm needles.

Back

Using 2¾mm needles and A, cast on 143[151 :159 :167] sts.
1st row K2, *P1, K1, rep from * to last st, K1.
2nd row K1, *P1, K1, rep from * to end.
Rep these 2 rows for 2cm, ending with a 2nd row.
Change to 3¼mm needles.
Commence main rib patt.

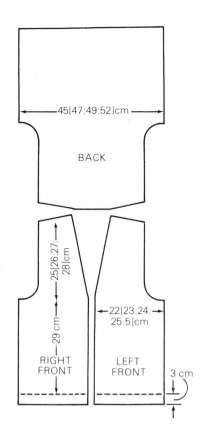

1st row (RS) K to end.
2nd row K1, *P1, K1, rep from * to end.
These 2 rows form patt. Cont in patt until work measures 29cm from beg, ending with a 2nd row.
Shape armholes
Cast off 7[9:10:11] sts at beg of next 2 rows. Dec one st at each end of next 5[5:7:7] rows, then at each end of every foll alt row until 103[107:111:115] sts rem. Cont without shaping until work measures 54[55:56:57]cm from beg, ending with a 2nd row.
Shape shoulders
Cast off 11[11:12:12] sts at beg of next 4 rows and 10[11:11:12] sts at beg of next 2 rows. Cast off.

Right front
Using 2¾mm needles and A, cast on 69[73:77:81] sts. Beg with a K row, work 9 rows st st.
Next row K to end to mark foldline. Change to 3¼mm needles. Commence patt.
1st row (RS) Using A, K to end.
2nd row Using A, P to end.
3rd row Using B, K4, *sl 1, K3, rep from * to last st, K1.
4th row Using B, K4, *sl 1 with yarn at front, take yarn to back, K3, rep from * to last st, K1.
5th row Using A, K1, *sl 1, K1, rep from * to end.
6th row Using A, P1, *sl 1, P1, rep from * to end.
7th row Using B, K2, *sl 1, K3, rep from * ending with K2.

8th row Using B, K2, *sl 1 with yarn at front, take yarn to back, K3, rep from * ending with K2.
9th and 10th rows Using A, as 1st and 2nd.
11th and 12th rows Using B, as 7th and 8th.
13th and 14th rows Using A, as 5th and 6th.
15th and 16th rows (B), as 3rd and 4th. These 16 rows form the patt. Cont in patt until work measures 29cm from hemline, ending with a WS row.
Shape armhole and front edge
Next row K2 tog, patt to end.
Next row Cast off 8[10:11:12] sts, patt to end.
Dec one st at armhole edge on next 5[5:7:7] rows, then on foll 8[8:7:8] alt rows, *at the same time* dec one st at front edge on 3rd and every foll 4th row until 34[36:39:39] sts rem, then on every foll 6th row until 30[31:33:34] sts rem. Cont without shaping until work measures same as back to shoulder, ending at armhole edge.
Shape shoulders
Cast off 10[10:11:11] sts at beg of next and foll alt row. Work 1 row. Cast off.

Left front
Work as for right front, reversing shaping.

Armhole borders
Join shoulder seams. Using 2¾mm needles, A and with RS of work facing, K up 181[187:195:199] sts round armhole. Beg with a 2nd row, work 7 rows rib as given for back welt. Cast off in rib.

Front band
Mark right front edge with pins to indicate button positions, the top one to be just below beg of front edge shaping and the last one to be 1cm above foldline, with 3 more evenly spaced between. Using 2¾mm needles and A, cast on 11 sts. Work in rib as given for back welt until band, when slightly stretched, fits up left front edge, across back neck and down right front edge. Make button-holes as markers are reached as foll:
1st buttonhole row Rib 4, cast off 3, rib to end.
2nd buttonhole row Rib to end, casting on 3 sts over those cast off in previous row.

To make up
Turn hem to WS at foldline and slip stitch in position. Join side and armhole border seams. Sew front band in position. Sew on buttons to correspond with buttonholes.

Crochet Introduction

Crochet has the great advantage of being very portable, money-saving and an immensely satisfying pastime. With a simple hook and yarn you can create fashion items for you and your family or furnishings for your home. Beginners will find these step-by-step courses clear and practical and an invaluable source of reference, while for those who are more experienced in crochet there are many fascinating new stitches and professional ideas for you to use.

Here, in twenty-nine graded courses, all the standard crochet techniques and more advanced skills are clearly explained. You are shown how to control your crochet hook and yarn, master stitches, techniques, tension, making-up and pattern adaptation, and how to apply these skills correctly and with confidence. Information is also given on making squares, circles and wheels, on working with colours in striped, chevron and checked patterns and on using unusual yarns like lurex and bouclé.

Each course is clearly illustrated with step-by-step photographs and has a special pattern for you to make as you practise the stitches and techniques. The patterns range from a simple cushion set to a beautiful rosy bed-spread, and from a child's Aran sweater to a lacy-look shawl. There is a favourite for all ages, from fashion wear to baby wear.

Step-by-step course -1

* The basis of crochet
* Making a double-crochet fabric
* Joining in a new ball of yarn
* Checking stitch tension
* Scatter cushions to make

Crochet is one of the most versatile and exciting skills to learn. If you need some inspiration, look at the samples on this page . . . just a few of the beautiful modern and traditional patterns you can create. Once you've mastered the basic stitches, it's an easy skill to develop and very quick to work.

Hooks

Crochet hooks are made in a range of sizes from a 0.60, used for fine lace crochet, to a 7.00, used in conjunction with thick yarns. The size is a metric measurement taken round the body of the shaft. All British manufacturers conform to this method of sizing, known as the International Size Range and sometimes shown as ISR in the instructions.

Yarns

Most yarns can be used for crochet, from the very fine cottons used in lace crochet to the really thick, knobbly yarns. It is best to buy all the yarn you will need for a particular design at the same time, to ensure that all the balls come from the same dye-lot; colours from different dye-lots vary considerably and this will show up badly on the finished fabric. Yarn is now sold in grammes rather than ounces, and is usually packed in 20, 25, 40, 50 or 100 gramme balls.

Alan Duns

The basis of crochet

1 To make a slip loop, first wind the yarn around your fingers like this.

5 Wind the yarn over the left-hand fingers. This is the recommended way, but as you practise you will find your own most comfortable position.

Making a double crochet fabric

Double crochet is the smallest stitch used in crochet. It gives a firm, closely woven fabric, with a pretty, seeded appearance, which looks equally attractive worked in a fine or chunky yarn.

Before beginning to work any crochet stitches extra chain are made in order to bring the hook up to the same height as the stitch being worked and to give the fabric a straight edge. They are always counted as the first stitch of every row and are called *turning chain*.

4 Wind the yarn clockwise round the hook as before.

2 Slide a length of yarn through the first loop.

3 Pull through the yarn to form the slip loop. Put the loop on the crochet hook and pull it tight.

4 Hold the hook in your right hand as you would a pencil, keeping the thumb and first finger as close to the hook as possible. Rest the hook against the second finger, keeping the shank firm.

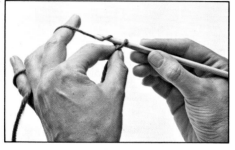

6 Hold the slip loop firmly in the left hand and wind the yarn in a clockwise direction over the shaft and round the hook.

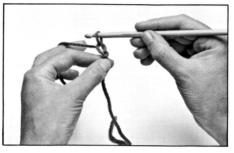

7 Draw the yarn through the loop on the hook. This makes one chain stitch.

8 Repeat steps 6 and 7 to make as many chains as you need. Always hold the chain as close to the hook as possible with the thumb and first finger of the left hand.

1 Make any length of chain. Insert the hook from front to back into the third chain from hook. The two missed chain are the turning chain.

2 Wind the yarn clockwise round the hook.

3 Draw the loop through the chain. There are now two loops on the hook.

5 Draw the yarn through the two loops on the hook. One double crochet made.

6 Insert the hook from front to back into the next chain.

7 Repeat steps 2 to 5 to make a double crochet.

continued

David Levin   Paul Williams

8 Continue to work one double crochet into each chain until you reach the end of the row.

9 To turn your work keep the hook in the right hand and turn the crochet over from right to left.

10 Work one turning chain, which counts as the first stitch. Miss first stitch of previous row and work into second stitch to keep edge of work straight.

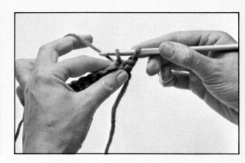

11 Insert hook from front to back into the second stitch *under* the two horizontal loops at the top.

12 Wind the yarn round the hook as in step 2.

13 Draw through the loop as in step 3.

14 Wind yarn over hook again and pull through to complete the first double crochet of the new row. Repeat to end.

15 Work the last double crochet into the turning chain of the previous row. Do this on every row to keep the edge straight.

16 After working required rows, fasten off by drawing yarn through last loop at end of row. Pull tight, break off yarn, darn in loose end with wool needle.

Keeping the edge straight

When you begin working a crochet fabric you may find it difficult to keep the edges straight. Don't worry – this is a common mistake. It happens because you are not working into the correct stitches at each end of the row. Remember to make a turning chain at the beginning of the row, work into the second stitch, missing the first stitch as in step 11. Work the last stitch into the turning chain at the end of the row as in step 15.

1 The fabric will slant inwards if you do not work into the turning chain at the end of the row.

2 The fabric will get wider if you do not miss the first stitch and work into the second stitch.

David Levin   Paul Williams

Joining in a new ball of yarn

A new ball of yarn should always be joined into the fabric at the side of the work, and never in the middle of a row. If you reach the middle of the row and have insufficient yarn to complete it, take the hook out of the working loop and unravel the yarn back to the side edge. Pick up the working loop to join in the new yarn. Remedy mistakes by unravelling the yarn in the same way.

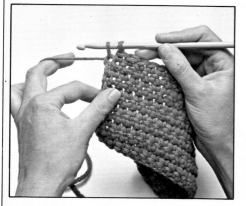

1   Work to the end of the row in the usual way until the two loops of the last stitch are on the hook.

2   Hold the fabric and yarn in left hand and loop the new yarn round the hook.

3   Draw new yarn through the two loops on hook. This completes the stitch and introduces the new yarn.

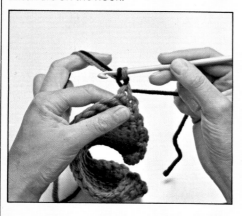

4   Turn work. Hold the old and new yarn together and work the turning chain with both yarns together to hold the new yarn in place. Pull the loose ends to tighten the stitch.

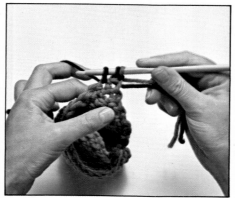

5   Work the next stitch using the new yarn alone.

6   Continue working with new yarn. When you have finished the piece come back to the two loose ends and darn in, using a blunt-ended wool needle.

Stitch tension

To make sure that your crochet is the correct measurement when completed, it is advisable to work a tension square in the hook and yarn stated to check your tension. If necessary you can alter the number of stitches by changing the hook size. Keep changing the hook size until your tension is correct.

Example : Your instructions quote 12 stitches to 10cm on a No. 5.50 hook using a chunky yarn. Make a piece with at least 24 stitches, not less than 10cm deep. Count up 12 stitches and mark with pins. Pin the piece flat and measure your 12 stitches.

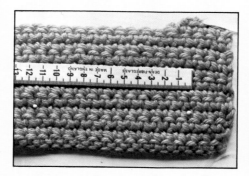

If the 12 stitches measure more than 10cm your tension is too loose and you must change to a smaller hook.

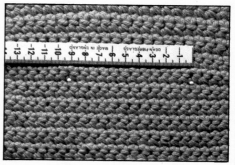

If the 12 stitches measure less than 10cm your tension is too tight and you must change to a larger hook.

Scatter cushions

Practice your stitches on one of these simple cushions or, maybe two or three . . . a colourful collection for your house or garden.

Size :
We give specific instructions to fit a cushion pad 41cm [16in] square (available from most needlecraft departments).

Materials
For 1 cover in double knitting yarn approx 180g
4.00mm crochet hook
For 1 cover in chunky knitting yarn approx 300g
5.50mm crochet hook
1 cushion pad 41cm square for each cushion

1   Make 69 chain for double knitting yarn or 55 chain for chunky knitting yarn.

2   Continue working in rows of double crochet, with 68 double crochet in each row for double knitting, or 54 in each row for chunky knitting yarn.
3   Work until fabric measures 38cm from beginning. Fasten off.
4   Darn in all loose ends of yarn using a blunt-ended wool needle. Make another piece in the same way.
5   Using either the same double knitting yarn, or a thinner yarn in a matching colour for chunky knitting yarn, oversew round three sides of cushion.
6   Insert cushion pad into cover. Oversew remaining seam.

☐ To calculate the size of cover for an existing cushion, measure the width and depth of your cushion and make the cover 2.5cm *less* all round. **Example**: for a cushion measuring 35.5cm square you will need a 33cm-square cover.

☐ To work out the number of stitches for any size cover: make a sample piece measuring approximately 10cm square, in the stitch and yarn you are using. Measure 5cm with a ruler and count the number of stitches. **Example**: if you have 10 stitches to 5cm (i.e. 2 stitches to 1cm) you will need to make 66 chain plus two extra for the turning chain, for a 33cm cover.

Peter Pugh-Cook

Step-by-step course – 2

Making a half treble fabric

1 Make any length of chain. Wind yarn clockwise round the hook.

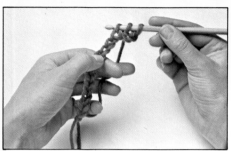

2 Insert the hook from front to back into the third chain from the hook. First two are turning chain.

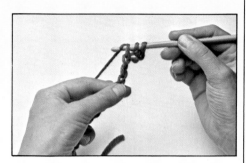

3 Wind the yarn round the hook.

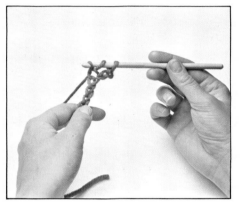

4 Draw the yarn through the chain. There are now three loops on the hook.

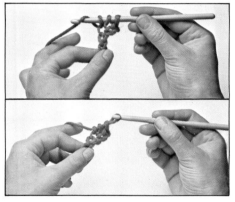

5 Wind the yarn round the hook and draw it through all three loops on the hook. One half treble has been made.

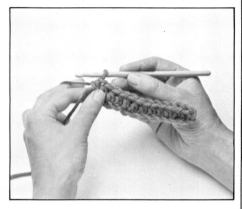

6 Repeat these actions into each chain to the end.

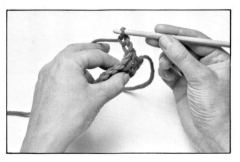

7 Turn work. Make **two** turning chain.

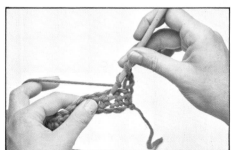

8 Miss the first stitch. Work the first half-treble as before into the second stitch. Work one half-treble into each stitch to the end of the row.

9 Work the last half-treble into the turning chain of the previous row. Repeat these last three steps for the number of rows you require.

David Levin   Paul Williams

The cosy baby bag

Warm as toast for chilly days — a snug sleeping bag worked in half trebles.

of row. Work last half-treble into turning chain of previous row. Turn.
Continue working in rows of half-treble in this way until back measures 56cm. Draw yarn through and fasten off.

Left front
Using No. 5.50mm hook make 18 chain. Work 1 half-treble into 3rd chain from hook, 1 half-treble into each chain to end. Turn. 17 half-treble.
Continue working in rows of half-treble as given for back.
Work until left front measures same as back. Draw yarn through and fasten off.

Right front
Using No. 5.50mm hook make 24 chain. Work 1 half-treble into 3rd chain from hook, 1 half-treble into each chain to end. Turn. 23 half-treble.
Continue working in rows of half-treble until right front measures same as back. Draw yarn through and fasten off.

Sleeves
Using No. 5.50mm hook make 24 chain. Work 1 half-treble into each chain to end of row. 23 half-treble.
Continue working in half-treble until sleeve measures 13.5cm. Draw yarn through and fasten off.

Base
Using No. 5.50mm hook make 9 chain. Work 1 half-treble into 3rd chain from hook, 1 half-treble into each chain to end. Turn. 8 half-trebles.
Continue working in rows of half-treble until piece measures 34cm. Draw yarn through and fasten off.

To make up
☐ With right sides of work facing, pin back and front pieces together with right front overlapping left front by approximately 5cm.
☐ Using a flat seam throughout join right and left shoulder seams for 9cm at each side. Mark a point 9cm from shoulder on side seams for armholes. With right sides facing sew sleeve tops in position along armhole opening.
☐ Join side and sleeve seams.
☐ Join right front to left front on the right side, for 9cm from bottom edge where they overlap. Sew the left front to the right front on the wrong side in the same way.
☐ Pin the base to the bottom of the bag matching side seams to centre of base ends.
☐ Sew in place using a flat seam.
☐ Sew two poppers at the inner and outer edge of the left front at the neck edge to hold in place. Repeat 3 more times at even intervals down the front opening.
☐ Thread ribbon through the last row of half trebles on the sleeves and draw up. Tie a bow at neck edge on right front at same place as poppers if required.

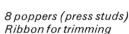

Size :
To fit a baby up to 6 months. Length to shoulder, 56cm. Sleeve seam, 13.5cm.

Tension
11 stitches and 9 rows to 10cm over half-treble worked on a No. 5.50mm hook.

Materials
300g Peter Pan Darling Chunky
1 No. 5.50mm crochet hook

8 poppers (press studs)
Ribbon for trimming

Back
Using No. 5.50mm hook make 38 chain. Work 1 half-treble into 3rd chain from hook, then 1 half-treble into each chain to end. Turn, 37 half-treble worked.
Next row work 2 chain to count as 1st half-treble, miss 1st stitch, work a half-treble into next and every stitch to end

Step-by-step course – 3

*Understanding correct tension
*How to check tension
*Using a substitute yarn

Understanding correct tension

Now that you have mastered the basic stitches in crochet it is vital to understand the importance of obtaining the 'correct tension' when working a pattern, as this can mean the difference between success and failure.

Most people think that tension refers to the ability to be able to make a smooth, even fabric, but this is not so. By 'correct tension' we mean working the same number of stitches and rows to a given measurement as the pattern designer used. This is usually worked out over 10cm. Remember that although you may not get the same number of stitches to begin with, this does not mean that your tension is 'wrong', but simply that you work either slightly more loosely or tightly than the designer. This difference can easily be remedied by changing to a different size hook.

Before beginning to work on a pattern the designer will crochet a square using the hook, yarn and stitch intended for the garment. The number of stitches in this square will determine the size and shape of the finished garment as all the measurements for it will be calculated from this figure. So, unless your tension is the same as in the instructions the garment will not turn out the same size as the original. Remember that a difference of even half a stitch over 10cm can alter the size of the finished fabric.

It is sometimes difficult to achieve the correct tension in both the stitches and rows, but it is more important to get the number of stitches right, since this determines the garment width. It is much easier to control the length of the garment, simply by working more or fewer rows, as necessary.

Checking your tension

The tension quoted for this sample is 15 stitches and 13 rows over half treble worked in double knitting yarn using a 4.00mm hook.

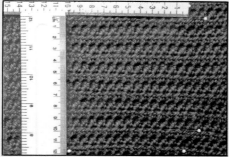

1 Make a tension square using a hook, yarn and stitch given in the tension, but work a few extra stitches.

2 The tension is gauged over 10cm, so make a square at least 10cm square to be able to check it correctly.

3 Pin the piece out on to a flat surface without stretching the stitches.

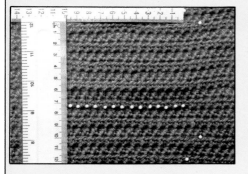

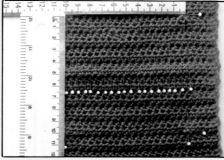

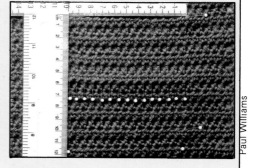

4 This sample has only 13 stitches to 10cm instead of the 15 quoted, so change to a smaller hook.

5 This sample has 19 stitches to 10cm, which is too many, so change to a larger hook.

6 Keep on changing to a smaller or larger hook until you achieve the correct tension as in this sample.

Paul Williams

Using a substitute yarn

If you are unable to buy the particular yarn quoted in your instructions it is sometimes possible to use a substitute, but it must be as near a match as possible.

To check your tension, work a 10cm square using the stitch and hook suggested, and measure to see if you need a larger or smaller hook size. If, by changing the hook size, you are able to obtain exactly the same tension as quoted it is all right to go ahead with the substitute yarn, although the garment will, of course, look and feel different from the original.

Step-by-step course – 4

* Making a treble fabric
* Joining with double crochet
* Scarf patterns

Making a treble fabric

A treble is the first of the long stitches used so frequently in crochet. It makes a more open fabric than double crochet and when used with fine yarns can produce a lattice effect. In filet crochet, for example, blocks of trebles are worked to form different motifs over an open lattice background. They can also be used in conjunction with double crochet and half-trebles to make shaped motifs such as shells.

Since the treble is a much longer stitch than a double crochet it is necessary to work three turning chain at the beginning of every row. Work the last stitch of every row into the top of the three turning chain of the previous row to keep the edge straight, and to prevent the yarn from pulling the work out of shape at the side edge.

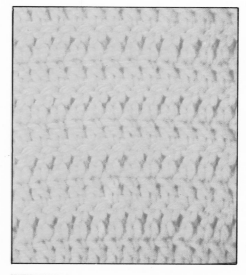

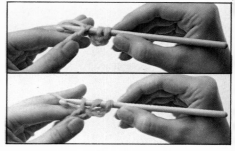

1 Make any number of chain, making two more chain than the number of stitches you will need, i.e. for 30 stitches make 32 chain. Wind the yarn round the hook. Insert the hook from front to back into fourth chain from hook.
2 Wind the yarn round the hook and draw through a loop. Three loops on hook.

3 Wind the yarn round the hook and draw it through the first two loops on the hook. Two loops remain on hook.

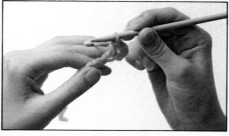

4 Wind the yarn round the hook and draw it through the last two loops on the hook. One treble made.

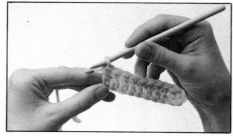

5 Work one treble in the same way into each chain to the end of the row.

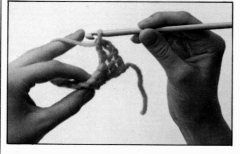

6 Turn work. Work three turning chain. Miss the first stitch. Work the first treble into the second stitch.

7 Work into each treble to end, work the last treble into the top of the turning chain of the previous row.

8 Continue to work in this way for the number of rows you need. Fasten off.

Paul Williams

Joining with double crochet

A decorative seam can be made by joining two pieces of fabric with double crochet. Make a feature of the seam by using a contrast-colour yarn. When worked on the wrong side of the fabric the seam gives a laced appearance on the right side.

1 Pin together two pieces of fabric to be joined just below the edge of the seam.

2 Insert hook through both thicknesses of fabric.

3 Loop the yarn round the hook and draw it through.

4 Work one chain with both ends of yarn and pull firmly to hold it in place.

5 Work one chain, one double crochet into next row end just below the edge.

6 Continue to work one double crochet into each row end to the end of the seam. Draw yarn through and fasten off.

7 When working with a treble fabric, work three stitches into every two row ends.

8 One chain can be worked between each stitch to spread the stitches along the seam.

Paul Williams

Scarves for all the family

Scarves that look good on all ages, worked in double knitting wool, using the stitches you have learnt so far. Turn back the bottom to make pockets joined with a decorative double crochet seam, or fold the scarf in half and join the two edges at the centre to make a cosy hood.

Scarf with pockets

Adult's scarf measures 20cm wide x 170cm long with pockets turned back.
Child's scarf measures 17cm wide x 122cm long with pockets turned back.

Tension
17sts and 10 rows to 10cm over treble worked on a 4.00mm hook.

Note follow the figures in brackets [] for the adult's scarf.

George Wright/accessories Fenwicks

Materials
8[10] 25g balls of double knitting yarn such as Sirdar Superwash Double Knitting.
4.00mm hook.
Small quantity of contrast colour yarn (optional).

To make scarf
Using a 4.00mm hook make 30 [36] chain.

☐ Work 1 treble into 4th chain from hook, 1 tr into each chain to end of row. 28 [34] treble.

☐ Continue working in rows of treble working 3 turning chain at the beginning of every row until work measures 154.5 [219] cm or the length you require. Fasten off. Darn in all ends.

To make pockets
Turn 14.5 [23] cm up at each end to form pockets and pin into place.
Join the pockets with double crochet.

☐ Work from right to left with the pocket facing you and folded edge to the right. Using a 4.00mm hook and contrast-colour yarn, insert hook from front to back through both thicknesses of scarf. Loop the yarn over the hook and draw a loop through. Work 1 chain using both ends of yarn to hold the stitch in place. Now work with 1 end of yarn only, work *1 chain, 1 double crochet into the next row end. Repeat from * to the end of the pocket, working the last double crochet into the corner of the pocket.

☐ Work the other side of the pocket in the same way, but beginning from the top edge of the pocket so that the front of the double crochet shows on the same side of the pocket.

☐ Work the other pocket in the same way. Darn in all ends.

☐ Press the scarf according to the instructions on the ball band.

Scarf with hood

Size
Adult's scarf measures 23cm wide x 162cm long.
Child's scarf measures 17cm wide x 142.5cm long.

Tension
17sts and 12½ rows to 10cm over double crochet worked on a 4.00mm hook.

Materials
7[11]x25g balls of double knitting yarn
4mm crochet hook
Note follow the figures in brackets [] for the adult's scarf.

To make scarf
Using a 4.00mm hook make 30 [41] chain.

☐ Work 1 double crochet into 3rd chain from hook, 1 double crochet into each chain to end. 29 [40] double crochet.

☐ *Work in rows of 3cm double crochet, 5cm half-treble, 7cm treble, 5cm half-treble. Repeat from * until work measures 142.5 [162] cm or length you require, ending with 3cm double crochet. Fasten off. Darn in all ends.

☐ Fold the scarf in half and pin seam together at centre for 18 [22] cm to form hood.

To join with double crochet
☐ Insert the hook from front to back at centre fold through both thicknesses of the scarf just below the edge of the seam. Loop the yarn over the hook and draw the yarn through. Wind 2 thicknesses of yarn round hook and draw through the loop to hold the yarn in place. Continue working through both thicknesses working 2 double crochet into each row end, for 18 [22] cm. Draw yarn through and fasten off. Darn in all ends.

☐ Press the scarf according to the instructions on the ball band.

Step-by-step course – 5

*Making a double treble fabric
*Making a triple treble fabric
*Fisherman's smock pattern
*Pattern for a tweedy-look tabard

Double and triple trebles, sometimes known as long trebles, are two of the longest of the crochet stitches and are made by winding the yarn two or three times round the hook before beginning to work the stitch.

When worked in a thick yarn they produce an open, chunky fabric that is very quick to make. They are more frequently used in fine lace crochet with other stitches to form either an openwork fabric or an interesting pattern.

It is important to remember that the turning chain must be lengthened to bring the hook up to the height of the stitch being worked; four chain are worked for a double treble and five for a triple treble. The chain counts as the first stitch.

Making a double treble fabric

1 Make any length of chain, making three more chain than the number of stitches you require, e.g. for ten stitches make 13 chain. Wind the yarn clockwise twice round the hook.

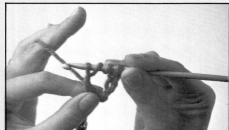

2 Insert the hook from front to back in to the fifth chain from the hook.

3 Wind the yarn clockwise round the hook.

4 Draw a loop through. There are now four loops on the hook.

5 Wind the yarn clockwise round the hook and draw it through the first two loops on the hook. Three loops left on the hook.

6 Wind the yarn clockwise round the hook and draw through the next two loops on the hook. Two loops left on hook.

7 Wind the yarn clockwise round the hook and draw it through the last two loops on the hook. One double treble has been made.

8 Work one double treble in the same way into each chain to end. Turn.

9 Make four turning chain.

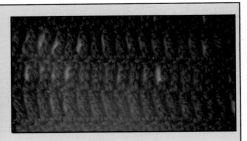

10 Miss the first stitch. Work one double treble into the second stitch, working under the two horizontal loops in the normal way.

11 Work one double treble into each stitch to the end of the row. Work the last double treble into the top of the turning chain of the previous row.

12 Repeat the last three steps for as many rows as you require. Draw the yarn through the loop and fasten off.

Making a triple treble fabric

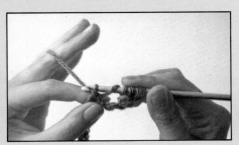

1 Make any length of chain, making four more chain than the number of stitches you require, e.g. for 12 stitches make 16 chain. Wind yarn clockwise three times round the hook.

2 Insert the hook from front to back into the sixth chain from the hook. Wind yarn round the hook and draw through a loop. Five loops on the hook.

3 Wind yarn round the hook and draw through first two loops. Four loops on the hook.

4 Repeat step 3 twice more. Two loops left on the hook.

5 Wind yarn round the hook and draw through last two loops on the hook. One triple treble made.

6 Work one triple treble in same way into each chain to end. Turn. Work five turning chain.

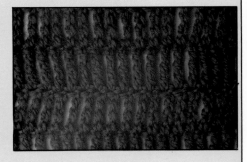

7 Miss the first stitch. Work one triple treble into second stitch, working under two horizontal loops in the normal way.

8 Work one triple treble into each stitch to end. Work last triple treble into the top of the turning chain of the previous row.

9 Repeat the last three steps for the number of rows required. Draw yarn through and fasten off.

Fisherman's smock

Get out and about in this simply styled cotton fisherman's smock. With draw-string waist and side-opening pocket it is made in double treble stitch – the sleeves and yoke are worked straight across from cuff to cuff.

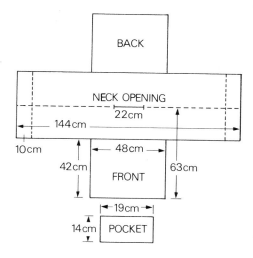

Size

To fit 87/92cm bust.
Length to shoulder, 63cm.
Sleeve seam, 48cm.
To make the top bigger add approximately 3 stitches for every extra 2cm to be added.

Tension

13 sts and 5½ rows to 10cm worked over double trebles on a 4.00mm hook.

Materials

650g of 3 Suisses Alezan Cotton
4.00 mm crochet hook

Back

Using 4.00mm hook make 65 chain.
Work 1 double treble into 5th chain from hook, then 1 double treble into each chain to end. Turn. 62 double trebles.
☐ Continue to work in rows of double treble with 4 turning chain at beginning of every row until piece measures 42cm from beginning.
☐ Draw yarn through and fasten off.

Front

Work in same way as for back.

Sleeves and yoke (worked in one piece)
Begin at cuff, work first sleeve, yoke,
then second sleeve and end at cuff.
☐ Using 4.00mm hook make 62 chain.
Work first row as given for back.
back until piece measures 61cm, ending
☐ Work in rows of double treble as for
back until sleeve measures 61cm, ending
at right-hand edge of right side of work.
This will be the lower edge of front yoke.

Shape neck

Work in double treble on first 29 stitches
only for front neck, leaving remaining 29
stitches unworked. Continue for 22cm,
ending at neck edge. Fasten off. Return
to the last complete row worked.
☐ Rejoin yarn to remaining stitches at
neck edge and work back yoke on these
stitches, working the same number of
rows as for front, ending at the *side
edge*. Turn.
☐ Work across 29 stitches of back yoke,
then across the 29 stitches of front yoke.
58 sts.
☐ Complete the yoke and sleeve on these
stitches.
☐ Continue for a further 61cm. Draw
yarn through and fasten off.

To make pocket

Using 4.00mm hook make 19 chain.
☐ Work 1 half treble into 3rd chain from
hook, 1 half treble into each chain to
end. Turn. 18 half trebles.
☐ Work 19cm on these stitches.
Draw yarn through and fasten off.

To make up

Darn in all loose ends of yarn on wrong
side of work.
☐ Mark a point with coloured thread on
both sleeves at front and back, 48cm
from edge of cuff.
☐ Using the markers as a guide, pin the
front to front yoke and the back to back
yoke and sew in place using a flat
seam.
☐ Join side and sleeve seams using a
back stitch seam, reversing the seam for
10cm at each cuff.
☐ Work a row of double crochet all
round pocket, neck edge, cuffs and welt.
☐ Sew on pocket to front at top and
bottom so that openings are at the side.
Turn back cuffs to right side.

To make the cord

Make a chain 117cm long.
☐ Insert hook into 2nd chain from hook
and draw yarn through both loops to
make 1 slip stitch. Work 1 slip stitch
into each chain to end.
☐ Fasten off and darn in loose ends.
Thread cord through double treble at
welt and draw up.

Country-life tabard

**Using double treble stitches, make this tweedy-look tabard
for out-of-doors days in country or town. Made out of two
simple rectangles, the shoulders are joined with fine double
crochet and the sides are laced with crochet chain.**

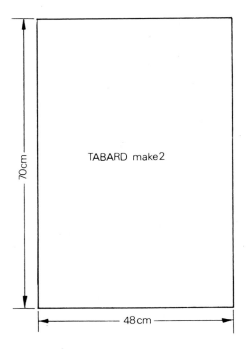

TABARD make 2

70cm

48cm

Size

The instructions given here are for a
medium size, 87/92cm bust.
Length to shoulder, 70cm.
To make the tabard bigger work
approximately 1 stitch more for every
centimetre you wish to add.

Tension

9 stitches and 3½ rows to 10cm over
double treble on a 5.50mm hook.

Materials

*750g of chunky knitting yarn such as
Hayfield Saxon
Small quantity of double knitting
wool in a contrast colour
5.50mm hook
4.00mm hook*

Front and back sections

Using chunky yarn and 5.50mm
hook make 47 chain for back. Work
1 double treble into 5th chain from
hook, 1 double treble into each chain
to end.
☐ Continue to work in rows of double
treble making 4 turning chain at the
beginning of every row, until the piece
measures 70cm from the beginning,
measured with work flat.
Draw yarn through and fasten off.

☐ Work the front in the same way.
☐ Darn in all the loose ends on the
wrong side of the work.

To work the edging

Join the chunky yarn to the right
side of one piece at the shoulder edge.
Work 1 chain, then 1 double crochet
and 1 chain down the side edge,
working into the double treble at the
end of each row.
☐ Work down other side edge in the
same way. Finish other piece to match.

Joining shoulders with crochet braid

By working a few rows of double crochet
in a fine yarn you can obtain a braid
effect on the edge of a chunky fabric
and it is possible to join two pieces
together by working through both the
edge stitches of one piece and the braid
stitches at the same time, to make a
contrasting seam.
☐ With the right side of the front
facing join double knitting yarn
to left shoulder edge. Using 4.00mm
hook make 1 chain, then work 1 double
crochet and 1 chain along the shoulder
edge for 13.5cm.

Lacing of tabard in another colourway.

☐ Turn and work 1 double crochet into each double crochet and chain to the end. Work 1 more row of double crochet in to these stitches.

☐ With the right side of the back facing match the shoulder edges of front and back. Insert hook through back and through first stitch of the edging just worked. Draw the yarn through and work a double crochet in the normal way through both thicknesses.

☐ Continue working in double crochet in this way to join the shoulder together, working into the corresponding stitches of back and front. When you have reached the shoulder edge, draw yarn through and fasten off.

☐ Work the other shoulder in the same way, starting from the neck edge.

☐ Darn in all the loose ends on the wrong side of the work using a wool needle.

Joining the sides with lacing

Mark a point 26cm from shoulder edge at either side for armholes.

☐ Using double knitting yarn and 4.00mm hook make 180 chain. Draw yarn through and fasten off. Make another chain in the same way. Lace the chain through the side seams to join them for 24cm.

Optional belt

If you wish to make a belt make a chain in the chunky yarn about 170cm long and work one row of double crochet then fasten off. Make another narrow belt in the double knitting yarn making a strip by working 4 double crochet for the same length. Fasten off.
Twist them together to make the belt.

Step-by-step course – 6

*Shaping with double crochet and half trebles
*Working a slip stitch
*Baby smock patterns

Shaping with double crochet and half trebles

Because of the height of most crochet stitches, it is important to take care when increasing or decreasing a stitch at the fabric edge, otherwise the edge may not be straight and smooth. You only have to miss one stitch at the beginning or end of a row when you are decreasing a stitch to get an edge that is uneven and stepped. This is not only unattractive, but also difficult to seam and happens particularly when working with half trebles. To avoid this a single stitch is usually decreased by working two stitches together, one stitch in from the edge. It is also better to increase one stitch on the second and second to last stitch in a row, to get a really smooth edge.

To decrease one double crochet at each end of a row

1 Work 1 turning chain at the beginning of the row and miss the 1st stitch in the usual way.

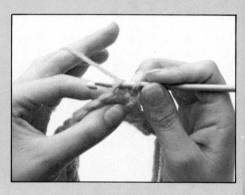

2 Insert hook from front to back into next stitch.

3 Wind yarn clockwise round hook and draw through a loop. 2 loops on hook.

4 Insert hook into next stitch. Wind yarn clockwise round hook and draw through a loop. 3 loops on hook.

5 Wind yarn round hook and draw through all 3 loops on hook. 1 stitch decreased.

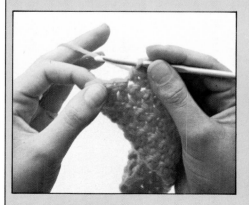

6 Work in double crochet to last 3 stitches.

7 Work the next 2 stitches together by repeating steps 2 to 5.

8 Work the last stitch into the turning chain of the previous row.

To decrease one half treble at each end of a row

1 Work 2 turning chain at the beginning of the row and miss the 1st stitch in the usual way.

2 Wind yarn round hook and insert hook into next stitch.

3 Wind yarn round hook and draw through a loop. 3 loops on hook.

4 Wind yarn round hook. Insert hook into next stitch.

5 Wind yarn round hook and draw through a loop. 5 loops on hook.

6 Wind yarn round hook and draw through all 5 loops on hook. 1 stitch decreased.

7 Work 1 half treble into each stitch to last 3 stitches.

8 Work next 2 stitches together by repeating steps 2 to 6.

9 Work the last half treble into the turning chain of the previous row. 1 stitch has been decreased at each end of row.

Paul Williams

163

To increase one double crochet at each end of a row

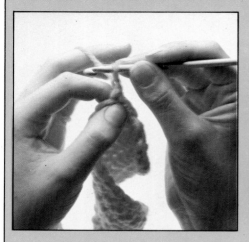

1 Work the turning chain at the beginning of the row in the usual way.

2 Miss first double crochet, work 2 double crochet into the 2nd stitch of the previous row.

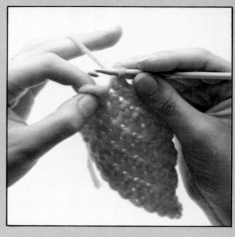

3 Continue to work into each stitch to the last 2 double crochet.

4 Work 2 double crochet into the next stitch.

5 Work the last double crochet into the turning chain of the previous row. 1 stitch has been increased at each end.

6 Work in exactly the same way for half trebles.

Working a slip stitch

It is possible to use crochet slip stitch in various ways, but however it is used the working method is always the same. Use it as a means of shaping: either by working over several stitches at the beginning of a row to decrease them, or as a means of getting from one point to another in a row (when making button-holes or shaping a neck).

Alternatively, slip stitch can be used for joining the two ends of a round when working circular motifs.

Slip stitch is seldom used on its own in a pattern, except for making a crochet cord. The shallowness of the stitch produces a firm cord, which is often used for fastening baby clothes.

To make a crochet cord

1 Make the length of chain you require. Insert the hook from front to back into the 2nd chain from hook.

2 Wind the yarn clockwise round the hook.

continued

continued : to make a crochet cord

3 Draw a loop through both loops on the hook. 1 slip stitch made.

4 Work 1 slip stitch into each chain to the end to make the cord.

5 To make a firmer cord with a plaited appearance work 1 slip stitch into each chain along the other side.

Paul Williams

Three baby smocks

Three pretty variations on the smock theme; one with sleeves, two without, worked in double crochet and trebles. Made in a fine, soft yarn, they are either plain or striped, with easy shaping on the skirt.

Baby's smock with sleeves

Size
To fit a baby up to 6 months old.
Length from shoulder, 28.5cm, excluding contrast edging.
Sleeve seam, 15cm.

Materials
100g of Pingouin Mademoiselle 4 ply
Small quantity of contrast colour for edging and back ties
1.75mm crochet hook
2.00mm crochet hook
Note you could make the smock striped by working every two rows in a contrasting colour.

Tension
24 stitches and 12 rows to 10cm over treble worked on a 1.75mm hook.

Kim Sayer/Dress — Harrods

To make smock front
Using 1.75mm hook make 58 chain. Work 1 treble into 4th chain from hook, 1 treble into each chain to end. 56 stitches.
☐ Work 20 rows in treble crochet, increasing one stitch at each end of every row by working 1 stitch into the first stitch after the turning chain instead of missing it at the beginning of the row and 2 stitches into the 2nd to last stitch at the end of the row. The skirt will measure approximately 17.5cm and there will be a total of 96 stitches in all.
Draw yarn through last loop and fasten off.

To make bodice
Return to chain at beginning of skirt. Miss first 7 chain for armhole. With right side facing, using 2.00mm hook, rejoin yarn to the 8th chain and work a row of double crochet across the chain, working the last double crochet into the 8th chain from the end, leaving the last 7 chain for the second armhole.
☐ Continue working in double crochet on these 44 stitches for 6cm.

To shape neck
Work across first 16 double crochet on next row, then turn and work on these stitches only for one side of neck.

165

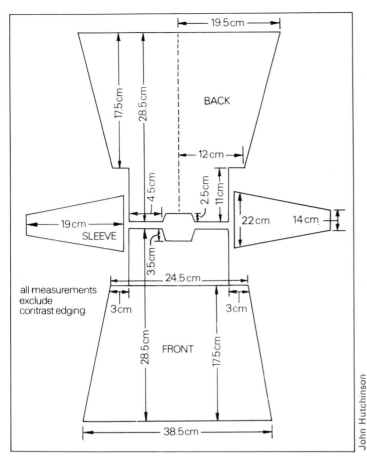

John Hutchinson

□ Decrease 1 stitch at the beginning of the next row for the neck edge, then continue in double crochet to the end of the row. Turn.

□ Continue to decrease 1 stitch at the *beginning* of every alternate row in the same way until 11 stitches remain. You will be decreasing 1 stitch at the neck edge. Draw yarn through the last loop and fasten off. Return to the stitches at the centre of the bodice.

□ With the right side of the front facing, miss the first 12 stitches for the centre neck and rejoin the yarn to the next double crochet.

□ Complete other side of neck to match the first, decreasing 1 stitch at neck edge on every alternate row, until 11 stitches remain.

□ Draw yarn through last loop and fasten off.

To make right back

Using 1.75mm hook make 29 chain. Work the 1st row as given for front. 27 stitches.

□ Increase 1 stitch at the beginning of the next row as given for front. Increase 1 stitch in the same way at the same edge on every row, keeping the other edge straight for centre back opening, until skirt measures the same as the back skirt. There should be 47 stitches. Draw yarn through last loop and fasten off.

To make bodice

Return to chain at beginning of skirt.

□ With right side of work facing and using a 2.00mm hook, rejoin yarn to 8th chain from shaped side edge, leaving the first 7 chain for armhole. Work in double crochet to end of row. 22 stitches.

□ Continue without shaping until bodice measures 8cm from beginning, ending at armhole edge.

To shape neck

Work across first 13 double crochet on next row, turn and leave remaining stitches for back neck.

□ Decrease 1 stitch at beginning of next and every following alternate row in the same way as for the front until 11 stitches remain and work measures the same as the front to shoulder. Draw yarn through and fasten off.

To make the left back

Work in the same way as the right back, but work increases at the end of the row instead of at the beginning, on the skirt. Miss 7 chain at the end of the row for the armhole, instead of at the beginning, to reverse the shaping. Work the neck shaping in reverse in exactly the same way.

To make the sleeves

Join shoulder seams using a back stitch seam.

□ Using a 1.75mm hook and with right side of the front facing, rejoin yarn to inside armhole at shaped side edge. Work 1 row of double crochet up one side of yoke, to shoulder then down other side of yoke to inside edge of armhole. 58 sts. Turn. Work 2 rows in treble on these stitches.

□ Continue working in treble, decreasing 1 stitch at beginning of every row until sleeve measures 19cm from beginning. Draw yarn through last loop and fasten off. Work 2nd sleeve in same way on other side of yoke.

To make up

Darn in all loose ends of yarn on wrong side of smock. Press lightly according to instructions on the ball band. With wrong side of work facing join top edges of sleeves to armholes at top of skirt, using a flat seam.

□ Join side and sleeve seams using a back stitch seam.

To work edging

Using main colour and 1.75mm hook and with right side of left back facing, join yarn to corner and work a row of double crochet all round, up right back, round neck and down left back to corner, working 3 double crochet into each corner stitch and missing 1 stitch at each corner of inside neck. Draw yarn through last loop and fasten off.

To make contrast edging and ties

With right side of work facing join contrast colour yarn to same corner as before.

☐ Work 1 double crochet all round hem and up back edge to point where skirt is joined to bodice, work 65 chain, then work 1 slip stitch into each chain just worked, back to edge again. This forms first tie.

☐ Continue to work in double crochet to first neck edge corner, then work another tie in the same way.

☐ Continue to work in double crochet round neck without missing 1 stitch at inside neck edges to next back edge corner. Work another tie in the same way at this corner. Complete the edging working another tie in the same way where yoke joins skirt. Draw yarn through last loop and fasten off. Darn in all ends on wrong side of work.

Baby's sleeveless smock

Size

To fit a baby up to 6 months old.

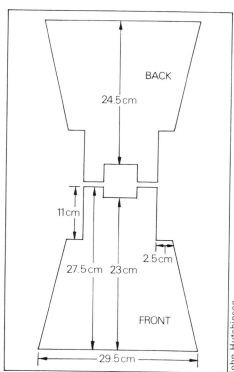

John Hutchinson

Tension

24 stitches and 12 rows to 10cm worked over treble on a 1.75mm hook.

Materials

50g of Pingouin Mademoiselle 4 ply in one colour for skirt, called A
50g of the same yarn in a contrast colour for the bodice, called B
The striped version also takes 50g of A and 50g of B
1.75mm crochet hook
2.00mm crochet hook

Steve Bicknell

Note to make the striped version work two rows in each colour down skirt, ending by working one row in the first colour used. Work the yoke all in one colour.

To make the front skirt

Using 1.75mm hook and A, make 58 chain.

☐ Work 1 treble into 4th chain from hook, 1 treble into each chain to end. Turn. 56 trebles. Continue to work in trebles, increasing 1 stitch at the beginning of every row by working 1 treble into the first stitch after the turning chain, until the skirt measures 12.5cm from the beginning. You should have worked approximately 21 rows and have 76 stitches in all. Draw yarn through last loop and fasten off.

To make the front yoke

Return to the chain at the beginning of the skirt.

☐ With the right side of the skirt facing, using B and 2.00mm hook, rejoin yarn to the 8th chain from the side edge, leaving the first 7 chain for the armhole. Work 1 turning chain, then 1 double crochet into each chain, working the last double crochet into the 8th chain from the end, leaving the last 7 chain for the second armhole.

☐ Continue working in rows of double crochet on these stitches for 6cm. Work across first 13 double crochet, turn and work on these stitches only for 3cm.

To shape neck

Fasten off. Return to stitches at neck edge. Miss first 18 stitches for centre neck. Rejoin yarn to next stitch and complete to

match first side. Draw yarn through and fasten off.

To make the back skirt

Work exactly as given for front skirt.

To make the back yoke

Work exactly as given for front, but work for 7.5cm before shaping the neck and work for 1.5cm only for neck so that the yoke is the same depth as front yoke.

To make up

Darn all loose ends in to wrong side of work. Press pieces lightly, following instructions on the ball band. Join side seams using a flat seam.

To work edging and shoulder ties

Using 1.75mm hook, B and with right side of front facing, join yarn to underarm at side seam. Work a row of double crochet round armhole to shoulder.

☐ Work 65 chain at corner of shoulder, turn and slip stitch into each chain just worked, back to shoulder to make the first tie. Work in double crochet to next corner and work another tie in same way. Continue to work round neck in double crochet, missing 1 stitch at inside neck corners, then work across shoulders, and make a tie at each of the corners as before.

☐ Work down the armhole and round back in the same way, making 1 tie at each corner on shoulders as before. Join the last double crochet to the first double crochet worked with a slip stitch. Draw yarn through and fasten off. Darn in any loose ends on the wrong side of the work using a blunt-ended wool needle.

Step-by-step course –7

*How to shape a treble or
 double treble fabric
*How to increase and
 decrease several stitches at
 each end of a row
*Pattern for an evening
 sweater

How to shape a treble or double treble fabric

Because of the depth of both the treble and double treble stitches it is important to take care when working your shaping, in order to achieve a neat, firm edge to your fabric.

Unless a pattern specifically states the method to be used, it is better to work the shaping one stitch in from the edge, in order to avoid making a step in your fabric, which is particularly noticeable when working long crochet stitches in thicker yarns, and can cause difficulties when making up your garment.

To increase a treble or double treble at each end of a row

Stitches are increased at either end of the row in exactly the same way as for double crochet or half trebles : work two stitches into the stitch after the turning chain at the beginning of the row : then work across the row until only two stitches remain, including the turning chain, then work two stitches into the next stitch ; finally, work the last stitch into the turning chain of the previous row. You will have increased two extra stitches – one stitch at each end of the row within a one-stitch border.

To decrease one treble at each end of a row

1 Make 3 chain at beginning of row where stitch is to be decreased.

2 Miss the first stitch in the normal way. Wind the yarn round the hook and insert hook into next stitch.

3 Wind yarn round hook and draw through a loop.

4 Wind yarn round hook and draw it through first 2 loops on hook.

5 Wind yarn round hook and insert it into next stitch.

6 Wind yarn round hook and draw a loop through.

Continued : decreasing one treble at each end of a row

7 There are now 4 loops on the hook.

8 Wind yarn round hook and draw it through first 2 loops on hook. 3 loops remain.

9 Wind yarn round hook and draw it through last 3 loops on hook. 2 treble have been worked together to decrease 1 stitch.

10 Work 1 treble into each treble until 3 stitches remain unworked. Do not forget to count the turning chain as 1 stitch.

11 Work the next 2 trebles together in the same way as at beginning of row. 1 stitch decreased at end of row.

12 Work the last treble into the turning chain of previous row.

To decrease one double treble at each end of a row

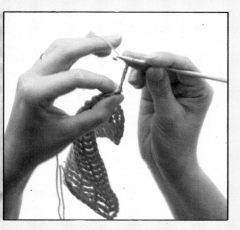

1 Work 4 chain at beginning of row where stitch is to be decreased.

2 Miss the first stitch in the normal way. Wind the yarn twice round the hook and insert the hook into the next stitch.

3 Wind yarn round hook and draw through a loop. 4 loops on the hook.

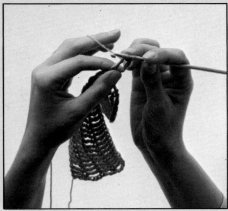

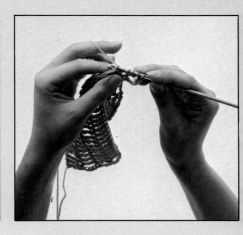

4 Wind yarn round hook and draw it through first 2 loops on hook.

5 Wind yarn round hook and draw it through next 2 loops on hook. 2 loops remain.

6 Wind yarn twice round hook and insert hook into next stitch.

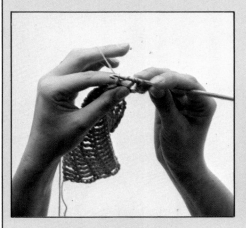

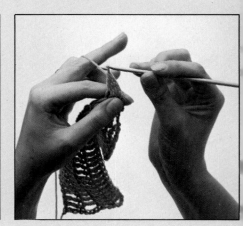

7 Wind yarn round hook and draw a loop through. 5 loops on the hook.

8 Repeat steps 4 and 5. 3 loops remain on hook.

9 Wind yarn round hook and draw through all 3 loops on hook. 2 double treble have been worked together to decrease 1 stitch.

10 Work 1 double treble into each stitch across row until 3 stitches remain unworked. Do not forget to count the turning chain as 1 stitch.

11 Work the next 2 double treble together in the same way as at beginning of row. 1 stitch decreased.

12 Work the last double treble into the turning chain at the end of the row.

How to increase or decrease several stitches at each end of a row

It is possible to increase several stitches at each end of a row by working extra chain for each additional stitch required. When increasing stitches at the beginning of the row you will also need to add extra chain to allow for the turning chain, remembering that the number of turning chain will vary according to the stitch being worked. For example, if you are going to add an extra four double crochet you will need to make five chain

in all, whereas for four treble you will need to make six chain in all. The method for decreasing several stitches at the beginning or end of a row is the same for all crochet stitches. Work in slip stitch over the number of stitches to be decreased at the beginning of the row, then work a slip stitch into the next stitch and make the correct number of turning chain before working across the row in the normal way. To decrease several stitches

at the end of the row simply leave the required number of stitches unworked, remembering to always count the turning chain as one stitch, then turn and work back along the next row. Since the technique used for increasing several stitches at each end of the row is the same for all stitches, follow the working method given for double crochet but substitute the correct number of turning chain for the stitch being used.

To increase several double crochet at each end of a row

1 Work the extra number of chain you require at the beginning of the row, e.g. 5 chain for 4 double crochet.

2 Work the first double crochet into the 3rd chain from the hook, then 1 double crochet into each extra chain.

3 Continue to work in double crochet across row until 2 stitches remain. This will include the turning chain.

4 Leave the working loop on a spare hook.

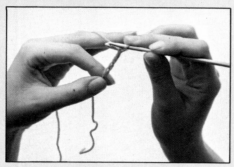

5 With a spare length of the correct yarn make a length of chain for the exact number of extra stitches, e.g. 4 chain for 4 double crochet.

6 Join this length of chain to the end of the row with a slip stitch. Fasten off yarn

7 Return to the working loop and work 1 double crochet into each of the last 2 stitches.

8 Work 1 double crochet into each of the extra chain. 4 double crochet increased at each end of row.

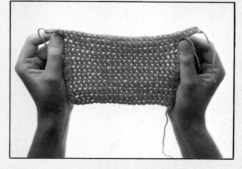

9 Work in double crochet across all stitches on the next row, including those just made.

Fluffy and flattering

Make something special for winter evenings. This glamorous mohair-look sweater, with batwing sleeves and bloused shape, has ribbons threaded through for added fashion interest.

Size
To fit 83 to 97cm bust.
Length to shoulder, 61cm.
Sleeve seam, 6.5cm.

Tension
9 stitches and 4 rows to 10cm worked over double treble on a 5.50mm hook.

Materials
Total of 325g of mohair-type yarn
such as Wendy Sorbet
4.00mm crochet hook
5.50mm crochet hook
9m of 2.5cm-wide ribbon

Back and front (made in one piece)
□ Begin at lower edge of front. Using 5.50mm hook make 42 chain loosely.
Shape front
□ Work 1 double treble into 5th chain from hook, 1 double treble into same chain to increase 1 stitch, 1 double treble into each chain until 2 chain remain unworked, work 2 double treble into next chain to increase 1 stitch, 1 double treble into last chain. Turn. 41 double treble.
□ Work 4 chain to count as first double treble, miss first double treble, 2 double treble into next double treble to increase 1 stitch, 1 double treble into each stitch until 2 double treble remain unworked, work 2 double treble into next stitch to increase 1 stitch, work last double treble into turning chain of previous row. Turn.
□ Repeat the last row 14 times more.

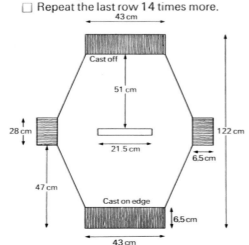

There will now be 71 double treble.
Work sleeves
□ Place a marker at each end of last row to denote beginning of sleeves.
□ Work 5 rows double treble without shaping.
Make neck opening
□ Work over first 26 double treble, work 19 chain loosely, then miss next 19 double treble for neck opening, work 1 double treble into each stitch to end of row. Turn. Work over first 26 double treble, work 1 double treble into each of next 19 chain, work 1 double treble into each stitch to end of row. Turn. 71 double treble.
□ Work 4 rows without shaping. Place a marker at each end of last row to denote end of sleeves.
Shape back
□ Work 4 chain to count as first stitch, work next 2 double treble together to decrease 1 stitch, work 1 double treble into each stitch until 3 stitches remain unworked, work next 2 double treble together to decrease 1 stitch, work last double treble into turning chain of previous row. Turn.
□ Repeat last row 15 times more. 39 double treble remain.
□ Draw yarn through and fasten off.

To make back welt
□ Using 4.00mm hook make 12 chain. Work 1 treble into 4th chain from hook, then 1 treble into each chain to end. Turn. 10 treble.
□ Work 3 chain to count as first treble, work 1 treble into back loop only of each stitch to end. Turn.
□ Repeat last row until welt is long enough to fit along lower edge.
□ Draw yarn through and fasten off.

To make front welt
Work exactly as given for back welt.

To make cuffs
□ Work as given for back welt until cuff fits along sleeve edge between markers.
□ Work another cuff in the same way.

To make up
□ Darn in all loose ends to wrong side using a blunt-ended wool needle.
□ Thread ribbon through (here over and under every 3 stitches, every 3rd row), secure the ends.
□ Using a flat seam sew welts to lower edge of back and front.
□ Using a flat seam sew cuffs to sleeves between markers.
□ Join underarm and side seams.

Step-by-step course – 8

* Working horizontal striped fabric
* Working vertical stripes — two methods
* Working diagonal stripes
* Start using abbreviations
* Pattern for a child's pinafore

Working horizontal stripes

Stripes are a good way to add extra colour or detail to a garment. They can be in sharp, contrasting colours or subtle shades. They can cross the fabric horizontally, vertically or diagonally. By varying the width of each stripe you can achieve a pleasing random effect.

Horizontal stripes are easy to work, especially if you use an even number of rows in each colour so that each colour begins and ends at the same edge. Our sample uses two colours, called A and B, and is worked in double crochet.

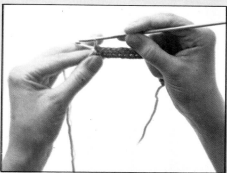

1 Make the desired number of chain with A. Work two rows with A, but do not complete the last stitch of the second row ; leave two loops on hook.

2 Loop B over hook and draw it through working loop. This completes the last stitch. Do not break off A.

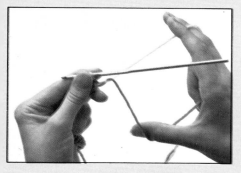

3 Turn the work. Twist B over and under A to hold A in place. Each colour is carried up the side of the work until it is needed again.

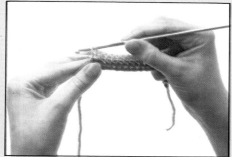

4 Work the next two rows in B. Do not complete the last stitch ; leave two loops on the hook.

5 Pick up A and complete stitch in A.

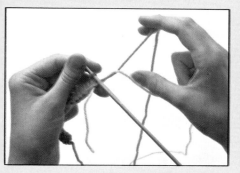

6 Turn the work. Twist A over and under B to hold B in place.

7 Continue to work stripes in A and B, carrying yarns up the side until the desired number of stripes have been worked. Fasten off.

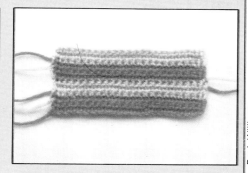

8 If you work an uneven number of rows in any colour you will need to break off the yarn and rejoin it at the other edge as shown.

Paul Williams

Working vertical stripes

This simple method is used where the stripes are only two or three stitches wide and the yarn is not too thick. The yarn is

The stranding method

carried across the back of the work. Our sample is made in double crochet and, uses two colours, A and B.

1 Make 19 chain with A ; with A work one double crochet.

2 Change from A to B on next stitch by completing stitch with B. The first three stitches (turning chain counts as first stitch) will be in A.

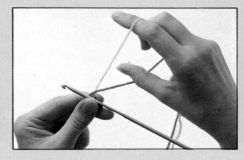

3 Wind B round A. Keep A at back of work.

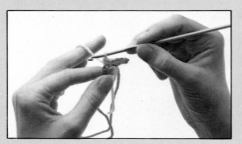

4 Work next two stitches in B.

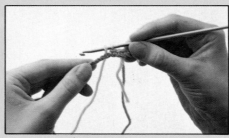

5 Insert hook into next stitch and draw through a loop. Leave B at back of work.

6 Pick up A. Carry A over B and complete stitch in A, taking care not to pull the stranded yarn too tight. There will be three stitches in B.

7 Continue to work three stitches in A and three in B across row in same way, but complete last stitch in B.

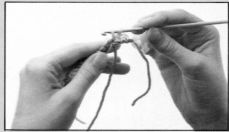

8 Turn and work first two stitches in B, insert hook into next stitch and draw through a loop. A will be at front of work.

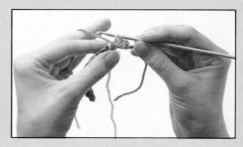

9 Bring B to front of work, then take A over B to back of work.

10 Complete stitch with A.

11 Continue to work in stripes across row, changing colours in same way each time, but complete last stitch in A.

12 Repeat these two rows until stripe pattern is complete. Fasten off.

The weaving method

The weaving method is used where the stripes are more than three stitches wide. The yarn being carried across the back of the work is linked in on top of one of the stitches in the stripe. The yarn is woven neatly into the back of the fabric.

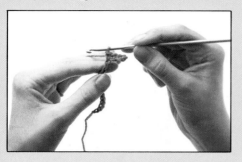

1 Work 21 chain in A, and work first three double crochet in A.

2 Change from A to B on next stitch by completing stitch with B. The first five stitches (including turning chain) will be in A.

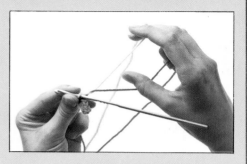

3 Wind B round A. Keep A at back of work.

4 Work next two stitches in B. As you work the third stitch in B, hold A against the top edge of the row and crochet over it with the next stitch, taking care not to pull the stranded yarn too tight.

5 Keeping A at the back, work two more stitches in B, changing to A on the second stitch. Five stitches have now been worked in A and five in B.

6 Continue to work five stitches in A and five in B across row in same way, linking in the colour being woven on the third stitch of every stripe, but complete last stitch in B.

7 Turn and work the first four stitches in B, remembering to count the turning chain as the first stitch, and noting that A will be at front of work.

8 Insert hook into next stitch and draw through a loop.

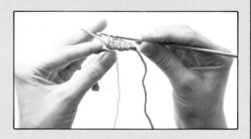

9 Bring B to front of work, then take A to back of work.

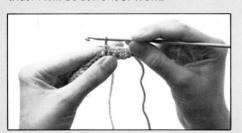

10 Complete stitch with A.

11 Continue to work in stripes across row, changing and linking in colours in the same way each time, but complete last stitch in A.

12 Repeat these two rows until stripe pattern is complete. Fasten off.

Paul Williams

Working diagonal stripes

These are worked in exactly the same way as vertical stripes, except that one stitch on each stripe is moved either to the right or to the left on every row to slant the stitches diagonally from right to left or left to right.

Strand the yarn across the back of the work and change the colours as needed in the same way as when working vertical stripes.

Start using abbreviations

Crochet has its own technical terms and a special language – a kind of shorthand – for describing instructions in a clear, concise way. Without this shorthand, the instructions for any but the simplest crochet are far too long and tedious to follow.

The abbreviations given here are for simple techniques that you already know: gradually these and other crochet notation will be introduced into patterns in the courses. As you become more practised at your crochet, you will find following the abbreviations becomes quite easy and automatic.

ch	=	chain
dc	=	double crochet
htr	=	half treble
tr	=	treble
dtr	=	double treble
tr tr	=	triple treble
st(s)	=	stitch(es)

Playtime pinny

What more could a small girl want? This practical pinafore dress is just the thing for a winter day's play. She will wear it time and again over jumpers, polo tops and blouses.

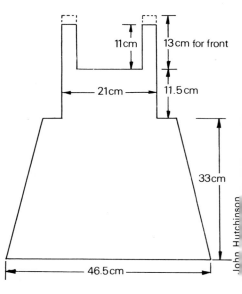

11cm

13cm for front

21cm

11.5cm

33cm

46.5cm

Size
To fit chest, 61cm.
Length, 56cm.

Tension
16sts and 14 rows to 10cm over htr on 4.00mm hook.

Materials
2 x 50g balls of Patons Fiona in main shade A, 1 ball each of contrasting colours B, C and D
4.00mm crochet hook
Waist length of elastic 15mm wide
2 buttons

Back

Using 4.00mm hook and B, make 74ch.
Base row Into 3rd ch from hook work 1htr, 1htr into each ch to end, joining in C on last htr. Turn.
Next row Using C, work 2ch to count as 1htr, 1htr into each htr to end, joining in A on last htr. Turn.
Continuing in htr, joining in colours as before, proceed as follows:
1st row Work with A.
2nd to 4th rows Work 2B, *3D, 3B, repeat from * to last 5sts, 3D, 2B.
5th row Work with A, but decrease 1htr at each end of row.
6th row Work with C.
7th row Work with B.
Working with A only, decrease 1htr at each end of 12th and every following 5th row until 57htr remain. Work 4 rows straight. Draw yarn through and fasten off.

Next row Miss first 12sts, join B to next st, 2ch, 1htr into each of next 32sts. Turn. Proceed on these 33sts as follows:
Next 3 rows Work 3B, *3D, 3B, repeat from * to end.
Work 1 row each in A, C, B and A.
Next 3 rows Work 3C, *3B, 3C, repeat from * to end.
Work 1 row each in A, D and B.
Next row Using C, work 2ch, 1htr into each of next 6htr. Turn.
Continue on these 7htr for strap, working in stripes of 1 row D, 1 row B and 1 row C until strap measures 11cm. Draw yarn through and fasten off.
Miss centre 19htr, join C to next htr, 2ch, 1htr into each of next 6htr. Continue on these 7htr to match first strap.

Front

Work as given for back, but make straps 13cm long instead of 11cm.

To make up

Sew in ends. Press lightly under a damp cloth with a warm iron. Using a flat seam, join the side seams.
Using B and with right side facing work a row of dc round outer edge of bib and straps.

Work herringbone casing over elastic on wrong side at waist. Sew 1 button to top of each back strap and use holes between htr on front straps to fasten.

Step-by-step course – 9

*Working with separate balls of yarn
*Working longer stitches
*Pattern for a shawl

A tremendous variety of shapes and patterns can be achieved in crochet by using different colours. The possibilities include motifs repeated at regular intervals across your fabric, large motifs such as diamonds or rectangles, blocks of colours worked in a random pattern and a variety of colours to produce a patchwork effect.

Working with separate balls of yarn

Where the motif being worked is small and is repeated several times at regular intervals across the fabric, the yarn can be carried across the back of the work in the same way as for vertical stripes. Large motifs or patchwork patterns, however, should be worked using separate balls of yarn for each colour. This avoids wasting unnecessary lengths of yarn.

The separate balls can be wound on to a shaped piece of card, which acts rather like a bobbin and helps to prevent the different colours from becoming tangled. Our sample shows the technique used in wide stripes of double crochet and uses two colours, called A and B.

1 Make 31 chain with A and work 30 double crochet into chain. Turn.

2 Work first nine double crochet with A.

3 Insert hook into next stitch and draw a loop through.

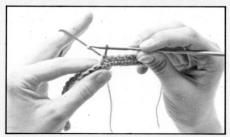

4 Draw next colour through working loop to complete stitch.

5 Wind B round A at back of work, passing B under and then over A. This winding of one yarn round the other prevents a gap where the stripes or shapes meet.

6 Work next nine double crochet in B, then change from B to second ball of A, repeating steps 3 and 4.

7 Repeat step 5 winding A round B.

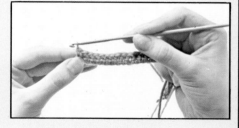

8 Work the last ten double crochet in A.

continued

Continued : working with separate balls of yarn

9 Turn and work first nine stitches in A. The wrong side of the work will be facing.

10 Insert hook into next stitch and draw a loop through.

11 Bring A to front of work, take B to back of work and complete stitch with B.

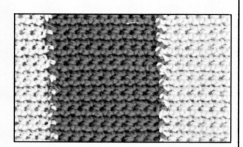

12 Continue to change colours at beginning of each stripe across the row in the same way, keeping the yarn not in use at the back of the work each time.

13 Work at least ten rows in this way so that you are familiar with the working method and can cope with both colours easily.

14 Sample showing the wrong side of the fabric.

Working longer stitches

Double crochet is really the ideal stitch for working motifs into a fabric. Because it is a shallow stitch, you can easily achieve a sloping edge on a motif ; whereas with deeper stitches, changes of colour made on a diagonal will produce a stepped effect. In working rectangles or squares, however, you can use treble or even deeper stitches effectively.

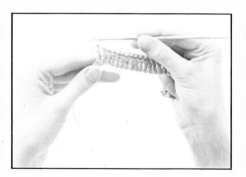

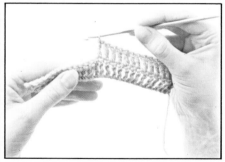

1 When working longer stitches such as double treble, work 31 chain, then work 28 double treble.

2 On the second row, work across the first 13 double treble (14 double treble including turning chain).

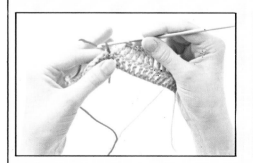

3 Insert hook into next stitch and work chain with next colour, to stand as next stitch (i.e. four for double treble).

4 You will now have two loops on the hook, one in each of the two colours.

5 Draw loop at top of chain through loop of first colour. Continue to the end of the row.

Paul Williams

Soft, muted shawl

Make this beautiful, soft shawl in muted shades as big as you fancy. Just work from the point upwards and finish when you like.

Size
Length at centre, 92cm.

Materials
Total of 350g of a mohair-type yarn such as Wendy Monaco
This shawl took 3 x 50g balls in each of colours grey-green and pink, 2 balls in cream.
5.00mm crochet hook.

Tension
11 double treble and $4\frac{1}{4}$ rows to 10cm.

To make shawl

Using green, make 5ch.
Base row Work 2dtr into 5th ch from hook. Turn.
Next row 4ch to count as first dtr, work 1dtr into first dtr – so increasing 1dtr, 1dtr into next dtr, 2dtr into the turning ch of previous row. Turn. 5dtr.
Next row 4ch, 2dtr into first dtr, 2dtr into each dtr to end. Turn. 9dtr.
Next row 4ch, 1dtr into first dtr, 2dtr into next dtr, work 1dtr into each dtr to within last 2dtr, work 2dtr into each of last 2dtr – so increasing 2dtr at each end of the row. Turn.
☐ Repeat the last row twice more, but join in pink on last dtr. 21dtr. Cut off green.
☐ Continuing to increase 2dtr at each end of every row. work in colour sections as follows :
Next row Work over first 9dtr, joining on cream on the 9th of these dtr (so having 11dtr worked in pink) : with cream work to end of row.
Work 3 more rows using pink and cream. Cut off yarns.
Work 4 rows using green and pink. Cut off yarns.
Work 4 rows using cream and green. Cut off yarns.
Work 4 rows using pink and cream. Cut off yarns.
Work 4 rows using green and pink. Cut off yarns.
Repeat the last 12 rows once more. Fasten off.

Gary Warren/accessories Harrods

Step-by-step course – 10

*Making geometric patterns working from a chart
*Pattern for a waistcoat

Making geometric patterns working from a chart

More complicated patterns are sometimes worked from a chart, which shows the motif or pattern on graph paper. This method of representing the motif eliminates the need for lengthy row-by-row instructions. The charts are really quite clear and easy to follow, so do not be deterred by their seeming complexity.

Each square on the graph represents one stitch, and each horizontal line represents one row. The motif as represented on the graph will not be in proportion, since a square will not be the same width or depth as a stitch, and so the chart should be used as a plan only.

Begin reading the chart from the bottom right-hand corner, so that the first row is read from right to left. This will be the right side of the work; the second row, which is worked on the wrong side, will be read from left to right.

Where a motif is to be repeated a number of times during the course of a row, the chart will show only one complete pattern repeat, plus the stitches to be worked at

each end of the row. The stitches within the pattern repeat should be repeated as many times as stated in the instructions, followed by the stitches to be worked at the end of the row. These end stitches will be the first stitches of the following row. Our sample is worked in two colours, coded A and B, in double crochet. A is represented by an X on the chart and B by a blank square. Carry the yarn not in use across the back of the work.

1 Make 11 chain with A; begin at bottom right-hand corner of chart and work two rows in A. These will be rows one and two on the chart.

2 Join on B ready for next row.

3 With right side of the work facing, work row three of chart from right to left.

Chart

A = ✖ MAROON
B = ☐ CAMEL

| Rows worked from left to right | | Rows worked from right to left |

Wrong side of work — Right side of work

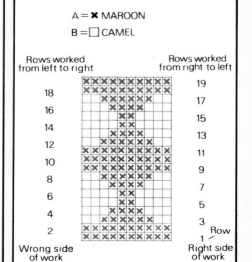

4 Turn. With wrong side of the work facing, work row four of chart from left to right.

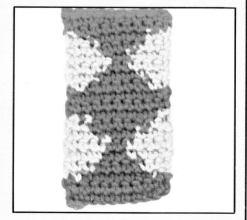

5 Continue to work each row in same way until motif is complete.

Home-spun waistcoat

Try out your own colour combinations and make this delightful patchwork-look waistcoat. A rich blend of colours gives it a really warm, home-spun look.

Sizes
To fit 83/87cm bust.
Length at centre back, 46cm.

Materials
Total of 250g of double knitting and Aran yarn such as Sirdar Superwash Wool Double Knitting and Sirdar Sherpa
This garment took 3 x 25g balls of double knitting yarn in rust and brick and 1 ball in camel ; also 2 x 50g balls of Aran yarn in brown tweed
3.50mm crochet hook
Five buttons

Tension
17 treble and 9 rows to 10cm.

Back
Using rust, make 61ch.
□ **Base row** 1tr into 4th ch from hook, 1tr into each ch to end. Turn. 59tr. Working in tr throughout proceed as follows :
□ Beginning with row 2 on chart, work patchwork design until row 11 has been worked. Work 2tr into first and last tr on next row – so increasing 1tr at each end of the row. Increase 1 tr at each end of the following 4 alternate rows. 69tr. Fasten off.
Shape armholes
Next row Join brown to 6th tr from side edge and work 3ch to count as first tr ; work to within last 5 tr. Turn. 59tr.
□ Continuing to follow the chart, work the first 2 tr and the last 2 tr together on the next row – so decreasing 1 tr at each end of the row. Decrease 1tr at each end of next 7 rows. 43tr. Work 9 rows straight. Fasten off.

Right front
Using rust, make 4ch.
Base row Work 2tr into 4th ch from hook. Turn. 3tr.
Beginning with row 2 on chart, work patchwork design shaping as follows :
□ Increase 2tr at each end of next 3 rows. 15tr. Now increase 2tr at end of next row and at this same edge on following row. 19tr.
Next row Work to end increasing 2tr at end of row ; do not turn work but make 11ch for side edge extension. Turn.
Next row 1tr into 4th ch from hook, 1tr into each ch and tr to end. Turn. 30tr.
□ Work straight until row 18 has been worked. Increase 1tr at end of next row

Read the diagram this way up

Richard Gliddon

LEFT FRONT

BACK

RIGHT FRONT

and on the following 2 alternate rows. 33tr. Work 1 row straight.

Shape front edge
Continuing to increase 1tr at side edge, decrease 1tr at the beginning of the next and following alternate row. 33tr. Fasten off.

Shape armhole
Next row Join camel to 6th tr from side edge; work 3ch to count as first tr, work to end. Turn.

□ Continuing to shape front edge on every alternate row, decrease 1 tr at armhole edge on next 8 rows. 16tr. Keeping armhole edge straight continue to shape front edge until 10tr remain. Work 1 row. Fasten off.

Left front
Work as given for right front, reversing shaping and working side edge extension thus : At the end of row 7 make 9ch using a separate ball of rust; fasten off and lay aside. Work row 8 to end of row, then work across the 9ch, so making 30tr.

The border
Join shoulder and side seams using a flat seam. With right side facing, join on brown and work a row of dc evenly all round outer edge, working 2dc into each st at front points and finishing by working a slip stitch into the first dc. Continuing to work 2dc into 2dc at points, work one round in rust, then one round in cream, making 5 evenly spaced buttonloops on the right front by working 2ch and missing 2dc. Next, work one round in brick working 2dc into each button loop, and one round in brown. Fasten off.

Armhole borders
Following the colour sequence as given for the border, work 5 rows of dc evenly all round armhole.

To make up
Press work using a warm iron over a damp cloth. Sew on the buttons.

Step-by-step course – 11

*Making a tubular fabric
*Two textured stitches
*Pattern for a striped bolster
*Pattern for a child's top

Making a tubular fabric

You've already learned to work in rounds, increasing on each round to make a flat motif. If you work in rounds without increasing, you can create a seamless tubular fabric of any width you like, which can be used to make a variety of garments, toys and household items, such as the multi-coloured bolster featured in this week's course. The tube is worked on to a basic circle, which should be the same size as the circumference of the article to be made.

Since the right side of the fabric will always be facing you, the stitches appear quite different from the way they look when worked in rows. However, if the work is divided at a given point, such as for the armhole shaping on a sweater, and then completed in rows, you must turn the work at the end of each round so that the stitches will always look the same throughout.

Try our sample using a double knitting yarn and 4.50mm hook.

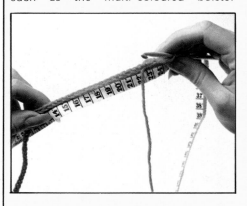

1 Make 45 chain. The length of chain should correspond exactly to the circumference of the circle to be made. Thus, if you were making a child's jersey measuring 60cm around the chest, you would need to begin by making a chain 60cm long. There is no need to add extra chain for turning.

2 Hold the hook in your right hand. Bring the free end of chain forward and up to the hook. Insert the hook into the first chain made. This prevents the chain from becoming twisted.

3 Wind the yarn over and round the hook from back to front and draw it through both loops on the hook to make a slip stitch.

4 Begin the round with the correct number of chain for the stitch being worked – in this case 3 chain for a treble. Hold the ring to the left of the hook and work 1 treble into the first chain to the left of these first 3 chain.

5 Work 1 treble into each following chain all the way round the circle so that you are working in a clockwise direction.

6 Join the last treble of the round to the 3rd of the first 3 chain – worked at the beginning of the round – with a slip stitch to complete the 1st round.

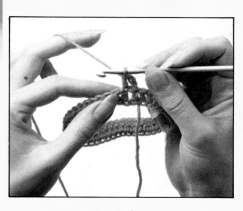

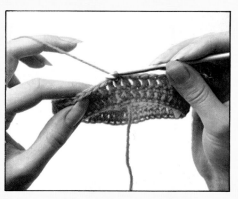

7 Begin the 2nd round by making 3 chain. Miss the first treble, which is the treble at the base of the first 3 chain. Now work 1 treble into the next treble.

8 Work 1 treble into each treble all the way round the circle and join the last treble to the top of the first 3 chain as before. By working continuously round the circle in this way you will always have the right side of the fabric facing you.

9 Where the fabric is to be divided at a given point the work must be turned at the end of each round. Work steps 1 to 6 as before. Do not continue to work round the circle, but turn the work so that the wrong side, or inside, of the tube is facing you.

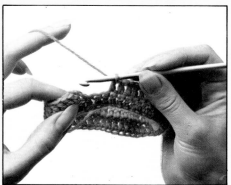

10 Now make 3 chain. The last stitch of the last round will now become the first stitch.

11 Now continue to work the next round as before, working in the same direction.

12 Continue to work as many rounds as required, remembering to join with a slip stitch and to turn the work at the end of each round until the section is completed.

Paul Williams

Two textured stitches

Here are two simple textured stitches for you to try. Both are worked in half trebles to give a firm, close fabric. You can make the samples in a double knitting yarn using a 4.50mm hook, or try using different yarns and hook sizes to see the varied effects which can be achieved with the same stitch.

Large granite stitch

This stitch should be worked over a number of chain divisible by two, with two extra for the turning chain.

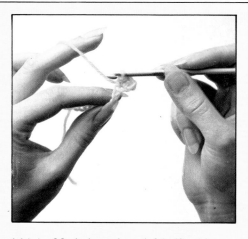

1 Make 22 chain and work 2 half treble into the 3rd chain from the hook. The first chain will count as the first htr of the row.

2 Miss the next chain and work two half treble into the next chain.

continued

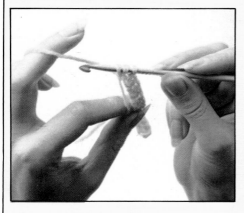

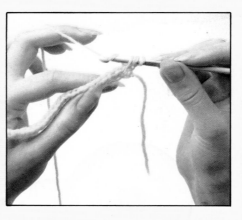

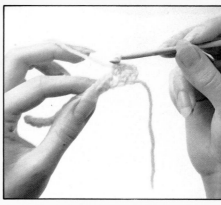

3 Repeat step 2 along the chain until 1 chain only remains unworked. Now work 1 half treble into this chain.

4 Turn the work. Make 2 chain to count as the first half treble. Now work 1 half treble between the first stitch at the edge of the work and the first half treble group. This will count as the first half treble group of the 2nd row.

5 Now work 2 half treble between the 2nd and 3rd half treble groups of the previous row.

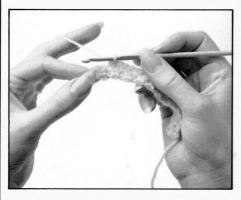

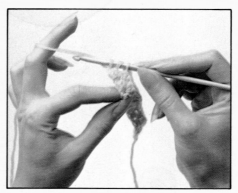

6 Continue to work in the same way as in step 5 between each half treble group of the previous row until the last half treble group has been reached.

7 Now work 1 half treble into the top of the 2 chain at the end of the row, to complete the 2nd row of the pattern.

8 Repeat steps 4 to 7 for every row, always working the first group as in step 4 and the last half treble into each turning chain of the previous row.

Crossed half trebles

This stitch makes use of a simple technique to produce a firm, thick fabric. The pattern is worked over a number of chain divisible by 2 plus 2 extra chain for the turning.

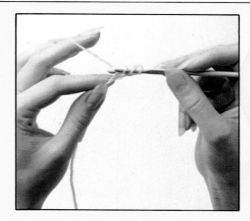

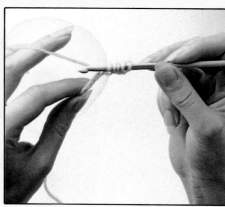

1 Make 22 chain for the base of the pattern. Wind yarn round the hook and insert it into 4th chain from hook. Wind yarn round hook again and draw through a loop so that there are 3 loops on the hook.

2 Wind yarn round hook again and insert it into the next chain. Wind yarn round the hook and draw a loop through once more. There are now 5 loops on the hook.

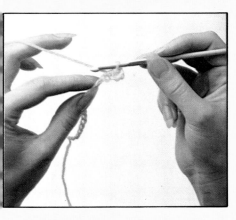

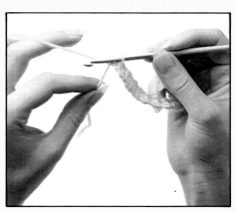

3 Wind the yarn round the hook and draw it through all 5 loops on the hook. You have now made a cluster group over 2 chain.

4 Now work one chain and then work another cluster group in the same way as before over the next 2 chain. Continue to work 1 cluster group over every 2 chain until only one chain remains unworked. Work 1 chain and then one half treble into the last chain.

5 Turn the work and make 3 chain which will count as the first half treble and 1 chain space. Wind the yarn round the hook and insert the hook into the first 1 chain space of the previous row. Now wind yarn round hook and draw through a loop.

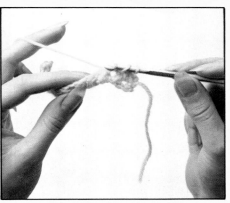

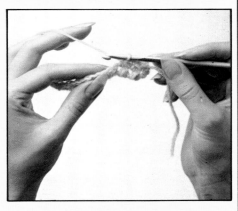

6 Complete the cluster group by working as before into the next 1 chain space in the previous row.

7 Make 1 chain. Now wind yarn round the hook and insert the hook into the same space as the last stitch just worked. Wind yarn round the hook and draw through a loop.

8 Wind yarn round hook and insert it into the next 1 chain space. Wind yarn round hook and draw through a loop.

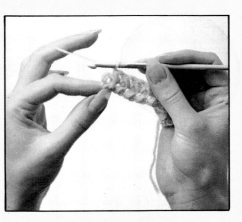

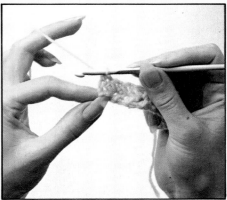

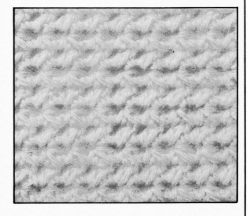

9 Repeat steps 7 and 8 across the row, beginning to work each group in the same space as the last stitch just worked until only the turning chain remains unworked in the previous row.

10 Make 1 chain. Now work 1 half treble into the top of the turning chain of the previous row to complete the 2nd row.

11 The 2nd row forms the pattern for this stitch. Repeat it for at least 10 rows to obtain the full effect of this stitch.

A bright way with stripes

You'll enjoy making this big bolster cover with its bright-coloured stripes, worked in rounds. It's a simple way to add a decorative – and practical – furnishing to your home.

Caroline Arber/accessories from John Lewis

Size
The cover measures 25.5cm in diameter x 77.5cm long.
The circles at the ends of the bolster are 25.5cm in diameter.

Materials
Total of 1000g of Aran yarn such as Lister/Lee Target Aran
Our cover took 350g of green, called A in instructions, 250g of yellow (B) and 400g of rust (C)
5.00mm crochet hook
Bolster to fit. The bolster should be 2.5cm larger in diameter and approx. 5cm longer than the cover to ensure a smooth fit.

Tension
18 sts and 20 rounds to 13cm worked over htr on a 5.00mm hook.

To make first circle
Work circle in stripes of 2 rounds A, 2 rounds B and 2 rounds C throughout. Using A, make 6ch, join into a circle with a ss.
1st round Make 2ch to count as first htr, now work 10htr into circle, join with a ss to 2nd of first 2 ch. 11 sts.
2nd round 2 ch to count as first htr, 1htr into first st ; now work 2htr in to each st round circle, join with a ss to 2nd of first 2ch. 22 sts.
3rd round 2ch, *1htr into each of next 2 sts, 2htr into next st, rep from * 6 times more, 1htr into st at base of 2ch ; join with a ss to 2nd of first 2ch. 30 sts.
4th round 2ch, 1htr into each of next 2 sts, 2htr into next st, *1htr into each of next 3 sts, 2htr into next st, rep from * 5 times more, 1htr into each of next 2 sts, join with a ss to 2nd of first 2ch. 37 sts.

5th round 2ch, 1htr into each of next 2 sts, 2htr into next st, *1htr into each of next 4 sts, 2htr into next st, rep from * 5 times more, 1htr into each of next 3 sts ; join with a ss to 2nd of first 2ch. 44 sts.
6th round 2ch, 1htr into each of next 2 sts, 2htr into next st, *1htr into each of next 5 sts, 2htr into next st, rep from * 5 times more, 1htr into each of next 4 sts, join with a ss to 2nd of first 2ch. 51 sts.
Continue to increase 7 sts in this way on every round, beginning each round as given for 6th round and working one more st between increases at the end of each subsequent round, until 17 rounds in all have been worked and there are 128 sts. Do not break off yarn.

To make bolster
Continue to work in rounds making a tube for main part of bolster.
Next round 2ch, miss first st, 1htr into each st all the way round the circle. Join last htr to top of first 2ch with a ss. 127 sts.

Work square pattern
Use separate balls of yarn for each block of colour, twisting the yarns at the back of the work when changing colours. You will need to turn the work at the end of each round, after joining with a ss, so that the different colours are in the correct position when working the following round.
1st round 2ch, miss first st, work 18 sts A, *3 sts B, 18 sts C, 3 sts B, 18 sts A, repeat from * once more. Now work 3 sts B, 18 sts C and 3 sts B. Join last htr to 2nd of first 2ch with a ss. Turn. There are 6 large blocks with a small block of B between each.
Work 19 more rounds in this way, keeping colour pattern correct, and turning work at the end of each round. Cut off additional balls of yarn. Turn work at the end of the last round so that you will be working the striped pattern in the correct direction.
Now continue to work continuous rounds in stripes of 2 rounds B, 8 rounds A, 2 rounds B, 8 rounds C and 2 rounds B. Repeat square pattern once more, but working C instead of A and vice versa. Turn work once more so that you are working in the right direction and work stripe pattern once more. Work 8 rounds in A. Draw yarn through and fasten off. Make a 2nd circle as given for first until 17 rounds in all have been worked, but working A in place of C and vice versa. Fasten off.

To make up
Darn all loose ends of yarn to WS of work Insert bolster in cover. With RS of 2nd

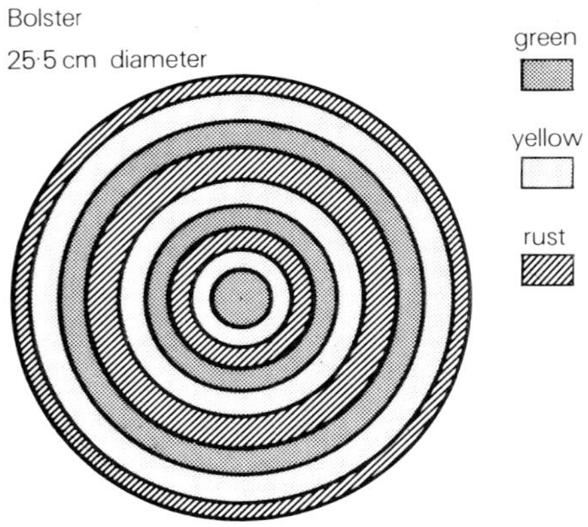
Bolster
25·5 cm diameter
green
yellow
rust

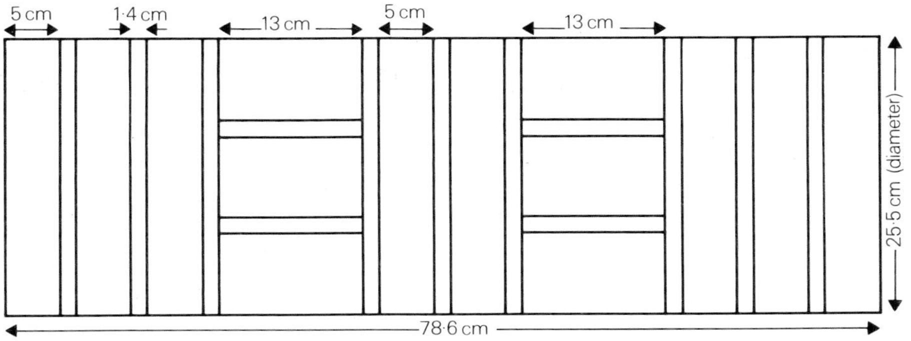
5 cm
1·4 cm
13 cm
5 cm
13 cm
25·5 cm (diameter)
78·6 cm

circle facing, rejoin A to a half treble on 17th round. Working through both thicknesses, join circle to top edge of bolster with dc. Work a round of dc in C through last round of first circle and first row of tube in the same way at other end.

To make your own filling
You will need a piece of foam rubber measuring approximately 2.5cm thick by 2.5m long by 78cm wide. Roll it into a tube so that it is approximately 28cm in diameter – that is, 2.5cm larger than the cover. Make a tube from a sheet of unbleached calico 85cm by 83cm to cover the foam rubber, with a circle at each end 31cm in diameter to complete the tube. (These measurements give you 1.5cm seam allowances.)

Rounds for applause

For playtime – or anytime – a child needs clothes with lots of 'give'. This comfortable sweater, crocheted in rounds, is sure to be an all-time favourite.

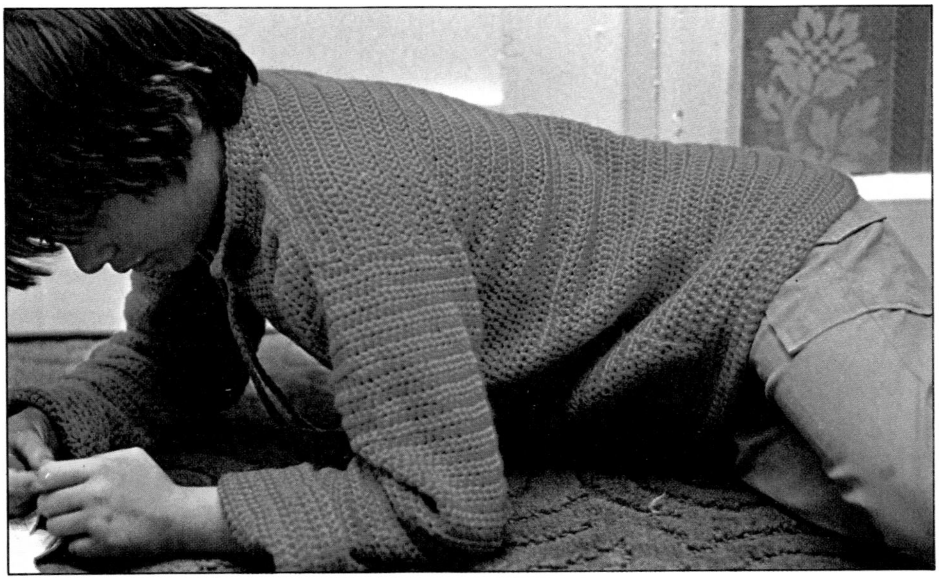
S. Wells

Size
To fit 51[56 :61 :66]cm chest.
Length, 34.5[42.5 :46.5 :52]cm.
Sleeve seam, 32.5[35 :37.5 :40]cm.
Note the instructions for larger sizes are given in square brackets [] ; where there is only one set of figures it applies to all sizes.

Materials
Total of 350[450 :500 :550]g of double knitting yarn such as Patons Behive double knitting
4.00mm crochet hook

Tension
17htr and 12 rows to 10cm worked on a 4.00mm hook.

Back and front (worked in a tubular fabric to armhole).
Make 96[104 :112 :120]ch. Join the last ch to the first with a ss, taking care not to twist the ch.
Base row 2ch to count as first htr, miss 1ch, work 1htr into each ch to end of round. Join with a ss to first ch. Turn.
1st round 2ch, miss first htr, work 1htr into each st to end of round. Join with a ss to first ch. Turn. Rep the 1st round throughout, turning the work at the end of each round until 26[30 :32 :36] rows in all have been worked. You can adjust the length at this point if necessary.

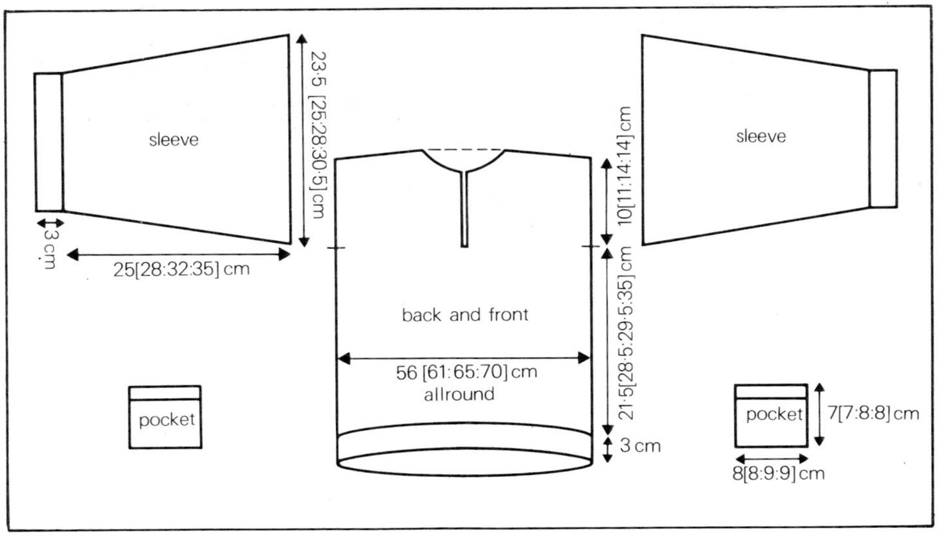
sleeve
23·5 [25:28:30·5] cm
3 cm
25[28:32:35] cm
10[11:14:14] cm
back and front
21·5[28·5:29·5:35] cm
56 [61:65:70] cm
allround
3 cm
pocket
sleeve
pocket
7[7:8:8] cm
8[8:9:9] cm
Brian Mavor

S. Wells

16[18 :20 :20]htr remain, ending at neck edge.

Shape shoulder

Work across first 8[9 :10 :10]htr, turn and leave remaining 8[9 :10 :10] sts unworked.

Work 1 more row. Draw yarn through and fasten off.

With right side of front facing, rejoin yarn at front neck opening. Complete the second half of front to match the first, reversing the shaping so that armhole and neck are worked in the correct position on this side.

Welt

Rejoin yarn to lower edge of body at side edge.

Next round 1ch, work 1dc into each st all round lower edge of sweater. Join with a ss to first ch. Turn.

Rep this round 4 times more. Draw yarn through.

Fasten off.

Sleeves

Join shoulder seams on wrong side of work. With right side of work facing, rejoin yarn to underarm. Work 40[44 :48 :52] htr evenly all round armhole ; join last htr to first with a ss, so forming a circle.

Continue in tubular fabric as given for body, decreasing one st at each end of every following 6th[7th :8th :8th] round until 30[34 :38 :42] sts remain.

Continue without shaping until 36[40 :42 :46] rounds an all have been worked.

You can adjust length here if necessary. Do not cut off yarn.

Cuff

Continue in rounds as before, work 4 rounds in dc. Draw yarn through and fasten off.

Neckband

With right side of front facing, rejoin yarn to right front at neck edge. Work 44[46 :48 :50]dc evenly round neck edge, ending at left front neck edge. Turn.

Work 4[4 :5 :5] rows in dc on these sts.

Do not fasten off. Continue to work 1 row in dc down one side of front opening, up . other side and round neck edge again. Fasten off.

Pockets (make 2)

Make 14[14 :16 :16]ch. Work 8[8 :10 :10] rows in htr, then 3 rows in dc on these sts. Fasten off.

To make up

Darn all loose ends in on wrong side of work. Press lightly under a damp cloth with a warm iron. Sew pockets to front. With double thickness of yarn make a chain 85[85 :90 :90]cm long. Using spaces between stitches at neck edge, lace cord up front opening as shown. Turn back cuff to required depth.

Divide for back

Work across first 48[52 :56 :60] htr, turn. Continue to work in rows on these sts for back with 2 turning chain at the beginning of each row. Work 12[14 :16 :16] more rows.

Shape shoulders

*Ss across first 8[9 :10 :10] sts, continue in pattern across row until 8[9 :10 :10] sts remain unworked, turn and leave these sts for 2nd shoulder. Rep from * once more, then draw yarn through loop on hook and fasten off.

Work front and divide for front opening

Return to remaining sts. Rejoin yarn at armhole edge and pattern across first 24[26 :28 :30] sts, turn and complete this side first.

Work 7[9 :11 :13] rows.

Shape front neck

Pattern across first 20[20 :22 :24] sts, turn and leave remaining 4[6 :6 :6] sts unworked.

Decrease 1htr at neck edge on next and every following row (by working 2htr together one st in from neck edge) until

Step-by-step course – 12

*Increasing within a row
*Decreasing within a row
*Pattern for a chevron-striped skirt

Sometimes you will need to increase or decrease within a row, instead of at the ends, in order to produce the shape required. On a skirt, for example, the fabric must be shaped smoothly from the waist over the hips. Increasing or decreasing within the row achieves this.

Another use for this kind of shaping is in making patterns, such as chevron stripes. By decreasing regularly at certain points you produce downward-pointing angles; by increasing regularly at intermediate points you produce upward-pointing angles, thus forming the familiar, wave-like pattern.

Increasing a stitch within a row

Increasing within a row is very simple: you just work two or more stitches into the stitch where the increase is required. It is a good idea to mark this stitch with a coloured thread, since you will probably have to increase again on subsequent rows above it. Our sample is worked in trebles, but the technique is the same for other stitches.

1 Make 14 chain and work two rows in treble. There will be 12 trebles in each row.

2 Work across the first four trebles of the next row: five trebles (counting the turning chain as one treble).

3 Work two trebles into next stitch. Place a marker in the increased stitch.

4 Work one treble into each treble to end of row. Turn.

5 Work across the first five trebles of the next row: six trebles (counting the turning chain as one treble).

6 Work two trebles into next stitch (the first of the two increased stitches).

7 Work one treble into each treble to end of row. Turn. Continue increasing in this way on the first of the increased stitches on the wrong side rows (this will be the second stitch on the right side rows). Note that the line of shaping produced in this way slants to the left on the right side of the fabric.

8 By increasing into the second of the two increased stitches on the wrong side (first of the increased stitches on the right side) you achieve a shaping that slants to the right. To keep the line of shaping vertical, increase in the first stitch and in the second on alternate rows.

Paul Williams

191

Decreasing within a row

The technique for decreasing within a row is essentially the same for each crochet stitch. Our sample is worked in treble, but you can adapt the method for other stitches using the detailed instructions for decreasing double crochet half trebles or double trebles at the end of a row.

1 Make 14 chain and work two rows in treble. There will be 12 trebles in each row.

2 Work across the first four trebles of the next wrong side row : five trebles (counting the turning chain as one treble).

6 Repeat step 3 into the *next* stitch. Wind yarn round hook and draw through a loop. There should be four loops on the hook.

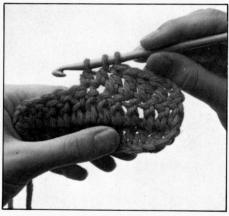

7 Repeat step 5. There will be three loops left on the hook this time.

8 Wind yarn round hook and draw through remaining three loops. One stitch has been decreased. Place a marker in the first stitch of the two you have worked together.

12 The line of decreases will slant to the left on the right side of the work.

13 To make the line of decreases slant to the right on the right side of the work, begin by repeating steps one to nine as before.

14 Work across four trebles of next row : five trebles (counting the turning chain as one treble).

3 Wind yarn round hook and insert hook into next stitch.

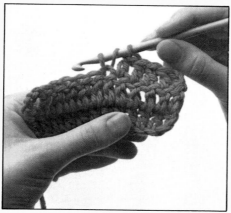

4 Wind yarn round hook and draw through a loop. There should be three loops on the hook.

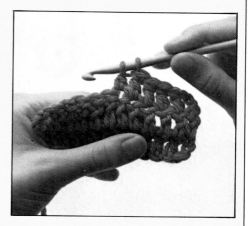

5 Wind yarn round hook and draw through first two loops on the hook. Two loops remain on the hook.

9 Work one treble into each treble to end of row. Turn.

10 Work across three trebles of next row : four trebles (counting the turning chain as one treble).

11 Work the next two trebles together as for previous row.
Work one treble into each treble to the end of the row.

15 Work the next two trebles together as before.

16 Work one treble into each treble to end of row.

17 Here the line of decreases slants to the right. To keep the line of shaping vertical decrease to the right and to the left on alternate rows.

Paul Williams

Chevron skirt

Flattering chevron stripes in four shades of brown and beige make a skirt you'll enjoy wearing time and time again. You'll also enjoy working the stripes and seeing their intriguing pattern emerge as you progressively increase and decrease the stitches.

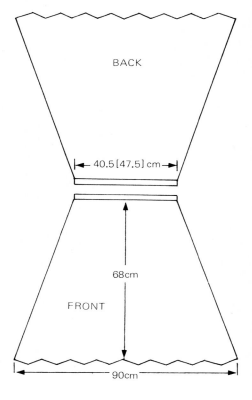

Sizes
To fit 91-97[102-107]cm hips.
Length when hanging, 68cm.

Materials
Total of 450 [600] g of double knitting yarn such as Pingouin Confortable
This garment took 3[3] x 50g balls in first colour, A
2[3] balls in 2nd colour, B
2[3] balls in 3rd colour, C
2[3] balls in 4th colour, D
4.00mm crochet hook
Waist length of 2.5cm wide elastic
18cm zip fastener

Tension
15tr and 7½ rows to 10cm over plain tr.
17tr to 10cm over chevron patt.

194

Back and front (alike)

Using A, make 148[172]ch.

Base row 1tr into 4th ch from hook, *1tr into each of next 10ch, work 3tr together over next 3ch, 1tr into each of next 10ch, 3tr into next ch, repeat from asterisk (*) to end, but finish last repeat 2tr into last ch instead of 3tr. Turn. 145[169]tr.

Next row 3ch to count as 1tr, 1tr into first tr, *1tr into each of next 10tr, work 3tr together, 1tr into each of next 10tr, 3tr into next tr, repeat from * to end, but finish last repeat 2tr into turning ch of previous row and join in B on last tr. Turn.

Repeat the last row, working 2 rows in each of B, C, D, A, B, C and D and join in A on last tr – so completing 16 rows from the beginning.

1st decrease row Using A, work 3ch, miss first tr, 1tr into each of next 10tr, *work 3tr together, 1tr into each of next 21tr, repeat from * to end, but finish last repeat 1tr into each of last 11tr. Turn.

Next row 3ch, 1tr into first tr, *1tr into each of next 9tr, work 3tr together, 1tr into each of next 9tr, 3tr into next tr, repeat from * to end, but finish last repeat 2tr into last tr, and join in B on last tr. Turn. Using B, repeat the last row twice more, joining in C on last tr of second row.

2nd decrease row Using C, work 3ch, 1tr into each of next 9tr, *work 3tr together, 1tr into each of next 19tr, repeat from * to end, but finish last repeat 1tr into each of last 10tr. Turn.

Next row 3ch, 1tr into first tr, *1tr into each of next 8tr, work 3tr together, 1tr into each of next 8tr, 3tr into next tr, repeat from * to end, but finish last repeat 2tr into last tr, and join in D on last tr. Turn.

Using D, repeat the last row twice more, joining in A on last tr of second row.

3rd decrease row Using A, work 3ch, miss first tr, 1tr into each of next 8tr, *work 3tr together, 1tr into each of next 17tr, repeat from * to end, but finish last repeat 1tr into each of last 9tr. Turn.

Next row 3ch, 1tr into first tr, *1tr into each of next 7tr, work 3tr together, 1tr into each of next 7tr, 3tr into next tr, repeat from * to end, but finish last repeat 2tr into last tr, and join in B on last tr. Turn.

Continue in this way, working in stripe sequence and pattern as now set, decreasing on every 4th row, as before, until 61[71] tr remain.

Work 7 rows, so ending 2 rows in D, joining in A on last tr of 3rd row.

Next row Using A, work 1ch, miss first tr, *1dc into next tr, 1htr into each of next 2tr, 1 tr into each of next 3tr, 1htr into each of next 2tr, 1dc into next tr, repeat from * to end, finishing 1dc into last tr. Turn.

Work 4 rows in dc. Fasten off.

To make up

Do not press. Using a backstitch seam, join side seams leaving 18cm from top edge open. Sew in the zip fastener. Work herringbone casing over elastic on wrong side at waist. Press seams lightly with a warm iron over a damp cloth.

Step-by-step course – 13

Practical and fashionable, these scarves illustrate the versatility of crochet. Three different kinds of yarn and three different stitch patterns create three individual styles.

Silky scarf

Size
18cm wide by 184 cm long, excluding fringe.

Materials
10 balls of Twilleys Lystwist (rayon yarn)
1.75mm crochet hook

To make
Using 1.75mm hook make 57ch.
1st row 1tr into 4th ch from hook, 1tr into each of next 7ch, *1ch, miss next ch, 1tr into each of next 17ch, rep

from * once more, 1ch, miss next ch, 1tr into each of last 9ch. Turn.
2nd row 3ch to count as first tr, 1tr into each of next 7tr, *1ch, miss next tr, 1tr into next sp, 1ch, miss next tr, 1tr into each of next 15tr, rep from * once more, 1ch, miss next tr, 1tr into next sp, 1ch, miss next tr, 1tr into each

of last 7tr, 1tr into the turning ch. Turn. Beg row 3, cont in patt working from chart until the 1st row of the 12th patt has been worked. Fasten off.

Fringe
Using three 45cm lengths of yarn tog knot fringe.

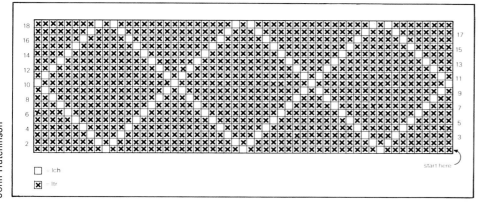

□ = 1ch
☒ = 1tr

start here

To make a knotted fringe

Cut the yarn into the required lengths. For the long, silky scarf you will need strands 45cm long. Take three strands together at a time and knot fringe as follows.

Holding the right side of the edge to be fringed so that it is facing you, insert a crochet hook through the edge from back to front, fold the three strands in half and place the loop on the hook.

Pull the hook towards you, so pulling the loop through the fabric.

Slide the hook upwards, around the six strands, and draw the ends of yarn through the loop. Pull the knot up tightly.

Knot each fringe in the same way at regular intervals along the edge.

Coral Mula

197

Mohair scarf

(See photo on page 196.)

Size
24cm wide by 224cm long.

Materials
7 x 25g balls of Hayfield Gossamer (mohair yarn)
4.00mm crochet hook

To make
Using 4.00mm hook make 46ch.
Base row 1tr tr into 8th ch from hook, *1ch, miss next ch, 1tr tr into next ch, rep from * to end.
Turn.
Patt row 6ch to count as first tr tr and 1ch, 1tr tr into next tr tr, *1ch, 1tr tr into next tr tr, rep from * to end, finishing 1ch, miss next ch, 1tr tr into next ch.
Turn. 20sps.
Rep the patt row until work measures 222cm from beg.
Edging row *4ch, 1dc into next sp, rep from * to end.
Fasten off.
Join yarn to base row and work edging row along this edge.

Triangular scarf

Size
80cm wide by 48cm deep, measured at widest parts.

Materials
2 x 25g balls of Jaegar Faeriespun (2 ply yarn)
2.00mm crochet hook

To make
Using 2.00mm hook make 6ch, join with a ss to first ch to form a circle.
1st row 5ch to count as first dtr and 1ch, work 1dtr, 1ch and 1dtr into circle.
Turn. 2sps.
2nd row 5ch, 1dtr into first sp, 1ch, 1dtr into same sp, 1ch, 1dtr into next sp, 1ch, 1dtr into same sp. Turn. 4sps.
3rd row 5ch, 1dtr, 1ch and 1dtr all into first sp, (1ch, 1dtr into next sp) 3 times, 1ch, miss next ch, 1dtr into next ch. Turn. 6sps.
4th row 5ch, 1dtr, 1ch and 1dtr all into first sp, now work 1ch and 1dtr into each sp to end, finishing 1ch, 1dtr into last dtr. Turn.
Rep the last row until there are 88 sps.
Now work edging thus :
Next round Work 3dc into each sp along the 3 sides and 6dc into each corner sp, finishing ss into first dc.
Next round 3ch, work 5tr all into first dc *miss next 2dc, ss into next dc, miss next 2dc, 6tr all into next dc, rep from * all round, finishing ss into top of the 3ch.
Fasten off.

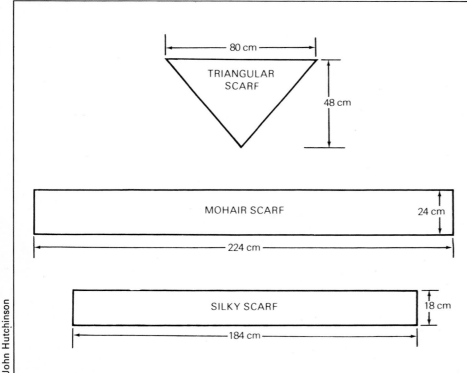

Step-by-step course – 14

Making a flat square motif

Many different motifs can be produced by working in rounds to create a flat shape, but possibly the best known and easiest to work is the granny square. The squares can be worked in either one or several colours and joined together to make a great variety of rugs, blankets, shawls and garments.

To make this sample use a 4.50mm hook and double knitting yarn.

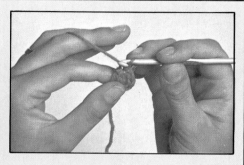

1 Make 8 chain and then loop the chain round to form a circle, inserting the hook from front to back into the first chain made.

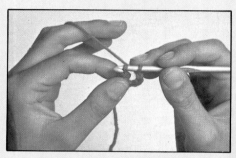

2 Wind the yarn round the hook and draw it through both the loops on the hook, so that the chain is joined together with a slip stitch.

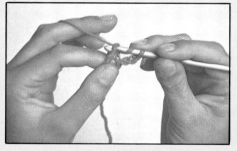

3 Work 3 chain, which will count as the first treble of the first round. Now wind the yarn round the hook and insert the hook from front to back through the centre of the circle – not into the chain stitch itself.

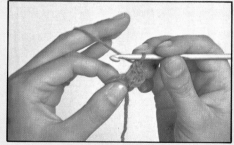

4 Complete this treble in the normal way and then work one more treble into the circle in the same way. There will now be 1 group of 3 treble, including the first 3 chain, worked into the circle.

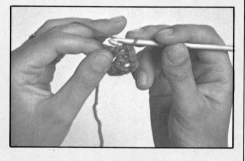

5 Make 2 chain. These 2 chain will be counted as the first corner of the square and will be called a 2 chain space. Now work 3 more treble into the centre of the circle as before.

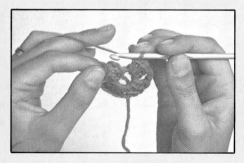

6 Repeat step 5 twice more, so that you will have 4 groups of 3 treble worked into the circle, and three 2 chain spaces. Work 2 chain for the last corner, and then insert the hook from front to back into the 3rd of the first 3 chain, worked at the beginning of the round.

7 Wind the yarn round the hook and draw it through both loops on the hook so that the beginning and end of the round are joined together with a slip stitch. This completes the first round of the square.

8 Continue to work round the square, without turning the work, so that the right side of the motif is always facing you. Unlike working in rows, there is a definite right and wrong side to the fabric when working in rounds. Begin the 2nd round by working 2 chain.

Frederick Mancini

continued

 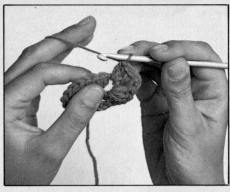 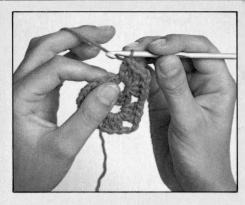

9 Work 3 treble into the next 2 chain space after the first block of trebles worked in the first round, inserting the hook from front to back under the 2 chain each time.

10 Make 2 chain and then work 3 treble into the same space as the 3 treble just worked. This will be the first corner group of the 2nd round. All the corners will be made in the same way on each round.

11 Make 1 chain and then work the next corner group as before into the next 2 chain space.

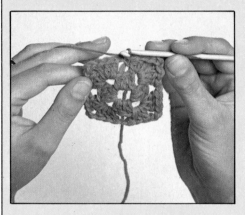  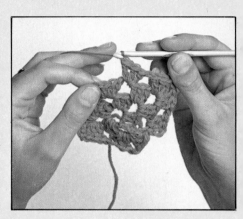

12 Complete the 3rd and 4th corners of the 2nd round in the same way. You will have now worked 4 corners in all with a 1 chain space between each corner. Join the end of the round to the beginning by working a slip stitch into the first of the 2 chain at the beginning of the round. The 2nd round has now been completed.

13 Work 3 chain to count as the first treble of the next round. Now work 2 treble into the first space after the slip stitch joining the previous round.

14 Work 1 chain and then work a corner group into the first corner space. Then work 1 chain, 1 group of 3 treble into the 1 chain space on the previous row, then 1 chain.

  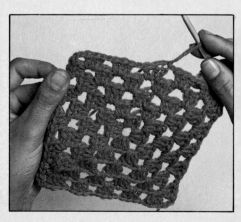

15 Complete the 3rd round in the same way, joining the last chain to the 3rd of the first 3 chain at the beginning of the round with a slip stitch.

16 The 4th round is worked in the same way, but with 2 groups of treble worked in each of the 1 chain spaces on each side of the square.

17 To make the sample bigger, continue to work as many rounds as you like for the size of motif required, working 1 more treble group on each side of the square on every subsequent round, with 1 chain between each group.

Introducing a new colour in a square motif

Follow this method if you want to introduce a new colour into the work without it showing in the previous round.

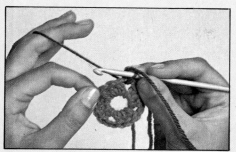

1 Complete the first round with the first colour. When you have worked the final slip stitch joining the beginning and the end of the round, draw the yarn through the last loop and fasten off. Cut off the yarn, leaving a length long enough to be darned into the back of the fabric when the motif has been completed.

2 Insert the hook into the centre of the next corner after the slip stitch that joined the ends of the last round together, and draw through a loop of the new colour. Remember to leave a length of yarn long enough to be darned in afterwards.

3 Work 1 chain with both ends of the yarn to hold it firmly in place. Now drop the free end of the yarn.

4 Work 2 more chain so that you have worked 3 chain in all, to count as the first treble of this round. Complete the round in the normal way with the new colour.

5 Change colour at the beginning of each round in the same way until the motif has been completed.

6 Darn all the loose ends in to the back of the fabric, taking care to sew each end into its own colour.

Sewing several motifs together

Use this method of joining motifs, such as granny squares, that have straight side edges.

1 Place two motifs together, right sides facing, so that the wrong side of each motif is on the outside. Pin them together along one side, about 1 round in from the edge.

2 For sewing the motifs together use a blunt-ended wool needle and the yarn used in the motif. If this is too thick, use a matching yarn in a finer ply. Begin at the right-hand edge of the square and oversew the two together, taking care not to pull the yarn too tightly.

3 Sew all the motifs together in the same way, sewing them first into horizontal strips and then sewing the strips together. By using this method, you will find it easier to get the seams to run straight.

Frederick Mancini

Giant cushions

These giant cushions are almost a substitute for sitting-room furniture. Make striking covers in bright-coloured stripes, or use more natural shades for a more subdued effect.

Multi-striped cushion

Size
Our cover has been made to fit a cushion pad measuring 91.5cm by 91.5cm square. It measures approximately 89cm by 89cm square, 2.5cm less than pad. Each square measures approximately 42cm by 42cm, excluding edging.

Materials
*25 x 50g balls of Pingouin Sport in blue
5 balls in white
4 balls in each of red, green and yellow
4.00mm crochet hook
A cushion pad 91.5cm by 91.5cm square*

Tension
18 htr and 11 rows to 10cm on a 4.00mm hook.

Note To make the cover for a different-sized pad or for an existing cushion, measure the width of your cushion pad and make your cover 2.5cm less. This ensures a smooth, snug fit. For example, a cushion measuring 63.5cm by 63.5cm square will need a cover measuring 61cm by 61cm square. Allow 2.5cm all round for edging and subtract this figure from the original size so that area for remaining squares will be 56cm by 56cm square.
Each square will therefore measure approximately 28cm by 28cm.

To make the striped square
We quote the colours used in our cushion. You can, of course, use any colour combination you like, but remember that you will need more of 1 colour than the others to make the back.
Using 4.00mm hook and red make 10ch, join with a slip stitch to first ch to form a circle.
1st round Work 2ch to count as first htr, then work 15htr into circle; join the last htr to the top of first 2ch worked with a slip stitch. There are 16htr.
2nd round Work 2ch, which will count as first htr; work 2htr into same place as slip stitch – 1 corner formed, * 1htr into each of next 3htr, 3htr all into next htr – corner formed, repeat from asterisk (*) twice more, then work 1htr into each of next 3htr, join last htr worked to top of first 2ch with a slip stitch. Fasten off.
3rd round Join white to 2nd htr of one corner group, 2ch, now work 1htr, 1ch and 2htr all into same htr, *(1ch, miss next htr, 1htr into next htr); work the section in brackets () twice; 1ch, miss next htr, work 2htr, 1ch and 2htr all into 2nd htr of next corner group, repeat from * twice more, (1ch, miss next htr, 1htr into next htr) twice, 1ch, join last ch worked to 2nd of first 2ch. You should have three 1ch spaces between each corner group.
4th round Using white, slip stitch over first 2htr and into the 1ch space at corner, 2ch, work 1htr, 1ch and 2htr all into same space, *1htr into each of next 2htr, (1htr into next 1ch space, 1htr into next htr) 3 times, 1htr into next htr, 2htr, 1ch and 2htr all into 1ch space at corner, repeat from * to the end of the round, but do not work the last corner group at the end of the last repeat, join the last htr worked to the 2nd of the first 2ch with a slip stitch.
Fasten off.
You should have worked 9htr between each corner group.
5th round Join blue to 1ch space at one corner, 2ch, now work 1htr, 1ch and 2htr all into same space, *(1ch, miss next htr, 1htr into next htr) to within 2nd htr of next corner group, 1ch, miss next htr, now work 2htr, 1ch and 2htr all into 1ch space at corner, repeat from * all round, but do not work the last corner group at the end of the last repeat; join the last ch worked to the 2nd of the first 2ch with a slip stitch. There should be 7 spaces between each corner group.
6th round Using blue, slip stitch over first 2htr and into the 1ch space at corner, 2ch, work 1htr, 1ch and 2htr all into same space, *1htr into each of next 2htr, (1htr into next 1ch space, 1htr into next htr) to within 2nd htr of next corner group, 1htr into next htr, 2htr, 1ch and 2htr all into 1ch space at corner, repeat from * to the end of the round, but do not work the last corner group at the end of the last repeat, join the last htr worked to the 2nd of the first 2ch with a slip stitch. Fasten off.
There should be 17htr on each side between corner groups.
Continue to work the 5th and 6th rounds alternately working in a colour sequence of 2 rounds yellow, 2 rounds green, 2 rounds red, 2 rounds white and 2 rounds blue until the 2nd round of the 3rd white stripe has been worked. Fasten off. This completes one square.
Work 3 more squares in the same way.

To make the plain square
Using blue throughout, work the first circle and first and 2nd rounds as given for striped square.
3rd round Slip stitch into top of 2nd htr of 3htr at corner, work 2ch which will count as first htr, now work 1htr, 1ch and 2htr all into same htr for corner group, *(1ch, miss next htr, 1htr into next htr) twice, 1ch, miss next htr, work 2htr, 1ch and 2htr all into 2nd htr of next corner group, repeat from * twice more, (1ch, miss next htr, 1htr into next htr) twice, 1ch, join last ch to 2nd of first 2ch worked.
There will be three 1ch spaces between each corner group.
4th round Slip stitch over first 2htr and into the 1ch space at corner, 2ch, work 1htr, 1ch and 2htr all into same space, *1htr into each of next 2htr, (1htr into next 1ch space, 1htr into next htr) 3 times, 1htr into next htr, 2htr, 1ch and 2htr all into 1ch space at corner, repeat from * to the end of the round, but do not work the last corner group at the end of the last repeat, join the last htr worked to the 2nd of the first 2ch with a slip stitch.
5th round Slip stitch over first 2htr and into the 1ch space at corner, 2ch, now work 1htr, 1ch and 2htr all into same space, *(1ch, miss next htr, 1htr into next htr) to within 2nd htr of next corner group, 1ch, miss next htr, now work 2htr, 1ch and 2htr all into 1ch space at corner, repeat from * all round, but do not work the last corner group at the end of the last repeat, join the last ch worked to the 2nd of the first 2ch with a slip stitch.
Continue working rounds 4 and 5 until square measures the same as the striped square. Fasten off.
This completes the first square.
Work three more squares in the same way.

To make up cushion
Darn all loose ends to the wrong side of each square, keeping each colour in its own stripe.
With the right side of two striped squares facing, using white yarn and a flat seam, join one edge of the squares together. Join the other two striped squares in the same way. Now join these two pieces together to make one large square. Join the plain squares in the same way.

The edging
With right side facing, insert hook into one corner space and draw a loop of blue through, 2ch, work 1htr, 1ch and 2htr all into same space, *(1ch, miss next htr, 1htr into next htr) along edge to corner, 1ch, miss next htr, work 2htr, 1ch and

2htr all into corner space, repeat from *
all round, but do not work corner group
at end of last repeat, join last 1ch worked
to 2nd of the first 2ch with a slip stitch.
Next round Work as given for 4th round
of plain square. Fasten off.
Work round outer edge of other square in
the same way.
Darn in all loose ends on wrong side of
work.

To join the squares together

With wrong sides facing join on blue;
working through double thickness work a
row of dc round 3 sides of cover, working
1dc into each htr and 2dc into each
space at corner. Fasten off. Insert
cushion pad, then join the remaining
seam in the same way.
You could insert a zip fastener into this
side if required.

Diagonally striped cushion

Size

Our cover has been made to fit a cushion
pad 91.5cm by 91.5cm square.
The cover measures approximately
89cm by 89cm square – 2.5cm less than
pad. Each square measures approximately
42cm by 42cm square, excluding edging.

Materials

*28 x 50g balls of Sunbeam Aran
Tweed in dark brown, A
11 balls in each of beige, B and grey, C
4.00mm crochet hook
A cushion pad 91.5cm by 91.5cm
square*

Tension

18htr and 11 rows to 10cm worked on a
4.00mm hook.

Note If you wish to alter the size of the
cover to fit a different-sized pad or to fit
an existing cushion, measure the width of
your cushion pad and make your cover
2.5cm less. For example a cushion
measuring 63.5cm by 63.5cm square will
need a cover measuring 61cm by 61cm
square. Allow 2.5cm all round for edging
and subtract this figure from the total
size so that the area for remaining squares
will be 56cm x 56cm. Each square will
therefore measure approximately 28cm x
28cm.

To make the striped square

Each square is worked in stripes on one
half, with the other half being worked
in one colour only. Take care when
changing colours to avoid making a hole
between the stitches.
Using 4.00mm hook and B, make 10ch,
join with a slip stitch to first ch to form
a circle.

1st round Work 2ch, which will count
as first htr, then work 15htr into the

circle; join the last htr to the 2nd of the
first 2ch worked with a slip stitch.
There are 16htr.
2nd round Work 2ch, which will count
as first htr, then work 2 htr into the same
place as slip stitch – 1 corner formed,
*work 1 htr into each of the next 3 htr,
3 htr all into next htr – corner formed,
repeat from asterisk (*) twice more,
work 1 htr into each of next 3 htr, join
the last htr worked to top of the first
2ch to complete the round. Commence
striped pattern.
3rd round Using B, work 1 slip stitch
into 2nd htr of group at corner, 2 ch,
1 htr into same place as slip stitch, (1 ch,
miss next htr, 1 htr into next htr) work
the section in brackets ( ) twice; 1 ch
miss next htr, now work 2htr, 1ch and
2htr all into 2nd htr of next corner group,
(1ch, miss next htr, 1 htr into next htr)
twice, 1 ch, miss next htr, work 2htr into
2nd htr of the next corner group, join
in second colour by drawing C through
working loop. Cut off B. Complete the
round in C by working 2htr into same
htr as last 2htr, (1ch, miss next htr, 1htr,
into next htr) twice, 1ch, miss next htr,
now work 2htr, 1ch and 2htr all into
2nd htr of the next corner group,
(1ch, miss next htr, work 1 htr into next
htr) twice, 1ch, miss next htr work 2htr
into same htr as first 2htr, 1ch, insert
hook into the 2nd of the first 2ch, and
draw B through. Cut off C.
There should be three 1ch spaces
between each corner group.
4th round Using B, work 2ch, 1 htr into
1ch space at corner, 1 htr into each of
next 2htr, (1htr into next 1ch space, 1 htr
into next htr) 3 times, 1htr into next htr,
now work 2htr, 1ch and 2htr all into
corner space, 1htr into each of next 2htr,
(1htr into next 1ch space, 1 htr into next
htr) 3 times, 1htr into next htr, 2htr into
1ch space at corner. Join in second
colour by drawing C through working
loop. Cut off B. Complete round in C by
working 2htr into same place as last
2htr, 1htr into each of next 2htr, (1htr
into next space, 1htr into next htr) 3
times, 1htr into next htr, now work 2htr,
1ch and 2htr all into next space at
corner, 1htr into each of next 2htr, (1htr
into next 1ch space, 1htr into next htr) 3
times, 1htr into next htr, 2htr into same
space as first 2htr, 1ch, insert hook into
the 2nd of the first 2ch and draw B
through. Cut off C.
5th round Work 2ch, 1htr into 1ch space
at corner, (1ch, miss next htr, 1htr into
next htr) to within 2nd htr of corner
group, 1ch, miss next htr, now work
2htr, 1ch and 2htr all into 1ch space at
corner, (1ch, miss next htr, 1htr into
next htr) to within 2nd htr of next corner
group, 1ch, 2htr into 1ch space at
corner. Join in 2nd colour by drawing A
through working loop. Cut off B.
Complete round in A, finishing by

working 2htr into same space as first
2htr, 1ch, insert hook into the 2nd of the
first 2ch and draw B through. Cut off A.
6th round Work 2ch, 1htr into 1ch space
at corner, continue to work as for 4th
round, working 1htr into each htr and
1ch space and 2htr, 1ch and 2htr all into
1ch space at corners. Remember to
change from B to A at corner, as before.
Continue to work stripes of 2 rounds in
each colour, keeping one half in B and
working the other half in colour sequence
of C, A and B throughout.
Make sure that the pattern is correct when
changing colours at corners. As the
square increases in size the length of each
stripe will also be extended. Continue to
work the square until it measures
approximately 42cm square. Fasten off.
Make one more square in the same way.
Make two squares, keeping the stripe
sequence the same but working the
plain half in C instead of B.
These 4 squares form the top of the
cushion.

To make the plain squares

Using A only throughout, work 4
squares as given for plain square on
multi-striped cover.

To make up

Darn all loose ends to the wrong side
of each square.
With the right side of two striped
squares facing, using the corresponding
colour and a flat seam join one edge of
the squares. Join the other two striped
squares in the same way.
Now join these 2 pieces together,
matching the stripes, to make one
larger square.
Join the plain squares in the same way.

The edging

With right side facing insert hook into
one corner space and draw a loop of A
through, 2ch, work 1htr, 1ch and 2htr all
into same space, *(1ch, miss next htr,
1htr into next htr) along edge to corner,
1ch, miss next htr, work 2htr, 1ch and
2htr all into corner space, repeat from *
all round but do not work corner group at
end of last repeat, join last 1ch worked to
2nd of the first 2ch with a slip stitch.
Next round Work as given for 4th round
of plain square. Fasten off. Work round
outer edge of other square in the same
way. Darn in loose ends on wrong side.

To join the squares together

With wrong sides facing join on A and,
working through double thickness, work
a row of dc round 3 sides of cover,
working 1dc into each htr and 2dc into
each space at corner. Fasten off. Insert
cushion pad, then join the remaining
seam in the same way.
You could insert a zip fastener into this
side if required.

Step-by-step course – 15

*Joining lace motifs
  with crochet
*Joining lace motifs to
  make a square fabric
*Joining simple squares
  with lace crochet
*Pattern for a lacy table
  cover

Joining lace motifs with crochet

Once you have completed the first motif of a lacy fabric, you can join the second and all subsequent motifs while working the last round of each. Working in this way not only maintains the continuity of the lace pattern but also greatly enhances the motifs themselves.

The beautiful bedspreads and lace table-cloths characteristic of traditional crochet are frequently worked in this way. Crochet patterns usually give detailed instructions on how to join the particular motifs you are working. They may appear complicated, but don't be put off.

If you follow the instructions carefully you will get beautiful results.
The step-by-step instructions given here are for joining two of the motifs used in the tablecloth featured in this course, but the principle is the same for any motif with lace edges.

1 Begin the sample by working the first motif from the table cloth instructions and the first 5 rounds of the second motif.

2 Hold the first motif behind the 2nd motif with the wrong side of each square facing. Match 1 corner picot of the first motif to the working loop at the end of the 5th round on the 2nd motif.

3 Work 1 double crochet through the corner picot of the first motif to join the squares together. The double crochet will count as the corner picot of the 2nd motif.

4 Leave the first motif. Make 2 chains and then work 3 treble into each of the next 3 treble on the 2nd motif, thus continuing to work the 6th round of the 2nd motif.

5 Hold the 2 motifs together again, matching the block of 3 treble just worked with the corresponding 3 treble on the first motif. Work 1 slip stitch into the first chain of the next 5 chain loop on to the first motif.

6 Leave the first motif. Work 4 chain and then 1 slip stitch into the next double crochet on the second motif.

continued

205

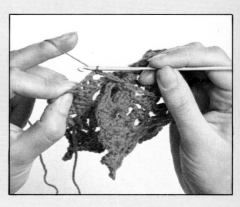

7 Work 1 chain, hold the 2 motifs together as before and work 1 double crochet into the next 4 chain picot on the first motif.

8 Leave the first motif and work 1 chain. Miss the next double crochet on the 2nd motif and then work 1 slip stitch into the next double crochet of the same motif.

9 Work 4 chain. Hold the 2 motifs together and then work 1 slip stitch into the last chain before the next 3 treble block on the first motif.

10 Leave the first motif. Work 1 treble into each of the next 3 treble on the 2nd motif. Work 2 chain. Hold the 2 motifs together and work 1 double crochet into the centre of the picot on the next corner of the first motif. One side of each square has now been joined.

11 Complete the 6th round of the 2nd motif in the same way as given for the second motif of the tablecloth. Join the last stitch to the first with a slip stitch.

12 Where the motifs are being joined in strips, each consecutive motif should be joined in the same way. Remember to work the first 5 rounds of the 2nd motif each time.

Joining lace motifs to make a square fabric

Where two sides of a motif are to be joined to produce a square fabric, the working method is exactly the same as for joining them in a strip, but it is important to work the joins in the correct order, so that the motifs are crocheted together evenly. The step-by-step instructions that follow relate to the table-cloth pattern, but apply to other square fabrics as well.

1 After completing the first row, or strip, of motifs, work the first five rounds of the first motif of the second row. Join one side of this motif to the lower edge of the first motif of the first row. Complete the sixth round.

2 Work the first five rounds of the next motif. With the wrong side of both motifs facing, hold the first and second motifs of this row together so that the bottom left-hand corner of the first motif corresponds to the working loop on the second motif.

3 Work 1 double crochet into the first corner picot of the first motif. This double crochet will count as the first corner picot of the 6th round on the second motif.

4 Now join the two motifs together on this side in the same way as before, making sure that you work the last double crochet on this side into the centre of the corner where the first 3 motifs meet. You will be working the 6th round of the 2nd motif at the same time as joining the two motifs together.

5 Turn the work so that the first row of motifs is at the top of your work and the first motif of the 2nd row on the right-hand side.

6 Now join the top of the 2nd motif of the 2nd row to the bottom of the 2nd motif of the first row in the same way as before, beginning by working 2 chain and then 3 treble into the first 3 treble on the 2nd motif.

7 Complete the 6th round of the 2nd motif, working round the remaining 2 sides of the square and joining the last stitch to the corner picot on the first motif.

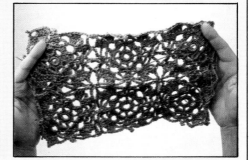

8 Work subsequent joins in the same way, making sure that you always work from the bottom left-hand corner of the motif to the right of the one to be joined, then up and across to the top left-hand corner of the motif being joined. In this way each motif will be joined correctly to the one before.

Joining simple squares with lace crochet

Square motifs with straight sides can also be joined with crochet by working a picot or decorative edging round the first square and then using the same edging to join the following motifs together. Once you have mastered the basic technique you will be able to join any square in the same way, using a variety of picot edgings. This will enable you to combine a motif and edging of your choice and create your own fabric.

The edging you use will depend on the size of motif you wish to make and the type of yarn being used. To follow these step-by-step instructions, first make two granny squares (Crochet Course 14 page 199). Work only 3 rounds for each motif.

1 With the right side of one motif facing, join the yarn to any corner space and make 4 chain. Work 1 double crochet into the 3rd chain from the hook to form a picot point. Now work 1 double crochet into the same corner space. This step will now be referred to as a 4 chain corner picot.

2 Work 1 double crochet into the next treble, then 4 chain and then 1 double crochet into the following treble. This makes one 4 chain loop.

continued

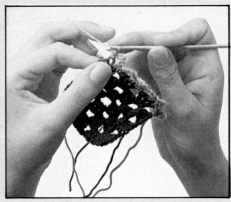

3 Work 4 chain and then 1 double crochet into the next chain loop on the previous round, making the 2nd 4 chain loop on the side of the square.

4 Repeat steps 2 and 3 once more and then step 2 once again. There will now be 5 loops on this side of the square.

5 Work 1 double crochet into the chain loop of the previous round at the next corner. Now work a 4 chain corner picot into the same loop.

6 Continue to work all round the square in the same way, making 5 loops on each side and one 4 chain corner loop on each corner. Join the last double crochet to the first chain worked at the beginning of the round. This completes the decorative edging for the first motif.

7 With the right side of the 2nd motif facing, join the yarn to any corner space and work 2 chain. Hold the first and 2nd motifs together with the wrong sides of each facing, and work a slip stitch into the top of the picot point at one corner on the first motif.

8 Work 2 chain and then 1 double crochet into the same space on the 2nd motif to complete the corner on the 2nd motif.

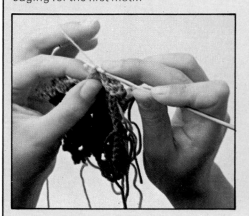

9 Work 1 double crochet into the next stitch on the 2nd motif, then 2 chain. Hold the motifs together and work a slip stitch into the top of the first loop on the first motif, working through the stitch rather than under the loop.

10 Work 2 chain and then 1 double crochet into the next treble on the 2nd motif. Now work 2 chain, then 1 slip stitch into the top of the next loop on the first motif.

11 Work 2 chain and then 1 double crochet into the next chain loop on the 2nd motif.

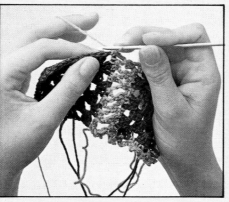

Paul Williams

12 Repeat steps 9 to 11 once more. Now work 1 double crochet into the next stitch.

13 Work 2 chain and then 1 slip stitch into the last loop on the side of the first motif. Now work 2 chain and 1 double crochet into the next stitch on the 2nd motif. Work one more double crochet into the next corner space on the 2nd motif and join it to the picot on the first motif as before, thus joining the two sides together.

14 Complete the picot edging round the remaining 3 sides of the 2nd square in the same way as given for the first motif. When joining the motifs on 2 sides, remember to start at the bottom left-hand corner of the motif to the right of the one being joined, then up and across to the top left-hand corner of the motif being joined.

The lacy look

Small motifs worked in a fine thread and crocheted together in strips make a lovely table cover. Lay it over a plain cloth in a contrasting colour to show off its delicate lines and texture.

Size
77cm at the widest part.

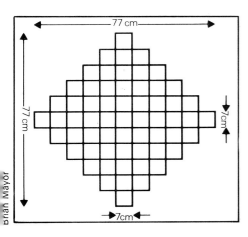

Brian Mayor

Materials
Total of 150g of crochet cotton such as Twilleys Lyscordet
2.00mm crochet hook

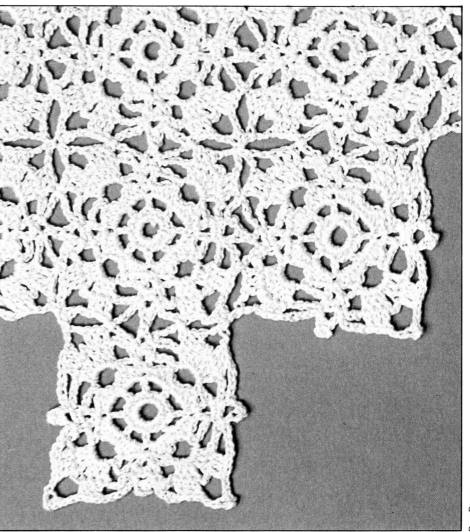

Ray Duns

Tension
1 motif measures 7cm square on 2.00mm hook.

First motif
Make 6ch, join with a ss to first ch to form circle.
1st round 2ch to count as first dc, work 15dc into circle, join with a ss to second of first 2ch.
2nd round 4ch to count as first htr and 2ch, *miss next dc, 1htr into next dc, 2ch, rep from * 6 times more, join with a ss to second of first 4ch.
3rd round Work *1dc, 1htr, 1tr, 1htr and 1dc all into next ch sp, 1ch, rep from * to end, join with a ss to first dc. 8 petals.
4th round 2ch to count as first htr, *3ch, 1dc into tr of next petal, 4ch, 1dc into tr of next petal, 3ch, 1htr into 1ch sp before next petal, 2ch, 1htr into same ch sp, rep from * twice more, 3ch, 1dc into tr of next petal, 4ch, 1dc into tr of next petal, 3ch, 1htr into last 1ch sp after last petal, 2ch, join with a ss to second of first 2ch.

5th round 1ch, *4ch, now work 3tr, 3ch and 3tr all into next 4ch sp to form corner, 4ch, 1dc into next htr, 1dc into next 2ch sp, 1dc into next htr, rep from * twice more, 4ch, now work 3tr, 3ch and 3tr all into next 4ch sp, 4ch, 1dc into next htr, 1dc into next 2ch sp, join with a ss to first ch.
6th round 1ch, *5ch, 1tr into each of next 3tr, 5ch, insert hook into 3rd ch from hook to form a little loop and work 1dc to form picot – called 5ch picot – 2ch, 1tr into each of next 3tr, 5ch, ss into next dc, 4ch, insert hook into 3rd ch from hook and work 1dc to form picot – called 4ch picot – 1ch, miss next dc, ss into next dc; rep from * twice more, 5ch, 1tr into each of next 3tr, work a 5ch picot, 2ch, 1tr into each of next 3tr, 5ch, ss into next dc, work a 4ch picot, 1ch, join with a ss to first ch. Fasten off.

Second motif
Work as given for first motif to end of round 5.
6th round (joining round) 1ch, *5ch, 1tr into each of next 3tr, 2ch, with right side of completed motif facing right side of second motif, which is to be joined, work 1dc into 5ch picot at corner of first motif, 2ch, 1tr into each of next 3tr of second motif, ss into first of 5ch after last tr on first motif, 4ch, ss into next dc of second motif, 1ch, 1dc into 4ch picot of first motif, 1ch, miss next dc on second motif, ss into next dc on second motif, 4ch, ss into last ch before next 3tr on first motif, 1tr into each of next 3tr on second motif, 2ch, 1dc into 5ch picot at corner of first motif, 2ch. One side has been joined. Complete motif as given for first motif. Fasten off.

☐ Make a strip of 11 joined motifs.
☐ Make and join 50 more motifs, placing them as shown in diagram. When two sides have to be joined, join the first side to the corresponding motif on the preceding strip and the second side to the preceding motif of the same strip.
☐ Pin out and press with a warm iron over a damp cloth.

Step-by-step course – 16

Working flat, circular motifs

Working circles in crochet is an important technique, since it is widely used to produce a variety of household items and fabrics.

The basic circle is made of a small number of stitches that are then increased evenly on each round until the motif is the size required. You can use any of a variety of yarns – dishcloth cotton, raffia and string, as well as fine crochet cotton – to achieve a variety of different effects with the same basic shape. In this course we show you how to work two of the simplest round motifs. Once you have mastered the basic technique, you can progress to a more complicated design.

1 Use a double knitting yarn and 4.50mm hook for this sample. Make 5 chain and join them into a circle with a slipstitch.

2 Make 3 chain to count as the first treble of the round. Now work 15 treble into the centre of the circle. You may have to push the stitches together while working to fit them all into the circle.

3 Join the last treble to the 3rd of the first 3 chain with a slip stitch. There will now be 16 treble in the circle, counting the first 3 chain as 1 treble.

4 Make 3 chain. Now work 2 treble into each stitch all the way round the circle. Complete the round by working 1 treble into the stitch at the base of the first 3 chain, and join this to the top of these chain as before. There should now be 32 treble worked in the 2nd round.

5 Begin the 3rd round by working three chain as before. Now work 1 treble into the next treble and then 2 treble into the next stitch on the previous round. The first increase has now been made.

6 Work round circle in the same way, working 2 treble into every other stitch. Work last treble into stitch at base of chain. Join last stitch to first 3 chain as before. There should be 48 treble in the circle.

7 Work the next round in the same way, but work 2 treble into every 3rd stitch, instead of every alternate stitch as on the previous round.

8 Work the last treble into the stitch at the base of the first 3 chain. Join with a slip stitch as before. There should now be 64 stitches in the circle.

continued

Paul Williams

211

Note Patterns for flat motifs are carefully devised to ensure that the motif does lie flat. If you are adapting or designing a motif of your own, you will need to pay special attention to the number of increases you make on each round: with too few increased stitches, the motif will curl up at the edges and with too many increased stitches, the finished motif will have a fluted appearance.

9 Continue to increase 16 stitches on each round in the same way, working 1 more treble between each increase on every subsequent round.

10 Work a total of 6 rounds for a motif approximately 16cm in diameter. There should be a total of 96 treble worked in the last round.

An openwork motif

This openwork motif demonstrates the use of spaces to make a flat circular shape, using the spaces for increasing on each round. Try working the motif in a different kind of material, such as a thick cotton or string; or work each round in a different colour to vary the completed motif.

1 Make 6 chain and join them into a ring with a slip stitch. Make 1 chain and then work 12 double crochet into the centre of the ring. You may have to push the stitches together while working in order to fit them into the circle.

2 Make 5 chain to count as the first treble and 2 chain space of the 2nd round. Miss the next stitch of the previous round and work 2 treble into the next stitch.

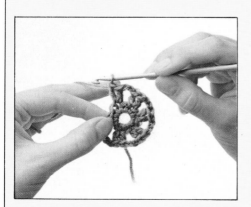

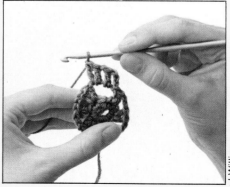

3 Work 2 chain. Miss the next stitch and work 2 treble into the following stitch. Repeat this step 3 times more.

4 Now work 2 chain and then 1 treble into the stitch at the base of the first 5 chain to complete the round. Join the last stitch to the 3rd of the first 5 chain with a slip stitch. There should be 6 groups of treble in all.

5 Begin the 3rd round with 3 chain. Now work 1 treble followed by 1 chain and then 2 treble all into the first space in the previous round.

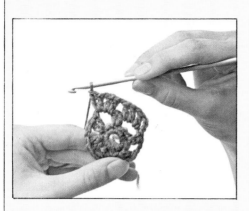

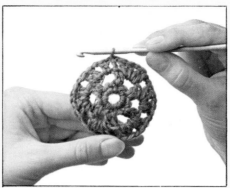

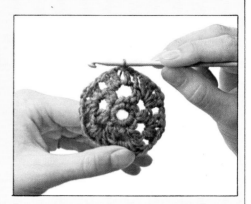

6 Make 1 chain ; then work 2 treble followed by 1 chain and 2 treble, all into the next chain space in the previous round.

7 Repeat step 6 into each space all the way round the circle. Complete the round with 1 chain and join this with a slip stitch to the top of the first 3 chain. There are now 12 groups of treble with 1 chain between each. This completes the 3rd round.

8 To begin the 4th round in the correct place, work a slip stitch across the next stitch and into the first chain space so that you will work the first stitch from this space.

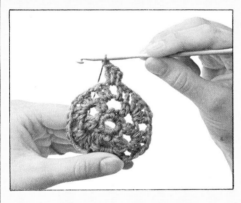

9 Work 3 chain for the first stitch and then 2 treble into the same space as the first 3 chain, making a group of 3 treble. Now work 1 chain.

10 Continue to work round the circle in the same way, working 3 treble into each space with 1 chain between each group of treble.

11 Work the last group of this round into the space before the block of 2 treble below the first 3 chain. Join the last chain to top of the first 3 chain with a slip stitch.

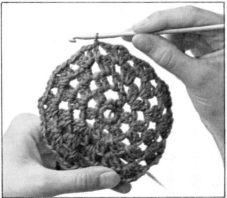

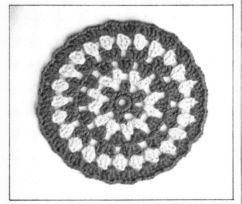

12 Begin the 5th round by working a slip stitch across the first treble block of the row below and into the first chain space. Now work 3 chain.

13 Repeat the 3rd round all round the circle, so that there are twenty-four 2-treble blocks. Join the last chain to the top of the first 3 chain with a slip stitch.

14 To make the motif bigger, repeat the 3rd and 4th rounds alternately until the motif is the required size. To work each round in a different colour, break off 1 colour at the end of the round and join next colour to first chain space of next round, so you need not work slip stitches at the beginning of the rounds.

Paul Williams

Working continuous rounds

An alternative way to work a circle is to crochet continuously round the centre circle, leaving the ends of each round unjoined, thus creating a spiral effect on your fabric. By working in this way it is possible to produce a six-sided motif in either a solid fabric – using double crochet or half treble – or a more open fabric with a lace pattern incorporated into the design. Try making several motifs, each in a different colour, and sewing them together to make an attractive piece of patchwork. This method of working is frequently used as a form of decorative shaping on the crown of a hat or beret, where the lines formed by the increases create a 'star' effect on the very top of the crown.

Our sample has been worked in a double knitting yarn with a 4.50mm hook.

1 Make 6 chain and join them into a circle with a slip stitch. Work 1 chain. Now work 12 double crochet into the centre of the circle. Do not join this or any of the following rounds.

2 Now work 2 double crochet into each double crochet of the previous round so that there are 24 stitches in all. Check at this point that you have the correct number of stitches.

3 Now work 1 double crochet into each of the next 3 double crochet of the previous round, and then work 3 chain.

4 Miss the next double crochet and work 1 double crochet into each of the next 3 double crochet. At this point, you have made the first space on the round. Now work 3 chain.

5 Continue to work all the way round the circle in the same way, working 3 double crochet between each space and missing 1 double crochet below each 3 chain worked until there are 5 chain spaces in all. Complete round by working 3 chain after last 3 double crochet. These chain will count as the 6th space on this round.

6 Begin the 4th round by missing the first double crochet and then working 1 double crochet into each of the next 3 stitches. Now work 2 double crochet into the first 3 chain space on the previous round.

7 Work 3 chain and then 1 double crochet into each of the next 3 stitches, followed by 2 double crochet into the next space. The first space of the 4th round is thus worked to the left of the space in the previous round to begin the spiral shape.

8 Complete this round, working in the same way all round the circle, ending with 3 chain, so that you have worked 5 complete spaces with the last 3 chain counting as the 6th space as before.

Paul Williams

9 Work the 5th round by missing the first double crochet and working 1 double crochet into each of the next 4 stitches. Now work 2 double crochet into the next space.

10 Work 4 chain and then repeat step 9 once more. Continue to work round the circle in the same way with four double crochet between each space, and end the round with 4 chain so that you will have worked 5 complete spaces with the last 4 chain counting as the 6th space as on the previous round.

11 Begin the 6th round by missing the first double crochet of the next block and working 1 double crochet into each of the next 5 double crochet. Now work 2 double crochet into the next chain space, followed by 4 chain.

12 Repeat step 11 all the way round the circle until you have worked 5 spaces with the last 4 chain counting as the 6th space as before.

13 Work the 7th round by missing the first double crochet and then working 1 double crochet into each of the next remaining double crochet in the next block, followed by 2 double crochet into the next space and then 5 chain. Work in the same way all round the circle, making 5 spaces as before and counting the last 5 chain as the 6th space.

14 Continue to repeat the last round 5 times more to make a motif approx. 20cm in diameter, always missing the first stitch on each block of double crochet in the previous round and then working into each remaining stitch in the block. There will be one more stitch worked in each block on every round.

Making a simple tassel

Follow these step-by-step instructions to make the tassel for the blue hat featured on page 216 You can alter the size of the tassel by changing the length of yarn cut and the number of lengths you use.

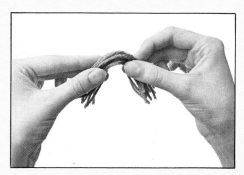

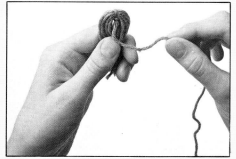

1 Cut 16 lengths of yarn, each approximately 12cm long. Fold the yarn in half.

2 Cut a length of yarn at least 30cm long and tie one end firmly round the centre of the lengths of yarn.

Paul Williams

continued

3 Wind the remaining length of yarn several times round the top of the tassel just below the centre fold, leaving enough yarn to be threaded into a needle.

4 Thread the yarn into a blunt-ended needle and insert the needle under the yarn wound round the tassel, and up through the middle of the tassel.

5 Catch the yarn with a slip stitch in the middle of the head of the tassel and then take it down through the centre so that it becomes one of the ends. Trim the ends if necessary.

Hats on !

If you've got a head for hats, make up one — or all three — of these crocheted charmers. Worked in rounds, they can be varied in all sorts of ways to team up with just about anything in your wardrobe.

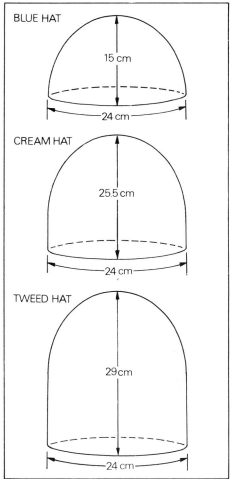

BLUE HAT
15 cm
24 cm

CREAM HAT
25.5 cm
24 cm

TWEED HAT
29 cm
24 cm

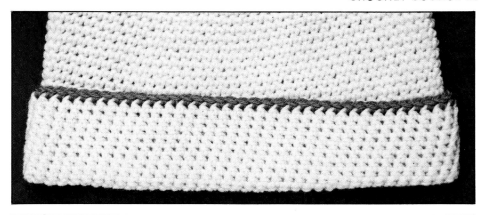

John Hutchinson

Sizes
To fit average size head : other measurements are shown on the diagrams.

Materials
Blue hat : total of 75g of double knitting yarn such as Patons Superwash Wool double knitting
Cream hat : total of 125g of double knitting yarn such as Patons Superwash Wool double knitting
An oddment of blue yarn
Tweed hat : total of 100g of double knitting yarn such as Patons Bracken Tweed
3.50mm and 4.00mm crochet hooks

Tension
18dc and 20 rows to 10cm.

Blue hat
*Using 4.00mm hook make 3ch, join with a ss to first ch to form a circle.
Next round Work 6dc into circle ; mark the first of these 6dc to denote the beginning of the round.
Working in continuous rounds, proceed as follows :
☐ Work 2dc into each of next 6dc to increase 6dc.
☐ Work (1dc into next dc, 2dc into next dc) 6 times.
☐ Work (1dc into each of next 2dc, 2dc into next dc) 6 times.
☐ Work (1dc into each of next 3dc, 2dc into next dc) 6 times.
☐ Work (1dc into each of next 4dc, 2dc into next dc) 6 times.
☐ Continue to increase in this way until 11dc have been worked between each increase ; you should have 76dc. *
☐ Work straight on these 76dc until work measures 15cm measured at centre.
☐ Change to 3.50mm hook and work 1 round. Fasten off.

Cord
☐ Using 3.50mm hook make 60ch, ss into each ch to end. Fasten off.
☐ Make 2 tassels and sew one to each end of cord.
☐ Sew centre of cord to top of hat.

Cream hat
☐ Using cream, work as given for blue hat from * to *.
☐ Work straight on these 76dc until work measures 25.5cm measured at centre. Fasten off.
☐ With wrong side of work facing join on blue and work 1 round of dc. Fasten off.
☐ Turn back 6cm for brim.

Ray Duns

Tweed hat
☐ Work as given for blue hat from * to *
☐ Work straight on these 76dc until work measures 29cm measured at centre. Fasten off.
☐ Fold back 15cm for brim.

Step-by-step course – 17

More about motifs

Now that you have mastered the basic principles of working a square motif, try making this pretty square with the Catherine wheel centre. The centre of the motif is worked in a circular shape with the corners and straight sides only being worked on the last two rounds – unlike the granny square, in which the four corners of the motif are made on the first round.

Our motif has been worked in a 4-ply yarn using a 3.50mm hook. Try making the same motif in several colours or using different yarns and hook sizes to see the variety of effects you can achieve. The same motif worked in a fine cotton will be very different when worked in a chunky yarn with a large hook.

1 Make 8 chain and join into a circle with a slip stitch. Now work 2 chain to count as the first treble, followed by 15 treble into the circle. Join the last treble to the first 2 chain with a slip stitch. Join each round in the same way.

2 Make 5 chain to count as the first treble and 2 chain space of the next round. Now work 1 treble followed by 2 chain into each stitch all round the circle. Join the last chain to the top of the 3 chain at the beginning of the round.

3 Work 3 chain to count as the first treble of the next round. Now work 2 treble into the first 2 chain space. This will be the first block of treble.

4 Work 1 chain, then 3 treble into the next 2 chain space.

5 Repeat step 4 all the way round the circle so that there are 16 blocks of trebles with 1 chain between each block. Join last chain to top of the first 3 chain.

6 Work 3 chain and then 1 double crochet into the next 1 chain space. Repeat this action twice more so that there are 3 loops on this side of the circle.

7 Work the first corner of the square by making 6 chain and then working 1 double crochet into the next 1 chain space.

8 Repeat steps 6 and 7 all round the motif so that there are three 3-chain loops on each side with a 6-chain loop at each corner, and 1 double crochet worked into each 1 chain space. Join the last chain to the base of the first three chain.

9 Work 3 chain to count as the first treble of the next round and then 2 treble into the first 2 chain space.

10 Now work 3 treble into each of the next two 3-chain loops on the side of the square.

11 Work 5 treble followed by 2 chain and 5 treble all into the next 6-chain loop at the corner.

12 Continue to work round the square in the same way, with three blocks of three treble on each side and 5 treble, 2 chain and 5 treble all into the 6-chain loop at each of the remaining 3 corners. Join the last treble to the top of the first 3 treble. This completes the motif.

Working a picot edging

There are various picot edgings which can be worked with a crochet hook directly on to the edge of the fabric, the simplest being that featured on the baby's carrying cape in this course. As they are worked into the edge of the fabric, they can be used not only as a decorative trimming but also as a means of neatening an uneven edge or hem on a crocheted or knitted fabric. They can be worked in either rows or rounds in any thickness of yarn, from a fine cotton for a delicate trimming on table linens to a thick wool for a chunky cardigan or tabard.

Our sample has been worked in a 4-ply yarn on a piece of double crochet fabric. Once you have mastered the working technique, try using a fine hook and crochet cotton for a different effect.

1 With the right side of the work facing, make 5 chain at the right-hand edge of the fabric to count as the first half treble and 2 chain space.

2 Miss the next 2 stitches and then work 1 half treble into the next stitch.

3 Make 2 chain and then repeat step 2 once more.

4 Repeat step 3 all along the edge of the fabric, working the last half treble into the turning chain at the end of the last row of the main fabric. You have now worked a series of 2 chain spaces with 1 half treble between each space.

5 Turn. Work 1 double crochet into the first space, inserting the hook from front to back under the 2 chain worked in the previous row.

continued

Fred Mancini

6 Make 3 chain and then work 1 slip stitch into the first of these 3 chain to form the picot point.

7 Work another double crochet into the same space, as before, so that 1 picot block has now been completed.

8 Continue to work 1 picot block in exactly the same way into each chain space to the end of the row to complete the edging.

Joining motifs with a slip stitch

Square motifs with straight side edges can be joined together with a slip stitch to make a very firm seam with a raised appearance. Use this method of seaming on something like a chunky rug or blanket to make sure that the motifs are joined firmly together and to make a feature of the seams.

1 Hold the two motifs to be joined with the wrong sides together and insert the hook through both corners.

2 Draw a loop of yarn through both corners and make 1 chain to hold the yarn in place.

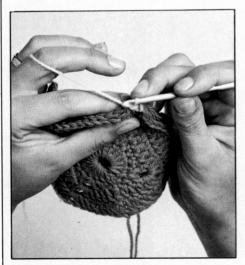

3 Work 1 slip stitch into the next stitch, working through both thicknesses.

4 Continue to work 1 slip stitch into each stitch along the edge of the motifs, taking care to work into the corresponding stitch on each motif.

5 When laid flat the seams thus joined are raised, producing a kind of lattice effect.

Cosy hooded cape

Sizes
To fit a baby up to 3 months old.
Length to shoulder, 49cm.
Length of hood to shoulder, 21cm.

What could be easier to make – or more comfortable for baby to wear – than this pretty cape? The pastel random yarn gives a soft effect to the motifs, which are sewn together in a simple rectangular shape. The picot edging is worked after the hood and cape have been joined.

Materials
*Total of 300g of double knitting yarn
    in a random shade such as Peter
    Pan Darling DK Random
3.00mm crochet hook
3.50mm crochet hook
1 button*

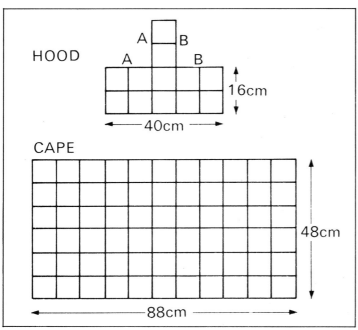

HOOD

A B
A   B

16cm

←—— 40cm ——→

CAPE

48cm

←——— 88cm ———→

Tension
1 motif measures 8cm square worked on a 3.50mm hook.

The motif
Using 3.50mm hook, make 6ch, join with a ss to first ch to form a circle.
1st round Work 3ch to count as first tr, then work 19tr into the circle, join the last tr to the 3rd of the first 3ch with a ss.
2nd round 1ch to count as first dc, 1htr into next tr, work 1tr, 3ch and 1tr all into next tr – corner formed, 1htr into next tr, *1dc into each of next 2tr, 1htr into next tr, now work 1tr, 3ch and 2tr all into next tr – corner formed, 1htr into next tr, rep from * twice more, 1dc into next tr, join last dc to the first ch with a ss.
3rd round 3ch, 1tr into each of next 2sts, work 2tr, 3ch and 2tr all into loop at corner – called 1 gr, *1tr into each of next 6sts, work 1gr into centre of loop at corner, rep from * twice more, 1 tr into each of last 3sts, join last tr to 3rd of first 3ch with a ss.
4th round 3ch, 1tr into each of next 4tr, 1gr into centre of gr at corner, *1tr into each of next 10tr, work 1gr into centre of gr at corner, rep from * twice more, 1tr into each of next 5tr, join last tr to 3rd of first 3ch with a ss. Fasten off.
☐ Make 65 more motifs in same way for cape and then make 12 for hood.

Cape
Darn in all loose ends to wrong side of motifs. Oversew motifs together, placing them as shown in diagram.

Edging
With right side of work facing, join yarn to first corner of 2nd motif on one long side and using 3.50mm hook work 1dc into this loop, *1dc into each tr to next

corner, 1dc into corner loop, then 1dc into corner loop of next motif, rep from * to end, working last dc into last corner loop. Turn.
Next row 1ch, (insert hook into next dc and draw a loop through) twice, yarn round hook and draw through all 3 loops on hook – one dc decreased ; decrease 1dc in this way over every 2dc to end of row. Fasten off.

Hood
Darn in all loose ends to wrong side of motifs. Oversew motifs together placing them as shown in diagram, sewing seams A to A and B to B.

Edging
With right side of work facing, join in yarn. Using 3.50mm hook work 1dc into each tr and loop along lower edge. Fasten off.

To join hood and cape
With right sides together join yarn to corner of first motif on cape and working through the double thickness join the lower edge of the hood to the top edge of the cape by working 1dc into each dc. Fasten off.

Edging
With right side of work facing, join yarn to lower edge at centre back and using 3.00mm hook work *1dc into each tr and 1dc into each corner loop along lower edge to corner, work 3dc into the corner loop, rep from * to corner at neck edge, work 3dc into corner, continue to work in this way round hood and down other side of cape to centre back ; join with a ss to first dc. Do not turn.
Next row 1ch, *1dc into each of next 3dc, 3ch, ss into top of last dc worked – 1 picot formed ; rep from * all round

edge of cape and hood, join with a ss to first ch. Fasten off.
☐ Sew a button to left front, 1 motif in from left front neck edge, and use corner sp on first motif on right for buttonhole.
☐ Press lightly on the wrong side using a warm iron over a damp cloth.

Ties
Using 3.50mm hook and yarn double throughout make a ch 42cm long. Fasten off.
☐ Make another tie in the same way.
☐ Sew 1 tie to each side of hood at neck.

More abbreviations to learn

ch	=	chain
dc	=	double crochet
htr	=	half treble
tr	=	treble
dtr	=	double treble
tr tr	=	triple treble
st(s)	=	stitch(es)

These are the abbreviations that you already know ; most refer to special crochet techniques. To keep instructions short and concise, a number of frequently recurring ordinary words are abbreviated to form part of the special crochet shorthand. Below is a list of some of these words in alphabetical order ; they will now appear in the patterns in the crochet courses so you can become familiar with them.

beg	=	beginning
foll	=	following
gr(s)	=	group(s)
rep	=	repeat
sp(s)	=	space(s)
ss	=	slip stitch

Step-by-step course – 18

*Making buttonholes
*Chain button loops
*Simple crochet rib
*Final list of abbreviations
*Pattern for a man's
 waistcoat

Making buttonholes

Both horizontal and vertical buttonholes are easy to make – either on the main fabric of your garment or on a separate band which can be sewn on afterwards. Your pattern will tell you how many buttonholes you should make for your garment. Before working the buttonholes, you should measure the length of the button band -- or the edge of your garment on which the buttons will be sewn – and mark the button positions on it, spacing them at equal distances from each other. Using these marks as a guide, you will know precisely where to make each buttonhole when working the buttonhole band.

Our samples were made with a 4.50mm hook and double knitting yarn, and the buttonhole measures approximately 2cm in length. You can vary the size of the buttonhole by using a different thickness of yarn or a different size hook, or by altering the number of stitches or rows in the buttonhole.

Horizontal buttonholes

1 Make 25 chain and work 4 rows in double crochet. When the buttonholes are being worked on the edge of the main fabric, always make sure that you finish the last row – the one before the buttonhole row – at the centre front edge.

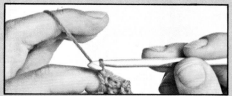

2 Turn and work 3 double crochet. Do not forget to count the turning chain as one stitch. The number of stitches worked at the edge of the fabric will depend on the thickness of yarn being used.

3 Now work 4 chain for the first buttonhole.

4 Miss the next 4 double crochet. Now work 1 double crochet into the next stitch. You can alter the number of chain made and stitches missed in the row below according to the size of buttonhole required.

5 Now work in pattern to the end of the row. Turn and work back to the point where the buttonhole has been made.

6 Work a double crochet into the stitch just before the chain made in the previous row.

7 Now work 1 double crochet into each chain made in the previous row, placing the hook through the middle of the chain each time. This completes the buttonhole.

8 Now work in pattern to the end of the row. The two buttonhole rows are now completed ; there should be the same number of stitches in the row as there were before you worked the hole.

9 Repeat these two rows each time a buttonhole is to be made. If you are making a separate buttonhole band, work the buttonholes in exactly the same way.

Fred Mancini

Vertical buttonholes

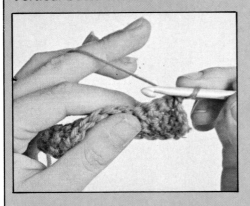

1 For this sample we have used a 4.50mm hook and double knitting yarn. Make 17 chain and work 4 rows in double crochet. When working on the main fabric make sure that you always finish the last row – the one before the buttonhole row – at the centre front edge.

2 Turn and work 4 double crochet. Do not forget to count the turning chain as one stitch. Now turn and leave the remaining stitches unworked.

3 Work 6 more rows on these 4 stitches for the first side of the buttonhole, so that you finish the last row at the buttonhole edge.

4 Do not turn. Work in slip stitch down the side of the buttonhole. Work the last slip stitch into the same place as the first double crochet worked for the first side of the buttonhole.

5 Make 1 chain. Now miss 1 stitch and work 1 double crochet into each stitch to the end. Work the last double crochet into the turning chain.

6 Now work 6 more rows on these 12 stitches so that this side has the same number of rows as the other side of the buttonhole. You should finish this row at the side edge of your fabric.

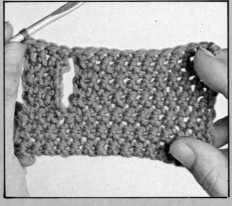

7 Turn and work back to the edge of the buttonhole. Now work 1 double crochet into the edge stitch on the other side of the buttonhole to join the two sides together.

8 Work in pattern to the end of the row to complete the first buttonhole. It is a good idea to count the stitches at this stage to make sure that you have the correct number.

9 Make all the buttonholes in the same way, whether working up the side edge of your fabric, or making a separate band which is to be sewn on afterwards.

Chain button loops

On some crochet fabrics it is not always necessary to make buttonholes since the spaces between the stitches can be used in place of buttonholes. The tiny buttons used on baby clothes can often be fastened through the fabric. However, if you are working an edging round a garment the depth of the edging may prevent your using the fabric in this way. In this case the simplest way to make a buttonhole is to work crochet loops at evenly spaced intervals down the side of your garment.

1 Work a row of double crochet down the side of the garment. Your pattern will tell you the stitch you should use and precisely how many rows to work before you make a button loop.

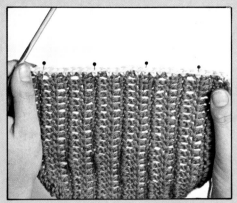

2 On the edge of the garment mark the positions of the loops by counting the stitches to be worked between loops.

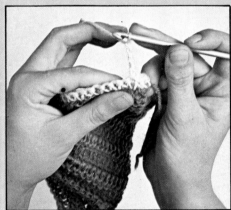

3 Work in double crochet to the point where the first button loop is to be made.

4 Now work 3 chain. You can alter the number of chain to make different sized button loops.

5 Miss the next 3 stitches on the previous row, and work 1 double crochet into the next stitch. The number of stitches you miss should always be the same as the number of chain you have just made.

6 Work in double crochet until you reach the marker for the next loop.

7 Now repeat steps 4 and 5 once more to make the second button loop.

8 Continue down the side of the fabric, working the loops in the same way until the edging is completed.

Fred Mancini

225

Simple crochet rib

Here is a simple form of ribbing, similar in appearance to knitted fisherman's rib, especially when worked in a chunky yarn. Although it does not have the same degree of elasticity as a knitted rib, it is still very useful for making collars, cuffs and welts. Used for the main fabric of a garment, the stitch makes a really attractive texture which is quick and easy to work.

The method of working differs from the usual way, in that the number of stitches needed to begin the pattern will correspond to the depth of the ribbing required, rather than the width. This means that you are, in effect, working from side to side, rather than from the lower edge to the top, so that it is only when the fabric thus made is turned sideways that the ribbed effect becomes apparent. You work round the garment, rather than starting at lower edge.

Try our sample using a chunky yarn and a 6.00mm hook.

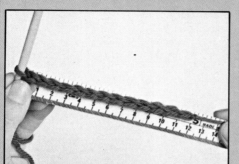

1 Make 13 chain for a piece of ribbing measuring approximately 12cm in depth.

2 Work 1 double crochet into 3rd chain from hook and then 1 double crochet into each chain to the end.

3 Turn 1ch. Miss the first double crochet. Insert the hook from front to back into the back, horizontal loop of the next stitch – not under both loops as in ordinary crochet.

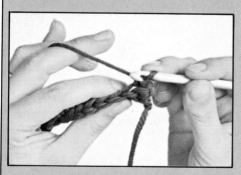

4 Draw the yarn through and complete the double crochet in the normal way.

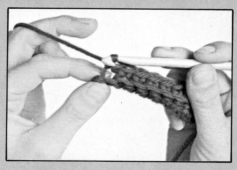

5 Continue to work a double crochet into each stitch, through the back loop only, in the same way, until only turning chain remains.

6 Work the last stitch into the back of the turning chain. If you work into the turning chain in the normal way you will find that the edge of your work becomes distorted.

7 Work each row in the same way until the piece is the required length. This should be the same length as the width of the garment you are making.

8 When the ribbing is to be used as a welt or cuff, turn the work at the end of the last row so that the rows just worked now run vertically rather than horizontally.

9 Continue to work along the side edge of the ribbing to begin the main part of the garment, working one stitch into each row end unless your instructions tell you otherwise.

Fred Mancini

Final list of abbreviations.

beg = beginning
ch = chain
dc = double crochet
dtr = double treble
foll = following
gr(s) = group(s)
htr = half treble
rep = repeat
sp(s) = space(s)
ss = slip stitch
st(s) = stitch(es)
tr = treble
tr tr = triple treble

The list on the left gives, alphabetically, the abbreviations you have learned so far. To complete your knowledge of crochet shorthand, we list the remaining commonly-used terms, along with their abbreviations. There are a few more crochet abbreviations for specialized terms, which will be introduced as they arise in the course. From now on, the course patterns will use all the standard abbreviations.

alt = alternate
cont = continu(e) (ing)
dec = decreas(e) (ing)
inc = increas(e) (ing)
patt = pattern
rem = remain(ing)
RS = right side
tog = together
WS = wrong side
yrh = yarn round hook

Shetland waistcoat

For keeping the winter chill out this waistcoat is ideal. It's made of warm Shetland wool in an easy-to-work pattern and trimmed with crochet ribbing.

Sizes
To fit 97[102:107]cm chest.
Length, 61[63:65]cm.
Note Instructions for larger sizes are in square brackets [ ]; where there is only one set of figures it applies to all sizes.

Materials
  10[11:11] x 25g balls of Templetons
    H & O Shetland Fleece
  3.50mm crochet hook
  4.00mm crochet hook
  5 buttons

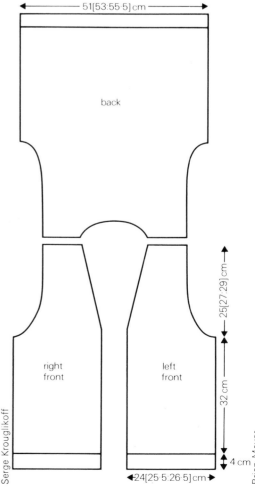

Serge Krouglikoff

Brian Mayor

Tension

18 sts and 20 rows to 10cm over patt worked on a 4.00mm hook.

Back

Using 3.50mm hook make 9ch for side edge of welt.

Base row 1dc into 3rd ch from hook, 1dc into each ch to end. Turn. 8sts. Commence rib.

Rib row 2ch to count as first dc, * 1dc into back loop only of next st, rep from * to end. Work last dc into back loop of turning chain. Turn.

Rep the last row 89[93 :97] times more. This completes ribbing for welt. Do not turn. Work along one long edge. Change to 4.00mm hook.

Next row 1ch, now work 1dc into each row end all along this edge. Turn. Commence patt.

Next row 2ch, miss first st, * miss next dc, work 2dc into next dc, rep from * to end. Turn.

This row forms the patt and is repeated throughout. Cont in patt until work measures 36cm from beg.

Shape armholes

Decrease 2sts at each end of next 2 rows, then one st at each end of next 6 rows. 72[76 :80]sts. Cont without shaping until armhole measures 25[27 :29]cm from beg.

Shape shoulders and neck

Next row Ss over first 5sts, 2ch to count as first st, now work in patt over first 16[17 :18]sts (remember to count the first 2ch as one st). Turn. Complete the right shoulder on these sts.

Next row Decrease one st, patt to last 5sts. Turn. Draw yarn through and fasten off.

Return to remaining sts. With RS of work facing, miss next 30[32 :34]sts, rejoin yarn to next st, 2ch, now work in patt to last 5sts, turn and leave these sts unworked.

Next row Ss over first 5sts, work in patt to last 2sts, work these 2sts together to decrease one st. Draw yarn through and fasten off.

Left front

Using 3.50mm hook make 9ch. Work

base row and rib row as given for back. Rep rib row 41[43 :45] times more. Do not turn but work along one long edge of welt as given for back. 44[46 :48]sts. Change to 4.00mm hook. Cont in patt as given for back until work measures same as back to armhole, ending at side edge.

Shape armhole and front edge

1st row Ss over first 2sts, 2ch, patt to last 2sts, work these 2sts together to decrease one st. Turn.

2nd row Work in patt to last 2sts. Turn.

Dec one st at armhole edge on next 6 rows, and *at the same time* decrease one st at front edge on every 3rd row until 20[21 :22]sts rem. Cont without shaping until armhole measures same as back to shoulder, ending at armhole edge.

Shape shoulder

Next row Ss over first 5sts, 2ch, work in patt to end of row. Turn.

Next row Patt to last 5sts, turn and leave these sts unworked.

Draw yarn through and fasten off.

Right front

Work as given for left front, but reversing shaping so that armhole and neck shaping are worked on the opposite side to left front.

Front border

Join shoulder seams on WS, using a back stitch seam. Using 3.50mm hook and with RS of right front facing, work a row of dc up right front, round neck and down left front, working 1dc into each row end. Work 7 rows in rib as given for back, making 5 buttonholes on 4th row, the first to come approximately 1.5cm from the lower edge, with 4 more evenly spaced up left front at approximately 7.5cm intervals as follows :

Work to point where first buttonhole is to be made, make 3ch and miss the next 3dc, cont in patt to the position for the next buttonhole, and work another one in the same way. The last buttonhole should be worked at the point where the front neck shaping begins. On the next row, work 1dc into each of the 3ch made in the previous row to complete the buttonhole. Draw yarn through and fasten off.

Armhole borders

Work as given for front border for 5 rows, omitting buttonholes.

To make up

Press work lightly under a damp cloth with a warm iron if necessary, omitting ribbing. Join side seams using back stitch seam. Press seams lightly. Sew on buttons to correspond with buttonholes.

Serge Krouglikoff

Step-by-step course – 19

*Crochet edgings
*Crab stitch edging
*Lace shell edging
*Scalloped shell edging
*Chain loop edging
*Pattern for child's apron

Crochet edgings

Crochet edgings are extremely versatile, giving you plenty of scope for adding your individual touch to the garment you are making.

In this course we show you how to work a selection of different edgings directly on to your fabric. These edgings can be used simply to neaten the edge of the fabric (for example, a plain crab stitch edging on a really chunky garment) or for decorative effect as well (for example, a delicate chain loop edge round a baby's shawl). The edgings may be worked on to crocheted or knitted fabric, using the same or a contrasting coloured yarn. It is important, however, to choose a type of yarn and edging appropriate to the garment you have made. Use a fine edging to go round a baby's dress or summer top and a heavier edging for a chunky jacket or coat.

If you are working down the side of your fabric, rather than into each stitch across the row, you may need first to work a row of double crochet to form a firm base for the edging. The number of double crochet you work down the row ends depends on the kind of stitch, hook and yarn used for the main fabric. Make sure you do not work too few stitches, as this pulls the edge and distorts the shape.

Crab stitch edging

This popular and very simple edging is an ideal way to give a firm neat edge to a chunky garment. The finished result is not unlike a form of blanket stitching, and for this reason it is particularly effective when worked in a chunky yarn on a thick fabric.

1 Work 1 row of double crochet as a base row along the edge of your fabric. Work the last double crochet into the corner of the fabric.

2 Do not turn the work as you would normally do. Keep holding the yarn and hook in the same hands as before, with the yarn to the left of the work.

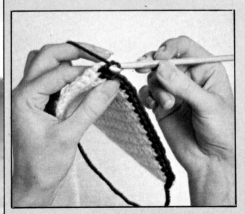

3 You now continue to work back along the row from left to right, rather than from right to left in the usual way. Begin by making 1 chain.

4 Miss the first stitch and insert the hook from front to back into the next stitch. Now place the hook over the yarn.

5 Draw the yarn through and complete the double crochet in the usual way. Work 1 double crochet into each stitch along the row in the same way. Fasten off.

Fred Mancini

229

Lace shell edging

This pretty lace edging looks best in a 4 ply or finer yarn. We show you how to work down the side of the garment, but you can, of course, work across the fabric, working into each stitch rather than each row end.

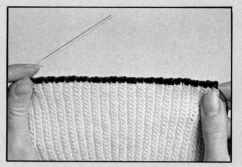

1 Work a row of double crochet along the edge of your fabric as a base row for the edging. This will also help to neaten the edge of your fabric.

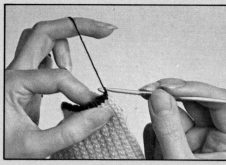

2 Turn the work so that you are ready to work back along the double crochet row in the normal way. Now make 1 chain, miss the first 2 double crochet.

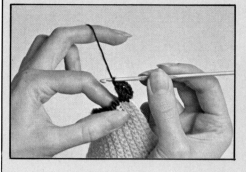

3 Work 2 treble, then 2 chain and 2 treble all into the next double crochet. Miss the next 2 double crochet.

4 Repeat step 3 all along the edge of the fabric until only one double crochet remains unworked.

5 Complete the edging by working a slip stitch into the corner of the fabric. Fasten off.

Scalloped shell edging

This edging is most effective when worked directly on to the fabric, rather than over a base of double crochet. It can either be worked into the stitches across the row or into the row ends and produces a scalloped effect on the edge of your garment.

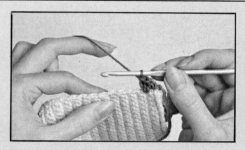

1 Join yarn to corner. Make one chain. Miss the next row end (or stitch) and work 3 treble into the following row end to form the first shell shape.

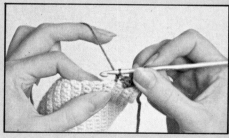

2 Now miss the next row end and work 1 double crochet into the following row end.

3 Miss the next row end and work 3 treble into the following row end for the 2nd shell.

4 Continue to repeat steps 2 and 3 all the way across the edge until the last shell has been worked.

5 Now miss the next row end and work the last double crochet into the corner of the fabric. Fasten off.

Chain loop edging

The pretty arched effect of this simple lace edging is achieved by working a series of chain loops on top of each other. You could make the edging deeper by working more chain loops until it is the depth you require.

1 Work a base row of double crochet down the side of the fabric. Make sure that you work an even number of stitches for this edging.

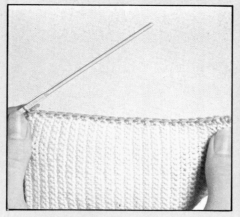

2 Turn and work 1 chain to count as the first double crochet. Now work 5 more chain. Miss the next double crochet and work 1 double crochet into the next stitch, thus forming the first arch.

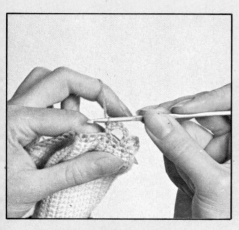

3 Work 5 chain. Miss the next double crochet and work 1 double crochet into the next stitch for the second arch.

4 Repeat step 3 all the way along the row, working the last double crochet into the corner of your fabric.

5 Turn the work. Now make 5 chain and then 1 double crochet into the centre of the first 5 chain loop of the previous row.

6 Make 5 chain. Now work 1 double crochet into the centre of the next 5 chain loop.

7 Continue to repeat step 6 all along the row until only 1 loop remains unworked in the previous row.

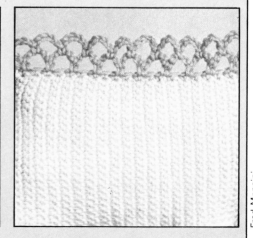

8 Work 5 chain as before. Now work a slip stitch instead of a double crochet into the centre of the last loop and fasten off the yarn.

Fred Mancini

Young Victoriana

For those special occasions, this apron will brighten up a plain dress. It is worked in a simple stitch and edged with shells around the straps and skirt.

Sizes
To suit 56[61:66]cm chest.
Length from shoulder, 47 [52:57]cm.

Note Instructions for larger sizes are in square brackets []. Where there is only one set of figures it applies to all sizes.

Materials
6[7:8] balls of Robin Suzette Crochet Courtelle
3.00mm crochet hook
2 buttons

Tension
22 sts and 22 rows to 10cm over patt worked on a 3.00mm hook.

Skirt
Using 3.00mm hook make 58 [64:70]ch.
Base row Work 1dc into 4th ch from hook, * now work 1tr into next ch, 1dc into next ch, rep from * to end. Turn. 56[62:68] sts.

Patt row 3ch to count as first tr, miss first dc, * work 1dc into next tr, 1tr into next dc, rep from * to end of row. Work last dc into turning ch, turn. The last row forms the patt and is repeated throughout. Cont in patt until work measures 24 [27:30]cm from beg.

Work edging
Do not turn work, but continue to work down side edge, working 1dc into each row end to lower edge, 1dc into rem loop of each ch along lower edge and 1dc into each row end up other side of work. Fasten off. With RS of work facing rejoin yarn to beg of edging and work 1ch, * miss next dc, work 2tr. 2ch and 2tr all into next dc to make a shell, miss next dc, 1dc into next dc, rep from * round 3 sides as before.
Fasten off.

Bib
Using 3.00mm hook make 30 [34:38]ch. Work base row and patt row as given for skirt. 28[32:36] sts. Cont in patt until bib measures 12[13:14] cm from beg.
Work straps
Patt over first 6 [6:8] sts, turn and leave rem sts unworked. Cont on these sts for 30 [32:34]cm. Fasten off.
Return to rem sts. Miss next 16[20:20] sts, rejoin yarn to next st and work in patt to end of row.
Complete as given for first strap.
Edging
Work edging as given for skirt along outer edges of bib and straps, and then along inner edge of 1st strap, across top of bib and along inner edge of 2nd strap. Fasten off.

Waistband and ties
Using 3.00mm hook make 9ch. Work 1dc into 3rd ch from hook, 1dc into each ch to end. Turn. 8 sts. Cont to work in dc until band measures 95 [100:105] cm from beg. Fasten off.

Pocket
Using 3.00mm hook make 18 [22:26] ch. Work base row and patt row as given for skirt. 16 [20:24] sts. Cont in patt until pocket measures 7 [8:9]cm from beg.
Shape top
Next row 1ch, 1dc into each of next 3 sts, * miss next tr, 1dc into each of next 3 sts, rep from * to end so that only 13 [16:19] sts rem.
Next row 1ch, miss 1 [0:0]dc, * work 2tr, 2ch and 2tr all into next dc, miss next dc, 1dc into next dc, miss next dc, rep from * 1 [2:3] times more, work 2tr, 2ch and 2tr all into next dc, miss 1 [1:0]dc, 1dc into turning ch. Fasten off.

To make up
Press work lightly, if you wish, under a dry cloth with a cool iron. Sew lower edge of bib to centre of waistband. Sew top of skirt to other side of waistband, gathering top slightly. Sew a button 7cm from each side of waistband and make a loop at end of each strap to fasten. Sew on pocket. Press seams.

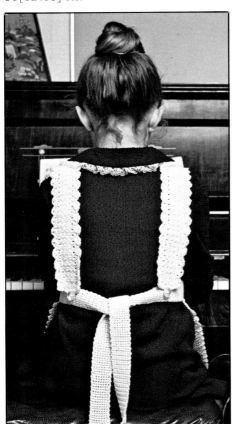

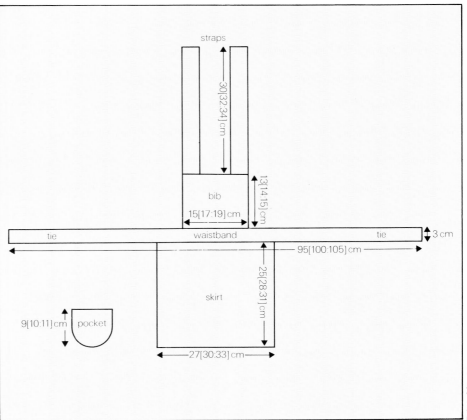

Brian Mayor

Step-by-step course – 20

An introduction to Aran-style crochet

'Aran' is a term which is rightly associated with knitting, rather than crochet. It refers to the intricate and highly textured knitting stitches that originated on the Aran Islands of Inishmore, Inisheer and Inishmaan, off the West Coast of Ireland.

Although crochet cannot duplicate exactly the appearance of Aran knitting, it can create patterns that resemble some of the Aran stitches, such as moss stitch, berry stitch and many others. This Aran-style crochet has its own appeal, and devotees of crochet appreciate its relative simplicity, compared to knitting, as well as its pleasing appearance.

The following step-by-step instructions are intended to help you work two of the more complicated stitches used to make the Afghan featured at the end of this course.

Uneven berry stitch

This simple, but effective, stitch is worked by drawing the yarn several times through the same stitch, then working all the loops off the hook to make a bobble or 'berry'. The size of the bobble depends on the number of times the yarn is drawn through the stitch (and also, of course, on the thickness of the yarn). Practise making the bobbles with an Aran-type yarn and a 6.00mm hook. Make 20 chain and start the sample by working 18 double crochet into the chain so that there are 19 stitches in all, including the turning chain.

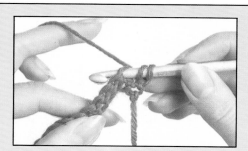

1 Begin the first row of the pattern with 1 chain. This will be the WS of the work. Miss the first double crochet. Now wind the yarn round the hook and insert it into the next double crochet.

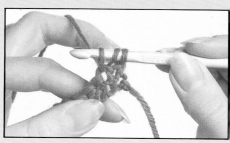

2 Wind the yarn round the hook and draw it through the stitch, pulling up the yarn so that the loop is quite loose.

3 Wind the yarn round the hook and draw it through the first loop on the hook. 3 loops now remain on the hook.

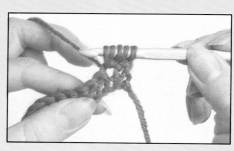

4 Wind the yarn round the hook and insert it once more into the same stitch as before. Repeat step 2 once more. 5 loops on the hook.

5 Wind the yarn round the hook and draw it through the first 4 loops. 2 loops remain. Now draw yarn in same way through last 2 loops to form bobble.

6 Work 1 slip stitch into the next double crochet to hold the bobble in place.

7 Work 1 bobble into next stitch, then 1 slip stitch into the next stitch, alternately until 2 stitches remain.

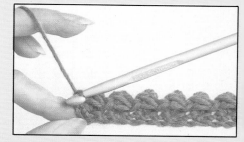

8 Work 1 bobble into the next stitch and then 1 double crochet into the turning chain to complete the first row.

continued

234

Continued : uneven berry stitch

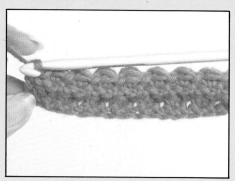

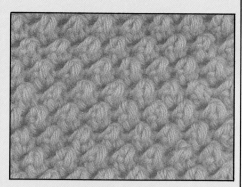

9 Turn. The 2nd row is worked on the RS of the work. Make 1 chain and miss the first double crochet. Now work a slip stitch into the top of each bobble and 1 double crochet into each slip stitch across the row. Work the last double crochet into the turning chain.

10 The 3rd row is worked like the first, but to alter the position of the bobbles, you must work 1 slip stitch into each slip stitch and 1 bobble into each double crochet of the previous row.

11 The bobbles are alternated in the same way each time. You work a slip stitch into each berry and a double crochet into each slip stitch on RS rows and a bobble into each double crochet and a slip stitch into each slip stitch on WS rows. Alter the row ends accordingly to keep pattern correct.

Lattice stitch

This highly textured stitch with a lattice or honeycomb effect is achieved by working double trebles on to the front of the fabric, working round the stem of the stitch rather than into the top of the stitches in the normal way. It is important to place the hook correctly, but once you have mastered this technique you will find the pattern quite simple to work. The step-by-step instructions show you exactly how this is done.

To work the sample make 22 chain, using a chunky or Aran-type yarn, and work 20 trebles into this chain, including the turning chain.

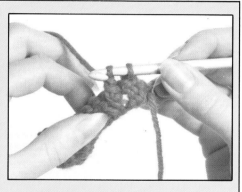

1 Begin to work the pattern on the front of these trebles. Wind yarn twice round the hook and insert hook into base of the 3rd treble, working from right to left so that your hook passes through the stitch.

2 Yarn round hook and draw a loop of yarn through the stitch to give 4 loops on hook. Now wind yarn round hook and draw it through first 2 loops. Repeat this action once more through second 2 loops. This makes 1 open double treble, leaving 2 loops on hook.

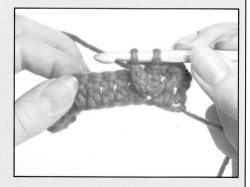

3 Insert the hook into top of the first treble of the row and draw through a loop. 3 loops on hook. Now wind yarn round hook and draw it through these 3 loops. This closes the first open double treble.

4 Work 1 double crochet into each of the next 2 stitches. The first of these stitches should be worked into the stitch behind the double treble.

5 Now work an open double treble as before into the same stitch as the last open double treble, so that you make a V-shape on the front of the fabric.

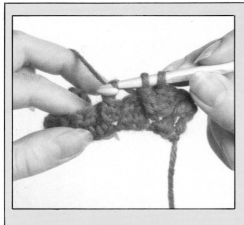

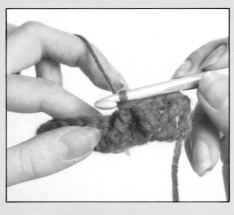

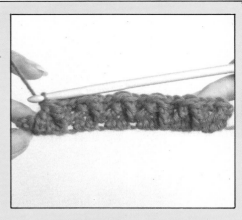

6 Miss the next 2 treble and work another open double treble into the base of the next stitch in the same way as before. 3 loops on hook.

7 Now insert the hook into the first stitch after the last double crochet worked and pull yarn through. Wind yarn round hook and draw it through all 4 loops on hook. This will be called close 2 double treble.

8 Repeat steps 4 to 7 four more times, so that you have worked 11 double trebles on the front of the fabric in all.

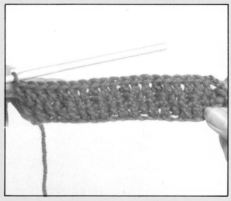

9 Repeat steps 4 and 5 once more. Now insert the hook into the next double crochet and draw a loop through. Now draw yarn through all 3 loops on hook. Work 1 double crochet into the turning chain to complete first row.

10 Turn. Make 3 chain. Now work 1 treble into each stitch to end of row. You should have 20 stitches in all.

11 Turn. Make 1 chain. Miss first stitch and work 1 double crochet into next stitch. Wind yarn twice round hook and insert it from right to left round the back of the first double treble 2 rows below.

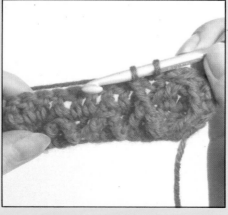

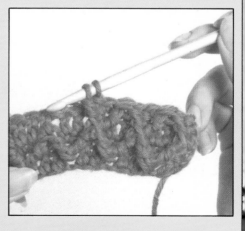

12 Complete the open double treble as before. Now work another open double treble, inserting the hook from right to left behind next group of 2 double treble where they meet at the top.

13 Repeat step 7 once more to close these 2 stitches. Repeat step 4 once more. Work an open double treble round same group as last double treble to make the first V-shape of this row.

14 Work 1 open double treble group round next group. Repeat step 7, then step 4 once more. Work an open double treble round same group as last double treble for next V.

continued

Continued : lattice stitch

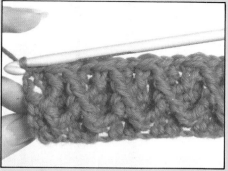

Fred Mancini

15 Continue to work across the row in this way until you have worked 2 open double trebles round last group and only the single double treble in the previous row remains unworked.

16 Work an open double treble round the last remaining double treble. Now repeat step 7 to close these 2 stitches, and work 1 double crochet into each of the last 2 stitches to complete the row.

17 This completed sample shows several rows of this stitch, worked so that you can see the full effect of working double trebles in this way.

Aran-style Afghan

The enduring appeal of Aran patterns — worked here in crochet — will make this Afghan a treasured family heirloom. Four different stitches are used to make the squares, and the completed squares are then joined together.

Size
143cm x 191cm, approx.

Note This Afghan is made up of four different patterned squares. For easy reference we have given them each a letter — A, B, C and D.

Materials
53 x 50g balls of Marriner Regency Aran Bainin
6.00mm and 7.00mm crochet hooks

Tension
A, 4 patt repeats to 6cm in width worked on 7.00mm hook
B, 3 patt repeats to 5cm in width worked on 7.00mm hook
C, 8 dc to 6cm in width worked on 6.00mm hook
D, 2 patt repeats to 5cm in width worked on 6.00mm hook

A (worked in even moss stitch)
Using 7.00mm hook make 31ch fairly loosely.
Base row (RS) Ss into 3rd ch from hook, * 1htr into next ch, ss into next ch, rep from * to end. Turn.
Patt row 2ch to count as first htr, miss first ss, *ss into next htr, 1htr into next ss, rep from * to within turning ch, ss into 2nd of first 2ch. Turn.
Rep the patt row until work measures 23cm from beg. Fasten off.
Make 11 more squares in the same way.

B (worked in uneven berry stitch)
Using 7.00mm hook make 30ch fairly loosely.
Base row (RS) 1dc into 3rd ch from hook, then work 1dc into each ch to end. Turn.
1st row 1ch, miss first dc, *yrh, insert hook into next dc and draw a loop through loosely, yoh and draw through one loop on hook (3 loops on hook), yrh, insert hook into same dc and draw a loop through loosely (5 loops on hook), yrh and draw through 4 loops on hook, yrh and draw through rem 2 loops on hook – called B1, ss into next dc, rep from * to last 2 sts, B1 into next dc, 1dc into 2nd of first 2ch. Turn.
2nd row 1ch, miss first dc, *ss into next B1, 1dc into next ss, rep from * to within last 2 sts, ss into next B1, 1dc into first ch. Turn.
3rd row 1ch, miss first dc, *ss into next ss, B1 into next dc, rep from * to within last 2 sts, ss into next ss, 1dc into first ch. Turn.
4th row 1ch, miss first dc, *1dc into next ss, ss into next B1, rep from * to within last 2 sts, 1dc into next ss, 1dc into first ch. Turn.
5th row 1ch, miss first dc, *B1 into next dc, ss into next ss, rep from * to within last 2 sts, B1 into next dc, 1dc into first ch. Turn.
The 2nd to 5th rows form the patt.
Cont in patt until work measures 23cm from beg, ending with 2nd or 4th row. Fasten off.
Make 11 more squares in the same way.

C (worked in rib)
Using 6.00mm hook make 32ch fairly loosely.
Base row (WS) 1dc into 3rd ch from hook, 1dc into each ch to end. Turn.
Patt row 1ch to count as first dc, miss first dc, 1dc into each dc to end, placing the hook into the horizontal loop under the normal ch loop of the dc, 1dc into turning ch, turn.
Rep the patt row until work measures 23cm from beg. Fasten off.
Make 11 more squares in the same way.

D (worked in lattice stitch)
Using 6.00mm hook make 29ch fairly loosely.
Base row (WS) 1tr into 3rd ch from hook, 1tr into each ch to end, turn.
1st row Working patt on front of the fabric work (yrh) twice, insert hook into base of 3rd tr on base row from right to left, yrh and draw a loop through, (yrh and draw through 2 loops on hook) twice – called 1 open dtr, insert hook into top of first tr, yrh and draw a loop through, yrh and draw through all 3 loops on hook – called close 1 dtr, 1dc in each of next 2tr, * 1 open dtr into base of same tr as before, miss next 2 tr, 1 open dtr in base of next tr, insert hook into top of tr after last dc worked, yrh and draw a loop through, yrh and draw through all 4 loops on hook – called close 2dtr, 1dc into each of next 2tr, rep from * to within last tr, 1 open dtr into base of same tr as before, close 1 dtr in last tr. Turn.
2nd row 2ch for first tr, miss first dc, 1tr into each dc to end. Turn. 28tr.
3rd row 1 ch for first dc, miss first tr, 1dc into next tr, inserting hook from right to left under first dtr 2 rows below, work 1 open dtr, then work 1 open dtr

under next gr of 2dtr, close 2dtr, 1dc
in each of next 2tr, * 1 open dtr under
same gr of 2dtr as before, 1 open dtr
under next gr of 2dtr, close 2dtr, 1dc
into each of next 2tr, rep from * to
within last 2tr, 1 open dtr, under same
gr of 2dtr as before, 1 open dtr under
last dtr, close 2dtr, 1dc into last tr. Turn.
4th row As 2nd patt row.
5th row 1 open dtr under first gr of
2 dtr, close 1dtr working into first tr,
1dc into each of next 2tr, * 1 open dtr
under same gr of 2dtr as before, 1 open
dtr under next gr of 2dtr, close 2dtr,
1 dc into each of next 2tr, rep from * to
within last tr, 1 open dtr under same gr
of 2dtr as before, 1 open dtr into last
tr, close 2 dtr. Turn.
The 2nd to 5th rows form the patt.
Cont to rep these rows until work
measures 23cm from beg, ending with a
5th row. Fasten off.
Make 11 more squares in the same way.

To make up
Join the squares tog with a flat seam
on the WS of the work, following the
diagram.

Border
With RS facing and using 7.00mm hook
join yarn to one corner and make 1ch
to count as first dc, work an uneven
number of dc evenly along each edge
with 3dc into the first 3 corners and 2dc
into last corner join with ss to first ch.
Turn. Work in uneven moss stitch as foll :
1st round Ss into centre dc at first corner,
1ch to count as first dc, * (ss into next
dc, 1htr into next dc) to centre dc at next
corner, 3dc into centre dc, rep from * all
round edge ending with a ss into first ss,
2 dc into same dc as ss, ss into first ch to
complete the round. Turn.
2nd round Ss into centre dc at first
corner, 1ch for first dc, * (1htr into next
dc, ss into ss, 1htr into next htr, ss into
next ss), to 3dc at next corner, 1htr into
next dc, 3dc into next dc, rep from * all
round edge ending last rep with 1htr into
first ss, 2dc into same dc as ss, ss into first
ch to complete the round. Turn.
3rd round Ss into centre dc at first
corner, 1ch, * (1htr into next dc, ss into
next htr, 1htr into next ss, ss into next
htr) to 3dc at next corner, 1htr into next
dc, 3dc into next dc, rep from * all
round edge ending last rep with 1 htr
into first ss, 2dc into same dc as ss, ss into
first ch to complete the round. Turn.
4th round Ss into centre dc at first
corner, 1ch, * (ss into next dc, 1htr into
next htr, ss into next ss, 1htr into next
htr) to 3dc at next corner ss into next dc,
3 dc into next dc, rep from * all round
edge ending last rep with ss into first ss.
2dc into same dc as ss, ss into first ch
to complete the round. Turn.
5th round Ss into centre dc at first
corner, 1 ch, * (ss into next dc, 1 htr into

next ss, ss into next htr, 1htr into next
ss) to 3 dc at next corner, ss into next dc,
3dc into next dc, rep from * all round
edge, ending last rep with ss into first
ss, 2dc into same dc as ss, ss to first ch
to complete the round. Turn.

Rep the 2nd, 3rd and 4th rounds once
more.
Fasten off.
Press work lightly on the wrong side
with a warm iron and a damp cloth, taking
care not to flatten the pattern.

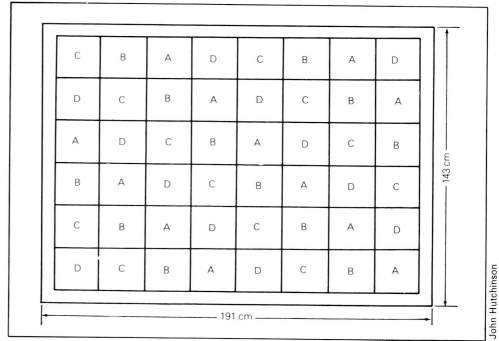

C	B	A	D	C	B	A	D
D	C	B	A	D	C	B	A
A	D	C	B	A	D	C	B
B	A	D	C	B	A	D	C
C	B	A	D	C	B	A	D
D	C	B	A	D	C	B	A

143 cm

191 cm

John Hutchinson

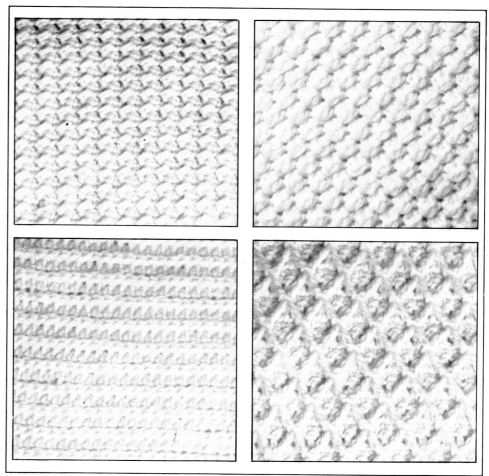

Step-by-step course – 21

More about Aran-style crochet

In the previous course we showed you how to work some of the background stitches which can be used in crochet to produce Aran-type fabrics. Here we concentrate on how to work cables and zig-zag patterns by working round the stem of certain stitches to produce a raised effect. Double crochet, half trebles

or crochet moss stitch are the best stitches to use for the background, since they make a firm, even fabric. Treble and double treble fabrics tend to be too open and therefore the motifs will not stand out so effectively against them. Once you have practised our samples, you will find it quite easy to experiment with the basic

working method. For example, simply by varying the number of rows worked before crossing a cable each time, you can alter its appearance considerably. Similarly, by working three or four stitches together in the zig-zag pattern, rather than separating the stitches each time, you will produce quite a different effect.

Simple zig-zag pattern

This pattern shows you how raised trebles can be made to slant alternately from right to left to produce a zig-zag effect. You can vary the pattern, either by working two or more raised stitches side by side for a more solid effect, or by working a stitch between each raised treble as shown here.

To make this sample use a chunky or Aran type yarn and a 5.50mm hook. Make 24 chain and work 23 double crochet into the chain (including the turning chain).

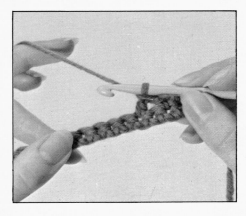

1 Begin the next row with 1 chain. Miss the first double crochet and work 1 double crochet into the next stitch. Miss the next double crochet and work 1 treble into the next stitch.

2 Keep the hook at the back of the work so that it is behind the treble just made. Wind the yarn round the hook and insert it from front to back through the stitch just missed.

3 Now complete this treble in the usual way. These 2 treble have been crossed at the back of the work.

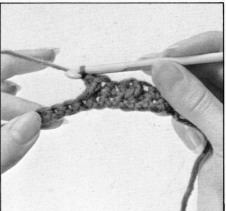

4 Work 1 double crochet into the next stitch and then cross the next 2 stitches at the back in the same way as before. This completes the first group of crossed trebles.

5 Work 1 double crochet into each of the next 2 double crochet. Now cross the next 2 trebles at the back of the work as before.

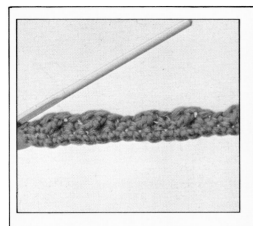

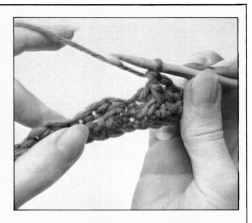

6 Continue to repeat steps 4 and 5 all the way across row, ending with step 4. Work 1 double crochet into the next stitch, then 1 double crochet into the turning chain. There should be 3 groups of 2 crossed trebles in all.

7 Turn. Make 1 chain. Miss the first stitch and work 1 double crochet into the next stitch. Miss next treble. Work 1 treble into next treble. Keep the hook at the front of the work. Wind yarn round hook and insert it from right to left round stem of missed raised treble.

8 Complete this treble in the usual way. These 2 trebles have now been crossed at the front (RS) of the fabric. Work crossed trebles at front in the same way each time.

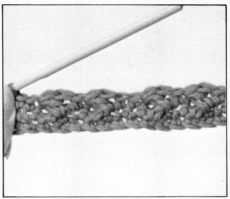

9 Work 1 double crochet into the next double crochet. Now cross the next 2 trebles at front (RS) of fabric as before.

10 Continue to work across the row in this way, with 1 double crochet worked into each double crochet and 2 trebles crossed at the front each time. Work last double crochet into the turning chain.

11 Turn. Now work 1 chain and first 2 stitches as in step 7. Keep hook at back (RS) of work. Wind yarn round hook and place hook round stem of missed raised treble on RS of work from right to left.

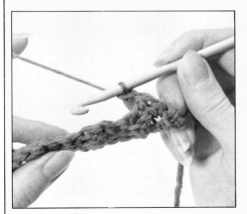

12 Wind yarn round hook and complete the treble in the normal way. This crosses the 2 trebles at back and slants them to the right on RS of fabric.

13 Continue to work 1 double crochet into each double crochet and cross two trebles at back (RS) of work each time. Work last double crochet into turning chain. Here we show you the completed row on the RS.

14 Each row is worked alternately to make the pattern, so that the trebles are crossed at the front when the RS is facing and at the back when the WS is facing.

Mike Berend

241

Mock cable panel

Here we show you how to work a cable on a half treble background. We use the same basic principle of working round the stem of the stitches in the row below to produce a raised effect. By using double trebles to cross the stitches you can achieve a cable effect, and you can vary the appearance of the cables simply by working fewer or more rows between each cross-over row.

To make this sample, first make 14 chain and work 13 half treble into the chain. We have used a 5.50mm hook and Aran type yarn.

1 Turn. Make 2 chain. Now work 1 half treble into each of next 3 stitches. Begin each cable row in the same way. Now wind the yarn round the hook and insert it round the stem of the next stitch from right to left.

2 Now complete 1 treble in the usual way. This completes the first raised treble. Work each raised treble in the same way.

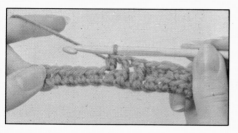

3 Work another raised treble round the stem of the next stitch. Now work 1 half treble into the next half treble. This stitch is in the centre of the cable and separates the raised stitches.

4 Work 1 raised treble round the stem of each of the next 2 stitches. Now work 1 half treble into each stitch to the end of the row (4 in all). Complete each cable row in this way.

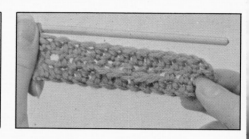

5 Begin the 2nd pattern row with 1 chain. Miss the first stitch and work 1 half treble into each stitch to the end so that there are 13 stitches. Work each alternate row in the same way.

6 Turn and begin cable row as before. Now wind the yarn round the hook and insert it from right to left round the raised treble worked in the previous cable row.

7 Complete the treble as before extending the yarn slightly to avoid distorting the fabric. Work another raised treble round the next raised treble in the previous cable row. Now work 1 half treble into the next (centre) half treble.

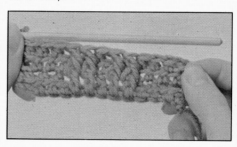

8 Work 1 raised treble round each of the next 2 raised trebles in the previous cable row. This completes the cable section for this row. Complete the row as before.

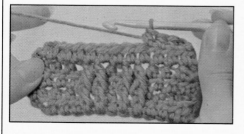

9 Turn and repeat step 5 once more. Now turn and work 4 half treble as before for the beginning of the next row.

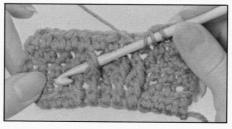

10 Miss the next 2 raised trebles in the previous row and the centre half treble. Wind yarn twice round hook and insert hook from right to left round next raised treble.

11 Complete 1 double treble in the normal way. Work another raised double treble round the next raised treble in the previous row. These 2 stitches now slant to the right.

Mike Berend

12 Hold the hook behind these 2 stitches and work 1 half treble into the missed (centre) half treble. Still keeping the hook behind the 2 double trebles, work 1 double treble round the first of the missed raised trebles.

13 Work another double treble in the same way round the 2nd of missed raised trebles. These 2 stitches slant from right to left behind first 2 double trebles.

14 Complete the row as before. Work the next cable twist by repeating steps 5 to 8 twice. Now repeat steps 9 to 13 once more. You have thus worked 5 rows in all before crossing the raised trebles again.

Stitch Wise

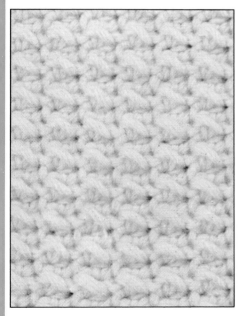

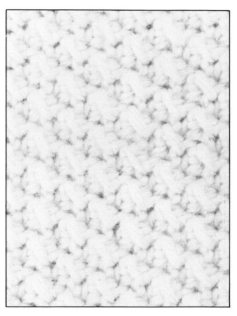

Even moss stitch
Make a length of chain which has a multiple of 2 stitches.
1st row Miss first ch, ss into next ch, *1htr into next ch, ss into next ch, rep from * to end. Turn.
2nd row 1 ch, miss first st, *1 htr into next st, ss into next st, rep from * to end of row, working last ss into turning chain. Turn. The 2nd row forms the patt. Repeat it each time.

Uneven moss stitch
Make a length of chain which has a multiple of 2 stitches.
Work the 1st and 2nd rows in exactly the same way as given for even moss stitch.
3rd row 2ch to count as first htr, miss first st, ss into next st, *1 htr into next st, ss into next st, rep from * to end of row, working last htr into turning chain. Turn.
4th row As 3rd.
5th row As 2nd row.
6th row As 2nd row.
The 3rd to 6th rows form the pattern and are repeated throughout.

Aran rib stitch
Make a length of chain with a multiple of 2 plus 1 extra chain.
1st row (RS of fabric) Work 1 htr into 3rd ch from hook, 1 htr into each ch to end. Turn.
2nd row 2ch, miss first st, *work 1 htr into horizontal loop (below two horizontal loops at top of stitch) at front of next htr, rep from * to end, working last htr into turning chain. Turn.
3rd row 2ch, miss first st, *work 1 htr into back loop of top two horizontal loops of next st, rep from * to end, working last htr into turning chain. Turn. 2nd and 3rd rows form patt and are repeated throughout.
This stitch gives the appearance of rib, although the WS of the fabric is flat.

Artful Aran

The intriguing textures of Aran-style crochet are used here to make a smart pullover for a child. The round neckline goes easily over a shirt and the saddle shoulders add extra style.

Sizes
To fit 66[71:76]cm chest.
Length, 42[46:50]cm.
Sleeve seam, 33[36:39]cm.
Note Instructions for larger sizes are in square brackets [] ; where there is only one set of figures it applies to all sizes.

Materials
17[19:21] x 20g balls of Robin Reward Double Knitting or 15[17:19] x 20g balls of Robin Reward Double Knitting and 2 balls in a contrasting colour 3.50mm and 4.00mm crochet hooks

Tension
18 sts and 18 rows to 10cm over moss stitch on 4.00mm hook.

Front and back (alike)
Using 3.50mm hook make 9[10:11] ch for side edge of welt.
Base row 1dc into 3rd ch from hook, 1dc into each ch to end. Turn.
Rib row 1ch, 1dc into back loop only of each dc to end. Turn.
Rep the rib row 57[67:73] times more. This completes ribbing for the welt. Do not turn but work along one long edge.

Next row 2ch to count as first dc, then 1dc into each row end to end. Turn.
59[69:75] dc.
Change to 4.00mm hook.
Next row (WS) 2ch to count as first htr, *ss into next dc, 1htr into next dc, rep from * to end, finishing ss into turning ch. Turn. Commence moss st patt.
Patt row 2ch, *ss into next htr, 1htr into next ss, rep from * to end, finishing ss into turning ch. Turn. This row forms the patt.
Cont until work measures 39[42:46]cm, ending with WS row. Fasten off.

Sleeves
Using 3.50mm hook make 8ch for side edge of cuff and work in rib as given for front until 29[33:39] rows in all have been worked, then work 1dc into each row end along one long side. Turn.
29[33:39] sts. Change to 4.00mm hook.
1st row 2ch, (ss into next dc, 1htr into next dc) 3[4:4] times, 1dc into next dc, (miss next dc, 1tr into next dc, keeping hook at back of work, work 1tr into last dc missed, so forming 2 crossed tr, 1dc into next dc) 1[1:2] times, (yrh, insert hook into next dc, yrh and draw a loop through, yrh and draw through one

loop on hook, yrh, insert hook into same dc, yrh and draw a loop through so having 5 loops on hook, yrh and draw through first 4 loops on hook, yrh and draw through rem 2 loops, called bobble 1, or B1, ss into next dc) 3 times, B1, (1dc into next dc, cross 2 tr) 1[1:2] times, 1dc into next dc, ss into next dc, (1htr into next dc, ss into next dc) 3[4:4] times. Turn.
2nd row 2ch, moss st 6[8:8], 1dc into next dc, (miss next tr, 1tr into next tr, keeping hook at front of work, work 1tr round the tr that was missed, called cross 2tr front, or Cr2F, 1dc into next dc) 1[1:2] times, (1dc into B1, 1dc into next ss) 3 times, 1dc into B1, (1dc into next dc, Cr2F) 1[1:2] times, 1dc into next dc, moss st to end. Turn.
3rd row 2ch, moss st 6[8:8], 1dc into next dc, (miss next tr, 1tr into next tr, keeping hook at back of work, work 1tr round tr that was missed, called cross 2tr back, or Cr2B, 1dc into next dc) 1[1:2] times, ss into next dc, (B1 into next dc, ss into next dc) 3 times, (1dc into next dc, Cr2B) 1[1:2] times, 1dc into next dc, moss st to end. Turn.
4th row 2ch, moss st 6[8:8], 1dc into next dc, (Cr2F, 1dc into next dc) 1[1:2] times, 1dc into next ss, (1dc into next B1, 1dc into next ss) 3 times, (1dc into next dc, Cr2F) 1[1:2] times, 1dc into next dc, moss st to end. Turn.
5th row 2ch, moss st 6[8:8], 1dc into next dc, (Cr2B, 1dc into next dc) 1[1:2] times, B1 into next dc, (ss into next dc, B1 into next dc) 3 times, 1dc into next dc, (Cr2B, 1dc into next dc) 1[1:2] times, moss st to end. Turn. The 2nd to 5th rows form the patt.
Cont in this pattern, increasing one st at each end of 2nd and every foll 6th row by working 2sts into the first and last sts, working the extra sts into moss st, until there are 47[51:57] sts. Cont without shaping until sleeve measures 33[36:39]cm from beg, ending with a WS row. Cut off yarn. With RS facing rejoin yarn to first dc at beg of panel, cont across panel sts only for 10[11:12]cm for saddle shoulder extension, ending with a WS row. Fasten off.

Neckband
Using 3.50mm hook make 8ch and work in rib as given for front for 36[39:42]cm. Fasten off.

To make up
Do not press. Sew saddle extensions to shoulder seams on front and back, then sew top of sleeves to sides of back and front. Join side and sleeve seams. Join short ends of neckband, then sew neckband to neck. Press seams lightly with a cool iron over a dry cloth.

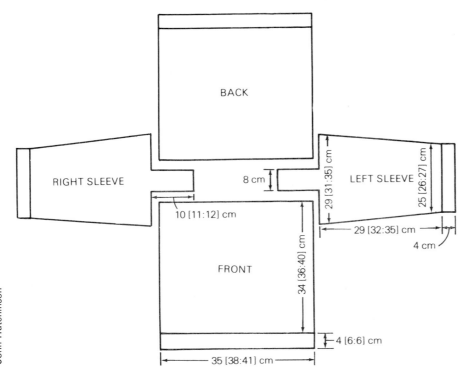

Step-by-step course – 22

*Basket weave patterns
*Working basic basket weave
*Stitch Wise : more basket weave patterns
*Pattern for a bath mat
*Pattern for a boy's jacket

Basket weave patterns

Once you have mastered the basic crochet stitches and developed a fluent way of working, you'll be amazed at the variety of patterns and stitches you can work – some lacy, others dense and firm. A perfect example of the latter kind of texture is the group of basket weave patterns in this course. Each of them produces a lovely, crunchy fabric with a heavily woven appearance.

Although it looks complicated, the basic basket weave pattern is not difficult to learn. You begin by working a row of trebles ; then on the following row you work round the *stem* of the next stitch, rather than under the top two loops as you would normally do when working a treble fabric. The woven effect is achieved by either working round the back of the stitch – which has the effect of pushing it

forward – or round the front of the stitch – the stitch pulling to the back.
Blocks of stitches are usually worked alternately forwards and then backwards across the row, the position being reversed on the following row, so that the stitches at the back are brought forward and vice versa. The number of stitches in each block can vary, depending on the fabric you wish to make.

Working basic basket weave

The best way to discover how the fabric is made is to try it yourself. Start by making our sample, using a double knitting yarn and a 4.50mm hook. Our pattern uses blocks of 3 treble and will therefore need a multiple of 3 chain, plus 2 extra for the turning chain (for the sample, 29 chain in all). If you wish, for example, to work 5 treble in each block, you will need to make a multiple of 5 chain plus 2 extra turning chain.

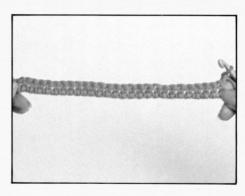

1 Work 1 row of treble (27 in all). Now turn and make 2 chain. Since you are working round the stem below the top of the stitch you need only make 2 chain instead of 3 as you would normally do when working a treble fabric.

2 Wind the yarn round the hook and insert it round the back of the stem of the 2nd treble, from right to left, taking the hook from the front of the work, through to the back and out to the front again, between the 2nd and 3rd trebles.

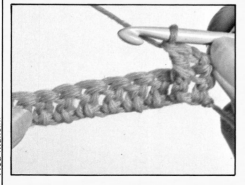

3 Wind the yarn round the hook, draw it through and complete the treble in the normal way. You will see that this treble has been pulled forwards to the front of the fabric.

4 Now work 1 treble round the back of the next treble in the same way to bring the next stitch forward. Including the first 2 chain, 3 stitches have now been worked to the front, making a vertical section. This stitch is called 'treble round front'.

5 Now begin the horizontal part of the pattern. Wind yarn round the hook, insert it from the back of the work, through to the front, round the stem of the next stitch to the left and through to the back of the work again.

Fred Mancini

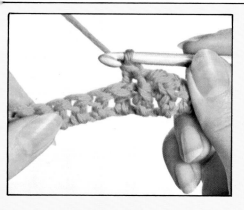

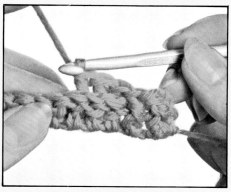

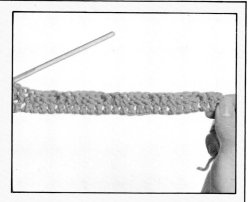

6 Now wind the yarn round the hook, draw it through the stitch, and complete the treble in the normal way, so pulling this treble to the back of the work. This method of working round the front of the stitch to bring it to the back is called 'treble round back'.

7 Work 1 treble in the same way round the front of the stem of each of the next 2 treble, repeating steps 5 and 6 each time. Keep the hook at the back of the work while working these trebles.

8 Work the next 3 treble to the front as before, repeating steps 2 and 3, then the next 3 treble to the back, repeating steps 5 and 6 alternately across the row. Work last treble to front, going round turning chain at end of row.

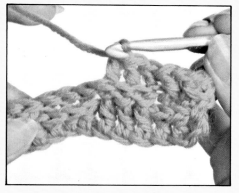

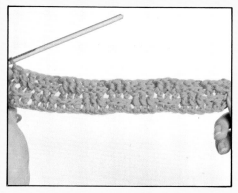

9 Turn and make 2 chain as before. The trebles which were at the front on the previous row now appear to be at the back and vice versa. Miss 1st (edge) stitch and work each of next 2 treble to front, repeating steps 2 and 3, so that they are now brought forward.

10 Now work each of next 3 treble to the back, repeating steps 5 and 6, so that they are taken to back of work. You will see that the fabric is reversible.

11 Continue to alternate the position of the blocks of trebles across the row, so that each forward block is taken back and vice versa. Work last treble round the turning chain in correct pattern sequence.

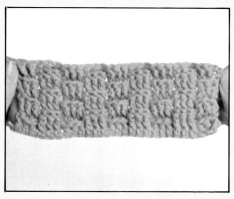

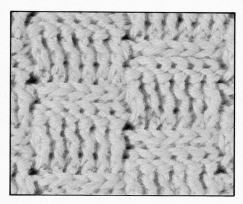

12 Work rows alternately in this way each time to create the woven effect. Several rows have been worked here, and you will see that where stitches have been worked to the back a ridge is formed running horizontally across fabric.

13 This sample shows blocks of 6 treble worked in same way, but with 2 rows worked before alternating position, so that the forward stitches will be kept back on the 2nd pattern row, before changing position on following row, to produce a strongly vertical pattern.

14 This sample shows the effect of working 1 treble to the front and then one to the back all the way across the row. The position of the trebles is reversed each time on every row to produce this woven, lattice effect.

Fred Mancini

Although they are worked in different ways, these three patterns all suggest basket work in their textures.

Elongated basket stitch

Here you must work into the row two rows below, placing the hook between the stitches each time to make the long trebles. The pattern is worked over a number of chain divisible by 6 plus 3, with 2 extra for the turning chain.

1st row 1 tr into 4th ch from hook, 1 tr into each ch to end. Turn.
2nd row 1 ch, miss first st, 1 dc into each st to end. Turn.
3rd row (WS) 3ch, miss first st, 1 tr into each of next 2 sts, *(yrh and insert hook between next 2 tr in row below, yrh and draw yarn up to same height as row

being worked, complete treble in normal way – called 1 tr below – 3 times, 1 tr into each of next 3 sts working in to top of stitch in normal way – called 1 tr top – rep from * to end, working last tr into turning chain. Turn.
4th row (RS) As 2nd.
5th row 3ch, 1 tr below between 1st and 2nd tr in row below, 1 tr below between next 2 tr, *1 tr top into each of next 3dc, (1 tr below between next 2tr) 3 times, rep from * to end, working last tr below between last tr and turning chain. Turn.
6th row As 4th.
3rd to 6th rows form patt and are rep throughout.

Basket weave variation

Unlike the basket weave stitches illustrated in the step-by-step photographs, this pattern has a definite right and wrong side to it. It is worked over a number of chain divisible by 10 plus 7, with 2 extra for the turning chain.

1st row (RS) 1 tr into 4th ch from hook, 1 tr into each ch to end. Turn.
2nd row 3ch, miss first tr, yrh and insert hook from right to left from back to front, round stem of next tr and to back of work again, yrh and draw through a loop, yrh and draw through 2 loops yrh and draw through rem 2 loops – 1 treble back; 1trB round each of next 4tr, *1 tr into each of next 5tr in normal way, 1trB round each of next 5tr, rep from * to end, 1 tr into top of turning chain. Turn.
3rd row 3ch, miss first tr, yrh, insert hook between 2nd and 3rd, from front to back, round stem of next tr and to the front again, yrh and draw through a loop, yrh

and draw through 2 loops on hook, yrh and draw through rem 2 loops – 1 treble front, or 1tr F – round each of next 4tr, *1 tr into each of next 5tr in normal way, 1tr F round each of next 5tr, rep from * to end, 1 tr into top of turning chain. Turn.
4th row As 2nd.
5th row 3ch, miss first tr, 1 tr into each of next 5tr in normal way, *1trF round each of next 5tr, 1 tr into each of next 5tr in normal way, rep from * to end, 1 tr into top of turning chain. Turn.
6th row 3ch, miss first tr, 1 tr into each of next 5tr in normal way, *1trB round each of next 5tr, 1 tr into each of next 5tr in normal way, rep from * to end, 1 tr into top of turning chain. Turn.
7th row As 5th.
8th row As 6th.
9th row As 3rd.
10th row As 2nd.
The 3rd to 10th rows form pattern. Rep them throughout until the fabric is the depth you require.

Raised treble pattern

Here trebles worked round the stem are worked alternately with trebles worked in the normal way to produce a highly textured, almost double fabric, similar in appearance to honeycomb stitch but made in squares rather than diamond shapes. The pattern is worked over an uneven number of stitches, and you should begin by making an uneven number of chain of any length.
1st row 1 tr into 4th ch from hook, 1 tr into each ch to end. Turn.
2nd row 3ch, miss first tr, *1 tr round stem of next tr inserting hook from right to left from the front to the back and round to the front of the work again—

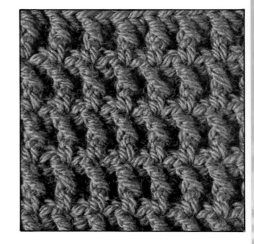

1 treble front – 1 tr into top of next st in normal way, rep from * to end, 1 tr into top of turning chain. Turn.
3rd row 3ch, miss first tr, 1 tr into top of next tr in normal way, 1trF round next tr, rep from * to last 2tr, 1 tr into next tr, 1 tr into top of turning chain. Turn.
4th row As 2nd row, but ending with 1trF, 1 tr into top of turning chain. Turn.
5th row As 3rd.
4th and 5th rows form pattern and are repeated throughout. Note that you alternate the trebles on each row by working 1trF into the normal treble worked in previous row and vice versa each time. Continue in this way to the required depth.

Mat finish

This bath mat is just the thing for catching splashes and drips. It is worked in a thick cotton with a sturdy basket weave pattern and is trimmed round three sides with a short fringe.

Gary Warren

Size
42cm wide by 69cm long, excluding fringe.

Materials
8 x 50g balls of Twilleys Dishcloth 77 cotton for mat ; 2 balls for fringe 3.50mm crochet hook

Tension
1 patt rep (12sts) to 6cm and 16 rows to 13cm over patt on 3.50mm hook.

To make
Using 3.50mm hook make 140 ch.
Base row 1tr into 4th ch from hook. 1tr into each ch to end. Turn.
Commence patt.
1st row (RS) 2ch, work *round* each of next 5tr by working yrh, insert hook from front to back between next 2tr, round tr at left and through work from back to front ; draw yarn through and complete tr in usual way—called treble round front (tr round Ft), work *round* each of next 6tr by working yrh, insert hook from back to front between next 2tr, round tr at left and through work from front to to back ; draw yarn through and complete tr in usual way—called 1 treble round back (tr round Bk), now work *6tr round Ft, 6tr round Bk, rep from * to within last 6sts, tr round Front to end. Turn.
2nd row 2ch, work 5tr round Bk, 6tr round Ft, *6tr round Bk, 6tr round Ft, rep from * to within last 6sts, tr round Bk to end. Turn.
3rd row As 1st row.
4th row As 1st row.
5th row As 2nd row.
6th row As 1st row.
These 6 rows form the patt. Rep them 7 times more, then work 1st to 3rd rows again.
Fasten off.

Fringe
Using four strands of yarn together, knot fringe into every alternate row end along each short edge and into every alternate st along one long edge.
Trim the ends.

One for the boys

This bomber-style jacket has a thick textured basket weave pattern for extra warmth. Contrasting collar, cuffs and welt add a touch of style.

Sizes

To fit 66[71 :76]cm chest.
Length, 42[46 :50]cm.
Sleeve seam, 38[40 :42]cm.
Note Instructions for larger sizes are in square brackets [] ; where there is only one set of figures it applies to all sizes.

Materials

12[13 :14] x 50g balls of Sunbeam Aran Knit in main colour (A)
2 balls in a contrasting colour (B)
4.50mm and 5.50mm crochet hooks
35[40 :45]cm open-ended zip fastener
10cm zip fastener for pocket

Tension

14 sts and 14 rows to 10cm over patt on 5.50mm hook.

Back

**Using 4.50mm hook and B, make 52 [56 :60] ch.
Base row 1dc into 3rd ch from hook, 1dc into each ch to end. Turn.
Next row 2ch to count as first dc, 1dc into each dc to end. Turn.
Rep the last row 4 times more. Cut off B, join to A. Change to 5.50mm hook.
Work 2 rows in dc**. Commence patt.
1st row (RS) 3ch to count as first tr, *1tr into next dc, work round next tr by working yrh, insert hook from front to back between next 2tr, round tr at left and through work from back to front ; draw yarn through and complete tr in usual way—called treble round front (tr round Ft), rep from * to within last 2dc, 1tr into next dc, 1tr into turning ch. Turn.
2nd row 2ch, 1 dc into each st. Turn.
3rd row 3ch, *work 1tr round Ft working round next tr on first row, miss dc above this tr, 1tr into next dc, rep from * to end, working last tr into turning ch. Turn.
4th row As 2nd row.
5th row 3ch, 1tr into next dc, *1tr round front working round next tr on 3rd row, miss dc above this tr, 1tr into next dc, rep from * to within turning ch, 1tr into turning ch. Turn.
The 2nd to 5th rows form the patt. *
Cont in patt until work measures 28[30 :32]cm from beg, ending with a WS row.
Shape armholes
Next row Ss over first 5sts, patt to within last 4sts, turn.

Serge Krouglikoff/kite from The Kite Shop

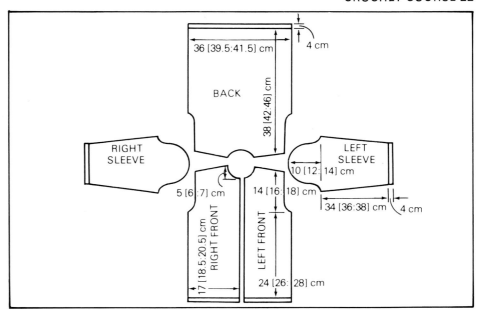

Diagram labels: 36 [39.5 :41.5] cm — 4 cm — BACK — 38 [42 :46] cm — RIGHT SLEEVE — LEFT SLEEVE — 10 [12 :14] cm — 5 [6 :7] cm — 14 [16 :18] cm — 34 [36 :38] cm — 4 cm — 17 [18.5 :20.5] cm — RIGHT FRONT — LEFT FRONT — 24 [26 :28] cm

Dec one st at each end of next 2 [3 :4] rows by working 2dc tog. 39 [41 :43] dc. Cont without shaping until work measures 14 [16 :18] cm from beg of armhole shaping, ending with a WS row.

Shape shoulders

Next row Ss over first 5 [5 :6] sts, patt over next 5 [6 :6] sts. Fasten off. Miss next 19 sts, rejoin yarn to next st, patt over next 5 [6 :6] sts. Fasten off.

Left front

Using 4.50mm hook and B, make 26 [28 :30] ch.

Work as given for back from **✱✱ to ✱✱**.

Cont in patt until work measures 14cm from beg, ending with a WS row.

Pocket row Patt over first 5 [6 :7] sts, make 15ch, miss next 15sts, patt over last 5 [6 :7] sts. Turn.

Cont in patt, working into ch on next row, until front measures same as back up to armhole, ending with a WS row.

Shape armhole

Next row Ss over first 5 sts, patt to end. Turn. 19 [20 :21] sts. Dec one st at armhole edge on next 2 [3 :4] rows. Cont without shaping until work measures 9 [10 :11] cm from beg of armhole shaping, ending with a WS row.

Shape neck

Next row Patt to within last 4 sts, turn. Dec one st at neck edge on next 5 rows, then cont without shaping until armhole measures the same as back, up to beg of shoulder shaping, ending with a WS row.

Shape shoulder

Next row Ss over first 5 [5 :6] sts, patt to end. Fasten off.

Right front

Work to match left front, omitting pocket and reversing all shaping.

Sleeves

Using 4.50mm hook and B, make 22 [24 :26] ch. Work base row as given for back, then work 5 rows in dc, inc

4 [4 :6] dc evenly on last row by working 2dc into a dc. 25 [27 :31] dc.

Cut off B, join on A. Change to 5.50mm hook and work 2 rows dc.

Cont in patt as given for back but in cone st at each end of 3rd and every foll 8th row until there are 35 [39 :43] sts. Cont wthout shaping until sleeve measures 38 [40 :42] cm from beg, ending with a WS row.

Shape top

Next row Ss over first 5 sts, patt to within last 4 sts. Turn. Work 1 row. Dec one st at each end of next and foll 3 [4 :5] alt rows, then at each end of every row until 9 sts rem. Fasten off.

Collar

Using 4.50mm hook and B, make 57 [61 :65] ch loosely.

Work base row as given for back, then work 3 rows in dc.

Next row 2ch, 1dc into each of next 5 [4 :5] dc, * work next 2dc tog, 1dc into each of next 12 [10-8] dc, rep from * 2 [3 :4] times more, work next 2dc tog, 1dc into each dc to end. Turn. 52 [55 :58] dc. Work 3 rows.

Next row 2ch, 1dc into each of next 5 [4 :5] dc, *work next 2dc tog, 1dc into each of next 11 [9 :7] dc, rep from * 2 [3 :4] times more, work next 2dc tog, 1dc into each dc to end. Turn. 48 [50 :52] dc. Work 1 [3 :5] rows.

Next row Ss over first 5sts, patt to within last 4sts. Turn.

Rep last row 3 times more. Fasten off.

To make up

Join shoulder seams. Set in sleeves, then join side and sleeve seams. Sew zip into pocket opening. Make pocket lining and sew in position.

Join on yarn and, using 4.50mm hook, work 2 rows of dc evenly along each front edge, matching colours. Sew in zip. Sew on collar. Press seams.

John Hutchinson

Step-by-step course – 23

Vertical chains worked on a crochet background

In this course we show you how to work crochet chains vertically on to a basic background fabric to make striped, checked and plaid patterns. These patterns are fun to work; you'll enjoy creating your own designs and using oddments of yarn in imaginative ways. Remember, though, that before you start you must work out the sequence in which the colours are to be used, since you could otherwise end up with a haphazard and untidy-looking fabric.

You can either work the background in a plain colour, using one or more contrasting colours for the vertical chains, or work it in a horizontal stripe pattern – again using contrasting colours for the chains – to create a more intricate pattern.

The fabric is worked in two stages. The first stage is to make a background, leaving spaces into which the chains can be worked. This can be an all-over lattice pattern, in which case you will need to work the lines of chain evenly across the width of the fabric, filling in all the spaces. Or it can consist of blocks of treble interspersed with lattice pattern so that the crochet chains will only be worked at intervals across the fabric. The second stage is, of course, to work the lines of chain vertically up and down or across the fabric.

Making the background fabric

For the sample in steps 1-6 use a double knitting yarn and 4.00mm hook.

1 Begin by making an uneven number of chain. Work 1 treble into the 5th chain from the hook. (These 5 chain count as first treble, missed chain and 1 chain). Make 1 chain. Miss next chain and work 1 treble into next chain.

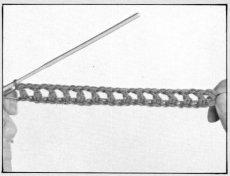

2 Now work 1 chain, miss next chain and work 1 treble into next chain all the way across the row, working last treble into last chain.

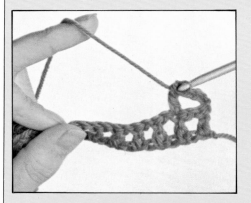

3 Turn and work 4 chain (to count as first treble and 1 chain). Miss first (edge) treble and space and work 1 treble into next treble.

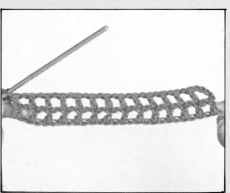

4 Continue to work 1 chain, miss 1 space and 1 treble into next treble all the way across the row. Work the last treble into the 4th of first 5 chain to complete the row.

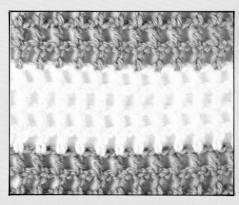

5 Continue to repeat steps 3 and 4, working last tr into 3rd of 4 chain, for each row of the lattice pattern. We used 2 colours for our sample, working 4 rows in each colour throughout. Fasten off.

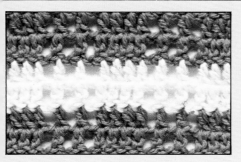

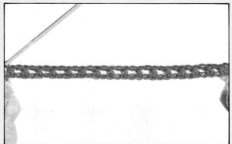

6 This sample shows a background fabric in which blocks of solid trebles and lattice stripes have been worked alternately across the row. In this case 4 treble have been alternated with 3 lattice spaces and worked in a striped pattern using two colours.

7 When using a 4-ply yarn it may be necessary to use half trebles in order to make the stitches the right proportion. A 4-ply yarn worked in trebles will tend to produce a rather loose fabric. Half trebles will make a firmer fabric and will leave shorter spaces which can be more easily filled with chain. In this case, work the background as before, substituting half trebles for trebles throughout. You will have to begin with an uneven number of chain and work the first half treble into fifth chain from hook.

8 On subsequent rows, work 3 chain to count as the first half treble and 1 chain at the beginning of the row, instead of the 4 chain worked when using trebles for the background.

Working the vertical chains

The chain stitch used is essentially the same as that used in embroidery, even though it is worked with a crochet hook. Normally a double thickness of yarn is used for the chains.

You can either use two balls of yarn at the same time, or – provided that the piece to be covered is not very long – cut a length approximately eight times the required length of the finished chain and fold it in half. (In this case you may not need to begin by making a slip loop, as in our sample, but can simply place the doubled yarn over the hook.)

1 Keep the RS of the background fabric facing you as you work. Make a slip loop on the hook, then insert the hook from front to back into the bottom right-hand corner space.

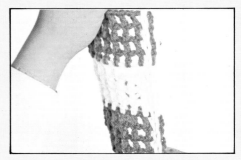

2 Wind the double yarn round the hook and draw it through the space and then through the loop on the hook. Always keep the ball of yarn at the back of the work.

3 Draw the loop up slightly and insert the hook from front to back into the next space. It is important to keep the yarn fairly slack when working each chain in order to avoid distorting the background fabric.

4 Repeat step 2 to complete this chain. Continue to work chains in this way all the way up the fabric, working into each space. Make the last chain over the top edge of the fabric and pull yarn through to fasten off.

Fred Mancini

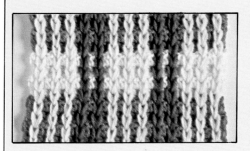

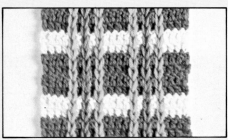

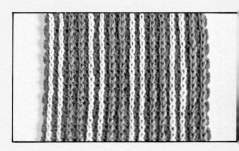

5 This sample shows each vertical line worked in chains, using one of the background colours and a contrast colour to create a simple check pattern. You will have to sew the spare ends of yarn to the WS of fabric when it is completed.

6 Here the background fabric previously worked, which combines blocks of trebles and lattice pattern, has been completed by working the vertical chain lines in two contrast colours to achieve a plaid effect.

7 A single thickness of 4-ply yarn has been used to make the chains on this sample, in which half trebles were used instead of trebles to create the background fabric. You will often find that you need to experiment with different-sized hooks and different background fabrics to obtain the desired effect in your chosen yarn. In some cases a single thickness of yarn works better than a double thickness.

Check mate

Your man won't mind being in check when he wears this smart slipover. Worked in half trebles, the fabric has contrasting checks, with the vertical lines worked in chain.

Sizes
To fit 97[102 :107 :112]cm chest.
Length, 61[62 :63 :64]cm.

Note Instructions for larger sizes are in square brackets []; where there is only one set of figures it applies to all sizes.

Materials
13[13 :13 :14] x 25g balls of Wendy
Nylonised 4 ply in main colour (A)
2 balls in each of 2 contrasting colours
(B) and (C)
3.00mm and 3.50mm crochet hooks

Tension
20 sts and 16 rows to 10cm over patt using 3.50mm hook.

Back
**Using 3.50mm hook and A, make 103[109 :115 :120]ch.
Base row 1 htr into 3rd ch from hook, 1 htr into each ch to end. Turn. 102[108 :114 :119] sts.
1st row (WS) 2ch to count as first htr, 1 htr into each of next 10[13 :13 :16] htr, *1ch, miss next htr, 1 htr into each of next 3 htr, 1ch, miss next htr, 1 htr into each of next 20[20 :22 :22] htr, rep from * twice

Victor Yuan/accessories from Howie

more, 1 ch, miss next htr, 1 htr into each of next 3 htr, 1 ch, miss next htr, 1 htr into each of last 11[14 :14 :17] htr. Turn.
2nd row 2 ch, 1 htr into each of next 10[13 :13 :16] htr, *1 ch, 1 htr into each of next 3 htr, 1 ch, 1 htr into each of next 20[20 :22 :22] htr, rep from * twice more, 1 ch, 1 htr into each of next 3 htr, 1 ch, 1 htr into each of last 11[14 :14 :17] htr. Turn.
3rd - 5th rows As 2nd row, but joining on B on last htr of 5th row.
6th row Using B, work as 2nd row, cut off B, do not turn, but return to beg of row, so working in the same direction as last row.
7th row RS facing and using A, work as 2nd row. Turn.
8th row As 2nd row, but joining on C on last htr. Turn.
9th row Using C, work as 2nd row, cut off C, do not turn but return to beg of row.
10th row RS facing and using A, work as 2nd row. Turn.
11th – 25th rows As 2nd row, but joining on B on last htr of 25th row.
The 6th to 25th rows form the patt. Cont in patt until work measures 37cm from beg. **

Shape armholes
Next row SS over first 5 htr, 2 ch, patt to within last 4 htr, turn.
Next row Ss over first 3 htr, 2 ch, patt to within last 2 htr, turn.
Work 2 htr tog (to dec one htr) at each end of next 2[3 :3 :4] rows, then at each end of foll 2[2 :3 :3] alt rows. 82[86 :90 :94] htr. Cont without shaping until work measures 24[25 :26 :27] cm from beg of armhole shaping.
Shape shoulder
Next row Ss over first 7[8 :8 :8] htr, 2 ch, patt to within last 6[7 :7 :7] htr, turn.
Rep this row twice more.
Next row Ss over first 6[5 :5 :7] htr, 2 ch, patt to within last 5[4 :4 :6] htr. Fasten off.

Front
Work as given for back from ** to **.
Shape armhole and divide for neck
Next row Ss over first 5 htr, 2 ch, patt 46[49 :52 :55] htr, turn.
Work on this set of sts first.
Next row Dec 1 htr, patt to within last 2 htr, turn.
Dec 1 htr at armhole edge on next and foll 1[2 :2 :3] rows, then on foll 2[2 :3 :3] alt rows *and at the same time* dec one htr at neck edge on every foll alt row until 23[25 :25 :27] htr rem. Cont without shaping until work measures 24[25 :26 :27] cm from beg of armhole shaping, ending with a WS row.

Shape shoulder
Next row Ss over first 7[8 :8 :8] htr, 2 ch, patt to end. Turn.
Next row Patt to last 6[7 :7 :7] htr. Turn.
Next row Ss over first 7[8 :8 :8] htr, 2 ch, patt to end. Turn.
Next row Patt to within last 5[4 :4 :6] htr. Fasten off. Rejoin yarn to rem sts at centre front neck and complete to match first side reversing all shapings.

To work vertical chains
Work chain stitch up the spaces in patt make a slip loop on hook as foll. Using B and keeping yarn at back of work insert the hook into the first sp and draw a loop through, *insert hook into next sp, yrh and draw a loop through the loop on the hook, rep from * working fairly loosely all the way up the garment. Fasten off. Cont to work into all the chain spaces across the row alternating B and C.

To make up
Press work with a warm iron over a damp cloth. Join shoulder and side seams.
Neck: Using 3.00 hook and A, work 4 rows of dc evenly all round neck edge working (2 dc together) twice at centre front on every row. **Armholes:** Using 3.00mm hook and A, work 4 rows of dc evenly all round armhole. **Welt:** Using 3.00mm hook and A, work 8 rows of dc evenly all round lower edge.

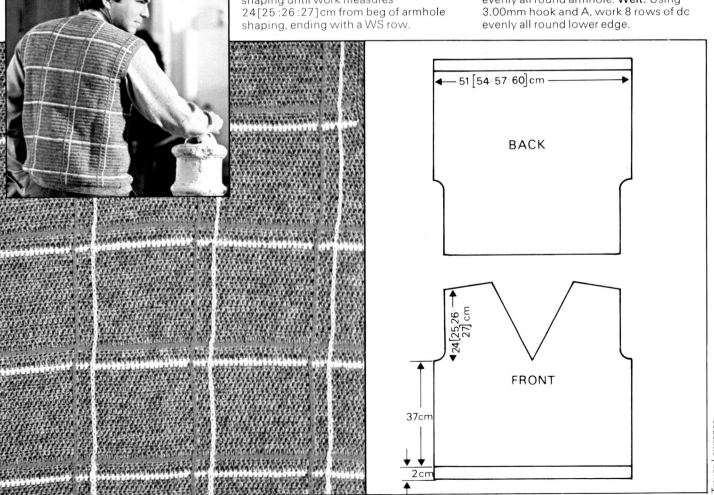

Step-by-step course – 24

Working shell patterns

Shell patterns are among the most popular crochet stitches, and fortunately, there is an amazing variety of them from which to choose. One advantage of shell patterns is that they look good whether worked in a fine cotton or in a thicker knitting yarn.

The basic principle of shell patterns – working three or more stitches into one stitch – can be used in many ways. If the stitches are all the same kind, the shell produced will be a simple fan shape. Alternatively, by working a series of different stitches which gradually increase and then decrease in height – for example, from a double crochet through to a double treble and back again to a double crochet – you can make a dome-shaped shell. For an open effect you can work one chain between each stitch. Whatever type of stitches are used, the pattern will normally call for an uneven number of them to be worked in each shell.

Here we give you step-by-step instructions for two different patterns. Once you have practised them you will find the shell stitch featured in the long-line waistcoat simple to work. On page 115 we introduce Stitch Wise, an occasional feature containing various stitch patterns.

Simple shell pattern

This pattern is a perfect example of trebles and double crochet used alternatively on each row to produce an all-over shell pattern. It is worked over a multiple of 6 chain with 2 extra for the turning chain. Our sample uses a double knitting yarn and a 4.50mm hook and is worked on a foundation of 26 chain.

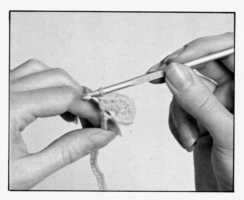

1 Make the first shell by working 3 treble, 1 chain and 3 treble all into the 5th chain from the hook. The first 4 chain will count as the first double crochet and 2 chain.

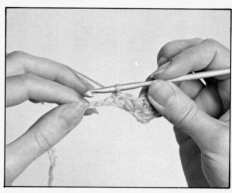

2 Miss the next 2 chain and work 1 double crochet into the following chain.

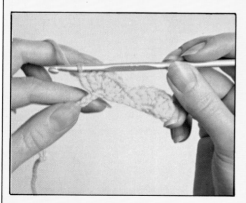

3 Miss the next 2 chain. Now work another shell in the same way as before into the next chain.

4 Continue to repeat steps 2 and 3 all the way along the chain until only 3 chain remain unworked. Miss the next 2 chain and work 1 treble into the last chain.

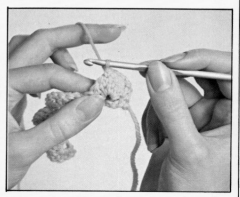

5 Turn and work 3 chain as the first treble. Now work 1 double crochet into the centre chain between the trebles in the first shell.

continued : Simple shell pattern

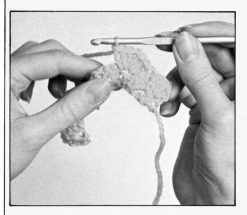

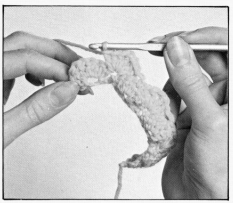

6 Now work 1 shell in the same way as before into the double crochet between the first and 2nd shells.

7 Continue to work 1 double crochet into the middle of each shell and 1 shell into each double crochet between the shells in the previous row until 1 shell remains unworked.

8 Now work 1 double crochet into the centre of the last shell.

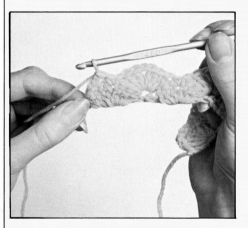

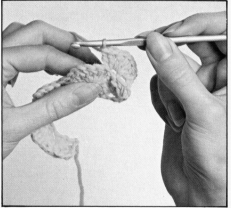

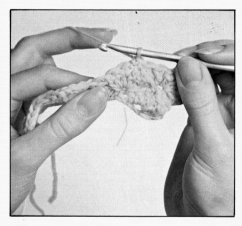

9 Work 1 treble into the turning chain of the previous row to complete the 2nd row.

10 Turn and work 2 chain to count as the first double crochet. Now work 1 shell into the first double crochet of the previous row.

11 Now work 1 double crochet into the centre of the next shell.

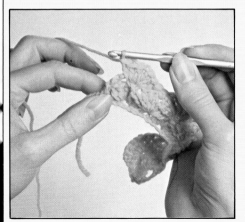

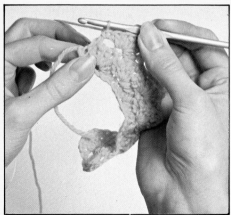

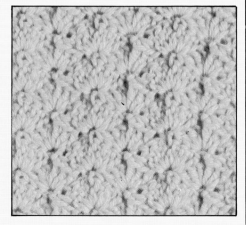

12 Continue to work across the row as before, working 1 shell into each double crochet and 1 double crochet into each shell until only the turning chain remains unworked in the previous row.

13 Now work 1 double crochet into the turning chain to complete 3rd row.

14 Continue to alternate the shell on each row in the same way, beginning each subsequent row with either 2 chain for a double crochet or 3 chain for a treble to keep the pattern correct.

Open shell pattern

This very simple pattern produces a pretty, open effect which is particularly effective when worked in crochet cotton. Our sample is based on 31 chain and worked in a 4-ply yarn with a 4.00mm hook. If you wish to make the sample larger or smaller, use any multiple of 4 chain plus 3 extra for the turning chain.

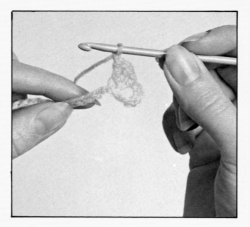

1 Make the first shell by working (1 treble and 1 chain) 3 times, all into the 7th chain from the hook.

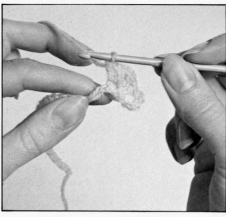

2 Now work 1 more treble into the same chain so that there are 4 trebles with 1 chain between each in the completed shell.

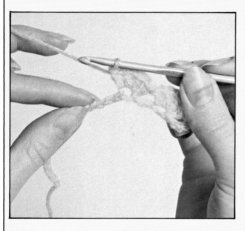

3 Miss the next 3 chain and work another shell in exactly the same way into the next chain. The centre of the shell is the 2nd 1-chain space.

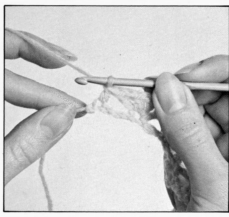

4 Repeat step 3 all along the chain until 4 chain remain unworked. Miss the next 3 chain and work 1 treble into the last chain to complete the first row.

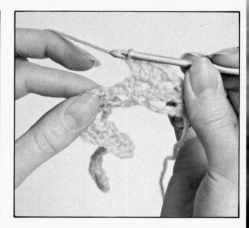

5 Turn and work 3 chain to count as the first treble. Work 1 shell in the same way as before into the centre 1-chain space of the first shell in the previous row.

6 Work 1 shell into the centre of each shell in the same way all along the row until the last shell only remains unworked.

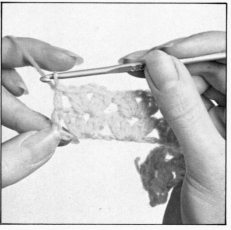

7 Work 1 shell into the last shell. Now work 1 treble into the turning chain to complete the 2nd row.

8 Continue to work each row in the same way, repeating steps 5-7 each time.

Stitch Wise

Shell Trellis Pattern

This classic pattern, in which the shells are worked in vertical lines with chain bars between each, has many variations. Our version combines trebles, double crochet and chain spaces to make a very pretty pattern, which looks equally good worked in a fine or thick yarn. Now that you have learnt the basic method for working shell patterns, try making a sample of this stitch for future reference. Make 32 chain.

Base row 1dc into 8th ch from hook, *3ch, miss next 2ch, 1dc into next ch, 2ch, miss next 2ch, 1tr into next ch, 2ch, miss next 2ch, 1dc into next ch, rep from * to last 6 ch, 3ch, miss next 2ch, 1dc into next ch, 2ch, miss next 2ch, 1 treble into last ch. Turn. 9h sp.

1st row 2ch, miss first 2ch sp, * work (2tr, 1ch, 2tr, 1ch, 2tr) all into next 3ch sp – called 1 shell – ; 1ch, 1dc into next tr in previous row, 1ch, rep from * to last 3ch sp, 1 shell into this sp, miss next 2ch, 1dc into next chain. Turn.

2nd row 5ch, * work 1dc into space between first 2 pairs of trebles in first shell, 3ch, 1dc into space between next 2 pairs of trebles in same shell, 2ch, 1tr into next dc in previous row, 2ch, rep from * to last shell, 1dc into space between first 2 pairs of trebles in last shell, 3ch, 1dc into space between next 2 pairs of trebles in same shell, 2ch, 1tr into turning chain. Turn. These last 2 rows form patt and are repeated throughout.

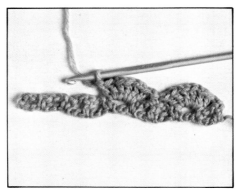

A shell worked into the 3 chain space made in the base row.

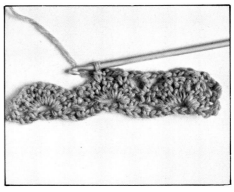

A double crochet worked into either side of the shell to form the base for the shell in the next row.

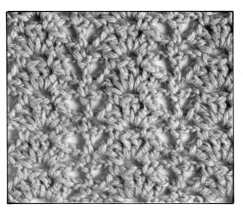

Several rows of the completed pattern.

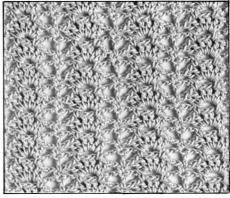

The versatility of crochet – the same stitch worked in a fine crochet cotton.

Long and lacy

The perennially popular waistcoat can be worn in many ways. Our version – worked in a shell stitch using a mohair type yarn – is shown here belted and bloused, but it looks just as good worn loose.

Sizes
To fit 87[92:97]cm bust.
Length, 81cm.
Note Instructions for larger sizes are in square brackets []. Where there is only one set of figures it applies to all sizes.

Materials
11[12:12] x 50g balls of Jaeger Gabrielle
5.50mm crochet hook

Tension
1 patt repeat measures 6cm in width and 2 patt repeats measure 6cm in depth worked on a 5.50mm hook.

Left front
** Using 5.50mm hook make 33[35:38] ch.
Base row 1dc into 3rd ch from hook, 1dc into each ch to end. Turn. 32[34:37] dc.
Next row 2ch to count as first dc, 1dc into each dc to end, working last dc into the turning ch. Turn.
Rep last row 3 times more. **
Commence patt.
The patt rows for each size are given separately. Follow the appropriate instructions for the size that you are making.
1st size only
1st row (RS) 3ch to count as first tr, * miss next 3dc, 7tr all into next dc –

shell formed, miss next 3dc, 1tr into each of next 2dc, rep from * twice more, miss next 3dc, 4tr into last dc – half shell formed. Turn.
2nd row 5ch to count as first dc and 3ch, *1tr into each of next 2 single tr, 3ch, 1dc into centre tr of next shell, 3ch, rep from * twice more, 1tr into last tr. Turn.
3rd row 3ch, *1 shell into next dc at centre of previous shell, 1tr into each of next 2tr, rep from * twice more, 4tr into 2nd of the 5ch. Turn.
The 2nd and 3rd rows form patt for the 1st size.
2nd size only
1st row (RS) 3ch to count as first tr, 1tr into each of next 2dc, *miss next 3dc, 7tr all into next dc – shell formed, miss next 3dc, 1tr into each of next 2dc, rep from * twice more, miss next 3dc, 4tr into last dc – half shell formed. Turn.

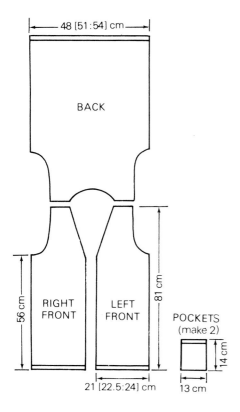

48 [51:54] cm

BACK

56 cm

81 cm

RIGHT FRONT

LEFT FRONT

POCKETS (make 2)

14 cm

21 [22.5:24] cm

13 cm

John Hutchinson

2nd row 5ch to count as first dc and 3ch, *1tr into each of next 2 single tr, 3ch, 1dc into centre tr of next shell, 3ch, rep from * twice more, 1tr into each of last 3tr. Turn.

3rd row 3ch, 1tr into each of next 2tr, *1 shell into dc at centre of previous shell, 1tr into each of next 2tr, rep from * twice more, 4tr into 2nd of the 5ch. Turn. The 2nd and 3rd rows form patt for the 2nd size.

3rd size only
1st row (RS) 3ch to count as first tr, 3tr into first dc, miss next 3dc, 1tr into each of next 2dc, *miss next 3dc, 7tr all into next dc – shell formed, miss next 3dc, 1tr into each of next 2dc, rep from * twice more, miss next 3dc, 4tr into last dc – half shell formed. Turn.

2nd row 5ch to count as first dc and 3ch, *1tr into each of next 2 single tr, 3ch, 1dc into centre tr of next shell, 3ch, rep from * twice more, 1tr into each of next 2 single tr, 3ch, 1dc into last tr. Turn.

3rd row 3ch, 3tr into first dc, *1tr into each of next 2tr, 1 shell into dc at centre of previous shell, rep from * twice more, 1tr into each of next 2tr, 4tr into 2nd of the 5ch. Turn.
The 2nd and 3rd rows form patt for the 3rd size.

All sizes
Cont in patt until work measures 56cm from beg, ending with a 3rd patt row.
Shape armhole
Next row Patt to last 9sts (including turning ch), turn and leave these sts unworked.

Shape neck
1st row Patt to within last 4ch, work 2tr into ch, now work 2tr tog.
2nd row 2ch to count as first st, 1tr into each of next 2tr, work in patt to end of row. Turn.
3rd row Patt to within last 2sts, work 2tr tog. Turn.
Cont to dec one st at neck edge on every alt row in the same way until 16[18:21] sts rem.
Next row 4ch, 1dc into centre tr of next shell, patt to end. Turn.
Next row Patt to within last dc, 4tr into last dc, 1tr into each of next 2ch. Turn. 16sts.
Rep these 2 rows until armhole measures 25cm from beg. Fasten off.

Right front
Work as given for left front from ** to **. Commence patt.
1st size only
1st row (RS) 3ch to count as first tr, 3tr into first st, miss next 3dc, *1tr into each of next 2dc, miss next 3dc, 1 shell into next dc, miss next 3dc, rep from * twice more, 1 tr into last tr. Turn.
This sets patt for the 1st size.
2nd size only
1st row (RS) 3ch to count as first tr, 3tr into first st, miss next 3dc, *1tr into each of next 2dc, miss next 3dc, 1 shell into next dc, rep from * twice more, 1 tr into each of last 3dc. Turn.
This sets patt for 2nd size.
3rd size only
1st row (RS) 3ch to count as first tr, 3tr into first st, miss next 3dc, *1 tr into each of next 2dc, miss next 3dc, 1 shell into next dc, miss next 3dc, rep from * twice more, 1tr into each of next 3dc, miss next 3dc, 4tr into last dc. Turn.
This sets patt for 3rd size.
All sizes
Cont in patt as set until work measures same as left front to armhole, ending with a 3rd patt row. Fasten off and turn work.
Shape armhole
Next row Miss first 9sts. Rejoin yarn to next st, 2ch, patt to end. Turn. Complete as given for left front, reversing neck shaping.

Back
Using 5.50mm hook make 73[77:83] ch. Work base row as given for left front. 72[76:82] sts. Work 4 rows in dc. Commence patt.
1st size only
1st row (RS) 3ch to count as first tr, *miss next 3dc, 1 shell into next dc, miss next 3dc, 1tr into each of next 2 dc, rep from * to within last 8dc, miss next 3dc, 1 shell into next dc, miss next 3dc, 1tr into last dc. Turn.
This sets the patt for the 1st size.
2nd size only
1st row (RS) 3ch to count as first tr,

1tr into each of next 2dc, *miss next 3dc, 1 shell into next dc, miss next 3 dc, 1tr into each of next 2dc, rep from * to within last dc, 1tr into last dc. Turn.
This sets patt for the 2nd size.
3rd size only
1st row (RS) 3ch to count as first tr, 3tr into first dc, miss next 3dc, 1tr into each of next 2dc, *miss next 3dc, 1 shell into next dc, miss next 3dc, 1tr into each of next 2dc, rep from * to within last 4dc, miss next 3dc, 4tr into last dc. Turn.
This sets patt for the 3rd size.
All sizes
Cont in patt as set until work measures same as left front to armholes, ending with a 3rd patt row. Fasten off and turn work.
Shape armholes
Next row Miss first 9sts, rejoin yarn to next st, work 2ch, patt to within last 9sts, turn and leave these 9sts unworked. Cont in patt until armholes measure same as left front, ending with a 3rd patt row. Fasten off.

Pockets (make 2)
Using 5.50mm hook make 21ch.
Base row 4tr into 3rd ch from hook, miss next 3ch, 1tr into each of next 2ch, miss next 3ch, 1 shell into next ch, miss next 3ch, 1tr into each of next 2ch, miss next 3ch, 4tr into last ch. Turn.
Work 6 rows in patt as set.
Next row Work 1dc into each st to end, decr 4sts evenly across the row. Turn.
Work 4 more rows in dc. Fasten off.

To make up
Do not press. Join shoulder seams.
Front border
With RS of right front facing and beg at lower edge, work a row of dc ip right front to shoulder, working 1dc into each row end of border and 2dc into each patt row end. Work 1dc into each st across back of neck and now work in dc down left front as before. Turn and work 4 rows in dc. Fasten off.
Armhole borders (alike)
Beg at side edge and work a row of dc round armhole edge, working 1dc into each st at underarm and 2dc into each patt row end.
1st row 1ch, now work 1dc into each of next 3sts, (work next 2dc tog) 3 times, now work 1dc into each dc until 10sts rem, (work 2dc tog) 3 times, 1dc into each of next 3sts, 1dc into turning ch. Turn.
2nd row 1ch, 1dc into each st to end. Turn
3rd row 1ch, 1dc into each of next 3sts, (work 2dc tog) 4 times, 1dc into each st until 11sts rem unworked, (work 2dc tog) 4 times, 1dc into each of next 2sts, 1dc into turning ch. Turn.
4th row As 2nd row. Fasten off.
Join side seams. Sew pockets to fronts.

Step-by-step course – 25

Working large lace patterns

There are several ways of making lace – on a loom or with bobbins, for example – but crocheted lace is probably the easiest method, since all you need is a crochet hook, some yarn and the ability to work all the basic crochet stitches that you have learned so far. The variety of patterns available is enormous, but basically they are all made in the same way: by building up groups of crochet stitches to form different shapes or motifs, such as shells or pyramids, and joining these with chain bars or single stitches. Don't be put off by the fact that some of these patterns appear complicated. They are much easier than they look, and as long as you follow the instructions carefully you will succeed in making a beautiful fabric. The type of lace fabric you make will, of course, depend on the thickness of yarn and the size of hook you use, but you will find that most of the patterns look equally good in a fine or a thick yarn.

Scallop shells

By working a simple pattern like the one shown here, you will begin to understand how large lace patterns are created. The basic principle is very similar however intricate the stitch might be, and thus, practising something quite simple like this scallop shell pattern will enable you to progress to a more complicated pattern without difficulty. To work this sample, first make 31 chain.

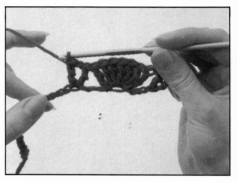

1 Work 1 double treble into 6th chain from hook. Miss next 3 chain and work 7 double treble into next chain for first shell. The chain are left unworked at each side of the shell or motif to create a space so that the motif can fan outwards and the fabric lies flat.

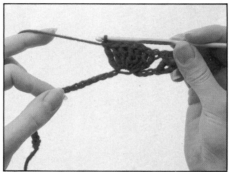

2 Miss next 3 chain. Now work 1 double treble, 1 chain and 1 double treble all into next chain. This 'V' group acts as a link between the shells. Lengths of chain and single stitches can also be used for this purpose, but you must still leave a space at either side of the group.

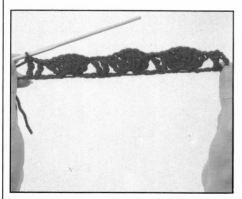

3 Work a shell and a V group alternately across the row in the same way. Make the last V group by working 1 double treble into the 2nd to last chain, 1 chain and the final double treble into the last chain. Most patterns will tell you exactly how to work the beginning and end of each row to maintain the continuity of the pattern.

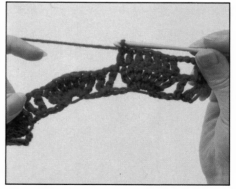

4 Begin next row with 3 chain. Now work 1 treble into the first chain space. Work 3 chain and work 1 treble into each stitch in the first shell. Thus you begin to build up and enlarge the original shape. One chain is sometimes worked between these trebles to fan the motif outwards even further.

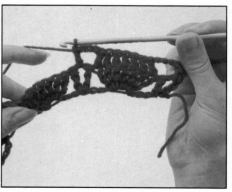

5 Make another 3 chain. Now work 1 treble into the centre of the next V group. The 3 chain and treble now form the link between the motifs in place of the V group, at the same time maintaining the open effect.

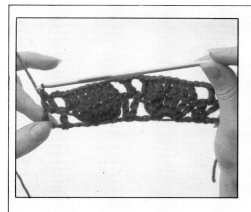

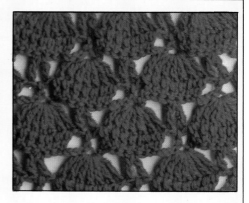

6 Continue to work into each shell and V group across the row, working 3 chain at each side. Finish the row with 1 treble into last space and 1 treble into turning chain. The last treble acts as the edge stitch.

7 The next row is worked in the same way as the first, except that the motifs are reversed by working a shell into each of the single trebles between the shells, and a V group into the centre stitch of each shell. To keep the pattern correct work 3 double treble at the beginning and end of the row to act as a half shell, since the full shell would be too wide.

8 As the pattern develops the shells and V groups are alternated so that they are positioned diagonally from one another. On other patterns more rows are required to build up the basic shape, and more chains are used, creating a really open lace fabric.

Japanese fan stitch

The soft fan shape of the shells in this pattern is achieved by working longer trebles than normal into one stitch. The resulting shell is much softer and thicker than it would normally be, creating a pretty, warm pattern, ideal for a cosy shawl.

The pattern is worked over a multiple of 14 chain plus 1. To make our sample work 30 chain (1 extra for the turning chain). Work 1 double crochet into 3rd chain and then 1 double crochet into each chain to end, so that there are 29 stitches in all. To make the sample wider, add 14 extra chain for each pattern repeat.

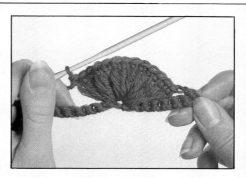

1 Turn and make 2 chain to count as first stitch. Miss next 6 stitches (7 including edge stitch). Now work 13 trebles into next stitch, drawing yarn out to about 1.25cm each time you work a treble, to make a long stitch. These 13 treble form first shell.

2 Miss next 6 stitches and work a double crochet into next stitch. Now miss next 6 stitches and work another shell into next stitch in same way as before. Miss next 6 stitches and work a double crochet into top of turning chain to complete first row.

3 Now turn and work **4** chain. Work a long treble as before into first (edge) stitch. Now make 5 chain and work a double crochet into 7th (centre) treble of next shell. Make 5 chain and work 2 long trebles into next double crochet between the shells.

4 Repeat these actions to complete the 2nd row, working 5 chain then a double crochet into the centre of the next shell; 5 chain and then 2 long trebles into top of the turning chain.

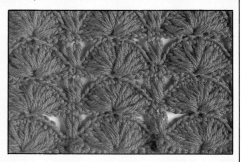

5 To continue pattern turn and make 2 chain. Now work a shell as before into double crochet worked in centre of each shell in previous row and a double crochet between trebles worked in previous row, working last double crochet into top of turning chain. Continue to alternate 2nd and 3rd rows.

Paul Williams

Two lace patterns

Try working one or both of these two lace stitches. The first, shell and chain pattern, uses the more conventional method of working shell shapes and interlocking chains to produce an open-work lace fabric which could be worked in a fine cotton or thicker crochet yarn.

By contrast, the second pattern, Window Panes, makes use of square blocks of trebles and chain bars to create an unusual lace effect, which would be ideal for a bedspread, worked in a fairly thick cotton.

Window panes

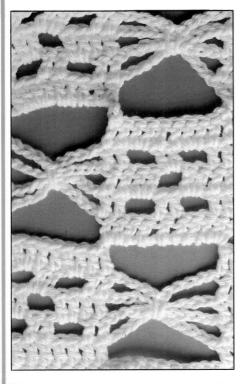

This pattern is worked over a multiple of 10 chain with 1 extra turning chain. We give instructions for working 3 blocks of pattern across the row. When using the pattern for a crochet fabric you will need to work extra stitches at either side to form a firm edge.

Make 31 chain ; work 29 double crochet into chain so having 30 stitches.

Base row 3ch, miss first st, 1tr into each of next 9dc, 10ch, miss 10dc, 1tr into each dc to end, working last tr into turning chain. Turn.

1st row 3ch, miss first st, 1tr into next st, *2ch, miss 2 sts, 1tr into each of next 2 sts, *, rep from * to * once more, 10ch, 1tr into each of next 2 sts, rep from * to * twice more, working last tr into turning chain. Turn.

2nd row 3ch, miss first st, 1tr into next st, * 2tr into next 2ch sp, 2ch, miss next 2 sts, 2tr into next 2ch sp, 1tr into each of next 2 sts*, 10ch, 1tr into each of next 2tr, rep from * to * once more, working last tr into turning chain. Turn.

3rd row 3ch, miss first st, 1tr into next st, *2ch, miss 2 sts, 2tr into next 2ch sp, 2ch, miss 2 sts, 1tr into each of next 2tr *, 4ch, insert hook under first 10 chain loop from front to back, work 1dc round all 3 loops at centre to draw them together – called 1dc round ch ; 4ch, 1tr into each of next 2tr, rep from * to * once more, working last tr into turning chain. Turn.

4th row 3ch, miss first st, *1tr into each tr and 2tr into each 2ch sp*, 10ch, rep from * to * once more, working last tr into turning chain. Turn.

5th row 3ch to count as first tr, 10ch, 10tr into next 10ch loop, 10ch, 1tr into turning chain. Turn.

6th row 3ch to count as first tr, 10ch, 1tr into each of next 2tr, *2ch, miss 2 sts, 1tr into each of next 2 sts, rep from * once more, 10ch, 1tr into 3rd of first 3ch. Turn.

7th row 3ch to count as first tr, 10ch, 1tr into each of next 2tr, 2tr into 2ch sp, 2ch, miss 2 sts, 2tr into 2ch sp, 1tr into each of next 2tr, 10ch, 1tr into 3rd of first 3ch. Turn.

8th row 3ch to count as first tr, * 4ch, 1dc round ch, 4ch*, 1tr into each of next 2tr, 2ch, miss 2 sts, 2tr into next 2ch sp, 2ch, miss 2 sts, 1tr into each of next 2 sts, rep from * to * once more, 1tr into 3rd of first 3ch. Turn.

9th row 3ch to count as first tr, 10ch, 1tr into each tr and 2tr into each 2ch sp, 10ch, 1tr into 3rd of 1st 3ch. Turn.

10th row 3ch, 9tr into 10ch loop, 10ch, 9tr into 10ch loop, 1tr into 3rd of first 3ch. Turn. (10tr in each lattice section as before.)

Rows 1 to 10 form patt and are rep throughout so that position of squares is reversed each time. To work more squares across, repeat the lattice and chain sections alternately as many times as required, only working the turning chain at side edge.

Shell and chain pattern

This pattern is worked over a number of chain divisible by 10, plus 1 chain and 5 extra turning chain.

Base row (RS) 1tr into 6th ch from hook, *3ch, miss 3ch, 1dc into each of next 3ch, 3ch, miss 3ch, (1tr, 3ch, 1tr) all into next ch, rep from * ending last rep (1tr, 2ch, 1tr) all worked into last ch. Turn.

1st row 3ch, miss first tr, 3tr into first 2ch sp, *3ch, 1dc into 2nd of next 3dc, 3ch, 7tr into next 3ch sp between tr, rep from * to end, ending by working 3tr (half shell) instead of 7tr into last sp between tr and turning chain and last tr into top of turning ch. Turn.

2nd row 1ch, miss first st, 1dc into each of next 3tr, *5ch, 1dc into each of next 7tr, rep from * to last half shell, 5ch, 1dc into each of next 3tr, 1dc into 3rd of first 3ch. Turn.

3rd row 1ch, miss first dc, 1dc into next dc, *3ch, (1tr, 3ch, 1tr) all into 3rd of next 5ch, 3ch, miss first 2dc of next shell, 1dc into each of next 3dc, rep from * ending last rep, miss next 2dc, 1dc into

next dc, 1dc into first ch. Turn.

4th row 1ch to count as first dc, *3ch, now work 7tr into next 3ch sp between tr, 3ch, 1dc into 2nd of next 3dc at centre of shell, rep from * to end, working last dc into first ch of previous row. Turn.

5th row 1ch to count as first dc, 2ch, * 1dc into each of next 7tr of shell, 5ch, rep from * to last shell, 1dc into each of the 7tr in last shell, 2ch, 1dc into first ch of previous row. Turn.

6th row 3ch to count as first tr, 2ch, 1tr into first st at edge of work, *3ch, miss 2dc, 1dc into each of next 3dc at centre of shell, 3ch, (1tr, 3ch, 1tr) all into 3rd of next 5ch, rep from * to end, ending last rep by working (1tr, 2ch, 1tr) all into first ch of previous row. Turn.

The 1st to 6th rows form the pattern and are repeated throughout.

Lacy luxury

A delicate lace pattern and a soft fine yarn make this pretty evening cover-up. Wear it in the daytime, too, when you want a bit of extra warmth.

Size
Length when hanging, 90cm excluding fringe.

Materials
*6 x 40g balls of Phildar Anouchka
3.50mm crochet hook*

Tension
1 patt rep measures 5.5cm in width and 6cm in depth worked on 3.50mm hook.

To make
Make 244 ch very loosely.
Base row 3tr into 4th ch from hook, *miss next 3ch, 1dc into next ch, miss next 3ch, 7tr all into next ch, rep from * to end, but finish last rep 4tr into last ch instead of 7tr. Turn.
1st row 4ch, miss first tr, *1tr into next tr, 1ch, rep from * to end, finishing 1tr into turning ch. Turn.
2nd row 1ch, 1dc into first sp, 3ch, 1dc into next sp, 3ch, *miss next tr, 1dc into next tr, 1ch, 1dc into next tr, 3ch, miss next sp, (1dc into next sp, 3ch) 4 times, rep from * to within last 6 sps, miss next tr, 1dc into next tr, 1ch, 1dc into next tr, 3ch, miss next sp, 1dc into next sp, 3ch, 1dc into last sp. Turn.
3rd row Ss into first 3-ch sp, 3ch, 1dc into next 3-ch sp, *2ch, (1dc into next 3-ch sp, 3ch) 4 times, 1dc into next 3-ch sp, rep from * to end, finishing 2ch, 1dc into next 3-ch sp, 3ch, 1dc into last 3-ch sp. Turn.
4th row Ss into first 3-ch sp, *3ch, 1dc into next 3-ch sp, rep from * to end. Turn.
5th row *5ch, miss next 3-ch sp, (1dc into next 3-ch sp, 3ch) twice, 1dc into next 3-ch sp, rep from * to end, finishing 5ch, miss last 3-ch sp, 1dc into ss.

Turn.
6th row *7ch, 1dc into next 3-ch sp, 3ch, 1dc into next 3-ch sp, rep from * to end, finishing 7ch, 1dc into the last dc of the 4th row. Turn.
7th row Ss over the 7ch and into 3-ch sp, 3ch, 3tr into same sp, *2ch, 1dc into 4th of 7ch, 2ch, 7tr into 3-ch sp, rep from * to end, but finish last rep 4tr into last 3-ch sp instead of 7tr. Turn.
Rep rows 1 to 7 until patt remains, ending with a 6th row. Fasten off.
Fringe
Using four 30cm lengths of yarn together, knot fringe evenly along the two side edges. Trim the ends.

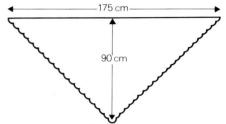

Brian Mayor

Step-by-step course – 26

Hints on making up

Sooner or later – and probably sooner – you will crochet a garment which involves detailed making up. Many people think that once they have completed making all the separate pieces of a garment, the task is virtually finished, and that all they need to do is quickly sew the seams together. This, of course, is not true; careful pressing and seaming are essential if you want your garment to have a really professional finish. After all, you've probably spent a considerable amount of time and care in working the crochet. A few extra minutes at the making-up stage may well make the difference between a finished sweater, jacket or dress which you'll be proud to wear and one that stays in the cupboard.

Blocking and pressing

Where the pieces of your garment are to be pressed before seaming, you must first pin each piece out to the correct size and shape on a flat, padded surface. This is known as 'blocking'. Some yarns can be pressed, and some cannot. On most ball bands you will find pressing instructions using the international symbols, shown overleaf. The ball band should also tell you whether the yarn should be wet or dry pressed. Many man-made fibres need no pressing at all and can be ruined if they come into contact with heat, so check the ball band carefully before pressing. If you are in any doubt about how the yarn should be treated, it is better not to press it at all to avoid disappointment.

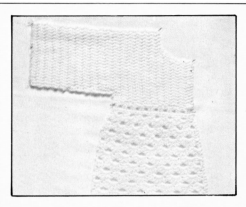

1 Place the piece to be pressed (RS down) on to a flat, well-padded surface. Your kitchen table covered with several layers of blankets and a sheet makes an ideal surface, since it is wider than an ordinary ironing board and provides plenty of room on which to lay the fabric out flat. Pin the piece at each corner as shown.

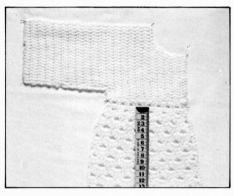

2 Now measure horizontally across the widest part and vertically down the centre of the fabric to make sure that the measurements are the same as those given in the instructions. If not, pat the fabric gently to the correct shape and size and pin once more at the lower edge.

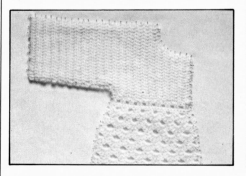

3 Now pin all round the fabric at intervals of about 2cm, taking care not to stretch the fabric, since this could result in a fluted edge. Check that each side measures the same and that stitches and rows are running straight before you begin to press.

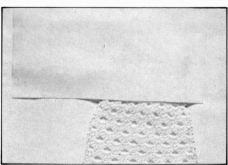

4 Place a clean, cotton cloth (either damp or dry depending on the type of yarn used) over the piece to be pressed. Remember that any ribbing on the garment should not be pressed, as this will flatten it, causing it to lose its elasticity.

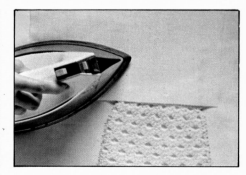

5 Pressing should always be done with a light touch, as over-pressing can easily ruin the soft, textured quality of crocheted fabrics. Set the iron at the correct temperature for the yarn, then press gently but firmly down on the cloth and lift the iron off again. Repeat this action all over the cloth, lifting and pressing, rather than pushing it over the cloth as when ironing. Allow the fabric to cool before removing the pins.

Special cases

Highly textured patterns, such as cluster patterns, are normally not pressed, for pressing may destroy their distinctive appearance. The same is generally true of lacy patterns. In some cases, however, (usually when a natural fibre has been used) the pattern will instruct you to press the garment lightly on the wrong side, taking care not to spoil the pattern. Block the garment over a folded towel and lay a damp cloth on top of it. Hold the iron so that it just touches the cloth and leave it there a second or so. Repeat over the whole surface of the piece – excluding ribbing, if any.

A lightly textured fabric may simply be blocked and pressed around the edges, as shown here.

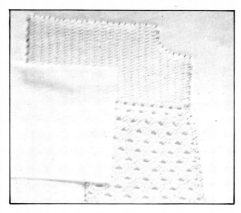

1 Block the piece to shape in the normal way, and then place a damp cloth over it.

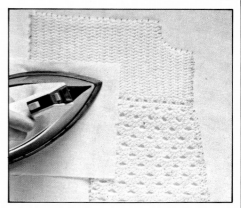

2 Press around the edges only. This creates a firm edge, making it easier to sew the pieces together. Allow the fabric to cool completely.

Ironing symbols

Iron with three dots: use a hot iron.

Iron with two dots: use a warm iron.

Iron with one dot: use a cool iron.

Iron with a cross through it: do not iron.

Sewing the pieces together

To sew crocheted fabrics together use a blunt-ended wool needle and the same yarn used for the garment. If this is too thick or unsuitable (a bouclé for example) you can substitute finer or more suitable yarn in a matching shade. Your instructions will usually tell you in which order the seams should be joined and the kind of seam to use for each piece. Remember that to avoid distorting the garment at the seams you must not draw the yarn too tightly through the fabric. Make sure that any patterns – such as shells or clusters – match exactly on each side of the seam before sewing the pieces together. You can, in some cases, use double crochet to join the pieces together. This is usually worked on the right side of the fabric with a contrasting coloured yarn to make a feature of the seam (See Crochet Course 4, page 155).

Back stitch seam

This seam is generally used for the main parts of the garment, such as shoulder, side and sleeve seams, on fabric that is closely woven or textured, such as double crochet, half treble or moss stitch fabrics. It creates a firm, strong seam ideal for sweaters and jackets.

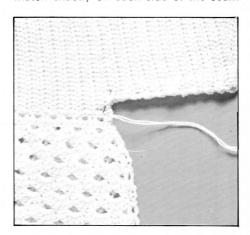

1 Pin the two pieces to be joined with RS together. Work the seam approximately one crochet stitch in from the edge. Begin by making 2 small stitches on top of each other at the starting point of the seam to hold the yarn in place.

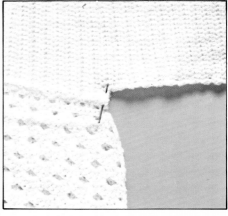

2 Insert the needle into the fabric again and bring it out slightly to the left of the fastening stitches. Now bring the needle to the right, insert it and bring it out a little farther to the left.

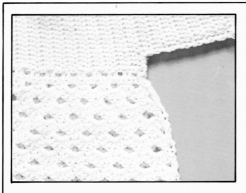

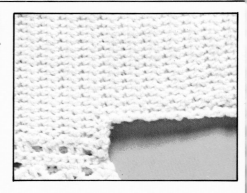

3 Continue to repeat step 2 all the way across the fabric, working in a straight line inserting the needle at the point where it emerged for the previous stitch, so that the stitches are all touching. Remember not to pull the yarn tightly.

4 If you are using this seam at the shoulder, work in a straight line from the outer (armhole) edge to the inner (neck) edge, rather than following the steps created by the shoulder shaping.

5 If you had a set-in sleeve this could be sewn in first before joining the side and sleeve edges, these edges could then be joined in one continuous seam. This method produces a firm neat seam as shown here.

Oversewn seam

This is an ideal seam for ribbing or very open lace patterns, since it does not make a ridge on the fabric. The yarn is taken over the top of the edge and then passed through the edge stitches.

On lacy patterns, which may have more spaces than stitches along the edge – ruling out a back stitch seam – oversewing is a practical alternative, for you need only pass the needle through the centre of the chain or edge stitch to join the two pieces. Match any pattern on your fabric carefully on each side of the seam before joining the pieces together.

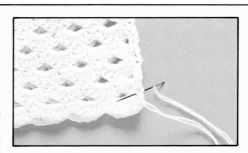

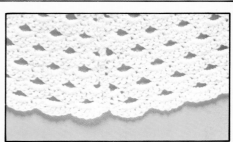

1 Place the two pieces with RS together. Using a blunt-ended needle and working from right to left make two small stitches at the beginning. With yarn at front of fabric pass the needle over the top of the two edges from front to back and insert the needle through the edges from back to front.

2 Now pull the yarn through firmly, but not too tightly, to complete the first stitch. Continue to work in same way across the fabric, working over the top across the fabric, working over the edges each time until the seam is complete.

Invisible seam

Here is another method of seaming which is also well-suited to very open lace crochet fabrics, since you can just catch the stitches at either side of the seam, rather than having to work through the double thickness of fabric each time. Because the seam lies perfectly flat, with no hard ridges, it is also ideal for baby clothes, in which comfort is extremely important. Unlike the other seams it is worked with the pieces lying flat, RS upwards.

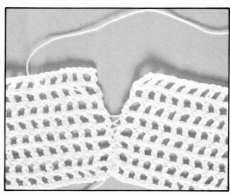

1 Place the two pieces of fabric edge to edge, RS facing upwards. Join the yarn on to one side of the seam, taking 2 small stitches to secure it. Now take the yarn over to the other side and pass the needle under one stitch. If the fabric is particularly fine, you can pass the needle under 1 loop only of the stitch.

2 Take the needle back to the other side and under the next stitch on this side in the same way. Pull the yarn through firmly so that the stitch becomes invisible. Continue to work along the seam, catching one stitch at either side until the seam has been completed.

Stitch Wise

Diagonal shell pattern

This pattern is worked over a multiple of 8 chain plus 7 extra chain, and shows how simple shells and chain links can be worked in diagonal, rather than vertical lines. Make sure that you work the base chain loosely.

Base row (RS) 1dc into 3rd ch from hook, *5ch, miss 3ch, 1dc into next ch, rep from * to end of ch. Turn.

1st row 3ch to count as first tr, 2tr into first (edge) dc – called half shell, 1dc into first 5ch loop, *5ch, 1dc into next 5ch loop, 5tr into next dc – called 1 shell, 1dc into next 5ch loop, rep from * to end, ending last rep with 5ch, 1dc into top of turning chain. Turn.

2nd row 3ch to count as first tr, half shell into first dc, 1dc into next 5ch loop, *5ch, 1dc into centre tr of next shell, 1 shell into next dc, 1dc into next 5ch loop, rep from * ending last rep with 1dc into top of turning chain. Turn.

3rd row 6ch, 1dc into first 5ch loop, *1 shell into next dc, 1dc into centre tr of next shell, 5ch, 1dc into next 5ch loop, rep from * to end, ending with 1 shell into last dc, 1dc into top of turning chain. Turn.

4th row 6ch, 1dc into centre tr of next shell, *1 shell into next dc, 1dc into next 5ch loop, 5ch, 1dc into centre of next shell, rep from *, ending with 1dc into centre tr of last shell, 1 shell into next dc, 1dc into 3rd of first 6ch. Turn.

5th row 3ch, half shell into first dc, 1dc into centre tr of next shell, *5ch, 1dc into next 5ch loop, 1 shell into next dc, 1dc into centre of next shell : rep from * ending last rep with 5ch, 1dc into 3rd of first 6ch. Turn.

2nd to 5th rows form pattern and are repeated throughout.

For the little one

Make a jacket and matching bonnet for the newcomer in the family. The lacy pattern is highlighted by using a yarn with a shiny thread running through it producing a slightly lustrous effect.

Sizes
Jacket fits 46[48]cm chest.
Length, 28[30.5]cm.
Sleeve seam, 12[13.5]cm.

Note Instructions for the larger size are in square brackets [] ; where there is only one set of figures it applies to both sizes.

Materials
Jacket *5[6] x 20g balls of Emu Treasure Ripple Quickerknit*
3.50mm crochet hook
4.00mm crochet hook
3 buttons
1m of 1cm wide ribbon
Bonnet *2 balls of yarn as above*
3.50mm crochet hook
1m of 1.5cm-wide ribbon

Tension
22 sts to 10cm and 22 rows to 13cm over yoke patt on 3.50mm hook.

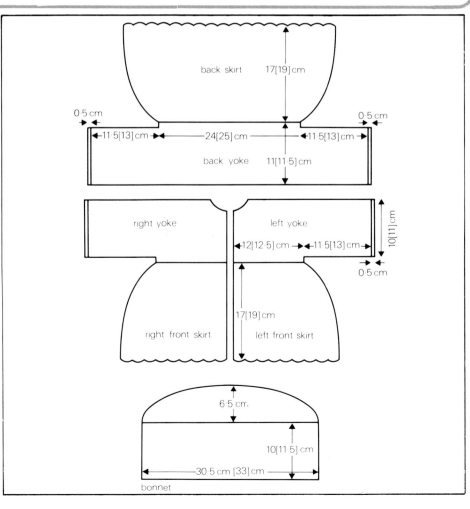

Jacket back yoke

Using 3.50mm hook make 23[26]ch for left cuff.

Base row (WS) 1 htr into 3rd ch from hook, 1 htr into each ch to end. Turn. 22[25] sts.

Commence patt.

1st row 2ch to count as first dc, working into *back* loops only, work 1 dc into each st to end. Turn.

2nd row 2ch to count as first htr, 1 htr into each st to end. Turn.

Rep the last 2 rows until work measures 11.5[13]cm from beg, ending with a 2nd patt row.

Next row Work 4ch for underarm, 1 dc in to 3rd ch from hook, 1 dc into next ch, patt to end. Turn. 25[28] sts.

Cont in patt until work measures 35.5[38]cm from beg, ending with a 1st patt row.

Next row Patt to last 3 sts, turn and leave last 3 sts for underarm. 22[25] sts.

Cont in patt until work measures 47[51]cm from beg, ending with a 1st patt row. Fasten off.

Left front yoke

Work as given for back yoke until front measures 1 row less than back yoke to first underarm, so ending with a 1st patt row. Fasten off.

Shape underarm

Next row Work 3ch, then patt across sts of sleeve. Turn.

Next row Patt across 22[25] sts, 1 dc into each of next 3ch. Turn. 25[28] sts.

Cont in patt over all sts until front measures 7.5[9]cm from underarm, ending with a 1st patt row.

Shape neck

Next row Patt to last 5[6] sts, turn. Dec one st at neck edge on next 3 rows. 17[19] sts. Work 4 rows without shaping. Fasten off.

Right front yoke

Using 3.50mm hook make 18[20]ch. Work base row as given for back yoke. 17[19] sts.

Next row (buttonhole row) 2ch, patt 1[2] sts, (2ch, miss 2 sts, patt 3 sts) 3 tines, patt 0[1].

Work 2 rows in patt, then inc one st at neck edge on next 3 rows, so ending with a 2nd patt row. Fasten off.

Shape neck

Next row Work 5[6]ch, patt across sts of front. Turn.

Next row Patt to last 5[6]ch, 1 htr into each of next 5[6]ch. Turn. 25[28] sts.

Cont in patt until front measures 7.5[9]cm from end of neck shaping, ending with a 1st patt row. Fasten off.

Next row Miss first 3 sts for underarm, rejoin yarn to next st, 2ch, patt to end. Turn. 22[25] sts.

Cont in patt until front measures 11.5[13]cm from underarm, ending with a 1st patt row. Fasten off.

Back skirt

Using 3.50mm hook and with RS of work facing, work 50[56]dc across lower edge of back yoke. Turn.
Next row (eyelet-hole row) 2ch, 1htr into next st, *1ch, miss next st, 1htr into each of next 2 sts, rep from * to end. Turn.
Next row 2ch, 1dc into each htr and ch of previous row. Turn. 50[56]dc. Change to 4.00mm hook. Commence patt.**

1st size only
Base row 2ch, 1dc into next st, *3ch, miss next st, 1dc into each of next 3 sts, rep from * to last 4 sts, 3ch, 1dc into each of last 2 sts. Turn.

2nd size only
Base row 2ch, 1dc into first st, *3ch, miss next st, 1dc into each of next 3 sts, rep from * to last 3 sts, 3ch, miss next st, 1dc into each of last 2 sts. Turn.

Both sizes
***1st row** 2ch, 1dc into next st, *5tr into 3ch sp, 1dc into centre dc of 3dc, rep from * to end, finishing with 1dc into last st. Turn.
2nd row 2ch, *3ch, 1dc into each of centre 3tr of group, rep from * to end, finishing with 2ch, 1tr into last st. Turn.
3rd row 3ch, 2tr into 2ch sp, *1dc into centre dc of 3dc, 5tr into 3ch sp, rep from * to end, finishing with 2tr into 3ch sp, 1tr into last st. Turn.
4th row 2ch, 1dc into next tr, *3ch, 1dc into each of centre 3tr of group, rep from * to end, finishing with 3ch, 1dc into each of last 2 sts. Turn.
The last 4 rows form the patt. Rep them 4 times more.

1st size only
Rep 1st row once more. Fasten off.
2nd size only
Rep 1st-3rd rows inclusive once more. Fasten off.

Right front skirt

Using 3.50mm hook and with RS of work facing, work 26[29]dc across lower edge of right front yoke. Work as given for back skirt from ** to **.
1st size only
Base row Work as given for back.
2nd size only
Base row 2ch, 1dc into next st, *3ch, miss next st, 1dc into each of next 3 sts, rep from * to last 3 sts, 3ch, miss next st, 1dc into each of last 2 sts. Turn.
Both sizes
Work as given for back skirt from *** to end.

Left front skirt

Work as given for right front skirt.

To make up

Press lightly on WS using a cool iron over dry cloth. Join shoulder and upper sleeve seams, then skirt and underarm seams.
Front and neck edging Using 3.50mm hook and with RS of work facing, work 1 row of dc up right front, round neck edge and down left front, working 3dc into each corner. Fasten off.
Using 3.50mm hook and with RS of work facing, rejoin yarn to top of right front and work round neck edge as foll : 1ch, *1dc into each of next 2 sts, 3ch, ss into first ch – picot formed, 1dc into next st, rep from * to top of left front. Fasten off.
Cuff edging Using 3.50mm hook and with RS of work facing, work 36[42]dc round cuff edge. Join with a ss into first dc.
2nd round Work in dc, dec 6 sts evenly.
3rd round Work picots as given for neck edging. Fasten off.
Sew on buttons to correspond with buttonholes. Thread ribbon through eyelet holes to tie at front.

Bonnet

Using 3.50mm hook make 68[74]ch. Work base row and patt 3 rows as given for jacket back yoke. 67[73]sts. Commence patt.
Base row 2ch, 1dc into next st, *3ch, miss 3 sts, 1dc into each of next 3 sts, rep from * to last 5 sts, 3ch, miss 3 sts, 1dc into each of last 2 sts. Turn.
Cont in patt as given for back skirt until bonnet measures 10[11.5]cm from beg, ending with a 2nd or 4th patt row.
Next row 1ch, 1dc into each dc and ch of previous row. Turn.
Work 3 more rows in dc.
Shape crown
1st row 2ch, 1dc into each of next 0[3]sts, (1dc into each of next 15 sts, work 2dc tog) 3 times, 1dc into each of next 15[18]sts. Turn. 64[70]sts.
2nd and every alt row 1ch, 1dc into each st of previous row. Turn.
3rd row 2ch, 1dc into each of next 0[3]sts, (1dc into each of next 7 sts, work 2dc tog) 7 times, 1dc into each of next 0[3]sts. Turn. 57[63]sts.
5th row 2ch, 1dc into each of next 0[3]sts, (1dc into each of next 6 sts, work 2dc tog) 7 times, 1dc into each of next 0[3]sts. Turn. 50[56]sts.
7th row 2ch, 1dc into each of next 0[3]sts, (1dc into each of next 5 sts, work 2dc tog) 7 times, 1dc into each of next 0[3]sts. Turn. 43[49]sts.
Cont to dec in this way on every alt row until 8[14]sts rem.
2nd size only
Next row (Work 2dc tog) 7 times.
Both sizes
Cut yarn, thread through rem 8[7]sts, draw up and fasten off securely.

To make up

Press as given for jacket. Join seam as far as start of crown shaping.
Edging Using 3.50mm hook and with RS of work facing, work one round of dc round front and neck edges. Fasten off.
Cut ribbon in half ; make a rosette at one end of each length and sew to bonnet as shown.

Step-by-step course – 27

Working cluster or bobble stitches

*Working cluster or bobble stitches
*Making a simple cluster group
*Raised bobbles
*Pineapple stitch
*Stitch Wise : more cluster patterns
*Pattern for a slipover

Cluster stitches – or bobble stitches as they are sometimes called – can be grouped together to form diamond or square shapes on a plain background, or incorporated into square, flat motifs, or used as an all-over pattern to produce a really chunky crochet fabric. There are various ways of making these stitches. The preferred method depends largely on the type of stitch being used for the background and on the kind of texture desired. Relatively few stitches, grouped together and interspersed with other stitches, will produce a softly textured fabric. Other techniques will produce large bobbles that stand out against the fabric, giving it a highly embossed appearance.

All kinds of cluster stitches are made in essentially the same way: by working a number of loops or stitches into the same place and then drawing them together with a chain to complete the group. In a pattern containing cluster stitches, the instructions will specify the particular method of working the clusters for that garment.

Making a simple cluster group

This is a simple stitch to work ; all you do is draw a number of loops through one stitch in the previous row, then draw the yarn through all the loops, gathering them together. The width of each cluster will tend to make a row of these stitches wider than the rest of the fabric. If you are working bands of clusters in a plain fabric, you should insert a row of double crochet between each two cluster rows to control the extra fullness and maintain the shape of the fabric.

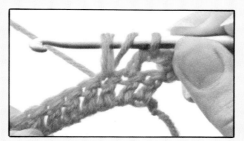

1 Work at least 2 treble at the beginning of the row where the cluster is to be made. This will be the RS of the fabric. Wind the yarn round the hook and insert the hook into the next stitch. Draw through a length of yarn, pulling it up to approximately 15mm, or so it is the same height as the previous stitch. There are now 3 loops on the hook.

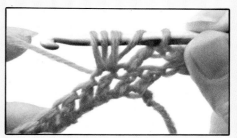

2 Wind the yarn round the hook and insert it into the same stitch as before. Now draw up another loop so that it is the same height as the first loop. There are now 5 loops on the hook.

3 Repeat step 2 twice more, so that there are now 9 loops on the hook. The number of times you repeat this step will depend on the size of bobble or cluster you wish to make.

4 Now wind yarn round the hook and draw it through all the loops on the hook to complete the cluster. Make 1 chain to hold the stitches firmly together.

5 Work at least 1 treble between each cluster all the way across the row and 2 treble after the last group to keep the edge straight. This sample shows several rows worked with 1 double crochet row between each cluster row. Work a double crochet into each treble and into the top of each cluster on the double crochet rows to maintain the number of stitches.

Paul Williams

Raised bobbles

The following method produces firm, raised bobbles made of trebles worked against a background of double crochet. You can work these bobbles to make an all-over pattern or group them into diamond or square shapes on a plain background. You will need to work at least 2 rows in double crochet before making the bobbles.

1 Work at least 2 double crochet at the beginning of the row. Now work 5 treble into the next stitch in the row below (placing the hook into the centre of the stitch), drawing the yarn up each time to the same height as the stitches in the row being worked.

2 Remove the hook from the working loop and insert it under the two horizontal loops of the first of these 5 treble. Take care not to pull the working loop back through the last stitch when withdrawing the hook.

  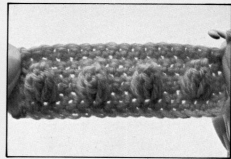

3 Now insert the hook once more into the working loop, so that the first treble and last treble of the group are both on the hook at the same time and the hook passes behind the 5 treble.

4 Draw the working loop through the first of these loops to complete the bobble. Make 1 chain to hold the stitches just worked firmly together.

5 Continue to work bobbles across the row ; miss the next stitch (the stitch missed in this row when 5 treble were worked into the row below) then work 1 double crochet into each of the next 3 stitches before making the next bobble in the same way as before. Finish the row by working at least 1 or 2 double crochet after the last bobble.

Pineapple stitch

This is a classic crochet cluster stitch in which loops are drawn through the vertical strand at the side of each group to make a horizontal rather than a vertical cluster. Pineapple stitch makes an ideal edging for a jacket or cardigan.
You will need to work at least one row in double crochet or trebles before working the cluster row, and you must have an even number of stitches on which to work it.

 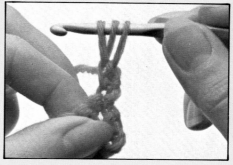

1 Work 2 chain at the beginning of the cluster row to keep the edge straight. Work a double crochet into the first (edge) stitch and then 1 chain. Now draw this chain (working loop) out loosely so that it is about 15mm long.

2 Wind the yarn round hook and insert the hook from front to back into the vertical loop at the side of the last stitch. Now draw through a loop loosely, extending it to the same height as before (3 loops on hook).

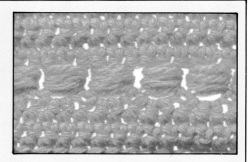

3 Repeat step 2 three times more (9 loops on hook). Pull each loop through loosely to prevent the cluster from becoming distorted. Miss next 2 double crochet. Insert hook into next stitch ; wind yarn round hook and draw it through this stitch and all loops on hook to complete first cluster.

4 To make the next cluster make 2 chain, drawing 2nd chain out to 15mm as before. Wind the yarn round hook and insert it from front to back into vertical loop at side of the last cluster into the loop made when first chain was worked after last cluster.

5 Complete this cluster as before. Make each cluster in the same way, inserting hook each time into vertical loop at side of last cluster worked. Finish the row with 1 chain and 1 treble into turning chain. For the next row, work 3 double crochet under top 2 loops of each cluster and 1 double crochet at each end.

Stitch Wise

Cluster stitch motif

Cluster groups worked in rounds have been used to make this highly textured square motif. You can make it in a fine or chunky yarn using either one colour, or changing the colour of the yarn at the end of each round for a really colourful effect.

Make 6ch and join into a circle with a slip stitch.

1st round 2ch to count as first dc, work 15dc into circle. Join with a ss to 2nd of first 2ch. 16dc.

2nd round 4ch to count as first cluster and 1 ch sp, * yrh and insert hook into next st, yrh and draw through a loop, yrh and draw through all 3 loops, called Cl1, 1 ch, rep from * to end of round. Join last ch to 3rd of first 4ch with a ss. 16 clusters.

3rd round Ss into first ch sp, 3ch, (yrh and insert hook into same sp, yrh and draw through a loop) twice, yrh and draw through all loops on hook, 2ch, * (yrh and insert hook into next 1 ch sp, yrh and draw through a loop) 3 times, yrh and draw through all loops on hook, called Cl3, 2ch, rep from * to end of round. Ss into 3rd of first 3ch.

4th round Ss into first 2ch sp, 3ch to count as first tr, 1 tr into same sp, (2tr into next 2ch sp, 1ch) twice, 1ch (Cl3, 2ch, Cl3) into next 2ch sp, called corner group, 1ch, *(2tr into next 2ch sp, 1ch) 3 times, 1 corner group into next 2ch sp, rep from * to end of round, working last corner group into sp before first 3ch in previous round and joining last ch to 3rd of first 3ch with a ss. Fasten off.

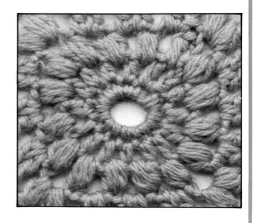

All-over cluster pattern

Several loops are worked into one stitch in the row below to create this really chunky cluster pattern. It may be substituted for the raised bobbles opposite. Make a number of chain divisible by 4 plus 1, with 1 extra for turning chain.

1st row (RS) 1dc into 3rd ch from hook, 1dc into each ch to end. Turn.

2nd row 1ch to count as first dc, miss first 1dc, 1dc into each dc to end, working last dc into turning chain. Turn.

3rd row 1ch, miss first dc, 1dc into next dc, *(yrh, insert hook into st in row below next dc, yrh and draw a loop through, extending it to the height of row being worked) 5 times, yrh and draw a loop through, extending it to height of row, 1 ch, called Cl1, miss next dc (this is the

dc missed when cluster was worked into row below), 1 dc into next dc, rep from * to end. 1 dc into turning chain. Turn.

4th row 1ch, miss first dc, 1dc into next dc, *1dc into top of next cluster, 1dc into dc between clusters, rep from * to last cluster, 1dc into top of last cluster, 1dc into next dc, 1dc into turning chain. Turn.

5th row 1ch, miss first dc, *Cl1 into next st in row below next dc, miss next dc (dc missed in this row when cluster was worked in row below), 1dc into next dc, rep from * to last 2dc, Cl1 into next dc, 1dc into turning chain. Turn.

6th row 1ch, *1dc into top of cluster, 1dc into next dc between clusters, rep from * to last cluster, 1dc into top of last cluster, 1dc into turning chain. Turn.

3rd to 6th rows form pattern.

Kim Sayer

John Hutchinson

BACK

35 [37] cm

6 cm

25 [27] cm

49 [54] cm

8 cm

FRONT

46 [49] cm

Soft clusters

This classic slipover made in a mohair-type yarn has bands of cluster stitches which give it an embossed look.

Sizes
To fit 82/87[92/97] cm bust.
Length, 57[62]cm.

Note Instructions for larger size are in square brackets []; where there is only one set of figures it applies to both sizes.

Materials
5[6] x 50g balls of Pingouin Poudreuse
4.50mm and 5.50mm crochet hooks

Tension
6 clusters and 10 rows to 10cm over patt worked on 5.50mm hook.

Back
**Using 4.50mm hook make 13ch for side edge of welt.
Base row 1dc into 3rd ch from hook, 1dc into each ch to end. Turn.
Next row 2ch to count as first dc, miss first st, *1dc into back loop only of next st, rep from * to end, working last st into back loop of turning ch. Turn. 12dc.
Rep last row 54[58] times more. This completes the ribbing for the welt.

Do not turn but continue to work down the long side edge of the ribbing. Change to 5.50mm hook. Working into the row ends, work 59[63] dc evenly along this edge. Turn.
Next row 2ch to count as first dc, 1dc into each dc to end. Turn. 59[63] dc. Commence patt.
1st row 4ch to count as first tr and 1ch, miss next dc, yrh, insert hook into next dc, yrh and draw a loop through, (yrh, insert hook into same dc, yrh and draw a loop through) 3 times, yrh and draw through all loops on hook, called Cl1, *1ch, miss next dc, 1 cluster into next dc, 1ch, miss next dc, rep from * to end, finishing 1ch, miss next dc, 1tr into turning ch. Turn. 28[30] clusters.
2nd row 2ch, *1dc into next ch, 1dc into top of next cluster, rep from * to end, finishing 1dc into each of next 2ch. Turn. 59[63] dc.
3rd row 2ch, 1dc into each dc to end. Turn.
These 3 rows form the patt. Cont in patt until back measures 32[35]cm from beg, ending with a 3rd patt row. **

Shape armholes
Next row Ss over first 9dc, 4ch, *miss next dc, Cl1 into next dc, 1ch, rep from * until 20[22] clusters in all have been worked, 1ch, miss next dc, 1tr into next dc, turn and leave rem sts unworked.
Cont in patt as set, working 43[47]sts in each dc row, until back measures 24[27]cm from beg of armhole shaping, ending with a 2nd patt row.

Shape shoulders
1st row Ss over first 8sts, patt to within last 7sts, turn.
2nd row Patt to end. Turn.
3rd row Ss over first 7sts, patt to within last 6sts. Fasten off.

Front
Work as given for back from ** to **.

Shape armhole and divide for neck
Next row Ss over first 9dc, work in patt until 10[11] clusters in all have been worked, turn and leave rem sts.
1st row Patt to end. Turn. 21[23] dc.
2nd row Patt to within last 3dc, work next 2dc tog to dec one st, 1dc into last dc. Turn. 20[22] dc.
3rd row 3ch, Cl1 into next dc, patt to end. Turn. 9[10] clusters.
4th row Patt to end. Turn.
5th row 2ch, dec one dc, patt to end. Turn.
6th row Patt to end. Turn.
Rep these 6 rows until 6 clusters rem, ending with a cluster row.

Shape shoulder
Next row Work 7[8]dc. Fasten off.
Return to rem sts. With RS of work facing, miss next dc, rejoin yarn to next st, Cl1, cont in patt until 10[11] clusters have been worked in all, 1ch, miss next dc, 1tr into next dc, turn and leave rem sts for armhole. Complete to match first side reversing shaping.

To make up
Join shoulder seams.
Neck border
With RS of left front facing and using 4.50mm hook, rejoin yarn to neck edge and work 33[37]dc down left front neck, miss centre st, work 33[37]dc up right front neck and 16[17]dc across back neck. Join with a ss to first dc. 82[91]dc. Working into back loop only, work 3 rounds in dc, dec 2sts at centre on each round by working 3dc tog at point of V on every round. Fasten off.
Armhole borders (alike)
Join side seams. With RS of work facing join yarn to underarm and using 4.50mm hook work 1dc into each st along underarm, then work in dc round armhole working 2dc into each cluster row end and 1dc for every 2dc row ends, then work 1dc into each st along underarm. Join with a ss to first dc. Working into back loop only, work 1 round in dc, ss into first dc.
Next round Work 7dc, now work 2dc tog to dec one st, work 1dc into each dc all round armhole to within last 10dc, work next 2dc tog, work to end, ss into first dc.
Next round 1dc into each of first 6dc, work next 2dc tog, 1dc into each dc to within last 9dc, work next 2dc tog, 1dc into each dc to end. Fasten off.

Step-by-step course – 28

*Shell fabric pattern
*Eyelet lace pattern
*Mother and daughter patterns : woman's shirt and girl's tunic.

Shell fabric pattern

This very simple shell stitch pattern has been used for the woman's shirt and the girl's tunic featured in this course. It has a slightly textured appearance without being too bulky. Because the pattern consists of two stitches worked into one, making a fan shaped group, it is important to work the foundation chain as loosely as possible.

Before making one of the garments in this course, make a sample to check your tension and see the over-all effect. If necessary, work the foundation chain with a larger hook than the one used for the pattern.

As you can see from the girl's tunic, it is possible to work bands of colour by introducing new colours at the end of a row. We worked one row in the first contrasting colour, followed by three rows in a second contrasting colour. The pattern is worked over an even number of stitches. We have made 25 chain and worked the first double crochet into the 3rd chain from the hook, so that there are 24 double crochet in the first row of the sample.

1 On the 1st row of this pattern you will not need to work any turning chain, since the first shell group is worked at the edge of the fabric. Begin by working a double crochet, chain and treble all into the 2nd stitch to form the first graduated shell.

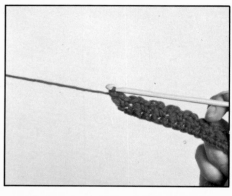

2 Now miss the next double crochet and work another group into the next stitch. Continue to work a group in the same way into every other stitch all the way across the row, working the last group into the top of the turning chain to complete the row.

3 Now turn the work and make 2 chain. From this point on, a turning chain is required at the beginning of every row. Miss the first treble and 1-chain space and work a group in the same way as before into the next double crochet. (This is the double crochet worked at the beginning of the last group in the previous row.)

4 Continue to work a group in the same way into each double crochet worked in the previous row until you reach the end of the row. The last group should be worked into the edge of the fabric this time, since there is no turning chain.

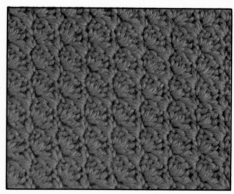

5 To continue the pattern, repeat the 2nd row each time, remembering that the last group should be worked into the top of the turning chain on subsequent rows.

Eyelet lace pattern

This fabric has a slightly lacy look and could be used for a summer blouse or an evening top. The pattern is worked over a multiple of 6 chain plus 3 extra. Our sample requires 27 chain in all, and is worked in a double knitting yarn with a 4.50mm hook, although this pattern looks equally good worked in a finer ply or a cotton yarn.

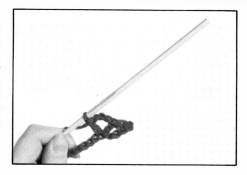

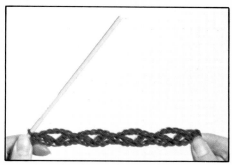

1 Work a double crochet into the 3rd chain from the hook. Now miss the next 2 chain and work 1 treble, followed by 3 chain and 1 treble, all into the next chain to create the first V-shaped group. Now miss the next 2 chain and work a double crochet into the following chain.

2 Continue to work a V group and a double crochet alternately across the row into every 3rd chain, completing the row by working a double crochet into the last chain. The pattern consists of these two simple steps worked alternately, reversing their position on every row.

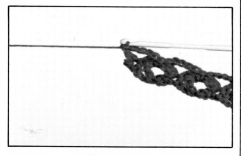

3 To keep the edge of the fabric straight and the pattern running in the correct sequence, you will have to work a half V at the beginning of the next row. This is done by working 4 chain to count as the first treble into the first stitch to complete the group. Thus the half group is achieved by working 1 chain in the middle of the 2 trebles instead of 3.

4 Now work a double crochet into the next 3-chain loop at the centre of the first V group, followed by a V group into the double crochet between the first two V groups worked in the previous row.

5 Continue to work a double crochet and a V group alternately across the row, completing the row by working a half V group consisting of 1 treble, 1 chain and 1 treble, all worked into the top of the turning chain.

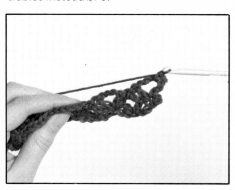

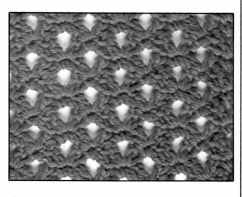

6 Begin the next row with 1 chain and then work a double crochet into the chain space in the centre of the first half V group at the edge of the work.

7 Now work a V group as before into the double crochet between the first and 2nd V groups in the previous row, thus reversing the pattern once more. Continue to work a V group and double crochet alternately across the row, finishing by working a double crochet into the 3rd of the first 4 chain, thus leaving the 4th of these chain to count as the 1-chain space in the V group of the previous row.

8 The all-over eyelet effect is created by alternating the rows in this way for the pattern, beginning one row with a half V group and the next with a double crochet.

Fred Mancini

Mother and daughter duo

A beautifully casual pair for mother and daughter, worked in a shell stitch fabric and trimmed with crochet-covered buttons. The girl's dress follows the lines of the shirt-style sweater, but has bands of colour across the chest.

Victor Yuan

Woman's shirt

Sizes

To fit 87 [92 :97] cm bust.
Length, 64[66 :68]cm.
Sleeve seam, 43[44 :45]cm.
Note Instructions for larger sizes are in square brackets [] ; where there is only one set of figures it applies to all sizes.

Materials

9[10 :11] x 50g balls of Pingouin Confortable Fin
3.00mm and 3.50mm crochet hooks
Cotton-wool for buttons

Tension

7½ groups and 18 rows to 10cm on 3.50mm hook.

Back

Using 3.50mm hook make 80 [84 :88] ch very loosely.
Base row 1 dc into 3rd ch from hook, 1 dc into each ch to end. Turn. 79[83 :87] sts. Cut off yarn and turn.

Shape lower edge

1st row Miss 24dc, rejoin yarn to next dc, 1ch, (1dc, 1ch, 1tr) ito next dc – called 1 group or 1gr – (miss next dc, 1gr into next dc) 14[16 :18] times, 1dc into next dc, turn (leaving 24 sts unused at end).
2nd row 2ch, miss first dc, (1gr into dc of next gr) 15[17 :19] times, ss into 1ch at beg of 1st row, (miss next dc, 1gr into next dc) twice, 1dc into next dc, turn (thus using 5 of the dc which were left at beg of 1st row).
3rd row 2ch, miss first dc, (1gr into dc of next gr) 17[19 :21] times, ss into 2ch at beg of last row, (miss next dc, 1gr into next dc) twice, 1dc into next dc, turn. Working 2 more gr on each row, rep the 3rd row 6 times more.
10th row 2ch, miss first dc, (1gr into dc of next gr) 31[33 :35] times, ss into 2ch at beg of last row, (miss next dc, 1gr into next dc) twice, turn.
11th row 1ch, (1gr into dc of next gr) 33[35 :37] times, ss into 2ch at beg of last row, (miss next dc, 1gr into next dc) twice, turn. 35[37 :39]gr.
You should now have used up all the dc which were left spare at the beginning, having used 5dc at the end of every row until the last 2 rows and 4 at the end of last 2 rows.
12th row 1ch, 1gr into dc of each gr to end. Turn.
Rep the 12th row until work measures 45cm from beg, (measured at centre).

Shape armholes

Next row Ss over 2gr, 1ch, patt to within last 2gr, turn.
Next row Patt to end. Turn.
Next row Ss over first gr, 1ch, patt to within last gr, turn.
Rep the last 2 rows twice more. 25[27 :29]gr. Cont without shaping until armholes measure 19[21 :23]cm.

Shape shoulders

Next row Ss over 2gr, patt to within last 2gr, turn.
Next row Ss over 2[3 :3]gr, patt to within last 2[3 :3]gr, turn.
Next row Ss over 3gr, patt to within last 3gr. Fasten off.

Front

Work as given for back until work measures 35cm from beg.

Divide for front opening

Next row Work 17[18 :19]gr, turn and cont on these sts until work measures the same as back to armholes, ending at side.

Shape armhole

Next row Ss over 2gr, 1ch, patt to end. Turn.
Next row Patt to end. Turn.
Next row Ss over first gr, patt to end. Turn.
Rep the last 2 rows twice more. 12[13 : 14] gr. Cont without shaping until armhole measures 14 [16 :18] cm, ending at armhole edge.

Shape neck

Next row Patt to within last 2[2 :3]gr, turn.
Next row Patt to end. Turn.
Next row Patt to within last gr, turn.
Rep the last 2 rows twice more, then cont on rem 7[8 :8]gr until armhole measures the same as back armholes ending at armhole edge.

Shape shoulder

Next row Ss over 2gr, patt to end. Turn.
Next row Patt to within last 2[2 :3]gr, turn.
Next row Ss over 3gr, patt to end. Fasten off.
Return to where work was left, rejoin yarn to next dc, 1ch, 1gr into next dc, patt to end. Turn. 17[18 :19]gr.

Complete to match first side, reversing shaping.

Sleeves

Using 3.50mm hook make 51 [55 :59]ch.
Base row 1dc into 3rd ch from hook, 1dc into each ch to end. Turn. 50[54 :58] sts.
1st row 1ch, miss first dc, 1gr into next dc, *miss next dc, 1gr into next dc, rep from * to end. Turn. 25[27 :29]gr.
2nd row 1ch, 1gr into dc of each gr to end. Rep the 2nd row until work measures 43[44 :45]cm from beg.

Shape top

Next row Ss over first gr, 1ch, patt to within last 2gr, turn.
Rep the last row 7[8 :9] times more. Fasten off.

Cuffs (make 2)

Using 3.00mm hook make 7ch.
Base row 1dc into 3rd ch from hook, 1dc into each dc to end. Turn. 6 sts.
Next row 2ch to count as first dc, 1dc into each dc to end. Turn.
Rep last row until cuff measures 18[19 : 20]cm. Fasten off.

Collar

Using 3.00mm hook make 13ch and work base row as given for cuffs. 12dc. Cont in dc for 36[38 :40]cm. Fasten off.

To make up

Do not press. Join the shoulder seams. Sew in sleeves, sewing the last 2cm of sleeve seams to the first 2gr of armhole. Join side and sleeve seams, leaving sleeve seams open for about 7cm from lower edge. Sew on cuffs, gathering sleeve edge to fit. Sew on collar

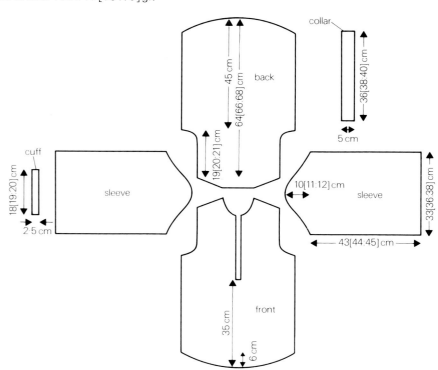

Brian Mayor

Front fastening

Starting at top of left front collar work 1 row of dc round front opening. Turn. Work another row of dc all round, making eight 5-chain buttonloops, first to come at neck edge and 7 evenly spaced down right front. Make 8 cotton-wool crochet buttons and sew to left front to match loops.

Child's tunic

Victor Yuan

Sizes

To fit 56[61 :66]cm chest.
Length, 46[51 :56]cm.
Sleeve seam, 22[24 :26]cm.

Note Instructions for larger sizes are in square brackets [ ] ; where there is only one set of figures it applies to all sizes.

Materials

4[4 :5] x 50g balls of Pingouin Confortable Fin in main colour (A)
1 ball in each of 2 contrasting colours (B) and (C)
3.00mm and 3.50mm crochet hooks
Cotton-wool for buttons

Tension

7½ groups and 18 rows to 10cm on 3.50mm hook.

Back

Using 3.50mm hook and A, make 51[55 : 59]ch.
Base row 1dc into 3rd ch from hook, 1dc into each ch to end. Turn.
1st row 1ch, miss first dc, (1dc, 1ch and 1tr) into next dc – called 1 group or 1gr, *miss next dc, 1gr into next dc, rep from * to end. Turn. 25[27 :29]gr.
2nd row 1ch, 1gr into dc of each gr to end. Turn.
Rep the 2nd row until work measures 33[37 :41]cm from beg.
Shape armholes
Next row Ss over 2gr, 1ch, patt to within last 2gr, turn.
Next row Patt to end. Turn.
Next row Ss over first gr, 1ch, patt to within last gr, turn.
Rep the last 2 rows once more. Now work 1[3 :5] rows without shaping. Cut off A. Join on B. With B work 2 rows. Join on C. With C work 6 rows. With B work 2 rows. Cut off B. Cont with C until armholes measure 13[14 :15]cm.
Fasten off.

Front

Work as given for back until work measures 28[32 :36]cm from beg.
Divide for front opening
Next row Patt over 12[13 :14]gr, turn and cont on these sts until work measures the same as back to beg of armhole shaping, ending at side edge.
Shape armhole
Next row Ss over 2gr, 1ch, patt to end. Turn.
Next row Patt to end. Turn.
Next row Ss over first gr, 1ch, patt to end. Turn.
Rep the last 2 rows once more. Now work 1[3 :5] rows without shaping. Cont in stripes to match back until armhole measures 9[10 :11]cm, ending at armhole edge.
Shape neck
Next row Patt to within last 2gr, turn.
Next row Patt to end. Turn.
Next row Patt to within last gr, turn.
For 3rd size only, rep the last 2 rows once more.
For all sizes, cont without shaping until armhole measures same as back. Fasten off.
Return to where sts were left, rejoin yarn to next dc, 1ch, 1gr into next dc, patt to end. Turn.
Complete to match first side, reversing shaping.

Sleeves

Using 3.50mm hook and A, make 31[35 :39]ch. Work base row as given for back. 15[17 :19] gr.
Cont in patt as given for back until sleeve measures 22[24 :26]cm from beg.
Shape top
Next row Ss over first gr, 1ch, patt to within last gr, turn.
Rep this row 4[5 :6] times. Fasten off.

Cuffs

Using 3.00mm hook and B, make 6ch.
Base row 1dc into 3rd ch from hook, 1dc into each ch to end. Turn. 5sts.
Next row 2ch to count as first dc, 1dc into each dc to end. Turn.
Rep last row until cuff measures 15[16 : 17]cm. Fasten off.

Collar

Using 3.00mm hook and B, make 11ch and work base row as given for cuffs. 10dc. Cont in dc for 26[28 :30]cm. Fasten off.

To make up

See women's shirt.

Front fastening

Using B, work front edging as given for mother's shirt, making six 5-chain buttonloops on right front.
Using C, make six small cotton-wool crochet buttons, and sew to left front to match loops.

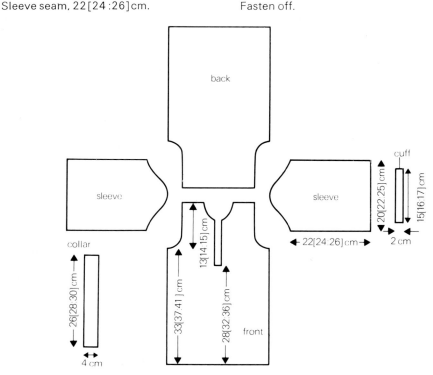

Brian Mayor

Step-by-step course – 29

Three-dimensional flower motifs

In this course we show you one of the most intriguing and unusual crochet techniques : working a three-dimensional flower motif. The flowers are most frequently worked as part of a crochet square such as the granny square featured in Crochet Course 14 (page 199), but they can, of course, be worked as separate motifs and sewn on to any crocheted or knitted fabric or on to clothes, as well.

Today, these flowers are usually worked in a knitting yarn or fairly thick cotton, and used to decorate bedspreads, rugs or elaborate shawls ; but in the past they were more often worked with a fine steel crochet hook in very fine crochet cotton and used on baby clothes, lingerie and fine lace collars. Such very fine crochet was particularly fashionable in the middle and late 19th century, when people were accustomed to spending long hours patiently doing intricate needlework.

Crocheted rose

These step-by-step instructions show you how to work the beautiful rose featured on the bedspread at the end of this course. In our sample – as in the bedspread pattern – each 2 layers of petals are worked in a different colour, but you could, of course, use just one colour.

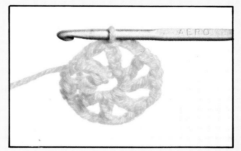

1 Begin the flower with 6 chain ; join them into a circle with a slip stitch. The first round is made by working 1 treble and 2 chain into the circle 8 times in all, thus making the 8 centre 'ribs' of the flower. First, make 5 chain ; these chain will count as the first treble and 2 chain space. Continue to work 1 treble and 2 chain around the circle, 7 more times. Finish the round by joining the last chain to the 3rd of the 5 chain with a slip stitch.

2 For the second round work 1 double crochet, 1 half treble, 3 trebles, 1 half treble and 1 double crochet into each 2-chain space of the previous round. Each of these groups of stitches forms a petal. Complete the round by using a slip stitch to join the last stitch to the slip stitch worked at the end of the previous round.

3 The next round consists of chains linking the petals already worked ; the chains are joined to the petals with double crochet. Begin by making 4 chain. Now insert the hook from back to front and round the stem of the first treble worked in the 1st round and work a double crochet in the normal way.

4 Keeping the 4 chain at the back of the petals all the time, work 4 chain and then a double crochet round the next treble in the first round all the way round the flower. Complete the round by working 4 chain and joining this with a slip stitch to the first chain at the beginning of the previous round.

5 Some patterns instruct you to turn the flower so the WS faces you when working the chains. In this case work the double crochet round the stem of the stitch worked in the previous round, then turn flower to RS again before you work the petals. Here we show the back of the flower with linking chains worked in a contrast colour.

continued

Fred Mancini

6 Now work a petal into each of the chain loops worked in the previous round. You should work 5 treble instead of the 3 worked in the previous petal round to increase the size of these petals. Use a slip stitch to join the last double crochet of the last petal to the first. You will see that the flower now has two layers.

7 Now work chain loops in exactly the same way as for the 3rd round, but work the double crochet linking each 4 chain loop round the back of the double crochet which you worked in the 3rd round. This has the effect of pulling the flower together at the back.

8 Work another round of petals into these chain loops as before, but this time work 7 trebles instead of 5 to make yet larger petals. If you need to make a smaller flower than the one we have made, you could finish the flower with this round.

9 Work another round of linking chains as before, working the double crochet round the back of the double crochet worked in the 5th round. Complete the flower with a final layer of petals, working 1 double crochet, 1 half treble, 2 treble, 5 double treble, 2 treble, 1 half treble and a double crochet for each petal.

10 The flower is now complete. You can use on its own by sewing it on to any fabric. If you prefer, enlarge the motif, giving it a granny-square type of background, as shown here. Begin by working the chain loops as before at the back. Work 3 treble, 3 chain and 3 treble into first loop for corner. Work 1 chain, 3 treble and 1 chain into next loop. Repeat alternately into each loop to make 4 corners.

11 On subsequent rounds you will work a corner into each 3 chain space, and a 3-treble group into each 1 chain space with 1 chain at either side, so that on each round you will be increasing a block of trebles on each side of the square. You can continue in this way until the square is as big as you require.

Simple primrose

Here is a much simpler flower which can also be worked with the same background. We have worked only two layers of petals, but you could make more for a larger flower.

1 Make 6 chain and join them into a circle with a slip stitch, as you would when working a square or circular motif. Now begin the first petal by working 1 double crochet, 3 treble and 1 double crochet all into the centre of the ring.

2 Make 2 more petals in exactly the same way and finish the round by joining the last double crochet to the first with a slip stitch. If you are using more than 1 colour, fasten off the yarn at this point by drawing it through the working loop. Make sure that this yarn is kept at the back of the work on following rounds.

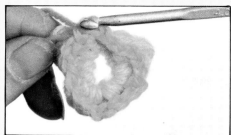

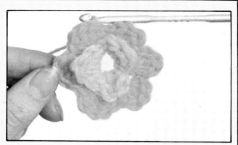

3 Turn the flower over so that the WS is facing you and rejoin the yarn to the back of the first double crochet. Make 3 chain and then work a double crochet into the back of the 2nd (middle) treble of the first petal, passing the hook behind the 2 back loops.

4 Make 3 more chain and work a double crochet round the stem of the 1st double crochet in the 2nd petal. Continue to work 3 chain and a double crochet in this way all the way round the flower so that you finish with six 3-chain loops in all. Join the last chain to the first with a slip stitch to complete the round.

5 Now turn the flower back so that the right side is facing you. (Cut off the yarn here if you wish to change colour and rejoin it to the first loop) Now work a petal into each of the 6 loops in exactly the same way as before. If you wish to make more layers, make another round of chain loops and work into these loops. You may have to increase the size of the petals by working 5 trebles instead of 3.

6 To begin the background turn the flower to the WS again and work a 3 chain loop between each petal, linking the chains by working a double crochet round the stem of the double crochet worked in the previous loop round. You should have 6 loops in all.

7 Now turn the flower to the RS again and make 3 chain for the first treble. Now work 2 treble, 2 chain and 3 treble all into the first loop. Make 1 chain and work 3 treble, 2 chain and 3 treble into each loop all the way round, with 1 chain between each loop, joining the round with a slip stitch.

8 To make the square, either slip stitch across to the first 2-chain space, if you are using the same colour, or join in a new colour to this space. Make 3 chain to count as first treble, then work 2 treble, 3 chain and 3 treble into first space. Work blocks of 3 treble into the two spaces, linked by 1 chain. Work another corner of 3 treble, 3 chain and 3 treble. This sets the pattern.

Fred Mancini

Stitch Wise

Pineapple square

The flower motif in the centre of this chunky pineapple stitch square is worked into the middle of the square after the square has been completed. By alternating a square with a flower and one without, you could make a very pretty bedcover or rug.

Make 8 chain and join into a circle with a slip stitch.
1st round *(Yrh and insert hook into circle, yrh and draw up a loop) 4 times, yrh and draw it through all 9 loops on hook, called pineapple 4, 2ch ; rep from * 7 times more. Join last chain to first pineapple with a ss. 8 pineapples in all.
2nd round Pineapple 4 into 2ch sp before ss, *2ch, pineapple 4 into next sp, 2ch, (1tr, 3ch, 1tr) into top of next pineapple

st, 2ch, pineapple 4 into next sp ; rep from *, ending last rep with (1tr, 3ch, 1tr) into next sp, 2ch. Join last ch to first pineapple with a ss.
3rd round Pineapple 4 into sp before ss, *(2ch, pineapple 4) into each sp to corner, 2ch, (1tr, 3ch, 1tr) into corner ; rep from * to end, 2ch. Join last ch to first pineapple with a ss.
Rep 3rd round for the size of square required.

To make the flower
Rejoin yarn to any 2ch sp on 1st round. Make 2ch to count as first dc, (yrh and insert hook into same sp, draw up loop) 3 times, yrh and draw through loops on hook, (pineapple 3), 1ch, pineapple 3 in same sp, 1ch, 1dc in same sp, *(1dc, pineapple 3, 1ch, pineapple 3, 1ch, 1dc) all into next 2ch sp in 1st round ; rep

from * all round motif. Join last dc to first with a ss. Fasten off.
There should be 8 petals in all.

This pretty, throw-over bedspread is just the thing for a little girl's bedroom. Alternatively, use it to bring a splash of colour to granny's bed-sitting room. The edges of the motifs are given gentle emphasis by being joined up with pink yarn. If pink does not suit your colour scheme, make it up in shades of yellow and gold.

We have simply laid a white sheet under the bedspread, but for extra colour you could use a pink sheet. If you prefer, line the bedspread with lining material from the furnishing fabric department—only the flat section need be lined and for this you will need 225cm of 115/120cm-wide fabric.

Everything's coming up roses

This splendid bedspread with its three-dimensional rose motifs will appeal to anyone's romantic nature. The rose motifs are alternated with plain motifs and the border is worked in rounds using each of the colours.

Size
To fit a single bed – 163cm by 230cm approx.

Materials
Wendy Courtellon Double Knit
43 x 20g balls in main colour (A)
17 x 20g balls in 1st contrasting
colour (B)
17 x 20g balls in 2nd contrasting
colour (C)
10 x 20g balls in 3rd contrasting
colour (D)

4.00mm crochet hook

Tension
One motif measures 19cm square.

Rose motif
Using 4.00mm hook and B, make 6ch, join with a ss to first ch to form a ring.
1st round 3ch to count as first tr, *2ch, 1tr into ring, rep from * 6 times more, 2ch, join with a ss to 3rd of first 3ch.
2nd round Work 1dc, 1htr, 3tr, 1htr and 1dc all into each 2ch sp, join with a ss to

Gary Warren

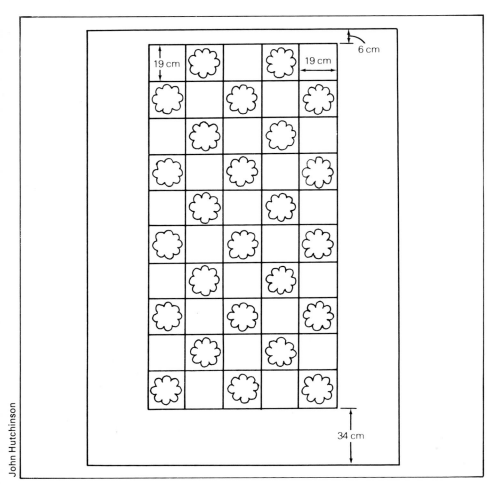

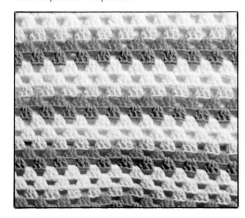

Work 6 more rounds, working 1 more tr group in each round between corner groups, so having six 3tr groups between each corner on last round. Fasten off. Make 24 more squares in the same way.

To make up
Placing motifs as shown in diagram, alternating one rose motif with one plain motif, join the motifs thus : with right sides together, using 4.00mm hook and B and working through the double thickness work 2dc into corner space, *working into the back loops only work 1dc into each of next 3tr, 1dc into next ch sp, rep from * 6 times more, 2dc into corner space. Do not fasten off but continue to join motifs until a row of 10 motifs have been joined. Being very careful not to let the motifs twist, join 4 more rows of motifs. Join the rows of motifs together in the same way.

The border
Working along two long sides and one short end work as folls.
1st row Join B to corner space and using 4.00mm hook work 3ch to count as first tr, 2tr into same space * ch, 3tr into next space, rep from * all round the three edges working 3tr, 3ch and 3tr all into the corner ch spaces. Fasten off.
2nd row Join on C and working into 3rd ch of first 3ch of previous row work 4ch, *3tr into next 1ch space, 1ch, rep from * all round the 3 edges working 3tr, 3ch and 3tr into the corner ch spaces. Fasten off.
3rd row Join on D and work as 1st row.
4th row Join on A and work as 2nd row.
5th row Join on A and work as 1st row. Cont in stripe sequence as set, patt 23 more rows.

Top border
Work in rows along top edge, working 2 rows in A, 1 row in B, 1 row in C and 1 row in D. Fasten off.

Lining
If you wish to line the bedspread, turn in a 2cm double hem all round fabric and slipstitch in place.

ss at end of first round.
3rd round Keeping each 4ch loop behind the petals of the 2nd round, work *4ch, placing hook from back to front work 1dc round next tr on 1st round, rep from * 6 times more, 4ch, join with a ss to ss at end of previous round.
4th round Work 1dc, 1htr, 5tr, 1htr and 1dc all into each 4ch loop, join with a ss to ss at end of 3rd round.
5th round As 3rd round working into the back of the dc of 3rd round. Cut off B.
6th round Join C to ss at end of last round, work 1dc, 1htr, 7tr, 1htr and 1dc all into each 4ch loop, join with a ss to ss at end of 5th round.
7th round As 3rd round working into the back of the dc of 5th round.
8th round Work 1dc, 1htr, 2tr, 5dtr, 2tr, 1htr and 1dc all into each 4ch loop, join with a ss to ss at end of 7th round. Cut off C.
9th round Join D to centre dtr of one petal, 1ch to count as first dc, then work 7ch, *keeping last loop of each on hook work 3dtr into the centre dtr of next petal, yrh and draw through all 4 loops on hook – called cluster 1 or Cl 1, 4ch, Cl 1 into same st as last Cl 1, 7ch, 1dc into centre dtr of next petal, 7ch, rep from * twice more, work Cl 1, 4ch and Cl 1 all into centre dtr of next petal, 7ch, join with a ss to first ch. Cut off D.

10th round Join A to one corner 4ch space, 3ch to count as first tr, 2tr into corner space, 3ch, 3tr into same space, 1ch, *(3tr, 1ch, 3tr and 1ch all into next 7ch space) twice, 3tr, 3ch, 3tr and 1ch all into corner 4ch space, rep from * twice more, (3tr, 1ch and 3tr all into next 7ch space) twice, join with a ss to 3rd of first 3ch.
11th round Ss over 2tr and into 3ch space, 3ch to count as first tr, 2tr into space, 3ch, 3tr into same space, (1ch, 3tr into next 1ch space) 5 times, * 1ch, 3tr, 3ch and 3tr all into corner 3ch space, (1ch, 3tr into next 1ch space) 5 times, rep from * 3 times, 1ch, ss into 3rd of first 3ch.
12th round As 11th round but working six 3tr clusters between each corner. Fasten off.
Make 24 more motifs in the same way.

Plain motif
Using 4.00mm hook and A, make 6ch, join with a ss to first ch to form a ring.
1st round 3ch to count as first tr, work 2 tr into ring, (3ch, 3tr into ring) 3 times, 3ch, join with a ss to 3rd of first 3ch.
2nd round Ss over next 2tr and into 3ch space, 3ch to count as first tr, work 2tr into same space, 3ch, (1ch, 3tr, 3ch and 3tr all into corner 3ch space) 3 times, 1ch, ss into 3rd of first 3ch.

Index